THE

PLAINS OF THE GREAT WEST.

THE

PLAINS OF THE GREAT WEST

AND

THEIR INHABITANTS

BEING

A DESCRIPTION OF THE PLAINS, GAME, INDIANS, &c.

OF THE GREAT NORTH AMERICAN DESERT

BY

RICHARD IRVING DODGE

Lieut. Colonel U. S. A.

WITH AN INTRODUCTION BY WILLIAM BLACKMORE

ILLUSTRATED

ARCHER HOUSE, INC., NEW YORK

PREFACE.

HUMAN NATURE is so liable to error, and to view facts through the medium of its own idiosyncrasies, that it is only by comparison of the opinions of different men that the world arrives at the truth of any subject.

There is scarcely a man who has reached the middle age of an active life whose experiences and the opinions formed upon them would not, if written out, be interesting and valuable to some portion of mankind.

To be valuable, however, it is of the utmost importance that the opinions be the result of intelligent observation or deduction of the person giving them.

In writing these pages I have carefully abstained from consulting 'authorities,' and have treated the different subjects from my own standpoint. Whether valuable or otherwise, the ideas are my own; and the beliefs expressed are the natural growth of long and varied experiences.

I have had ample opportunity to study the Indian character and habits in his own native wilds.

I have 'nothing extenuated nor set down aught in malice.'

THE AUTHOR.

CONTENTS.

PART I.

THE PLAINS.

PART II.

GAME.

PART III.

INDIANS.

LIST OF ILLUSTRATIONS.

INTRODUCTION.

THE truism that 'good wine needs no bush,' is 'equally applicable to the fact that a good book requires no introduction. In the present instance, I have been induced to depart from this sound maxim at the instance of the publishers, who, from my bibliographical and personal knowledge of the Aborigines of North America, have requested me to give a brief sketch of some of the principal Indian tribes, referred to in this book; the chief events of the last fifteen years; and the probable fate of the red man. With reference to my knowledge of the North American Indians, I may mention that during the last thirty years it has been my constant effort to collect and read all that has been written relative to these Aborigines, whilst during the last eight years I have personally had opportunities of seeing in their own homes some of the principal tribes between the British Possessions and Lake Superior in the North, and the Indian territory in the South; the Great Missouri and Mississippi Rivers in the East, and the Pacific in the West. During the latter period it has been my good fortune to number amongst my acquaintances some of the principal chiefs of several of the most important tribes, amongst whom I can name 'Red Cloud,' 'Red Dog,' and 'Two Lance,' three of the principal chiefs of the Ogallalla Sioux; 'Spotted Tail,' head chief of the Brulé Sioux; 'Ouray,' the head chief of the Utes; 'Washakie,' the principal chief of the Shoshones; 'Little Raven' and

' Bird Chief,' principal chiefs of the Arrapahoes ; 'Little Robe,' head chief of the Cheyennes; in addition to which there are many of the leading chiefs and warriors of the Kiowas and Comanches, Osages, River and Mountain Crows, Pawnees, Apaches, Navajoz and Pueblo Indians, who are personally well known to me.

DESTRUCTION OF BUFFALO.

But before referring to the Indian tribes, I desire to add my testimony to that of Colonel Dodge as to the wholesale and wanton destruction, during the last few years, of the buffalo. When one reads of the total destruction during the three years (1872-3 and 4) of four millions and a half of the 'Black Cattle of Illinois,' out of which number upwards of three millions have been killed for the mere sake of their hides, it is at first almost impossible to realise what this slaughter represents, and how much good and nutritious animal food, which would have fed the red men as well as the hardy settlers of the ' Great West,' has been wasted.

The figures speak for themselves. When in the West in 1872, I satisfied myself by personal inquiries that the number of buffalo then being annually slaughtered for their hides was at least one million per annum. In the autumn of 1868, whilst crossing the Plains on the Kansas Pacific Railroad—for a distance of upwards of 120 miles, between Ellsworth and Sheridan, we passed through an almost unbroken herd of buffalo. The Plains were blackened with them, and more than once the train had to stop to allow unusually large herds to pass. A few years afterwards, when travelling over the same line of railroad, it was a rare sight to see a few herds of from ten to twenty buffalo. A like result took place still further southwards, between the Arkansas and

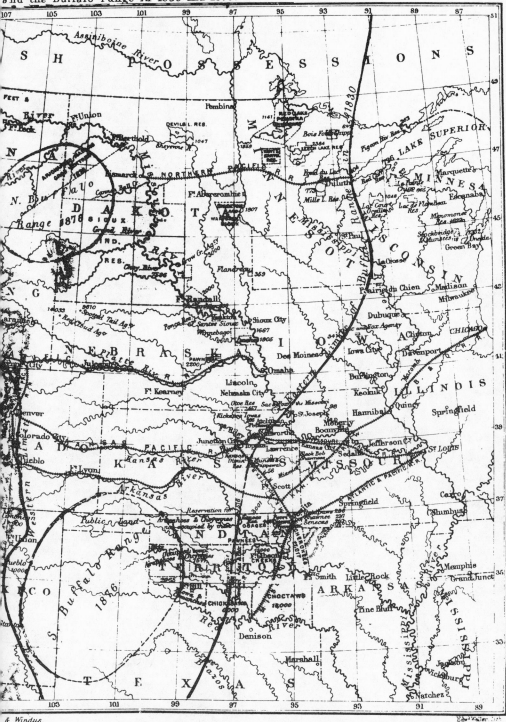

Territories of the United States and the Buffalo range in 1830 and 1876

POSSESSIONS

Assiniboine River

Pembina

LAKE SUPERIOR

RED LAKE Reservation

M I N N E S O T A

Marquette
Escanaba

DEVILS L. RES.
Cheyenne R.
1047

Bois Fort Chip.

LEECH LAKE RES.

Duluth

F.t Berthold
Bismarck

NORTHERN PACIFIC

Fond du Lac

St. Paul

W I S C O N S I N

La Pointe
Lac Court Oreilles Res.
Lac de Flambeau Res.

Menomonee Res.
Stockbridge & Oneida

Green Bay

D A K O T A

SIOUX
Grand River
IND.
RES.
Clay River

Crow Creek Agy.

Flandreau
359

La Crosse

Prairie du Chien

Milwaukee
Madison

F.t Randall
Yankton
Santee Sioux
Winnebago
1667
Omaha 1805
Sioux City

Red Cloud Agcy.
Spotted Tail Agcy.
Ponca Agy.

N E B R A S K A

I O W A

Des Moines
Iowa City

Dubuque
Fox Agency

Clinton
Davenport

CHICAGO

Platte River
PAWNEE
2200

Lincoln
Nebraska City

Otoe Res.
1467
Kickapoo Iowas
F.t Kearney

Omaha

Burlington
Keokuk
Hannibal

I L L I N O I S

Quincy
Springfield

Denver
Colorado City

K A N S A S
PACIFIC
Kansas River

Junction City
Lawrence

F.t St. Joseph
Atchison
F.t Leavenworth on the Missouri
Moberly
Boonville

Jefferson C.y
Sedalia
St. LOUIS

M I S S O U R I

Pueblo
F.t Lyon

Arkansas River

Black Bob
Chippewa
Miami
F.t Scott

ATLANTIC & PACIFIC R.R.

Springfield

Cairo
Columbus

Public land

Reservation for
Arapahoes & Cheyennes
occupied by other

I N D I A N

OSAGE

Senecas

F.t Smith
Little Rock

A R K A N S A S

Memphis
Grand Junct.

PAWNEE

T E R R I T O R Y

CHICKASAW

CHOCTAWS
18000

Pine Bluff

M I S S I S S I P P I

Red River
Denison

Brazos River

T E X A S

Marshall

Jackson
Vicksburg
Natchez

North Buffalo Range 1876

South Buffalo Range 1846

Buffalo Range in 1830

Cimarron Rivers. In 1872, whilst on a scout for about a hundred miles south of Fort Dodge to the Indian territory, we were never out of sight of buffalo. In the following autumn, on travelling over the same district, whilst the whole country was whitened with bleached and bleaching bones, we did not meet with buffalo until we were well into the Indian territory, and then only in scanty bands. During this autumn, when riding some thirty to forty miles along the north bank of the Arkansas River to the East of Fort Dodge, there was a continuous line of putrescent carcases, so that the air was rendered pestilential and offensive to the last degree. The hunters had formed a line of camps along the banks of the river, and had shot down the buffalo, night and morning, as they came to drink. In order to give an idea of the number of these carcases, it is only necessary to mention that I counted sixty-seven on one spot not covering four acres.

But this great loss of good and wholesome animal food, all of which with a little judgment and foresight could have been utilised, will be better understood by reference to the statistics of cattle in other countries. On reference to the official agricultural returns of Great Britain, the United Kingdom, British Possessions, and Foreign countries, it will be seen that the wanton and wasteful slaughter for the three years in question (and in making the comparison I am keeping to the *illegitimate* slaughter for hides, and not *legitimate* slaughter for food) swept away more buffalo than there are cattle in Holland and Belgium, or as many as three-fourths of the cattle in Ireland, or one-half of those in Great Britain.

The result, therefore, would be the same as if a fearful murrain in one year had destroyed the whole of the cattle in Holland and Belgium, or, in the same time, if either three-fourths of the cattle of Ireland, or one-half of those of Great Britain, had been swept away by a plague as great as that of Egypt.

The citizens of the United States will better realise this great waste, if they consider that this destruction amounted annually to more than double the number of the annual drives of cattle from Texas, which range from 350,000 to 500,000 head per annum ; or that it would have been the same during the three years as if half the cattle of Texas or all the cattle in Canada had been carried off by some dire disease.

The mere loss of food, however, is not the only evil which has resulted from this wanton wastefulness. Many of the wild Indians of the Plains, deprived of their ordinary sustenance, Government rations not being forthcoming, and driven to desperation by starvation, have taken to the war path ; so that during the present war many of the Cheyennes and Arrapahoes, and some of the young braves from the friendly ' Red Cloud ' and ' Spotted Tail ' agencies have left their reservations, and joined the hostile Sioux under ' Sitting Bull.' The hardy settler and pioneer of the Plains who always looked to the buffalo for his winter supply of meat, has been deprived of this resource, and complains most bitterly of this slaughter for pelts.

In 1873, when the settlers in Kansas were suffering from the destruction of their crops by the ravages of the grasshoppers, troops were considerately sent by the Government to the Republicans to kill meat for the starving families. When the soldiers arrived, however, at their hunting-grounds, there was but little meat for them to kill, as the 'buffalo skinners' had anticipated them and had slaughtered nearly every buffalo in the district.

With the great economy endeavoured to be introduced into each department of the Government of the United States, it is difficult to understand how the Executive, whilst they enforce a heavy tax upon each seal which may be killed in Alaska, has neglected to avail themselves of such a fruitful source of revenue as that which might be derived from buffalo pelts. A tax of $5 on each skin, which could have been easily imposed and collected, under heavy penalties and forfeiture of all buffalo skins not having the Government duty stamp thereon, would realise not less than $1,000,000 per annum, even supposing that the number of buffalo annually killed for their skins were only 200,000 in lieu of upwards of a million. A tax of this amount would have realised upwards of fifteen millions of dollars on the buffalo ruthlessly slaughtered for their hides.

I suggested this remedy at the time, but, although referred to by the press, it was not attended to, and it is now almost too late. It is of little use ' to lock the stable door after the steed has been stolen.'

Such a tax, moreover, would have been fair and equitable ; as it is not reasonable that a few needy citizens should monopolise for their own private benefit the public property of the State. If the same principle were carried out with regard to the public lands, timber, and mines, a few citizens of the United States, similar in character to the buffalo skinners before referred to, would take more than the lion's share of the public property.

THE INDIANS OF NORTH AMERICA.

The number of Indians of all descriptions at present inhabiting the United States is estimated at about 300,000. Two centuries ago they numbered upwards of two millions. Everywhere, and amongst all tribes, with the exception, perhaps, of the Dakotahs or Sioux, they are rapidly decreasing in numbers. This decrease arises from various causes; amongst the principal of which may be mentioned contagious diseases, intemperance, and wars, both amongst themselves and with the whites. The steady and resistless emigration of white men into the territories of the West, restricts the Indians yearly to still narrower limits, and, destroying the game, which in their normal state constituted their principal means of subsistence, reduces them to a state of semi-starvation and desperation. The records of every tribe tell the same story of their gradual decrease and probable extinction.

The Indians of the United States are placed under the management of the Indian Bureau, a branch of the Interior Department of the Government, and are governed by means of superintendents and agents especially appointed for this purpose, the department being divided into superintendencies and agencies.

There are fourteen superintendencies, viz. Washington, California, Arizona, Oregon, Utah, Nevada, New Mexico, Colorado, Idaho, Dakotah, Montana, Northern, Central, and Southern; whilst there are several independent agencies.

In California, Washington, and Oregon territories there are about 50,000 Indians.

Arizona and New Mexico contain a like number, consisting principally of the *Navajoes*, *Apaches*, and *Pueblo* Indians.

Nevada, Utah, and Colorado contain about 35,000, consisting of the different tribes of *Utes*, *Shoshones* or *Snake* Indians, and *Bannocks*.

Dakotah, Montana, Wyoming, and Idaho, the homes of the *Dakotah* or *Sioux*, *Black-feet*, and *Blood* Indians, contain about 70,000 of the most warlike and uncivilised Indians of the Plains; whilst the Indian territory which is situated to the west of the State of Arkansas and between Texas and Kansas, contains about 70,000, consisting principally of the semi-civilised tribes, including the

Creeks, *Cherokees*, *Choctaws*, *Chickasaws*, *Osages*, *Seminoles*, *Winnebagoes*, *Pawnees*, *Pottawatomies*, and the *Sacs* and *Foxes*.

The wild *Kiowas* and *Comanches*, and the *Arrapahoes* and *Cheyennes*, who, with some of the bands of the *Dakotahs*, inhabit the country lying between the west of the Indian territory and the eastern slopes of the Rocky Mountains, number about 10,000.

In addition to the tribes previously enumerated, there are also the *Chippewas*, or *Ojibbeways*, numbering some 20,000, who roam about the shores of Lake Superior and the banks of the Upper Mississippi ; whilst the *New York* Indians, consisting of the remnants of the celebrated *Six Nations*, together with other miscellaneous wandering tribes, number less than 10,000.

No satisfactory classification of the Indian tribes has yet been made. That, however, which has been most generally adopted is the following :—

1. The *Algonquin* or *Ojibbeway Confederacy* occupied all the country to the frozen regions, north of a line commencing near Cape Fear, on the Atlantic, thence extending westerly to the mouth of the Illinois River, thence along that river and by way of Lake Michigan, Falls of St. Mary, Lake Superior, and rivers and portages to the Lake of the Woods, and thence westerly to the Rocky Mountains.

2. The *Mobilian*, or *Cherokee Confederacy*, occupying the country south of the line running westerly from Cape Fear to the north line of Tennessee, thence west to the Mississippi, thence by the Mississippi, Arkansas, and Canadian Rivers to the Rocky Mountains.

3. The *O-chunk-o-raw*, or *Winnebago Confederacy*, extending from Lake Superior to the Arkansas River, including the Wisconsin River and Lower Ohio, and extending west to the Rocky Mountains.

4. The *Dakotah*, or *Sioux Confederacy*, extending west to the Rocky Mountains from a line running from Kewenaw Bay to the north-eastern corner of the present State of Iowa.

The lines between the different confederacies must be understood as only approximating to correctness, as Indian boundaries were never well defined.

These confederacies were generally not confederacies of Government, but were divided into a number of independent bands or tribes, often at open war with each other, and frequently unable to speak each other's dialects.

The Dakotahs, or *Sioux.*—The *Dakotahs*, more frequently termed *Sioux*, and also called by the French ' *Les Coupe-gorge*,' or ' Cut-throats,' from their sign or symbol, which consists of drawing the lower edge of the hand across the throat, are the most powerful and warlike of all the Indian tribes. They are divided into the *Santees*, or Upper Bands, and the *Tetons*, or Lower Bands.

They are called by the Algonquin nations *Nadonessioux*, or ' Enemies,' which was subsequently abbreviated or corrupted to ' Sioux,' a common name for the tribe among the English and French traders for the last 200 years; it is, however, a mere nickname, and excessively disagreeable to the tribes to which it is applied.

The Santees, or Upper Bands, consist of the following bands :—

1. The *Wahpakoota*, or ' Leaf-shooters.'

2. *Mdewakanton*, or the ' Village of the Spirit Lake,' or *Mille Lacs*.

3. *Wahpaton*, or the ' Village in the Leaves ;' and

4. *Sisseton*, the ' Village of the Marsh.'

The first two of these bands resided, in 1862, in Minnesota, and originated the massacre. They are called

'Santees,' from Isanti, because they once lived near Isant Amde, one of the *Mille Lacs.*

The Tetons, or Lower Bands, comprise the following bands :—

1. *Yankton,* or ' The Village at the end.'
2. *Yanktonai,* or ' One of the End Village.'
3. *Brulé,* or ' Burnt-thighs.' (' Spotted Tail's ' band.)
4. *Two-kettle,* or ' Two Boilings.'
5. *Sisapapa,* or ' Black-feet.'
6. *Minnecongou,* or ' Those who plant by the water.'
7. *Oncpapas,* or ' They who camp by themselves.'
8. *Sans-Arcs,* or ' No Bows.'
9. *Ogallallas,* or ' Wanderers.' (' Red Cloud's ' Band.)
10. *Assineboins,* or ' Pot-boilers.'

All of whom reside in Dakotah, Montana, and Wyoming.

These Indians, comprising 17 different bands, are the most numerous tribe in the United States. Forty-six thousand seven hundred and fifty-three received rations from the Government at eleven different agencies during the year 1874. The wilder portions of this tribe, who have as yet consented to visit an agency only on an occasional raid for rations, are variously estimated from 5,000 to 10,000, making the whole number of Sioux not far from 53,000. As a whole, the Sioux are as yet un-reached by civilisation, except so far as their necessities and inclinations have led them to receive rations and annuity goods from the hands of Government agents.

All the separate bands of the Sioux form a confederacy similar to that of the ancient confederacy of the Iroquois Indians. Amongst the Indians of the United States they are the only tribes which have increased in population. They are most aggressive, and wage a constant warfare against their weaker neighbours. Amongst their hereditary and implacable enemies are the Pawnees, whom they have almost exterminated, the River and Mountain Crows, who act as a frontier police between the Northern Sioux and the white settlers of Montana, the Shoshones or Snakes, and the Utes.

Amongst their leading chiefs are ' Sitting Bull,' now engaged in hostilities in Montana with the United States troops, under Generals Terry, Crook, and Gibbon ; ' Red Cloud ' and ' Red Dog,' chiefs of the Ogallalla Sioux ; and 'Spotted Tail,' chief of the Brulé Sioux. 'Little Crow,' who was the leader in the massacre in Minnesota of 1862, was the head chief of the Minnecongou Sioux ; and up to the time of the outbreak had always been re-garded as the friend of the whites.

The Sioux and the Cheyennes are about the finest in *physique*, and most independent, warlike, and self-reliant of all the tribes of the continent, and there is as much difference between them and some of the inferior tribes as there is between an American horse and an Indian pony.

The Cheyennes.—The Cheyennes, also called *Paikan-doos* or ' Cut-wrists,' are described by Catlin as a small tribe about 3,000 in number, living as neighbours to the west of the Sioux, between the Black Hills and the Rocky Mountains. ' There is no finer race of men than these in North America, and none superior in stature, excepting the Osages, there being scarcely a man in the tribe full-grown who is less than six feet in height. They are undoubtedly the richest in horses of any tribe on the continent, living in the country, as they do, where great herds of wild horses are grazing on the prairies, which they catch in great numbers and vend to the Sioux, Mandans, and other tribes, as well as to the fur-traders. These people are a most desperate set of horsemen and warriors also, having carried on an almost unceasing war with the Pawnees and Black-feet from time out of mind.'

At present they number about 2,000.

The principal chief of this tribe is Ta-ke-ho-ma, or 'Little Robe.'

Moke-to-ve-to, or 'Black Kettle,' the head chief, as well as their most distinguished war chief, was killed at the battle of Washita.

The Arrapahoes.—The Arrapahoes, sometimes called 'Dirty-noses,' from their sign, which consists in seizing the nose with the thumb and fore-finger, are described by Burton as follows :—

'The Arrapahoes, generally pronounced Rapahoes (called by their Shoshone neighbours Sháretikeh, or Dog-eaters, and by the French *Gros Ventres*), are a tribe of thieves, living between the south fork of the Platte and the Arkansas Rivers. They are bounded north by the Sioux, and hunt in the same grounds with the Cheyennes. This breed is considered fierce, treacherous, and unfriendly to the whites, who have debauched and diseased them, while the Cheyennes are comparatively chaste and uninfected. The Arrapahoe is distinguished from the Dakotah by the superior gauntness of his person, and the boldness of his look; there are also minor points of difference in the mocassins, arrow-marks, and weapons.'

The Rev. Dr. Morse thus speaks of these Indians in 1820 :—'Their number is estimated at 10,000. Their country extends from the head-waters of the Kansas, south to the Rio del Norte. They are a warlike people, and often make predatory and murderous excursions on their eastern and northern neighbours.'

The tribe has, since 1820, from wars and that terrible scourge the small-pox, greatly decreased, and is now almost extinct. They now number only 1,500.

Their head chief is '*Oh-nas-tie*,' or 'Little Raven.' Mr. Richardson, who was in the habit of seeing him frequently in 1865, describes him as being the nearest approximation he ever met to the ideal Indian. He had a fine manly form, and a humane trustworthy face ; he has associated freely with the settlers in Colorado ever since the gold discoveries of 1858. He has always been on good terms with them, and in several instances prevented outbreaks of his people, who wished to avenge real or fancied injuries. In 1860, he received a medal from President Buchanan, and has been honoured in other ways by the military commanders on the Plains. When speaking of the future of his people, ' Little Raven ' is always despondent, as he plainly sees that the Indian is doomed to destruction, and that a few generations at furthest will see the race extinct. Other chiefs are ' Bird Chief ' and ' Yellow Bear.'

The Kiowas and Comanches.—The Kiowas and Comanches are wild and roving Indians, whose range extends over a large part of Western Texas and the southeastern portion of New Mexico and Northern Mexico.

The two tribes in 1867 numbered 2,800. The Kiowas, or ' Prairie men,' make the signs of the prairie and of drinking water. Catlin, when he visited them, describes them as being a much finer race of men than either the Comanches or Pawnees, tall and erect, with an easy and graceful gait, and long hair, cultivated frequently so as to reach nearly to the ground. He states that they have usually a fine and Roman outline of head, and are decidedly distinct from both the Comanches and Pawnees, both in appearance and language. The Kiowas have the reputation, and doubtless deserve it, of being the most rapacious, cruel, and treacherous of all the Indians of the Plains. They range mainly south of the Arkansas, and south of the Rio Grande. They have the credit of influencing the Comanches to do whatever they suggest.

The Comanches, or Camanches (*Les Serpents*), imitate

LITTLE ROBE (TAK-KEE-O-MAH), CHIEF OF THE CHEYENNES.

LITTLE RAVEN, HEAD CHIEF OF THE ARRAPAHOES.

by the waving of the hand or fore-finger, the forward crawling motion of a snake. In stature they are rather low, and in person often approach to corpulency. These fierce, untamed savages roam over an immense region, living on the buffalo, and plundering Mexicans, Indians, and whites with judicial impartiality. Arabs and Tartars of the desert, they remove their villages (pitching their lodges in regular streets and squares) hundreds of miles at the shortest notice. The men are short and stout, with bright copper faces and long hair, which they ornament with glass beads and silver gewgaws.

On foot slow and awkward, but on horseback graceful, they are the most expert and daring riders in the world. In battle they sweep down upon their enemies with terrific yells, and, concealing the whole body, with the exception of one foot, behind their horses, discharge bullets or arrows over and under the animal's neck rapidly and accurately. Each has his favourite war-horse, which he regards with great affection, and only mounts when going to battle. With small arms they are familiar; but 'gun-carts,' or cannons, they hold in superstitious fear. Even the women are daring riders and hunters, lassoing antelope and shooting buffalo. They wear the hair short, tattoo their bodies, have stolid faces, and are ill-shapen and bow-legged.

These modern Spartans are most expert and skilful thieves. An old brave boasted to General Marcy that his four sons were the noblest youths in the tribe, and the chief comfort of his age, for they could steal more horses than any of their companions. They are patient and untiring—sometimes absent upon war expeditions for a year, refusing to return until they can bring the spoils of battle. When organising a war party, the chief decorates a long pole with eagle-feathers and a flag, and then, in fighting costume, chants war songs through his village.

He makes many raids upon white settlers ; but his favourite victims are Mexicans. Like all barbarians, he believes his tribe the most prosperous and powerful on earth, and, whenever the Government supplies him with blankets, sugar, or money, attributes the gifts solely to fear of Comanche prowess. Never tilling the ground, insensible alike to the comforts and wants of civilisation, daring, treacherous, and bloodthirsty, they are the Bedouins of the frontier, and the mortal terror of weaker Indians and of Mexicans. According to tradition, their ancestors came from a far country in the west, where they expect to join them after death.

Catlin says of them :—' In their movements they are heavy and ungraceful ; and on their feet one of the most unattractive and slovenly-looking races of Indians I have ever seen ; but the moment they mount their horses, they seem at once metamorphosed, and surprise the spectator with the ease and grace of their movements. A Comanche on his feet is out of his element, and comparatively almost as awkward as a monkey on the ground, without a limb or branch to cling to ; but the moment he lays his hand upon his horse, his *face* even becomes handsome, and he gracefully flies away like a different being.'

The Kiowas number at present about 2,000 and the Comanches 3,000.

The principal chiefs of the Kiowas are ' Lone Wolf' and ' Satanta,' or ' White Bear.' The latter in cunning and native diplomacy has no rival. In wealth and influence the Dakota chief, ' Red Cloud,' is his rival ; but in boldness, daring, and merciless cruelty, ' Satanta ' is far his superior. If a white man does him an injury, he never forgives him ; but if, on the other hand, the white man has done him a service, death alone can prevent him from paying the debt. Mr. Kitchin, who visited him in 1864, describes him as ' a fine-looking Indian, very energetic, and as sharp as a briar. He and all his people treated me with much friendship. I ate my meals regularly three times a day with him in his lodge. He puts in a good deal of style—spreads a carpet for his guests to sit on, and has painted fire-boards, twenty inches wide and three feet long, ornamented with bright brass tacks driven all round the edges, which they use for tables. He has a brass French horn, which he blew vigorously when the meals were ready.' General Custer, in his 'Life on the Plains,' speaking of 'Satanta,' says :—'Aside from his character for restless barbarity and activity in conducting merciless forays against our exposed frontiers, "Satanta" is a remarkable man—remarkable for his powers of oratory, his determined warfare against the advances of civilisation, and his opposition to the abandonment of his accustomed mode of life, and its exchange for the quiet, unexciting, uneventful life of a reservation Indian.' He and 'Lone Wolf' were captured by the United States troops in 1868, and suffered imprisonment in Texas for some years ; but were afterwards released.

Other important chiefs of this tribe, are 'Son of the Sun,' 'Dog Eater,' and 'Sleeping Wolf,' all of whom have visited Washington.

Some of the principal chiefs of the Comanches are 'Ten Bears,' 'Silver Brooch,' 'Wolf's Name,' 'Little Horse,' and 'Iron Mountain.'

PRINCIPAL INDIAN EVENTS SINCE 1862.

The principal Indian events which have occurred within the last fifteen years are the following :—

1. The Sioux massacre of whites in Minnesota in 1862, which resulted in the deaths of 644 men, women, and children, killed in the several massacres, and of 93 soldiers killed in battle.

2. The Sand-Creek or Chivington's massacre of Indians, which took place on November 29, 1864, when about 130 of the Cheyennes (principally women and children) were killed at Sand Creek, on the Little Arkansas River, by a large body of men under Colonel Chivington and Major Anthony.

3. Fetterman's massacre, which occurred on December 21, 1866, near Fort Phil Kearney, and resulted in the annihilation, by some of the Sioux Indians, under their celebrated chiefs, ' Red Cloud ' and ' Red Dog,' of Colonel Fetterman's command, consisting of 80 men and several officers. Colonel Fetterman and his men were led into an ambuscade, and not one was left to tell the tale of their slaughter by the Indians.

4. The Indian war with the Cheyennes, Arrapahoes, some of the Brulé and Ogallalla Sioux Indians, and Kiowas and Comanches in the autumn of 1868.

The principal events of this war was Colonel Forsyth's fight in September on the Arickara Fork of the Republican River, when with 51 scouts he succeeded in maintaining his position for eight days against the attacks of from 800 to 1,000 Indians under ' Roman Nose,' until his force was relieved by troops sent from Fort Wallace. Of the 51 men engaged in this fight 23 were either killed or wounded, Lieutenant Beecher and Surgeon Movers being amongst the killed, whilst Colonel Forsyth was seriously wounded.

And the battle of Washita, on December 23, 1868, when the United States troops, under the late General Custer, captured and destroyed the united winter camp of the Cheyennes under ' Black Kettle,' of the Arrapahoes under ' Little Raven,' and the Kiowas and Comanches under ' Satanta,' ' Satanka,' and ' Lone Wolf.' The result of this fight was 103 warriors left on the ground, and the capture of a large number of prisoners, together with 875

Indian ponies, and the whole of the winter supplies of the Indians. The victory, however, was not purchased without its sacrifices: amongst the killed being Major Elliott, Captain Hamilton, and 19 enlisted men; of the wounded were Major Barnitz and 13 enlisted men.

Major Elliott and the men under his command, in a charge against the Indians, became separated from the other troops, were surrounded by an overwhelming force of Indians, and cut off to a man. When their bodies were discovered, a few days after the battle, it was found that they had been horribly mutilated.

The decisive character of the victory, and the severe blow sustained by the Cheyennes, may be judged from the number of 'big' chiefs, war chiefs, and head men killed in the battle of the Washita. It was learned from the squaws, by means of Mr. Curtis, the interpreter, that the following were killed:—

Cheyennes—'Black Kettle,' chief of the band; 'Little Rock,' second chief; 'Buffalo Tongue,' 'Tall White Man,' 'Tall Owl,' 'Poor Black Elk', 'Big Horse,' 'White Beaver,' 'Bear Tail,' 'Running Water,' 'Wolf Ear,' 'The Man that hears the Wolf,' 'Medicine Walker.'

Sioux—'Heap Timber,' and 'Tall Hat.'

Arrapahoes—'Lame Man.'

On Christmas Day a detachment of troops under Colonel Evans captured a Comanche village of sixty lodges, who surrendered after only a feeble resistance. In the meantime other troops had succeeded in capturing Satanta and 'Lone Wolf,' and on January 1 General Sheridan, in his despatch to General Sherman, was enabled to report as follows:—

'The destruction of the Comanche village by Colonel Evans's command on Christmas Day gave the final blow to the backbone of the Indian rebellion. At midnight on December 31, 1868, a delegation of the chief fighting men of the Cheyennes and Arrapahoes, twenty-one in number, arrived here on foot, their animals not being able to carry them on. They said they ruled the village, and begged for peace, and for permission for their people to come in, and asked no terms, but only for a paper to protect them from the operations of our troops while *en route.* They report the tribes in mourning for their losses. Their people are starving, having eaten up all their dogs and finding no buffalo. We had forced them into the cañons on the eastern edge of the " Staked Plains," where there was no small game or buffalo. They are in a bad fix and desire to surrender unconditionally. I acceded to their terms, and will punish them justly ; and I can scarcely make an error in any punishment awarded, for they all have blood upon their hands.'

Thus ended the Indian campaign of 1868, and another laurel was added to the numbers already gained by the hero of a hundred battles, who first commenced his military career of success by a dashing charge on Indians in Oregon.

5. The massacre of the Piegans under Colonel Baker, on January 23, 1870, when 173 were killed, amongst whom were 53 women and children.

6. The brutal murder on April 11, 1873, at the Klamath Agency, of General Canby and Dr. Thomas, when engaged as Commissioners in a peace conference with ' Captain Jack ' and other representative men of the tribe ; Mr. Meachan, another of the Commissioners, was severely wounded. After seven months' fighting, the Indians were subdued by the military, and ' Captain Jack ' and three of his principal men were tried by Court-martial and executed.

7. The war of 1876 against the Northern Sioux under the leadership of ' Sitting Bull.' This last Indian campaign, in consequence of the disastrous massacre of

General Custer and all the troops that were with him, has created so much excitement in the United States, and will probably lead to the almost immediate solution of the Indian question, that I have ventured to give a condensed account of the two principal events in the campaign; namely the fight on Rosebud Creek, on June 17, 1876, with the column under the command of General Crook; and the massacre of General Custer and his brave companions in arms on Sunday, June 25. The United States troops were divided into three columns, which were set in motion to converge on the country held by the Sioux. One of these columns came from the West under General Gibbon, down the valley of the Yellowstone, along the left bank of the river from Fort Ellis, the march being commenced on April 1. Another column came from the East under the officer in supreme command, General Terry. He passed over the Powder River mountains into the valley of the Yellowstone; and, his march being the shorter and easier, he did not leave Fort Lincoln till May 11. The third column, under General Crook, came up from the South, having left Fort Fetterman on May 15. Thus these expeditions were moving on a common centre from hundreds of miles apart. As they approached the country of the hostile Indians, the object was to feel for the enemy, and to sweep by means of scouts large tracts of these wild mountainous and desert lands. Gibbon had to make sure that there were no Indians on the left bank of the Yellowstone, that they had not passed over that river and moved north; and Terry, after he got on the scene, commenced feeling up the southern tributaries of the Yellowstone and seeking trails. When Gibbon reached the point where the Rosebud Creek flows into the Yellowstone, he found the Indians on the opposite side encamped eighteen miles up the creek. Here he was joined by General Terry,

who had ascended the river in the steamer *Far West.*
The valleys of five branches were searched, and gradually
the fighting district was narrowed till it centred in the
valley of the Rosebud, and the valley of the Big Horn.
On Terry's column, which was almost wholly composed
of Custer's regiment, the 7th Cavalry, reaching this tract,
the two columns occupied a position to the north of the
fighting men under 'Sitting Bull,' while Crook, in
command of the 3rd—the strongest column—was to the
south of the hostile Indians. The Sioux were therefore
between the two—Terry, Gibbon, and Custer being in the
valley of the Yellowstone, at the mouths of the tributaries;
while Crook was at the head-waters of these streams.
The object of the combined movement was for each column
to drive the Indians before it, till the retreat of the Sioux
was checked by the advance of one of the others ; but 'Sitting Bull' seems to have early concentrated his warriors,
heavily reinforced by the Cheyennes, Arrapahoes, and other
tribes. He therefore held a commanding position, which
he has thus far turned to account. When Crook arrived
at the head-waters of the Rosebud, learning that the
camp of the Indians was in that valley as Gibbon
had discovered, some eighteen miles from the mouth of
the river, he immediately advanced by forced marches to
attack the village ; but 'Sitting Bull,' aware of his movement, took up a position, and, instead of Crook surprising
'Sitting Bull,' the latter surprised him. The battle that
ensued was long and furious, and the loss on both sides
severe. Crook fell back to his camp, and the Indians
struck their camp and hurried away to the Little Horn
River, a tributary of the Big Horn.

Meanwhile, Custer encamped at the mouth of the
Rosebud, and General Gibbon broke up his camp on
the north or opposite bank of the Yellowstone, and
marched up the stream to the confluence of the Big

Horn, when the steamer *Far West* arrived, and with her assistance he was enabled to cross. Custer, having got all ready for the attack on the Indian camp, drew up his column on June 22, consisting of the twelve troops of the 7th Cavalry—some 14 officers and 600 men, with 180 packed mules, loaded with fifteen days' rations. On the next, the 23rd, the trail discovered by Colonel Reno was found and followed. It turned off from the Rosebud, leading over the divide to the Little Horn, where the scouts reported a large village. Custer marched all night as well as all the day of the 24th ; and on Sunday morning, June 25, the village was declared to be only a few miles ahead. Custer rode in advance with his orderlies, but failed to detect any trace of what the scouts declared to be plainly visible. The village of 'Sitting Bull' was on the left bank of the Little Horn, about fifteen miles from its confluence with the Big Horn. The river on that side is fringed with timber, from the edge of which to the hills on the left—that opposite to Custer's advance—spreads a plain some miles long of bottom-land. By the bank of the river ran the tents of the Sioux, the largest village ever seen in the West, extending nearly four miles, and containing 6,000 or 7,000 people, of whom 4,000 were warriors. On the right, or the side which Custer approached, is a range of bluffs, which the cavalry crowned, and then they looked down upon 'Sitting Bull's' concentrated strength. It is probable that Custer did not correctly estimate the number of the enemy ; for a considerable portion was hidden behind the wood. As he looked down the whole expanse was in commotion. Mounted bands were riding furiously around, and columns of dust arose in every direction, from out of which would shoot single warriors mounted on their swift ponies, and the cry was raised that the Indians were retreating. It may be that Custer was deceived into this belief; for, detaching several troops, he ordered Colonel Reno to pass up, enter the valley, ford the river, and ride down on the village, while he, making the *détour* below, crossed the river and rode up, thus to hem the Sioux between the meeting squadrons. On the bluff he left four troops in reserve, with his pack mules and all the material. At the head of five troops, as the General rode down the ridge he raised his hat to the comrades he left behind, who returned the salute with a loud cheer—the last they ever saw of Custer.

Reno moved up the ridge in compliance with the instructions he had received, descended the valley, forded the river above the village, and formed in open column. Then he advanced at a trot, the pace gradually increasing until it broke into a gallop. The resistance was not serious for a considerable distance, and the first intimation of real danger was in the masses on the bluffs of the valley, opposite those down which the cavalry had descended. The fire became heavier and heavier on the flank of the column as it moved, while gradually the Indians gathered in force in front. The pressure became greater and greater, till it pushed the column towards the river, for all round the front and the left flank the Indians had become massed in overwhelming strength. Then, in order to secure the shelter of the woods, Reno dismounted his party. The Indians, in their efforts to dislodge the whites, charged across the plain, up and into the very trees. On they came, riding ponies, or running on foot, at each charge leaving many of their number before the wood from which they had recoiled; till, what happened in the advance recurred in this attempt to defend an untenable post. Soon the forest was penetrated at every point, and the attack then was in flank and in rear as well as in front.

Vain were the attempts of the officers to keep the Indians from the commanding points. They were soon again in possession of every post, and then Reno saw that he must mount and charge through timber, or, surrounded, be cut off from the reserves. The retreat became a wild scramble for life, the Indians rising up on every side, and each trooper as he galloped was the target for a dozen rifles. But fast as he pressed his horse the Indian pony was swifter still, and often the cavalryman had to contend with five or six painted warriors. Thus the retreat, at first hurried, assumed the aspect of a rout, and really became a race for the ford and life. The Indians fell fast under the revolvers of the cavalry, as they followed undaunted in pursuit. A strong party of the Red Men holding the ford attempted to bar the passage, but were ridden down in the wild flight; then the troopers crossed the river and dashed up the opposite bank under a deadly fire of the Sioux, now filling the woods which skirt the river. It was at the ford, which is narrow, that the loss was heaviest, for the crush prevented a quick passage; but as soon as the foremost soldiers crowned the hill they dismounted and opened fire on the Indians to cover the passage of their comrades, and presently the reserve left on the bluffs came up. The Indians crowded into the river both above and below the ford, and drawing together charged the hill, when they met with severe punishment at the hands of the fresh troops now brought into action.

A troop was detached along the crest of the hill to obtain intelligence of Custer; but at every step opposition strengthened till the officer was recalled in the fear his men would be surrounded and cut off. For some time Reno was left in comparative peace. Two hours passed; still there was no news of Custer. Another hour; and then Reno began to devise means for an

advance along the ridge, which he found almost impossible, hampered as he was with wounded. The officers
were discussing the feasibility of such a movement when
the Indians in large numbers were observed coming up
the valley. The attack on Custer had evidently been
concluded, and they now hoped to complete the destruction of the 7th Cavalry by the annihilation of Reno's
party. The ground was hard, and the shelter imperfect;
yet attempts had been made to dig rifle pits; so when the
fresh assault had been delivered, the soldiers were in a
measure prepared. Yet for a few minutes the lives of
all hung in the balance, so desperate was the charge of
the blood-stained Sioux. Hand to hand the struggle was
maintained; some of the Indians who had expended their
ammunition, entering with clubbed rifles, even hurling
stones: and it was long before the Red Men drew off
exhausted and cowed by the loss inflicted.

No sooner had the day dawned than the attack was
renewed with deafening war-whoops, and now all the
Indians, numbering 3,000 to 4,000, appeared to be
gathered around Reno. The men had been without water
36 hours, and, as the sun grew hot, the suffering increased,
and the animals showed signs of perishing, while around
rose the piteous cry of the wounded for the water which
flowed in a limpid stream below at a distance of some
200 yards. Though every inch of the ground was commanded by Indian sharp-shooters, Reno determined to
procure a supply at all hazards. Suddenly a party sprang
out of the entrenchments and rushed down the hill as if
to repeat the charge on the valley. The attention of the
Indians being diverted by this unexpected attack, another
party with camp-kettles and canteens ran into the river,
where a storm of bullets passed over their heads, for their
comrades were firing at the Indians across the stream,
while the Indians were firing at them. So quickly and

well was this gallant act performed that a full supply was obtained at the cost of five lives. As Dr. De Wolf had been killed, Dr. Porter alone remained to attend to the wounded, the number of whom increased rapidly. About noon on the 26th a change became evident. The Indians, who had covered the country for miles and had blocked every avenue, vanished from the bluffs and all the ground around—presently the valley became the scene of renewed commotion; the lodges were pulled down, and in groups the Red Men hurried away and disappeared in the wild hills. Until dark the stampede continued, and before the night fell, Reno's front was clear, and his command passed a quiet night. Nor was an Indian to be seen when the next day dawned.

It was eleven A.M. on June 26, that Gibbon's column, which had recommenced its forced march, observed a heavy smoke up the Little Horn about fifteen miles distant—taken to be an encouraging sign, but the scouts reported a great battle ending disastrously to Custer. The command reached the river about one P.M., and, having crossed at a good ford, was again in motion by five o'clock. Two scouts with messages for Custer were sent out, but both soon returned pursued by the Sioux who covered the hills. They began to appear on the bluffs to the right, and the column moved along prepared for battle. The force was then in a level bottom-land of considerable width, with the Little Horn on the left, and steep bluff-like lands on the right. It was in these hills the Indians were most numerous, and at nightfall heavy bodies of them were visible. General Gibbon halted, and encamped in a square, well out of rifle range from both river and bluff, the men lying on their arms. With great care the column moved with the light of the next morning up the river, the bluffs narrowing as it passed till the defile opened into a valley beyond. It was in that valley that Custer had fought, and evidences of the struggle soon became visible to the advance guard. The scouts saw they were approaching an Indian village, and Terry received a message from the front that the advance had come on the bodies of 190 troopers, and, judging from what had been seen, there were as many more in the hills near by. As the column proceeded, it came on the remains of an immense and hastily-abandoned Indian village. Buffalo robes, elk-skins, kettles, the camp utensils used by Indians covered the ground. Wounded Indian ponies struggled here, and dead ones lay there, mixed with the bodies of horses branded 7th Cavalry. There, too, lay the head of a white man, but nowhere the body, and close by, stretched, face on ground, lay a trooper with an arrow in his back— the top of his skull crushed in. Two Indian lodges of fine white skins were next passed, around which, in funeral array, were the bodies of the horses killed, for inside were grouped a band of the slain warriors, in war paint and costume, whose spirits had gone to the happy hunting ground mounted on the spirits of the horses outside. On a shirt deeply stained with blood was written—'Lieutenant Sturgis, 7th Cavalry.' And now a horseman was seen riding at speed down the valley. He came to tell how Reno's command had been found on a hill three or four miles farther up, with all that remained of the 7th Cavalry. In traversing the ground the bodies of the fallen soldiers and their horses were passed, horribly mutilated, and offensive from the heat. Where Reno had fought the dead lay mingled together in the wild confusion in which they had fallen in the *melée*, and about three miles down the valley they had ascended, on the other side of the river, was the scene of General Custer's last defence, presenting an appearance even more horrible. On one spot lay 115 soldiers of the 7th, and near the top of a little knoll in the centre of the plateau Custer's unmutilated remains reclined as if in sleep, his face calm, and a smile on his lips. Around were the bodies of 11 officers; on his left was his brother, Captain Thomas Custer; on his right Captain Miles Keogh. Almost at his feet lay a handsome boy of 19, his nephew Reed, who insisted on accompanying the general. Not far away was the corpse of Boston Custer, another brother, and near him was Lieut. Calhoun, the husband of Custer's sister, a lady who lost in that desperate charge her husband, three brothers, and a nephew. And there, too, was Kellogg, the *Herald's* correspondent, while in various parts of the field were strewn the corpses of the officers and men lying as they fell in that fatal fight. Custer rode at the head of five troops numbering 240 men, not one of whom survived. In all, 261 were buried, and 52 wounded were brought away. The officers killed were General Custer, Colonel L. Custer, Colonel Keogh, Colonel Cooke, Colonel Yates, Lieut. Porter, Lieut. Smith, Lieut. McIntosh, Lieut. Calhoun, Lieut. Hodgson, Lieut. Riley, Lieut. Sturgis, Lieut. Crittenden. Lieut. Harrington and Assistant Surgeon Lord are missing.

An old trapper of the Yellowstone country, named Ridgely, who was a prisoner in ' Sitting Bull's ' camp, is probably the only white man alive who witnessed the Custer Massacre. He was taken by the Indians in March last, and was detained, though kindly treated. Custer's movements had been closely watched for days; and the division of the force into detachments was noted with satisfaction. Ambuscades were prepared. There were two villages, the smaller only being visible to Custer, consisting of 25 tepees; but there were 75 double tepees behind the bluff. Custer attacked the smaller village, and was opposed by 1,500 to 2,000 Indians in regular order of battle. The fight was commenced in the ravine, near the ford, and fully half of Custer's command seemed to be unhorsed at the first fire. The action only lasted 55 minutes. Ridgely's account of what followed is thus told :—' After the massacre of Custer's forces the Indians returned to camp with six soldiers as prisoners, and delirious with joy over their success ; those six were tied to stakes at a wood pile in the village, and were burned to death. While the flames were torturing them to death, the Indian boys fired red-hot arrows into their quivering flesh until they died. " Sitting Bull " was met after the fight, and he exultingly remarked that he had killed many soldiers and one damned general, but he did not know who he was. The squaws then armed themselves with knives, visited the battle-field, and robbed and mutilated the bodies of the soldiers. While those soldiers were being burned the Indians turned their attention to a force, evidently Reno's, attacking the lower end of the village.' Ridgely says Custer's command had been slaughtered before a shot was fired by Reno's force, which attacked the lower end of the camp about two o'clock P.M. The Indians returned in the evening and said the men had fought like the devil, but Ridgely says they did not make a statement of their losses. They said the soldiers had been driven back twice, and they piled up stones and the attack was unsuccessful. The prisoners were kept burning for over an hour, but Ridgely was not permitted to speak with them ; so we are unable to state who they were. One was noticeable from his small size and grey hair and whiskers. Reno killed more Indians than Custer, who fell in the midst of the fight ; and two captains, believed to be Yates and Keogh, were the last to die. The night after the massacre the Indians were wild with delight, and many were drunk on whisky stolen from the whites. The squaws performed the duty of guards for the prisoners, and, becoming drowsy,

Ridgely and two companions escaped, securing ponies, and began their long journey homeward.

But as a pleasing contrast to this horrible massacre and disastrous campaign by the United States troops against their hostile Indians, I turn to the more fortunate and successful campaign of the present autumn by the British against some of the Indian tribes in Canada. Recent reports of this campaign are as follow :—

' Lieutenant-Governor Morris and half-a-dozen officials have been away in the north-west territory during the past six weeks, hunting up our Indians, armed with treaties and presents, and, so far as heard from, their success has been remarkable. They have met the Indians in large numbers at different points in the territory, and we hear that on every occasion they have come off victorious—carrying away with them, as the result of each encounter, treaties signed by the chiefs of tribes, ceding their rights over immense districts of territory, and leaving behind them nothing worse than cartloads of presents for the Indians, and the memory of a visit pleasant and profitable on both sides. It is thus we hope to fight and win all our Indian campaigns. To the United States we will leave the exclusive employment on such occasions of horse, foot, and artillery. We shall be content with a contract, reduced to writing, and signed by both parties. Confidence begot of faith kept and justice observed, has ever been and will ever be, we trust, the bond of union between Canada and her red children.'

CAUSES OF INDIAN WARS.

The three principal causes of wars with the Indians are :—

First. Nonfulfilment of treaties by the United States Government.

Second.   Frauds by the Indian agents, and

Third.   Encroachments by the whites.

With reference to the first cause of war, namely, *breach of treaty obligations by the Government*, it is only necessary to observe that it would be extremely difficult to find *any* treaty entered into by the Government with the Indians during the last twenty years, which has been strictly and honourably fulfilled.   At the same time, however, that the United States Government have not fulfilled their engagements, they have not insisted, as they might and should have done, on a strict compliance with treaty obligations by the Indians.

The philanthropic Bishop H. B. Whipple, of Minnesota, who is the champion of the peace policy with the Indians, in an important letter which he has recently addressed to the President with reference to the cause of the existing Indian war, in condemning the breach of the treaty obligations with some of the hostile tribes by which the nation's faith was pledged that no white man should enter the Indians' territory, pertinently remarks :—
' The nation has left 300,000 men living within its borders, without a vestige of government or personal rights of property, or the slightest protection to person, property, or life.   We told these heathen tribes they were independent nations, and sent out the bravest and best officers whose slightest word was as good as their bond, because the Indian would not doubt a soldier's honour, and they made a treaty pledging the nation's faith that no white man should enter that territory.   I do not discuss the wisdom of this treaty, that being for others to decide, but it is the supreme law of the land, and a violation of its plain provisions is deliberate perjury.   General Sherman reports that " *civilisation makes its own compact with the weaker party; it is violated, but not by the savage.*"
It is done by a civilised nation.   The treaty has been

universally approved, because it ended a shameful Indian war, which cost $30,000,000 and the lives of ten white men for every Indian slain. The whole world knows we have violated the treaty, and the reason of the failure of the negotiations last year was because our own Commissioners did not have authority from Congress to offer the Indians more than one-third the sum for their lands they are already receiving under their old treaty.'

The Bishop in continuation, and in contrasting the position and treatment of the Indians by the United States Government with that of the Indians living in British possessions, paints the following two pictures, describing most forcibly the advantages of fulfilment over nonfulfilment of treaties :—

' On one side of the line is a nation that has spent $500,000,000 in Indian wars; a people who have not one hundred miles between the Atlantic and the Pacific which has not been the scene of an Indian massacre; a Government which has not passed twenty years without an Indian war; not one Indian tribe to whom it has given Christian civilisation; and which celebrates its Centenary by another bloody Indian war. On the other side of the line are the same greedy, dominant Anglo-Saxon race, and the same heathen. They have not spent one dollar in Indian wars, and have had no Indian massacres. Why? In Canada the Indian treaties call these men " the Indian subjects of Her Majesty." When civilisation approaches them they are placed on ample reservations, receive aid in civilisation, have personal rights in property, are amenable to law, and protected by law, have schools, and Christian people send them the best teachers. We expend more than $100 to their $1 in caring for Indian wards.'

There is not a tribe but could furnish its list of breaches of treaty obligations; but probably in no case could they be found greater than in the instance of the Absaraka or Crow Indians, who have always been at peace with and the friends of the whites, and have acted as the protectors of the settlers in Montana against the incursions of the hostile Northern Sioux; and yet, after having surrendered to the United States Government the greater portion of their lands in Wyoming and Montana, they have not had a single condition of the last treaty entered into with them fulfilled. I may notably mention that the Government having undertaken to educate their children, and to provide at least *thirty* schools for the tribe, had when I was in Montana, a few years ago, provided only *one*, and that of a most inferior character.

The Indians themselves are keenly alive to the non-fulfilment by the Government of their treaty stipulations. At a recent council with the Brulé Sioux held at the Spotted Tail Agency, with the view of inducing the Indians to remove from their present reservation to the Indian territory, ' Spotted Tail,' referring to the white man's broken faith, addressed the Commissioners as follows:—

' We have come here to meet you, my friends. We have considered the words you brought us from the Great Father, and I have made up my mind. This is the *fifth* time words have come to us from the Great Father. At the time the first treaty was made on Horse Creek there was a promise made to borrow the overland road of the Indians, and though I was a boy then they told me that promises were made to last fifty years. These promises have *not* been kept.

' The next conference we had was held with General Maynadeer, when there was no promise made, but we made friends and shook hands.

' Then there was the treaty made by General Sherman, General Sanborn, and General Harney, when we were told we should have annuities and goods for thirty-five years.

They said this, but did not tell the truth. At that time General Sherman told me the country was mine and I should select any place I wished for my reservation. I said I would take the country from the head of the White River to the Missouri. He said he would give us cows to raise cattle, mares to raise horses, and oxen and waggons to haul logs with, to haul goods and earn money that way. He said, also, there should be issues of such things as we needed to learn the arts with, and, besides that, money to every one. He told us each of us should have $15 for an annuity. He told me these things should be carried out, and for me to go to the mouth of Whitestone and locate my people, and these things should be fulfilled to me. *But it was not true.*

' When these promises failed to be carried out I went myself to see the Great Father, went to his house and told him these things. The Great Father told me to go home and select any place in my country I chose for my home, and go there and live with my people. I came home and selected this place and moved here. They told me if I would move here I should receive a fulfilment of the promises made to me, but all I got was *some very small cows and some old waggons that were worn out.*

' Again, last summer you came to talk about the country, and we said we would consider the matter. We said we would leave it to the Great Father for him to settle. In reply to that he has sent you out this summer.

' When a man has a possession that he values, and another party comes to buy it, he brings with him such good things as he wishes to purchase it with. You have come here to buy this country of us, and it would be well if you would come with the goods you have promised to give us, and to put them out of your hand so we can see the good price you propose to pay for it. Then our hearts would be glad.

' My friends, when you go back to the Great Father I want you to tell him to send us goods ; send us yokes and oxen and give us waggons, so we can earn money by hauling goods from the railroad. This seems to me to be a very hard day; half of our country is at war, and we have come upon very difficult times. This war did not spring up here in our land : it was brought upon us by the children of the Great Father, who came to take our land from us without price, and who do a great many evil things. The Great Father and his children are to blame for this trouble. It has been our wish to live here peaceably ; but the Great Father has filled it with soldiers, who think only of our death.'

The treaty was subsequently concluded, but in signing ' Two Strike,' one of the leading chiefs, representing one of the sub-bands of the tribe, said :—' The reason we are afraid to touch the pen and are silent before you is, because we have been deceived so many times before. If we knew the words you tell us were true, we should be willing to sign every day.'

The frauds of the Indian Agents.—These are so notorious that it is scarcely necessary to revert to them. The most significant fact, however, is that an Indian agent, with a salary of only $1,500 or $2,000 a year, ordinarily retires in the course of a few years with a large fortune.

Congress honestly grants the appropriations due to the Indians, but as a rule not more than from five to twenty per cent. of the actual amount due ever reaches these unfortunate wards of the Government. Usually the actual amount received by the Indians approximates more closely to the smaller than the larger per centage I have named.

Encroachments by the Whites.—These gradual occupations of the lands of the Red Men by the whites within the last thirty or forty years are apparent to any one who will take up a map of the United States, and contrast what was *then* and what is *now* the home and hunting grounds of the Indian.   The Indians have been removed or driven from time to time still farther west, and the fertile States of Illinois, Wisconsin, Minnesota, Iowa, and parts of Missouri, have been carved out of their ancient territories.   This rapid occupation of their lands cannot be better described than by quoting the testimony of an old Sioux chief, given at an Indian Council not many years since.   The chief is reported to have said : ' When I was a young man (and I am now only fifty years old), I travelled with my people through the country of the Sac and Fox tribe to the great water Minne Toɴkah (Mississippi), where I saw corn growing, but no white people.   Continuing eastward we came to the Rock River Valley, and saw the Winnebagoes, but no white people. We then came to the Fox River Valley, and thence to the great lake (Lake Michigan), where we found a few white people in the Pottawatomie country.   Thence we returned to the Sioux country at the Great Falls (Falls of St. Anthony), and had a feast of green corn with our relations who resided there.   Afterwards we visited the pipe clay quarry, in the country of the Yankton Sioux, and made a feast to the " great medicine," and danced the " Sun-dance," and then returned to our hunting grounds on the Prairie.   And now our "father" tells us the white man will never settle on our lands and kill our game ; but see ! the whites cover all these lands that I have just described, and also the lands of the Ponchas, Omahas, and Pawnees.   On the south fork of the Platte the white people are finding gold, and the Arrapahoes and Cheyennes have no longer any hunting-grounds.   Our country has become very small, and before our children are grown up, we shall have no more game.'

Florida, also, was wrested from the Seminoles, and

there is now not one of the aborigines to be found in this State. At the close of the Seminole war, which lasted nearly six years, ' Coacoochee,' or ' Wild Cat,' one of the most distinguished chiefs and warriors of the tribe, after having been captured by Colonel Worth, thus pathetically describes the treatment his people received at the hands of the whites, and the latter's occupation of the lands of his nation :—

' I was once a boy,' said he, in subdued tones. ' Then I saw the white man afar off. I hunted in these woods, first with a bow and arrow, then with a rifle. I saw the white man, and was told he was my enemy. *I could not shoot him as I would a wolf or a bear ; yet like these he came upon me.* Horses, cattle, and fields he took from me. He said he was my friend. He abused our women and children, and told us to go from the land. Still he gave me his hand in friendship. We took it. Whilst taking it he had a snake in the other. His tongue was forked. He lied and stung us. I asked but for a small piece of these lands, enough to plant and to live upon, far south—a spot where I could lay the ashes of my kindred. And even this has not been granted to me. *I feel the irons in my heart.*'

The Black Hills, although solemnly reserved by treaty for the sole occupation of the Sioux, have during the last two years, in spite of the efforts of the Government to prevent them, been taken possession of by miners, whilst the same thing has occurred still farther to the north-west in Northern Wyoming and Montana, where miners and others have settled in the best hunting grounds of the Crows ; the only difference in these two instances being that the Sioux, being the more warlike race, have resented these encroachments, and killed as many miners as they could ; whilst the Crows, on the other hand, who have always been at peace with and the allies of the whites, have acquiesced in these encroachments, or restricted themselves to remonstrances to their agents.

INDIAN ATROCITIES AND WESTERN REPRISALS.

In order to attain a true knowledge of the North American Indian, it is necessary that he should be described as he really is—

> A stony adversary, an inhuman wretch,
> Incapable of pity, void and empty
> From every drachm of mercy.

One of his most striking characteristics is the ferocity and cruelty which he displays against his enemies, be they red or white. It would be as true to depict the tiger as quiet and docile, as to represent that the Indian has one particle of consideration, feeling, or mercy towards either his enemy or captive.

The atrocities committed by the Indians against the whites in the various attacks which they have made on the emigrant trains and their capture of white women, or their raids on the settlements, are so horrible that they cannot well be described. Colonel Dodge in his book has given in the 36th and 40th chapters a few instances. The Indian records teem with these barbarities, and the western man, knowing from past experience the treatment which he and his family will receive at the hands of the Indians if captured, always, if he has the opportunity, makes arrangement to kill himself, wife, and children, rather than any of them should fall into the hands of Indians on the war path. Even officers of the United States have not disdained when engaged in Indian warfare to carry with them a small pocket Derringer pistol, loaded, to be used in the event of capture as a *dernier ressort*, so as to escape by self-inflicted death the torture to which captives are invariably subjected.

Instances of the brutal treatment of white women, captured by the Indians, are unfortunately only too numerous. I may, however, here refer to the case of Mrs. Blynn and child, who were captured by 'Satanta,' chief of the Kiowas, near Fort Lyon, while on their way to their home in the States. 'Satanta' kept her as his captive until the time of the fight of the United States' troops with the Kiowas in 1868, when, in order to prevent her recapture, she was ruthlessly murdered. When the bodies were discovered by the troops there were two bullet holes penetrating the brain, and the back of the skull was fearfully crushed, as if with a hatchet; whilst the marks on the child led to the conclusion that she had been seized by the feet and dashed against a tree.

Another case was that of the Germaine girls, who were captured on the banks of Smoky Hill River in Western Kansas, on September 10, 1874. The family consisted of father, wife, and seven children; six of whom were girls, whose ages ranged between five and twenty-one years. The following is the account given by Catherine, of the attack and of the treatment which she and her sisters received :— 'The next morning I went down the river's bank to drive up the cattle, and when returning heard shouts and yells. Running towards the waggon I saw my poor father shot through the back and my mother tomahawked by a big Indian. They were both scalped while yet living. An old squaw ran up and stuck an axe into my father's head and left it there. Rebecca seized an axe and attempted to defend herself. She was soon overpowered, and knocked down insensible. While lying on the ground covered with blood, several Indians outraged her person. Then they tore her clothes off and covered her up with bed-clothes from the waggon. These were set on fire, and my darling sister was burned to death. Stephen was killed next, his scalp being taken. Sister

Johanna and myself were placed side by side, and they came up to inspect us and see which one they should kill. The choice fell on poor Johanna, and she was shot through the head. Tying us—Sophia, Lucy, Nancy, and myself— they hurried us across the prairie, going south. My clothes were torn from me. I was stripped naked, and painted by the old squaws, and made the wife of the chief who could catch me when fastened upon the back of a horse which was set loose on the prairie. I don't know what Indian caught me. I was made the victim of their desires—nearly all in the tribe—and was beaten and whipped time and time again. They made me carry wood and water like the squaws. I had to kill dogs and cook them for the Indians to eat. We had nothing but dog-meat and horse-meat. During the time we were away from the home camp on the Staked Plains I nearly froze. The snow was very deep, and I had nothing to keep me warm but a blanket. Both feet were frozen, and my nails came off from my feet. Sophia was with me but little of the time—where she went I don't know. I am positive I can identify every one of the seventeen members of the party that murdered my family. "Medicine Water" was with them, and I believe was the leader.'

Atrocities such as have been here indicated have roused the indignation and passion of the frontiersman beyond control, and as this feeling is reciprocated by the Indian who sees his hunting-grounds occupied and food destroyed, it has become almost impossible to exaggerate the antipathy existing between the settlers of the Western Plain and the aboriginal inhabitants. A bloody feud, and a strife utterly implacable, with the mutual purpose of extermination, exists between the two races. The Red Men wage a pitiless and incessant war of treachery against the whites. They never spare; they come in darkness and by stealth, with rifle, tomahawk, and scalping knife;

they creep up under the shadows of woods and by night to the lonely hamlet or solitary cabin, and not a man, woman, or child is left alive or unmutilated. The settler, in his turn, is equally determined and merciless. As evidence of this relentless war I would refer to the following resolutions, not many years since passed by the Idaho Legislature, for the extermination of all Indians :—

‘ Resolved—That three men be appointed to select twenty-five men to go to Indian hunting, and all those who can fit themselves out shall receive a nominal sum for all scalps that they may bring in, and all who cannot fit themselves out shall be fitted out by the committee, and when they bring in scalps it shall be deducted out.

‘ That for every buck scalp be paid 100 dollars, and for every squaw 50 dollars, and 25 dollars for everything in the shape of an Indian under ten years of age.

‘ That each scalp shall have the curl of the head, and each man shall make oath that the said scalp was taken by the company.’

It will be observed that the hunting of men, women, and children is put on a par with the extermination of noxious and dangerous beasts, the males being designated as ‘ bucks’ and the wretched young barbarians, consigned to massacre by this Herodian decree, as ‘ everything in the shape of an Indian under ten years of age.’

The opinion of a friend of General May who passed twenty-five years among the Indians gives so good an illustration of Western ideas and correct mode of treatment of the Indians, that I cannot do better than give it :—

‘ “ They are the most onsartainest varmints in all creation, and I reckon tha’r not mor’n half human ; for you never seed a human, after you’d fed and treated him to the best fixins in your lodge, jest turn round and steal all your horses, or ary other thing he could lay his hands on. No, not adzackly. He would feel kinder grateful, and ask you to spread a blanket in his lodge ef you ever passed that a-way. But the Injun he don't care shucks for you, and is ready to do you a heap of mischief as soon as he quits your feed. No, Cap.," said the western to General May, "it's not the right way to give um presents to buy peace; but ef I war governor of these yeer United States, I'll tell you what I'd do. I'd invite um all to a big feast, and make b'lieve I wanted to have a big talk; and as soon as I got um all together, I'd pitch in and sculp about half of um, and then t'other half would be mighty glad to make a peace that would stick. That's the way I'd make a treaty with the dog'ond, red-bellied varmints; and as sure as you're born, Cap., that's the only way." I suggested to him the idea that there would be a lack of good faith and honour in such a proceeding, and that it would be much more in accordance with my notions of fair dealing to meet them openly in the field, and there endeavour to punish them if they deserve it. To this he replied, " 'Tain't no use talk about honour with them, Cap.; they hain't got no such thing in um; and they won't show fair fight any way you can fix it. Don't they kill and sculp a white man when-ar they get the better on him? The mean varmints, they'll never behave themselves until you give um a clean out-and-out licking. They can't onderstand white folks' ways, and they won't learn um; and ef you treat um decently, they think you are afeard. You may depend on't, Cap., the only way to treat Injuns is to thrash them well at first, then the balance will sorter take to you and behave themselves." '

Only a few years ago in one of the Western territories, whilst conversing with some of the leading settlers in the neighbourhood, I heard a somewhat similar plan proposed. In the instance, however, to which I refer, the speaker stated that his remedy and settlement of the Indian question would be to place all Indians on reservations, and then, strictly confining them to their reservations, feed them with rusty bacon and condemned flour; adding that he believed that in less than a year they would all die off like rotten sheep.

With the existence, then, between them of such feelings of antipathy and animosity, it is impossible for the savage Indians and semi-civilised white men to occupy the same country. All authorities who have investigated the subject are unanimous in predicating that the Red Men are a doomed race. The edict has gone forth, ' *Delenda est Carthago* ;' and the Indians will as surely disappear before the progress of the more energetic and aggressive Anglo-Saxon, as the snows of winter melt away before the summer sun.

But sad as the fate of the Red Man is, yet, even as philanthropists, we must not forget that, under what appears to be one of the immutable laws of progress, the savage is giving place to a higher and more civilised race. Three hundred thousand Red Men at the present time require the entire occupation of a continent as large as Europe, in order that they may obtain an uncertain and scanty subsistence by the chase. Ought we, then, to regret if in the course of a few generations their wigwams, tepees, and mud lodges, rarely numbering more than one hundred in a village, are replaced by new cities of the West, each equalling, perhaps, in magnificence, in stately structures, and in population (exceeding that of all the Indians), either St. Louis or Chicago? Or if in supplanting less than 300,000 wandering, debased, and half-naked savages we can people the self-same district with a population of many tens of millions of prosperous and highly civilised whites?

The countless herds of buffalo, which formerly ranged the plains, will be superseded by treble their number of improved American cattle; the sparse herds of the smooth-haired antelope will be replaced by countless flocks of woolly sheep; and the barren prairies, now covered with the short buffalo grass, yellow sunflower, and prickly cactus, barely sufficient to support the wild denizens of the Plains, will under cultivation teem with yellow harvests of wheat and corn, providing food for millions; so that in a few years the only reminiscence of the Red Men will be the preservation of the names of some of the extinct tribes and dead chiefs in the nomenclature of the leading cities, counties, and States of the Great West.

WILLIAM BLACKMORE.

LONDON: *October 5, 1876.*

PART I.

THE PLAINS.

(*The Great Divide.*)

'This is the highest point. Two ways the rivers
Leap down to different seas, and as they roll
Grow deep and still; and their majestic presence
Becomes a benefaction to the towns
They visit.'   LONGFELLOW.

EARLY DAYS IN DENVER (1859).
Now a city containing upwards of 20,000 inhabitants.

THE PLAINS.

CHAPTER I.

GENERAL DESCRIPTION.

WHEN I was a schoolboy my map of the United States showed between the Missouri River and the Rocky Mountains a long and broad white blotch, upon which was printed in small capitals 'The Great American Desert—Unexplored.'

What was then 'unexplored' is now almost thoroughly known. What then was regarded as a desert supports, in some portions, thriving populations. The blotch of thirty years ago is now known as 'The Plains.'

Like an ocean in its vast extent, in its monotony, and in its danger, it is like the ocean in its romance, in its opportunities for heroism, and in the fascination it exerts on all those who come fairly within its influence.

The first experience of the plains, like the first sail with a 'cap' full of wind, is apt to be sickening.

This once overcome, the nerves stiffen, the senses expand, and man begins to realise the magnificence of being.

At no time, and under no circumstances, can a man feel so acutely the responsibility of his life, the true grandeur of his manhood, the elation of which his nature is capable, as when his and other lives depend on the quickness of his eye, the firmness of his hand, and the accuracy of his judgment.

There is no lack of such occasions on the plains.

The whole western portion of the North American Continent, from the Isthmus of Darien to Behring Straits, from the Missouri River to the Pacific Ocean, is a vast plateau, more or less elevated, through the general level of which many mountain ranges and systems push their heads to the limit of perpetual snow.

The term 'The Plains' is, however, specially applied to a comparatively restricted portion of this great area, extending from the Guadalupe Mountains of Texas on the south to the British line on the north—from the Missouri River on the east to the Rocky Mountains on the west—from the thirtieth to the fiftieth parallel of latitude, and from the ninety-fifth to the one hundred and fifth degree of longitude.

To the scientific geologist the plains is a most interesting and exhaustive field. Its prominent geological features have not been so confused and defaced as in the other elevations, and the problems presented appear so comparatively easy as to attract the interest and attention of even the most unscientific observer.

The first great upheaval—that which lifted from the waters the great mass of the Rocky Mountains—must have resulted in mountain heights to which those now on earth are comparatively molehills.

From the ruins of these mountains the foundation of the plains was to be formed. Their bases ceaselessly lashed by the ever restless ocean, their summits beaten by the deluges of rain which must have marked that early epoch, they were torn to fragments, and the detritus, carried nearer or farther by the currents, were deposited in the layers where they now appear in a new creation of solid rocks.

At their base, and stretching far to the eastward, are now miles upon miles of rounded stones, pebbles, and sand, the washings of ages, deposited at the mouths of rivers and streams in form of bars, or piled in measureless heaps by the action of glaciers.

Almost the whole eastern foot of the mountain is now bounded by this formation. If forms the whole country known as the 'Divide' between the waters of the South Platte and those of the Republican rivers. Near Colorado Springs it is very marked, the bar being hundreds of feet in thickness, and of unknown extent to the eastward; while to the southward it follows the trend of the mountain range crossing the Arkansas, building the plateau on which now stands the new town of Pueblo, until it is finally lost in the volcanic regions about the head of the Cimarron River. How high the original and principal upheaval must have been to have furnished such an amount of detritus and washings is beyond computation.

A little to the southward of the Spanish Peaks appear the first evidences of fire; but, from that starting-point, far to the south and west, there is abundant proof that at one time in Earth's history Nature made it 'very warm' for whatever was in that vicinity. The whole surface is a mass of partially molten rocks, of lava and volcanic tufa. Hundreds of extinct volcanoes dot the country, some of which are even yet remarkable for their beauty and symmetry of form. Of these the most remarkable is the 'Capulin,' near the head of the Cimarron River. Rising sheer from a nearly level plateau, and built by and for itself of molten material to a height of 1,000 feet,[1] it has exactly the form, and nearly the perfect symmetry, of a lady's thimble.

The western side is partially broken down by the last eruption, affording a comparatively easy access to the crater; and, fortunately, owing to its position, it does not in the least detract from the beauty of the cone. Three miles to the south-west is Mount Tilden, appearing from the road an almost perfect hemisphere. It is only 700 or 800 feet high; but the ascent is exceedingly trying, from the fact that the whole surface is composed of loose materials, into which the foot sinks at every step.

[1] The general level of the plateau from which these vo'can es rise is at least 6,000 feet above tide-water.

How a mountain composed of such materials should have
retained for ages its perfect shape is one of Nature's
secrets.

The crater is very perfect, and the specimens of lava
and tufa are the finest to be found in any of the volcanoes. In this crater is growing a large cedar-tree,
which, judging from its external appearance, must be
more than a hundred years old.

From evidence which will appear farther on, there
is no doubt that the plains were for myriads of ages
the *sport* of nature, and were successively upheaved
and submerged partially or wholly; how often can
probably never be known to human intelligence. I
think, however, that every portion of land in this basin,
not of the first grand mountain upheaval, can be referred
to one of three subsequent horizontal upheavals which fix
the distinctive character of the country, and each leaves its
peculiar marks.

The *first* of these, occurring probably about the
period of fire, brought up the immense plateau called the
'Raton Mountains,' the 'Mesa de Maio,' the 'Mesa
Grande,' on which is Fort Union, and many other more
or less isolated plateaus, now having an elevation of from
6,000 to 8,000 feet.

The peculiarity of this first horizontal elevation, is,
that its upper surface is still a plain marked with ridges
of burnt and half-molten rocks, and covered everywhere
with lava and volcanic tufa, so hard as to defy the action
of the elements.

The land elevated by this upheaval rose perpendicularly from the sea, the upper surface remaining nearly
horizontal, but inclining slightly to the eastward. The
precipitous sides, formed of the hard igneous rock, show
scarcely any evidence of wear even by the ages of
exposure to the elements; and, although the ocean still
washed its foot, this plain gave off no detritus. It rises
from the plain below, almost as sheer and unmarked by

the elements as if upheaved but a year ago. Wherever found in the volcanic regions, the distinctive features of this first plain are always the same.

Farther north, out of the region of fire, this upheaval brought up the same rocks, though unburned, and preserved the same characteristic perpendicularity of elevation. This has, however, been very greatly modified by the subsequent action of the elements ; and while the upper surfaces even yet retain their general level, their sides are scored with ravines, and the *débris* falling from the top has rounded out the bottoms into almost the semblance of ordinary hills.

The *second* great horizontal upheaval pushed still farther above tide-water, the continent already formed, and added to it an immense area, forming what is now known as the ' High Plains,' with a present elevation of from 4,000 to 7,000 feet.

Like the first upheaval, it evidently rose sheer from the water; but being of softer material it is, except in some marked places, washed by rains and the action of the sea into an apparent continuation of the third or lowest plain. In many places this second plain stands up almost as sharp and straight as the first, from which, however, it is readily distinguished by the more recent character of the rocks. It is through this second plain that the streams have cut the deep cañons which are so marked a feature in plains scenery; and when, as sometimes happens, a stream has had to work its way through the mass of material forming both first and second plains, the cañon formed is often sublime in its magnificent profundity.

The *third* plain, comprising all the portion from 3,000 or 4,000 feet above tide-water to the general level of the Mississippi and Missouri Valleys, appears to have been very recently formed of material brought from the mountains and upper plains, and to have been slowly and gradually lifted, or rather silted, out of the waters. The general features and appearance give the idea of a subsidence of the waters rather than an elevation of the land, though the latter has been the process of its development.

This plain is greater in extent than either of the others, and of an uniformity and sameness not only uninteresting, but monotonous. About sixty miles from Fort Lyon, on the new road to Fort Union, is one of the most magnificent and instructive views that ever met the eye of a lover of nature.

Standing on the second plain and looking west, the horizon is bounded by the long line of peaks of the 'Snowy Range,' towering to the skies and glittering in everlasting white. Apparently at their feet, though more than a hundred miles from them, and looking like a black table against a white wall, are the Raton Mountains, the first plain or horizontal upheaval. A little to the right, and apparently very near, are the 'Cumbres Espagnoles,' 'Spanish Peaks,' and still farther to the north-west the Sangre de Christo, Greenhorn, Cheyenne, and a vast succession of mountain upon mountain, range after range, the whole overtopped by the magnificent mountain called 'Pike's Peak,' so appropriately and significantly named after its original discoverer, then Lieutenant, but subsequently General Zabulon Pike.

To the south-west, and within five or six miles, the 'Mesa de Maio,' an interrupted continuation of the Raton plain, rises like a huge blank wall 1,000 feet from the high (or second) plain upon which we stand ; and which to our rear, by a sudden and precipitous plunge of 800 to 1,200 feet, reaches the third or lowest plain—the basin proper of the Mississippi and Missouri—which stretches in limitless expanse to the eastward.

From this position can be seen in plainest form, and with all their marked peculiarities, the result of Nature's handiwork in the four great general upheavals, which in my opinion brought this portion of the continent from the depths of ocean.

In some portions of the middle plains Nature seems to have endeavoured to outdo her previous efforts, and to try how many and varied forms the surface of the earth could be forced to assume by means of partial upheavals. Some of the most curious of these formations are to the west of the Laramie plains.

The ground is broken in every possible way, the lines of upheaval running at all points of the compass, and parallel, perpendicular, or oblique to neighbouring mountain ranges.

One very remarkable peculiarity presents itself in several ranges of hills in the vicinity of Fort Fred Steele. Extending sometimes for miles, a portion of earth, more or less broad, is as it were turned on edge, as one might partially open the cover of a book lying on a table. The lifted edge rises almost perpendicularly from the earth, showing the stratification; while the other face of the hill thus formed is the natural surface of the ground, covered with prairie grass, shrubs, &c.

Immediately behind this long narrow hill, and probably by the same convulsion, is elevated another similar hill, with one sheer stratified face, the other not so steep, and with a natural surface. This is continued, and I have seen as many as five distinct ranges of hills, each one in rear overtopping that in front; all the front faces being masses of stratified rocks, whilst all the rear faces are the natural surface of the ground. The front face of the range opposite Fort Fred Steele is not more than seventy feet in height, while the summit of the last is at least 600 feet above the plain below.

The Rattlesnake Hills present another curious feature. They are a series of four or five ranges of hills, from 600 to 800 feet in height, parallel to, and the nearest from half a mile to a mile distant from, the great Medicine Bow Range of the Rocky Mountains. They are separated from each other by ravines 300 or 400 feet deep, and from 200 to 400 yards wide. I once described this formation to Professor Agassiz. Without seeing, he could not accurately account for it ; but his hypothesis was, that Nature by her slow processes had built up immense beds of secondary rocks about the foot of the great wedge-shaped mass of the Medicine Bow Range. A convulsion uplifted the mountain, forcing it through the portions of secondary resting on its shoulders, turning over a great mass as the plough turns the earth from the furrow. Subsequently there came another upheaval, lifting the mountain higher, and turning another parallel mass from its sides. He considered that the number of parallel hills showed the number of lifts that the mountain had received before arriving at its present elevation.

Twenty miles south of Rawlin's Springs is another curious freak of nature, the parallel ridges being overturned, not by the upheaval of a wedge-shaped mountain, but by the successive lifts given to a huge plain (part of first plain). A succession of parallel ranges of barren rocky hills is finally greatly overtopped by what appears, looking at its face, to be a fine mountain range, it being 8,000 or 9,000 feet high, and on this face looking north can all the year round be found patches of snow. Reaching its summit with difficulty, one is surprised to find stretching far to the south and west an apparently boundless plain, with a gentle declination from the northern face. Proceeding a mile or two south, this plain begins to be broken with the shallow depressions deepening gradually into ravines, the beds of beautiful streams (full of fine trout), the heads of the Muddy, a tributary of Green River.

In the ravine formed by the grand northern face of this magnificent plain and the parallel range on the north, runs the old overland stage road ; and the ravine itself is Bridger's Pass, celebrated in the olden time for its natural difficulty, and its danger from Indians. In the ordinary sense of the word it is no pass at all; that is, it crosses no mountain range. It is, as already stated, simply a ravine between two parallel ranges. The road was made through it in consequence of its supply of water. The Union Pacific Railroad runs parallel to, and almost within sight of, the old waggon road, for several hundred miles west from Laramie City, the rail crossing a succession of comparatively level plains, while the waggon road was obliged to wind its way close to the great ranges, climbing and descending rough and difficult foot hills, crossing deep and dangerous ravines, increasing greatly the distance, and a hundredfold the difficulty: attributable to that prime necessity 'water.'

The 'Church Buttes,' still farther west, are another remarkable feature. The bed of a great lake—probably of fresh water—has been thrust up, so that it now stands from 100 to 200 feet above the surrounding plain.

This elevation must have taken place before the material had time to solidify into rock. Though stratified, the 'Buttes' are quite soft, and filled with remains of reptiles, &c. The faces of the 'Buttes' are still nearly perpendicular; and, however long they may have been exposed to the elements, not a very great deal of the material has been washed down, the surrounding plain appearing to be of very different composition. At a little distance—from half a mile to a mile from the 'Buttes'—the plain is covered with agates and petrifactions. Some of the most beautiful specimens of moss agates come from this plain.

Every one has heard of the 'Bad Lands,' a singular formation which appears at intervals from the Loup River to the mouth of the Yellowstone. This was all, undoubtedly, once the bed of a very shallow lake, or inland sea, which must gradually have subsided, since it remained for ages a marsh. The whole formation is full of the bones of animals, the larger of which are generally found in nearly a naturally upright position, as if the animals had mired in the morass.

On a foundation of stiff clay, or other hard material, a deposit of soft and loose materials, arranged in layers or strata, varying in thickness from thirty to 600 feet, has been made.

The curious peculiarity of the ' Bad Lands' formation is, that the channels cut by rains and frost in this soft deposit have almost invariably perpendicular sides, and differ from ordinary ravines in that there is no gradual deepening. They appear to cut at once through the whole thickness of the deposit, are exceedingly tortuous, and vary in width with the nature of the particular locality, or with the length of time that the process of erosion has been going on.

With this general peculiarity, the 'Bad Lands' vary in the most extraordinary degree. In some localities the upper plain appears at a little distance unmarked; but an attempt to pass over it discloses the fact that it is scored in every direction by innumerable narrow crooked channels, from thirty to 100 feet in perpendicular depth, and from a few inches to eighty or 100 feet in width. Through such 'bad lands' no one but the most experienced plainsman can hope to make headway.

In process of time the narrow grass-covered portions of plain between the channels are gradually cut away into backbones, at first very sharp and narrow getting broader, however, as more of the material is washed away. This is called the 'Hogs back' Bad Lands, and in most of its stages is utterly impassable. When most of the material inside a particular bed has been washed out, and the Hogsbacks levelled with the foundation plain, the 'Bad Lands' present their most striking characteristics.

Imagine an immense irregular bowl-shaped depression in the earth, from four to ten miles in diameter; the sides, from 100 to 600 feet high, cut by the action of water into myriads of forms, 'regular, irregular, and fantastic.' The general bottom of the bowl is level; and scattered over it, in most picturesque irregularity, are hills and mounds, with their almost perpendicular faces cut into every conceivable and inconceivable design—castles and towers, domes and pinnacles, obelisks, monuments, and pyramids. The palace and the Indian 'tepee' are here side by side, and all the varied forms are fluted by water, and frescoed in variously-coloured earths, forming a grand and wonderful *coup d'œil* that no man can imagine or realise until he sees it.

Travel through these 'Bad Lands' is not difficult. The ground is covered with fragments of the bones of animals and reptiles; and the man must indeed be insensible who can pass unmoved through these most magnificent burying-grounds of animals extinct before the advent of his race.

Almost everywhere throughout the whole length and breadth of the plains are found, in greater or less profusion, animal remains, fossils, shells, and petrifactions. Bones are very numerous and in great variety, from the Saurion and Mastodon to the minutest reptile, ranging in point of time from the remotest ages to the present day.

When the Union Pacific Railroad was building, an attempt was made to obtain water for the engines by sinking a well at Julesburg. No water was obtained ; but many interesting facts were developed, during the progress of the work, as to the nature of the great plains deposit. When the shaft had been sunk to a great depth (I think between 200 and 300 feet), the workmen came to an immense deposit of bones of animals in every state of preservation or decay. These, as they were brought to the surface, were eagerly picked over by curiosity-hunters, and the most perfect carried off. Some time after this I was so fortunate as to be stationed at Fort Sanders, when that post was honoured by a visit from Professor Agassiz. He had hardly been at the post twenty-four hours before (as, I am told, was usual with him) he had converted the whole garrison into enthusiastic naturalists, and everything rare or curious was brought to him for examination and explanation. One of the officers had a bone from the Julesburg well, which, after some trouble, was fished out of a box of similar treasures, where, carefully labelled, it had been stowed away as something most especially worth preserving. This was brought to the Professor, who examined it carefully, while we stood around in eager expectation. 'It is,' said he—in the broken English which gave additional charm to his most interesting and instructive conversation—'it is the bone of an antelope.' 'How,' exclaimed several, in disappointed surprise, 'could an antelope bone get three hundred feet under ground?' 'Ah! that,' answered the Professor, 'I do *not* know; but I do know that this is the leg-bone of an antelope.'

At many times, and in widely separated localities, I assisted at the unearthing of bones of extinct monsters, or turned over piles of curious fossils, or great beds of shells, which, I regret to admit, I was too ignorant to classify or fully appreciate. One of the most remarkable of plains phenomena is the wide dissemination of petrifactions. It is scarcely possible to examine any piece of pebbly ground without finding numbers of specimens, some of them extremely perfect and beautiful. Sometimes acres of a plain will be covered with specimens of 'wood agates' of almost every shade of colour, from pure white to jet black, from almost perfect transparency to thickest opacity, all solidified in the hardest of quartz, but showing the annual rings of woody fibre as clearly as if the specimen had just been torn from its native tree. Sometimes whole forests appear to have been converted into stone. In a small ravine, a dry tributary of 'Two Butte Creek,' I once came upon what appeared to be a sort of raft or obstruction of logs. As it is a perfectly treeless country, I was led to a closer examination, and to

my surprise found that the logs were stone. Never elsewhere have I seen petrifactions so large or so perfect.
One huge trunk of a pine-tree was about six feet in
diameter and ten or twelve feet long. It was hollow, and
a portion of the hollow part had been burned away. The
bark, the wood, the hollow, the marks of fire, were all
perfectly natural, yet the log was solid stone. Many
other trunks, branches, and broken portions were lying
about or heaped in a sort of dam across the ravine, which
even if full of water could scarcely have floated away the
smallest of them as wood. One broken piece of heart-
pine was as perfect as if just split from the log, with the
' fat yellow ' resin exuding between the layers; but all was
stone. The place where these now lie is on what I
designate as the ' second plain.' a high, and here nearly
level, tableland. At this time I doubt if there is a growing pine-tree within fifty miles of the spot, and I have
never seen growing, in the most protected cañon of the
Rocky Mountains, so large a pine-trunk as this petrifaction. The process of petrifaction seems in many cases to
be inexplicable. Once marching with a command near the
Medicine Bow Creek, I was searching for a crossing over
a deep and difficult ravine for my waggons, when I came
to a stump of a pine-tree about two feet high and twelve
inches in diameter. About it were lying large chips such as
none but an experienced axeman and a good axe take
from trees in felling ; something attracted my close attention to the stump, which I found to be of stone. On dismounting and picking up the chips, I found that they also
were stone. This tree had undoubtedly been cut down
by a white man, probably since the exodus of the
Mormons. The petrifaction of the stump is easily accounted for ; but how account for the conversion to stone
of the scattered chips, lying on the hard dry surface of the
ground away from moisture ! I filled my saddle-pockets
with these chips, and subsequently distributed them among
friends, scientific or otherwise. I have recently learned

that the stump has been dug up and sent to some scientific establishment in the east.

Some portions of the plains seem to be entirely underlaid by a mass of gypsum. The streams tributary to the Cimarron on both sides, east of 100° longitude, cut their way through immense deposits of this mineral. North of the Great Salt Plain of the Cimarron the deposit seems to attain its greatest thickness. Though the ' divide ' is high, and the country very broken, the rains in many places do not reach the principal channels by ravines, but through caves and tortuous caverns cut underground by the dissolution of the gypsum. From these hills I have taken out beautiful specimens of selenite transparent as glass. Here are also fair samples of alabaster, though not to my knowledge in masses sufficiently large to be of commercial value. The water impregnated by the gypsum is sweet and sickly to the taste; it fails to satisfy thirst, and warrants a constant admixture of some corrective.

The Great Salt Plain of the Cimarron is a curiosity well worth travelling many miles to see. For thirty or forty miles the bed of the stream is an expanse of sand half a mile wide, in many places so loose as to form quicksands. This is so impregnated with salt that the buffalo lick it up greedily. Near the mouth of Buffalo Creek a number of springs rise from the bed, the water of which is a saturated solution of almost pure salt. A great area of nearly a hundred acres is floored to unknown depths with most beautifully crystallised rock salt, as clear and apparently pure as that taken from the evaporating pans at Syracuse, in the State of New York. It can be quarried out in lumps and boulders of any size. These splendid natural salt works are unfortunately situated in the Indian Territory, and have not yet been in any way developed.

The hills in this gypsum region along the Cimarron are covered with splendid buffalo grass, the streams bordered by beautiful trees and shrubs in great variety, and, bad as is the water, this country abounds in game, and is a favourite wintering-place of the Cheyenne and Airapahoe Indians.

In strong contrast to the beauty of this well-watered gypsum country is the horrible sterility of the alkali plains. West of the North Platte, towards Green River, there stretches one of the most horrible of these deserts, called the ' Bitter Creek Country.' Scarcely a shrub or blade of grass relieves the eye. The dry earth is covered with a whitish efflorescence, and every puff of the sultry wind fills each pore with an acrid caustic dust, irritating and inflammatory to an intolerable degree. The skin cracks; the eyes becoming inflamed, bloodshot, and watery, cannot bear the horrible glare; the tongue swells, the lips bleed, and the throat is parched. The water quenches not the thirst, but irritates the alimentary canal, disarranges the whole internal economy; and many days of travel in this country sometimes brings the hapless traveller to an end, as full of suffering and torture as could be devised by the most inventive Indian.

Almost similar, though not quite so bad, is the alkali desert of the Upper Red River. Numberless others, of greater or less extent, give a not always pleasurable variety of travel on the plains.

About twenty-five miles from Fort Lyon, on the Purgatory River, is a curious picture on stone. The rocky bluff is of carboniferous sandstone, about fifty feet high, and nearly perpendicular. Somewhat less than half way up is the picture of a bear rudely drawn, and a little larger than life size. Scientific men have examined it, each of whom had a different opinion. The yellowish grey rock is blackened to the depth of about two inches. It is not painted, it is not an infiltration. The composition of the blackened rock is the same as that not discoloured. One savant claimed that it is a photograph of a bear taken by lightning on the rock! Whatever it is, it certainly is a remarkable freak of nature.

Coal of good quality is found in many places on the plains. Building-stone is confined to a comparatively few localities. On the middle plains, about the Smoky, Pawnee Fork, and the Arkansas, there is an unlimited supply of a rock about equally a limestone and a sandstone. In some places on the Arkansas, as at Old Fort Lyon, it comes from the quarry in such perfect cubes or parallelopipeds, that without cutting it may be placed in a wall like bricks. In other places the strata is much thicker; but the rock itself, when taken from the quarry, is so soft that it can be cut into any desired shape with a common handsaw. This, though it makes a pretty building, is not so durable as the harder stone of the thinner strata.

A volume might be written of the curious features and formations of the plains. Enough, however, has been said to invite the attention of scientific men to this vast and most instructive field.

CHAPTER II.

SURFACE.

It is the common opinion among persons who have never been in the Great West, that the plains are a vast limitless expanse, as level as an Eastern meadow. Nothing could be farther from the truth. Nature abhors a level as it does a vacuum; or I should more truly say that nature, in striving to bring all things to a general level, is constantly antagonistic to partial levels. The general surface of each of the three great plains was undoubtedly nearly a level; all, however, having a decided inclination from the mountains. This general surface is now broken in three ways: by local convulsion and partial upheavals, by superposition of portions of an upper plain, and by the action of water.

The great convulsion which upheaved the first plain raised up at the same time other grounds, some of which must have been islands in the deep; and yet others farther away from the fire region, which, unprotected by lava and partially molten rocks, have been gradually rounded into long ranges which now stand as hills above the general level of the second plain.

The 'Two Buttes,' the 'Potato Butte,' and many similar lone flat-topped peaks, are fine specimens of the islands of the first upheaval, while the heavy ridge stretching along the north bank of Ceriso Creek (near the Mesa de Maio) is undoubtedly attributable to the same upheaval, though its distinctive features have been somewhat marred by ages of exposure to the elements So with the second plain, which at the time of its upheaval was undoubtedly much more extensive than at present. The line of demarkation between the second and third plain is most distinctly indicated in the country south and west of Fort Lyon, the second plain rising by a sudden jump of from 500 to 1,000 feet from a general level of the 'third. For from twenty to thirty miles from this present line the surface of the third plain is broken by large masses of the second plain, some still almost perpendicular, other almost rounded into hills, but all having the general level of the second plain.

Standing, therefore, on either of the lower plains, anywhere in the comparative vicinity of its junction with the plain above it, our horizon will be bounded more or less by hills all referable to the next plain above.

Away from the vicinity of the junction of the plains we appear to be surrounded on all sides by a boundless expanse of dead level. This appearance is due to the fact that in looking at it the eye catches only the higher lines of the upper surface of a plain which was originally almost a dead level. I have already said that the inclination of all the plains is from the mountains. How decided this inclination must have been at first is proved by the peculiarity of the streams. The larger rivers, the Platte, the Arkansas, and the Canadian, taking their rise in the mountains, were already pouring their waters towards the ocean in tortuous channels scarcely yet worn through the new upheaval. They kept a general course down the inclination; the Arkansas alone swerved from its direct course by a mass of hilly country (which will, I think, be found to be referable to the second plain). The first rains which fell upon the newly-raised lands had to make channels for themselves. They naturally sought the greatest inclination. It was from the mountain. An examination of a good map will show how completely the streams appear to ignore each other, and how each independently takes its own course towards the sea.

Rain which falls within 400 yards of the Arkansas runs into Pawnee Fork, keeping nearly parallel to the larger stream for 200 miles, before finally uniting with it. These rains falling on and running over the newly upheaved and soft materials of the plains, have rounded the higher portions into long and gentle slopes, each, however, terminating in a ravine, which becomes deeper, wilder, and more tortuous until it has entirely cut its way through the second plain. When the ground is high and the 'divides' between the streams narrow, these streams are exceedingly precipitous and difficult, and to travel through them with waggons is a work of art.

The streams which take their rise in the mountains cut their way through the second plain in cañons more or less wide and deep, depending on the nature of the material encountered. The South Platte (at first deflected from its natural course, and sent to the northward by the immense mass of *débris* washed from the mountains and deposited in the sea as a bar) gets through with difficulty, but cutting no very remarkable cañon, the materials through which it made its way being of such a nature as to be rapidly rounded into hills and easily worn away into slopes.

The Arkansas cuts through the same 'bar,' but encounters from the second plain a more rigid resistance than the Platte, and it gets a long way from the mountains before fairly out of cañon.

The tributaries of the Arkansas, which take their rise in the mountains, cut splendid cañons for their passage. Of these the finest is that of the 'Purgatory,' which for more than fifty miles is almost shut out from the light of day by beetling cliffs of red sandstone, 800 to 1,000 feet high, and in many places within a very few hundred feet of each other.

The Cimarron, rising on the west side of the great first plain or Raton Mountains, runs at first to the southward; then, turning abruptly to the east, cuts its way through the immense depth of both first and second plains by one of the most magnificent cañons east of the mountains.

The Canadian acts in the same way; but, having to cut through only the second plain, its cañon, though fine, is not comparable to that of the Cimarron.

So long as these streams are in the second plain they are rapid, deep, have high steep banks, narrow but fertile bottoms, lands covered by a thick growth of cotton-wood and other soft-wood trees, with bushes and shrubs in great variety, with plums, grapes, cherries, gooseberries, and some other wild fruits and berries.

As soon as they emerge on the third plain their character changes; their current is less rapid, the banks are low, the bed is wide, shallow, and filled with sand. The bottom lands are very broad, without trees or shrubbery, except occasionally a small growth of willow, scarcely larger than switches. The bottom is an alluvial deposit of from one to six feet, underlaid by sand. When the river rises and the current increases in power, this sand is washed out from below, the bank falls in, and the stream is never, for two consecutive years, in the same bed, the current eating the alluvium on one side to deposit great bars on the other. These in a very few years gain a scanty vegetation, another slight deposit of alluvial soil, to be again destroyed by another freak of the ever-changing current. One of the most striking peculiarities of these rivers is that they rise downward.

In April the Arkansas, at Fort Dodge, is a sandy bed, a fourth of a mile in width, and with possibly an average of three or four inches of water. In June, when the mountains send forth their floods of melted snow, the river swells, the current increases in power, and washes out long channels in the sandy bed. When the banks show a rise of two feet the waters cut channels in the sand five or six feet deep, and covering probably a full third of the distance from bank to bank. At these times the current may be said to be a huge wave of sand surging, rolling, turning, and shifting with incessant activity. Where there is six feet of water in the morning, there may by noon be a bar with but an inch. By night the bar may be gone and a deep channel in its place. These channels are from ten to thirty feet wide, with generally perpendicular sides. Some force will set a current in a particular direction across a bar. In a few moments a channel from three to six feet deep is cut, through which the water pours as in a mill-race. A shift or change above diverts the current to some other direction, and in almost as few moments the recent channel is filled up to within a few inches of the surface of the water. As the currents by turns set in almost every conceivable direction with reference to the general course of the stream, so the channels may be parallel, oblique, or even perpendicular to that general course. Even leaving out of consideration the danger of quicksands, it can be readily seen that the crossing of such a stream is no child's-play. A good place of entrance being found, the horse and rider, stripped of every superfluous article, wade in. For a few paces the horse steps along in water but a couple of inches in depth. Without a moment's notice or preparatory deepening, his fore feet go down under him, and he plunges head first into swimming water with a tremendous current. He has hardly recovered the shock, and struck out fairly in swimming, before his chest strikes a wall of sand, on which, after many struggles and plunges, he finally succeeds in obtaining a footing. Again he walks on in shallow water, again to be plunged suddenly into a treacherous channel, again to scramble, plunge, and strain to get out of it. Imagine this done over and over again for twenty or thirty times, and with an infinity of variations, and an idea can be formed of the crossing of a plains river in high water. All the streams which come from the mountains are the same in this peculiarity.

One summer I had a small row-boat on the South Platte opposite 'Fort Sedgwick.' Every day some one used it in crossing the river, and though the boat drew but about four inches of water, and though the river was impassable to animals except by swimming channels for nearly a third of the distance, the crossing could never be effected twice on the same line. The boatmen soon learned to know the position and contour of a bar by the appearance of the ripples on the surface of the water. The boat, in making its journey from side to side, not unfrequently had to make three or four times the distance up or down, seeking a passage through the constantly shifting bars. It can be readily seen from this description that no permanent ferry is possible on such rivers. Much money was spent, and time lost, in the effort to establish a flying bridge by boats at Fort Dodge. The effort failed of course. The first boat launched in deep water was fast aground in an hour or two, and its wreck now lies imbedded in sand, exactly where the launch took place.

An ordinary flat boat may be used to great advantage in crossing these streams, provided there be men enough to manage it. After loading, a rope as long as possible, not less than 200 or 300 feet, is attached to one corner. The other end is carried the full length up the bank. Half-a-dozen good swimmers then take hold near this end, and start into the water, wading when possible, and swimming when necessary. They find a good foothold well out in the river, when twenty more men are sent out to man the rope. Such of these as cannot swim must hang on to the rope in crossing the channels. The rope being manned (by groups at intervals for mutual assistance in case of danger), a couple of good men armed with long poles are placed on the boat, and when all is ready it is swung off. As it floats towards the middle of the river, the swimmers at the far end of the rope constantly gain ground towards the other bank, swimming or wading, all the other men attached to the rope necessarily following. The bars being of such loose shifting materials, the boat can, if there be men enough, and a good foothold for them, generally be forced over them, the corner to which the rope is attached acting as a wedge in opening a way, which the men with poles constantly widen, by pushing the stem of the boat up or down stream, working it sideways while the ropemen pull. If the bar cannot be forced in this way, the boat is either pulled up stream, or allowed to drop down, until the bar can be turned. It is a tedious process and dangerous for men, but is often absolutely necessary as the only means of crossing the stream. A raft on such a stream would be utterly useless, even could the timber to make it be found. The great danger of these rivers is not only from swift channels and quicksands, but from the great weight of the current, loaded as it is with sand. A man caught in one of these moving sand-waves seems to lose the power even of struggling. Some soldiers were one day fishing with a seine in the South Platte, where the water was two or three feet deep. The three men farthest from the bank suddenly went down. One was caught by a comrade and saved. The others were never seen again either in life or in death. The sand never gives up its dead.

There are many varieties of quicksand. Sometimes the bottom seems to fall out and leave horse and rider in a void of sand and water. This, though disagreeable, is not very dangerous. At other times a horse will sink to his knees, or to his belly, before finding a firm bottom, the sand closing tenaciously to his legs and feet. If he be new to the experience and the sand bad, he will probably drown or cripple himself by straining. The most dangerous and treacherous are those which not only catch and grip tenaciously, but in which the victim sinks deeper and deeper, slowly but most certainly, until buried in unknown depths. A man or animal caught in one of these has no hope but from outside assistance. Fortu-

nately the most dangerous sands are moderately firm on
the surface, and a man has usually sufficient warning to
enable him, with ordinary presence of mind, to escape.
Besides this, from his broader foot and quicker movements, a man does not sink in quicksands so rapidly as a
horse or mule, and men will walk with impunity around
a waggon sunk to its bed, or drag out a mule sunk to its
haunches.

The streams which take their rise in the second plain,
as the Loup, the Republican, Smoky, and the more
easterly tributaries of the great rivers, have nearly the
same peculiarities as their more ambitious compeers. At
their heads they round off the broad expanse into long
slopes. Gradually deepening, they cut their way through
more or less pretentious cañons, with narrow, fertile,
alluvial bottoms, gorged with vegetation, charming in
grace of outline, and beautiful in variety of scenery.
On arriving at the third plain, they take the characteristics of the larger rivers in that plain, and, on a smaller
scale, are just as bare, as monotonous, and as dangerous.
This third plain was probably once the almost desert
shore of a shallow sea, or arm of the Gulf of Mexico,
into which was poured the rich treasures of alluvial soil
brought from the mountains, gradually filling it up and
forming a great marsh. It is the most barren and least interesting of the plains, and sinks gradually towards the east
and south, becoming finally merged in that great alluvial
deposit now the Mississippi Valley proper. The transition
from the bare, sandy monotony of the one, to the luxu-
riant, almost tropical, vegetation of the other, is generally
too gradual to be fully appreciated. Occasionally, however, it is so abrupt as to be almost startling, giving rise
to a thousand conjectures as to the cause of the remarkable phenomenon.

I have heretofore intimated that there are no really
level plains. This is a truth to which there are exceptions.
Portions of the surface of the great first plain, within the

fire limit, are yet very nearly level, having been protected from the action of the elements by the lava and half-molten rocks with which they are covered.

Portions of the second plain are also yet found which are not broken by ravines. These were probably very level areas of the original ocean-bed, which in the upheaval were lifted so horizontally that the rains found no inclination, and were absorbed by the porous soil before having time to make one. Even when they occur, these level plains are very limited in extent, and generally have one, or many, depressions in their surface of greater or less extent, which are lakes after rains.

On this kind of prairie are found the curious depressions called ' buffalo wallow.' These are formed in the following manner : A heavy rainfall deluges the hard and level prairie. The water is soon absorbed by the thirsty soil, or licked up by the hot sun-rays; a portion of the soil, a little more moist than that adjoining, opens in cracks, such as can be seen in any ordinary dried-up mud hole. Another hard rain comes : these cracks are filled up by earth washed from their edges, which, packed more tightly, and retaining moisture longer than before, cracks again wider in drying. This process is repeated again and again, until quite a depression is made into the soil, which is now so tightly packed as to retain water for a considerable time. When the buffalo is shedding his coat in the spring, he is constantly endeavouring to get rid of the superfluous hair, and, in the absence of trees against which to rub, he is frequently rolling and rubbing himself on the ground. These small water-holes are his especial delight. He throws himself into them with the greatest satisfaction, rolling and plunging, and rounding out the hole until it is of a size to fit comfortably his huge proportions. Sometimes the prairie will be dotted for a mile with these holes, which are generally oval in shape, five to ten feet long, three to five broad, and from six inches to two feet in depth.

The buffalo is in no way necessary to the formation
of the 'buffalo wallow,' it being found in parts of the
country where there are no buffalo. He simply uses the
mud bath provided by nature, and in doing so renders his
tub more shapely and symmetrical. The process of formation is exactly similar to that of the 'hog wallow' of
Southern Texas. Given certain conditions of soil, position,
and rainfall, and prolific nature does the rest. Besides its
use as a bath the 'buffalo wallow' is an admirable reser-
voir for the preservation of water. The high levels on
which they occur are frequently far from natural springs
or water-courses, and the buffalo and other game would
suffer greatly but for the water stored and retained in
these holes. Often when marching in unknown regions,
across the hot and dusty plain, with men and animals
suffering for water, I have hailed with delight the appearance of these natural tanks, and many a pleasant camp
have I made beside one, the fuel for cooking being the
ample store of dried buffalo droppings, or chips in profusion over the prairie.

The plains proper are treeless. The high first plain
affords in its deep cañons protection to a growth of
small pine and cedar. The second plain is entirely
bare on its surface. The gorges cut by the streams
(whether rising in the mountains or in its own bosom)
are filled with a fine growth of large trees, cotton-wood,
hockberry, elm, with shrubs, bushes, vines, and a profusion of flowers. As the gorges widen the timber grows
more and more scarce, and by the time the stream
arrives at the third plain, there is scarcely a tree or
even a shrub to be found on its banks. The Platte, the
Arkansas, and the Cimarron, filter their waters for hundreds of miles through the sands of their shallow beds,
without a tree to give life and variety to the scene. Their
tributaries murmuring brooks, embowered in shade, picturesque with festooned vines, lovely with flowers and
vocal with the songs of myriads of birds; while the cañons

of the second plain are bare, monotonous, and lifeless as the third.

Many scientific reasons have been given for the treeless condition of the prairies, none of which, that I have seen or heard, meet all the points of the problem. It is easy to account for the treeless character of the high plains ; but why one portion of the lower plain should be bare while a contiguous portion apparently exactly similar in soil and position is covered with a fine forest, is a problem which I believe will never be satisfactorily solved.

From the evidence of practical farmers I am convinced that the soil of the second plain is naturally as good for agricultural purposes as any to be found. It is a deep, rich loam, containing all the ingredients necessary for the best farming lands. All it needs is water. Along the railroads which cross this plain, wherever there is water sufficient for irrigation, fine gardens are made. The trees set out are healthy and grow rapidly, if only supplied with enough water and protected from the winds. Many of the streamlets of the second plain, rising apparently on its surface, probably owe their origin to the strata from the first plain. They sometimes meander for miles in meadow-like plains, or through gentle undulations, before cutting cañons for themselves. The soil is perfect, the water abundant, yet there is not a tree, scarcely a bush. As soon as the brook has cut a narrow and deep cañon, every available space is probably crowded with vegetation—trees, shrubs, and vines. The soil is the same, the water the same ; the only difference is, that one portion is exposed to the wind, whilst the other is not.

The Indians burn portions of the prairie every fall, setting the fires so as to burn as vast an extent of country as possible, and yet preserve unburned a good section in the vicinity where they purpose to make their fall hunt. The buffalo, finding nothing to eat on the burnt ground collect on that unburnt—reducing greatly the labour of the hunt. These prairie fires, which were formerly supposed to account for the treelessness of the plains, have really comparatively little to do with it. On the high prairie the grass is very short. When on fire, the blaze, from six to fifteen inches high, moves over the ground slower or faster, according to the wind, but not with vitality or heat enough to seriously injure a bush of a few inches in diameter. Yet the high prairie is bare. In the cañons the grass is often five to ten feet high, and dried leaves, shrubs, bushes, vines, furnish a storehouse of fuel, sufficient to make a roaring vortex of twenty feet of flame. And yet the cañons are full of vegetation. The only occasion where fire acts a prominent part as a cause of the treelessness is at the lower ends of the cañons, where the bottoms widen out, and the hills, becoming lower, are more remote, and afford less protection from the wind. Trees will grow in such positions, but not so stubbornly as in the cañons. The fire in the long grass about their trunks, fanned by the winds to which they are exposed, will destroy the smaller, and so burn the trunks and branches of the larger trees as frequently to kill them. In many such places the islands in the stream which fire cannot reach will be covered with fine trees and thick vegetation, while the contiguous banks are as bare as any portion of the high prairie. On many streams, particularly on the North Platte, some of the narrow bottoms of the cañons are covered with splendid trees, large and old, without any small young trees, or a particle of underbush. This is undoubtedly the effect of fire, and proves, I think, that prairie fires were not so frequent a hundred years ago as now.

As the settlements creep up the stream, and care is taken to prevent fires, the young trees spring up, and, as the growth of the cotton-wood is extremely rapid, all the ground suited to their propagation is soon covered.

Another great enemy to the trees is the beaver. This animal is very plentiful on all the streams where there is sufficient vegetation for his sustenance. The wooded islands in the larger streams are a favourite home for him; for, though extremely active and industrious on occasions, he does not make a dam except when forced to do so by the scarcity of water. He works from necessity, not from the love of labour. The amount of damage a family of beavers can do in the way of cutting down trees is wonderful. They eat only the bark of the more tender branches, and a good-sized tree lasts but a little while. Many islands are kept denuded of trees by these animals, and they do vast damage even in the thicker and more vigorous growth of the cañons.

The treelessness of the high plains is caused by the lack of water, and high winds; of the lower plains, by wind, fire, and beaver. As the third plain gradually blends with the great alluvial deposit of the Mississippi Valley, the timber increases in variety, size, and vigour of growth.

The broadest expanse of the second plain extends from the great central mass of mountains in a direction a little east of south, including the Staked Plain, and terminating in the so-called Guadalupe Mountains of Texas. It is perfectly treeless, except on its south-easterly edge, where it is marked by two extraordinary belts of woods called the ' *Cross Timbers.*'

The larger of these belts is about an average of twelve miles broad, the smaller about eight miles. The 'timber' is composed of a great variety of trees and shrubs, oak predominating. It is not a heavy growth; but many of the trees are of good size, and the whole is a fair average forest. Starting on the high arid edge of the Staked Plain, these belts pursue a course from north-west to south-east. This outline is very irregular, but they keep a general parallel course at an average distance of some fifteen miles apart, never, I am told, once joining each other until both are finally blended and lost in the heavy timber lands of the Brazos and Trinity Rivers. I have crossed these belts but once, many years ago. They were to me then, and are still, one of the most remarkable and unaccountable freaks of nature on the plains. The soil and general surface inside and outside the timber are apparently the same. The belts cross streams which just above and below are as bare as any other portion of the plains. Water does not widen them; the high dry plain does not contract them. They are inexplicable.

Except the arid alkali deserts, and those given over to sand and sage-brush, the whole prairie is covered with grass. Even the lava-covered tops of the first plain furnish sufficient soil to dress them with a ragged coat of green, while the cañons are frequently fairly supplied with nutritious grasses. The higher portions of the second plain are covered with the famed buffalo-grass. It covers the ground very thickly, to the exclusion of other grasses, or even of flowers. The blades are short, but two or three inches long, and curl upon themselves, forming a thick close mat of beautiful sward, green as emerald in early spring, but of a yellowish grey later in the season. This grass is extremely nutritious, and a favourite with graminivorous animals at all times and seasons. Its best quality is that it does not, like other grasses, dry up and become withered and lifeless from the dry heat of summer, but seems to cure itself as hay uncut, and preserve through the fall and winter all its nutritive qualities.

In Texas there is a fine grass growing to the height of two, and under very good conditions of three, feet, called the 'gramma-grass.' The 'buffalo-grass' of the high plains and this 'gramma-grass,' though entirely different in growth and appearance, are really identical. This I discovered accidentally. At Fort Dodge I had a small piece of ground covered with sods of buffalo-grass taken from the high prairie. It was watered daily, and otherwise well cared for. To my great astonishment it appeared to change its whole nature, grew tall and rank, and in due time developed the seed-heads of the true 'gramma-grass.' The buffalo-grass is uninviting to the eye, being so very short that an inexperienced man in search of pasture for animals would pass it without consideration. It makes up in thickness what it lacks in length, and horses and cattle not only eat it greedily, but fill themselves much quicker than would seem possible.

The Arkansas Valley at Fort Lyon is covered with tall, fine-looking grass, which the large herds of domestic cattle will scarcely touch, preferring to go eight or ten miles away from the river to feed upon the buffalo-grass of the high plain. Another curious fact in this connection is, that the cattle under such circumstances return to the river for water only on alternate days.

Another good grass is called 'bunch-grass.' Neither this nor the buffalo can be cut for hay, which, if required, must be cut from the taller but coarser and greatly less nutritious grasses from the bottoms.

Another phenomenon of the plains is the sand-hills. Commencing sometimes high up on the second plain, the sand is arranged or disposed in what may be termed sand-streams. The ground covered varies in width from a few yards to thirty or more miles. Sometimes the sand is piled in oval or conical hills, from ten to 200 feet in height; at other times it seems to cover the ground to a greater or less depth in an almost level mass. These sand-streams pursue an almost unbroken course in a general easterly direction, sometimes, but not invariably, following the course of the larger water-courses. The edges or boundary of the sand are clear cut and well-defined—a remarkable fact, since the sand is so light as to be the sport of every wind. It is in colour from bright yellow to pure white, and the particles of fine sand are so very minute that a handful thrown into the air disappears entirely.

One of these sand-streams takes its rise in the high land known as 'The Divide,' keeps an easterly course parallel to a tributary of Big Sandy, called Rush Creek, crosses the Big Sandy, and makes a sharp bend to the south, following the direction of the Big Sandy to its junction with the Arkansas. It then crosses the Arkansas, and is joined on its south bank by another similar but smaller sand-stream, which, taking its rise in the high table-land between the Purgatory and Arkansas Rivers, follows the general course of the latter stream.

The Rush Creek and Big Sandy branch has a very regular width of about twelve miles. The sand is disposed in small hummocks, covered with broom-sage (a tall, stiff-jointed grass common on the abandoned fields of Virginia and North Carolina). It is loose and deep, making travel extremely laborious and difficult. The Purgatory branch varies from a quarter of a mile to three miles in width, and is better to travel over than the other. These streams when united follow the right or south bank of the Arkansas in a belt of from five to thirty miles in width. Sometimes this belt will leave the river for a few miles; at other times the sand-bluffs stand sheer from the water to the height of 200 feet.

The sand takes every variety of form. At one place the long gentle slopes, covered with grass, give at a little distance no indication of the nature of the ground beneath; at another, the high bare knolls, cut in rifts by the wind, look in the sunlight like huge snow-drifts. In some places the 'hills,' or knolls, change their forms with every wind; in others, the wind seems to have no effect whatever. The most curious fact connected with these sand streams, or ranges of knolls, is that, however much they may and do vary in form, however they may be and are shifted by the ever-changing winds, all variations and changes take place within the regular limits or boundaries.

The south bank of the Arkansas is bounded by these hills for more than 300 miles. The wide sand-bed of the river itself is in many places perfectly dry for a month or more of each year. The prevailing winds during the summer and fall—the dry season—are from the south-west; yet, however much the form and position of the sand-hills on the south side of the river may change, there is scarcely a particle of sand to be found on the north bank, nor a single sand-dune formed outside of what can readily be distinguished as the old limits or boundaries of the sand-stream. Just opposite Fort Dodge this stream narrows in one place to a few yards. The waggon road to Camp Supply crosses at this narrow place, and saves many miles of weary labour. Twenty-five miles below Fort Dodge the Arkansas bends to the north-east; the sand-stream attempts to follow, but, apparently unable to turn so sharply, compromises the matter by keeping near the river with the northern edge, while the south edge stretches in nearly a straight line to the east in continuation of its former course. The consequence is, that the sand-stream becomes nearly forty miles wide, and so extremely difficult to cross with loaded waggons, that buffalo-hunters, and other people of that section, prefer to turn it by the longer road, *viâ* Fort Dodge.

Another of these sand-streams follows the general course of the Cimarron. Another, and an especially bad one, passes eastward between Wolf Creek and the Canadian. Numberless others could be mentioned if necessary. Their general characteristics are the same as of the example given.

I must mention one, more remarkable than any other of which I have knowledge, which, though lying in the limits of the second plain, is not within the limits of the United States. Starting in the south-west of the territory of New Mexico, and running in a south-easterly direction through the Mexican State of Chihuahua, nearly parallel to and from fifty to seventy miles from the Rio Grande, this sand-stream has a length of over 100 miles by a breadth of twelve or fourteen. This stream is a succession of bare rounded hillocks, twenty or thirty feet high, of loose white sand, crowded together with most irregular regularity. The outside limits are perfectly defined, the country through which the 'stream' passes being generally a plain, from the level of which the 'hills' rise abruptly. Standing upon one of those hillocks the view is a most remarkable one. Along the length of the stream, as far as the eye can reach, can be seen only a succession of conical hillocks, crowded together without order in position, but each perfect in form, and white as the driven snow. The sand is so light and so loose, and shifts so constantly, that there can scarcely be said to be a road across it. A road enters and a road leaves it, but all traces of the heaviest train are soon effaced and buried in the sand. The passage is said to be dangerous. I have crossed it but once. Before entering it, our leader, an old freighter who had spent many years in that country, mounted a dune, and looked long and anxiously at the sky. The day was bright, the air still and clear. Deciding to risk it, he gave the order, and our waggons at once plunged to the hubs in the yielding sand. We were not heavily loaded, and every man was required to walk, yet the teams could make only 100 or 200 yards before stopping to blow and rest. Our leader, keeping ahead on the summits of the hillocks, directed the movements, and with great difficulty, and by sometimes doubling teams, we finally gained the hard ground on the west side, making the distance of about twelve miles in just about as many hours.

Wherever sand-streams are covered with grass the surface is undermined by a beautiful little animal called the gopher (on the high plains a small striped squirrel, on the southern plains a pouched rat). This animal feeds on the roots of the grass, on seeds, &c., which he stores in cavities dug out of the soft sand. His labours not only render travel more difficult, but exceedingly dangerous, especially to a rapidly-moving horse. It is this animal that gives the danger to buffalo-hunting.

The prairie dog digs a deep hole with a wide mouth, and piles up around the orifice a mound of earth. It can be seen and avoided in the sharpest chase. The gopher digs a blind pitfall without external opening, and neither man nor horse have any warning of danger. Galloping, or running eager and excited, the horse suddenly plunges to his knees, turns a somersault, and if both horse and rider regain their feet without a broken bone they are fortunate.

CHAPTER III.

CLIMATE.

EXTENDING over nineteen degrees of latitude, and varying in altitude from almost the sea level to 8,000 feet, the plains present every variety of climate.

Summer brings its torrid heats, its miasmas and fevers, to that portion of the third plain which joins the great alluvial deposit; while the Arctic region itself can scarcely exceed the rigour with which winter lays its icy hand on the high plains.

Besides the variation resulting from latitude and altitude, the yearly and even the daily extremes of temperature are most remarkable, and would seem to result not only in very great discomfort, but in constant sickness to those subjected to them. This, however, is not the case. No part of the world can be more healthy than the middle plains; and, probably from the dryness of the atmosphere, the extremes of heat produce less effect on the human body than in the Eastern States.

A summer's day with the thermometer at 110° is felt about as it is in New York when the thermometer indicates 90°; and, no matter how hot the day, the mercury goes down with the sun. One is always sure of a delightful evening, when he can sit out bareheaded and enjoy the pure delicious air without the discomfort of dew, or the danger of ' coughs, colds, and consumptions,' and of a most glorious night's sleep under at least one blanket. Refreshed and invigorated by such a night's rest, the frame can stand a vast amount of daily heat.

The winters are peculiar. For a week each day will be clear, calm, and like a mild October day of the East. No overcoat is needed, and the presence of winter is scarcely recognised. Then comes a storm; the icy wind cuts like a knife, no clothing seems to keep it from the person, and penetrating to every part it drags out every particle of vital heat, leaving but a stiffened corpse of him who is so unfortunate as to be exposed to it.

An exposure to the full force and fury of a violent 'plains Norther' would be certain death to any indigenous animal. Buffalo and antelope fly before it, and seek protection in the deepest and most wooded cañons. Near Julesburg, I once saw the snow dotted with the bodies of a great number of snow-birds frozen to death in a storm of a few days before. Men suffer more than other animals. Lacking the instinct of the latter, which enables them to presage the coming storm, men new to plains life, misled by the mildness of the ordinary winter weather, expose themselves possibly in light clothing on the plains, are caught in a storm, and perish miserably in a few hours.

A gentleman, competent and in a position to form a correct estimate, once told me that at least 100 buffalo-hunters had perished from cold in the country, within 100 miles of the Arkansas River, in two years. During the winter of 1872-3 I was in command at Fort Dodge, Kansas. At least seventy capital amputations were performed by the post surgeon on citzens who were buffalo-hunters or railroad *employés*, whilst a much greater number of frozen men were sent East for treatment. I think it safe to say that over 200 men in that vicinity lost hands or feet, or parts of them. One poor fellow had both hands and both feet taken off, and not only recovered, but was a few months ago in good health and attending to his usual business.

Fortunately for the habitability of the plains, these excessively severe storms occur only a few times during a winter, and are generally of but a few days' duration.

The cold itself is not intolerable. The danger is from the sharp wind, which drives the cold like icy daggers through the body. Great suffering can always be avoided, if it be possible to get out of the wind. A day which would be death on the high plain, may scarcely be uncomfortably cold in a thicket at the bottom of a deep narrow cañon. Indians and old plainsmen understand this perfectly, and nothing but absolute necessity will force either to encounter the risks of a journey on the plain during a storm. At the first symptom of its approach, all speed is made for the nearest deep-wooded cañon, where they lie still until the storm is over.

The army frequently suffers greatly from these storms. It sometimes happens that a marauding and murdering band of Indians escapes during the summer the punishment which it deserves. It cannot travel in winter, not only because the Indian is more susceptible to cold than the white, but because his ponies are too poor and weak to carry him. A winter campaign is determined upon. Encumbered with trains, limited in rations, and most especially in forage, it is not always practicable for the troops to halt until the storm expends itself, even did a perfect knowledge of the country enable the officer in command to find a suitable place. At other times some military necessity, arising either from the Indians or from complications of the Indian Department, requires the movement of troops in mid-winter. The amount of suffering in all such cases can hardly be exaggerated.

While in command of Fort Sedgwick, in 1867, I was required to send a company of the 2nd Cavalry to the Republican River in February. It had been gone but a few days when a most violent storm set in. At the proper time the company returned without the loss of a man, but this result was due entirely to the indomitable will and pluck of the captain in command. The company had to march for thirty miles in the teeth of the most terrific gale and blinding snow-storm, and in at least eighteen inches of snow. The men were made to dismount, and each, leading his horse, to take turns in opening the way through the snow. The cold and suffering were so intense and the toil so great, that some of the men refused to do more, and, throwing themselves into the snow, declared their intention of dying there rather than make another effort. Orders, entreaties, and threats, all proving alike unavailing, the captain finally fell upon them with the flat of his sabre, belaboured them into the ranks, and brought all in safety to the post.

In the winter of 1865-6 a considerable command was caught on the Cimarron, and barely escaped total destruction. An officer who was with it describes the sufferings as most fearful. Many men were more or less frosted, and about 600 animals frozen or starved to death.

The recent sufferings of a command sent into the Black Hills are fresh in the minds of all. It is easy, seated in a comfortable office, and by a good fire, to give orders for a winter campaign or movement of troops on the plains, but it usually means death to somebody. This is of course a part of the soldier's bargain, and it is the pride of our soldiers to obey orders, whether they lead to death by the cold of a plains storm, or by the heat of the Indian stake. But such men deserve that there shall always be a necessity.

The reports published yearly by the Surgeon-General give the accurate facts relative to the thermometric variations of the plains. I mention one or two simply as illustrations. At Fort Lyon, on the Arkansas River, on the second plain, at an altitude of about 4,000 feet, the daily variation in summer is not unfrequently 40°; and on one occasion, in winter, the maximum thermometer at 11 o'clock A.M. was about 65°, while the minimum sometime during the same night was 15° below zero—a variation of 80° in twenty hours.

The city of Omaha, on the third plain, and not exceptionally blessed or cursed with variation, had the thermometer at 120°, in the coolest places to be found, for several days during the summer of 1874, while the winter of the same year sent the mercury down to 28° below zero—a yearly variation of 148°. Omaha, like most other points of the third plain, has but little daily variation, the nights of summer being nearly as hot as the days, while the days of winter are nearly as cold as the nights.

CHAPTER IV.

THE atmospheric phenomena of the plains are on the most magnificent scale. Thunderstorms are rare on the high plains, but when they do occur they excel in all the elements of grandeur and sublimity. Nowhere is the lightning-flash a more vivid and blinding glare. Nowhere is the crash of the thunder more stunning, nor its roll more deep and prolonged. Nowhere does a man feel more intensely the nearness and power of the Creator. For at least six months, from November to April, of every twelve, 'the wind is never weary on the high plains,' and wind-storms may occur at any season. The storms of each locality generally come from one particular direction, and, at whatsoever season occurring, are often perfect tornadoes, overturning and destroying everything movable.

Scarcely a military post on the plains but suffers yearly from these storms in torn roofs and wrecked houses. In May and June these storms are not unfrequently accompanied by hail. For fury, destructiveness, and size of the stones, the hailstorms of the country about Fort Lyon far excel any it has ever been my misfortune to encounter. Two occurred in the summer of 1870, which did immense damage, splitting the shingles of the roofs, breaking palings or fences, killing wild birds, domestic fowls, and all young or small animals exposed to them. It was estimated that at least a hundred calves were killed by these two storms.

Many of the hailstones were three—some four, five, and even six inches in circumference—and in many cases they were not rounded stones, but irregular shapeless masses of ice.

There is still another storm to which the plains are subject, called a ' sand-storm.' It is not necessary that the wind should blow particularly strong to bring on one of these, but that it have an inclination to the ground. A terrific wind-storm may sweep over and parallel to the surface, without much disturbing the dust; but one of these impinging winds picks up everything—dust, sand, and pebbles of the size of a pea—drives them through the air, rendering it most painful, and even dangerous, to open the eyes, and shutting out almost entirely the light of day. These storms are of frequent occurrence all over the plains, and are exceedingly disagreeable, though easily avoided by getting into a ravine. I have frequently watched through a window the phenomena of these ' sand-storms.' Even though the wind did not appear to blow hard, and the surface passed over seemed to offer but little of dust or sand, the cloud of flying particles was so thick, that at many times it was impossible to see twenty feet ahead. No crevice is too small for many of these particles, which penetrate into even the most tightly closed room, and no end of anathemas and feminine ' bad words ' have been lavished on these ' sand-storms ' by the fair followers of the drum.

All these storms are exceptional, the summer and fall weather of the high plains being as near perfect as it is possible to imagine.

CHAPTER V.

TRAVEL.

THE ordinary uneducated plainsman travels, like the Indian, by landmarks; making, however, unlike the Indian, some use of the sun and the stars. The more educated use the compass and maps. All classes are greatly dependent on instinct. A good plainsman 'is born, not made.' He must have within him a something unaccountable even to himself, which, however variable and circuitous the path of his wanderings, tells him constantly the direction of his return. A small natural aptitude in this may be greatly improved by cultivation and practice; but a total lack of the peculiar faculty can never be replaced by practice, study, or science.

One of the best of the explorers of twenty-five years ago, a man who in his day, and for the length of his service, added as much as any to our knowledge of the 'Great West,' who, if but armed with his compass, sextant, and chronometer, plunged fearlessly into any unknown wilderness, would sit on the ground and yell lustily for assistance if by accident he found himself without instruments, out of sight of his tent or party. Under ordinary circumstances a partially skilful plainsman will not care for a compass, except on cloudy days, or when intending to march accurately on some given point. The sun and natural instinct, quickened by practice, are sufficient for all ordinary plain travel. Under some circumstances, however, instinct, practice, sun, compass, and head, all fail. Few persons, with any

knowledge of geography or of the points of the compass, have travelled at all without having at some time
experienced the curious sensation of being 'turned round.'
A man is going up the Hudson River in a steam-boat, and,
walking from the cabin to the guards, finds himself apparently going down the river. A traveller looks from
his book or paper out of a car window, and finds to his
disgust that he seems to be going back towards his
starting-point.

This feeling is sometimes so strong that I have seen
passengers really alarmed, being sure that they must have
taken a wrong train. I myself have been so 'turned
round' on Broadway, that it required all my knowledge
of the street, of its tremendous tide of population, which
constantly rushes along its west side, and the comparatively few people on the other, to force me against feeling
an instinct in the direction I ought to go.

No power of mind or will can change this feeling,
which, however, generally goes off of itself after a while, as
mysteriously and with as little cause as it came. It does
not always go off, and a wrong impression once made
may cling through life, as to me Detroit is always in
Canada, and New Orleans always on the right bank of
the Mississippi, because I happened to be 'turned round'
when I first arrived in those cities. Under such curious
circumstances the features of the best known localities
become strange; everything looks different from what
it ought to look. This is 'getting lost' in the plains
sense.

To the man whose 'head is level,' the mere being in
an unknown locality, or not knowing exactly where he is,
amounts to nothing. This is something that happens
every day, and no amount of turning among deep cañons,
or wooded ravines, ever interferes with the instinct of the
true plainsman. Sometimes, however, he will arrive at a
stream which he knows ought to run in a particular
direction. To his astonishment it is running the other

way. On some morning the sun will rise in what to him appears the south or west.

The old plainsman knows what this means at once ; and unless he has a compass, or is as sure of his locality as a resident in New York would be on Broadway, he accepts the situation, goes into camp, and waits until he gets all right again.

Fortunately, this hallucination being an affection of the mind without external cause, no two persons of any party are likely to be affected at the same time, and in the same way. Fortunately, too, all persons are not subject to it, at least to the same extent; and some old plainsmen (in whom instinct supplies the place of imagination and knowledge) profess to regard it as a weakness or evidence of ' greenness.'

The man who travels by compass, whose full reliance is on the mysterious needle—more true than any human mind—saves himself great trouble, though not necessarily from the annoyance of the feeling.

I have, however, seen intelligent men, accustomed to plains life and to long journeys over the ' trackless wastes,' so completely ' turned round ' as to lose all confidence in the compass, to declare it was wrong, that some local attraction affected its accuracy, &c. Two gentlemen, by no means new to the plains, were once with me on a hunt. They became separated from the party, and, after wandering about for some time, sus- pected they might be lost. They compared compasses, made up their minds that both compasses were wrong— ' locally attracted '—got into a discussion as to the route, which led to a quarrel, and finally to a separation, each pursuing what seemed to him the true route. Both were wrong. The compasses were right. One got into camp by accident ; the other had to be hunted up and brought back.

The effect on some minds of being really and thoroughly lost or ' turned round ' on the plains is most appalling. Everything appears changed and unnatural; the most ordinary events appear to possess unusual significance; the nerves become unstrung, and the man soon loses control of himself entirely. I have been told of two instances where lost men, when found and approached by parties sent in search of them, made off in the greatest terror, escaping by almost superhuman efforts from their friends, to die of starvation in the wilderness.

When serving in Texas, a soldier of my company became 'lost' while returning to the post from a small village two miles off. A party was sent out to search for him, and on the second or third day came upon him almost naked in a little thicket. As soon as he discovered the party, he bounded off like a deer and was pursued. After an exciting chase he climbed a tree, from which he was taken by force, and with the greatest difficulty—struggling, striking, and biting like a wild animal. He was brought back to the post perfectly wild and crazy, confined, and watched and attended with the greatest care for over a month before he recovered his mind. He was an excellent man, more than usually intelligent; but I doubt if he ever fully recovered the shock. He recollected nothing but going a little distance off the road for something and getting 'turned round' and realising that he was lost.

Once in Texas, when quite a young man, I went hunting with the acting post surgeon, an enthusiastic sportsman, but a very nervous excitable man. After we had been out a few hours a heavy fog settled down upon us, completely shutting out the sun and all landmarks. On examining our pockets we found we had left our compasses at home. The doctor became very much excited, and soon developed a symptom of the plains insanity—'to keep moving.' We were in a triangle formed by two large branches of a stream crossed by a road, and I explained to him that we could not possibly have any difficulty in returning to our post as soon as we could see the sun. My plan was to find a comfortable position, go into camp, and remain quiet until the sun appeared. He would not hear of it; and I had to go with him to save him from himself. He believed his horse would take us out, and gave him his head. For several hours the horse travelled at a good walk, when we came upon the trail of two horses. As Indians were bad, I examined the trail carefully, and found it was our own.

We were wandering objectless in a circle. After a great deal of persuasion I got the doctor to go into camp. We had nothing to eat, and had found no water. He could not sleep, and by morning was almost insane. The fog still enveloped us, but he would not remain in camp ; and I thought action best for him, who was, in addition to his other troubles, now tormenting himself with the certainty of dying of hunger and thirst. We saddled, and let the horses have their heads to search for water. In a short time I killed a fine buck, of which the doctor, in his half-crazy excitement, ate huge chunks, raw and warm ; not that he was particularly hungry, but that he feared he would be so. Taking each a goodly quantity of meat, we started again. About three o'clock we found a little water-hole, went into camp, made a fire, cooked some of our venison, and at dark I went to sleep. About 3 A.M. I was roused by the doctor, who, with the most frantic exclamations and even tears of delight, pointed out to me the stars, which were showing brightly above us. The fog had lifted. Nothing could have kept him in that camp ; nor was I loath to move towards comfort and plenty. By noon we arrived at our post. We had wandered through the glades of the chaparral thickets for more than twenty-five miles from the post.

Though never ' turned round ' or lost in the plains sense, I have, on several occasions during the first year of my service, lost my reckoning so far as to sleep out for a night or two.

One of these occasions might easily have had a tragic termination, and was so full of adventure that I relate it, not as a model of good travelling, but as a specimen of plains life.

I was a lieutenant, temporarily attached to a cavalry company. We were returning from a long scout, and had to cross a portion of the Guadalupe Mountains. These mountains were at that time a stronghold of the Texas plains Indians, who, hid in their fastnesses, watched their opportunities for raids on the settlements below, using most frequently the Bandera Pass on their return with stolen stock. In the hope of bagging some ducks, I went off alone to the right of the command, following for some distance the branches of the Perdinales. I was mounted on a powerful mule, an excellent riding and hunting animal. My eagerness for game led me farther than I intended, and though I took the proper direction, and kept a sharp watch for the trail, night overtook me in the wilderness. I found a good place in a deep ravine with plenty of wood, picketed my mule, and went into camp. The frame of my tent was made of sticks, stuck in the ground in a circle and bent together at the top. Over these was placed my wide india-rubber pouches, and over the slit in the top I fastened my hat. My bed was the saddle-blanket, my pillow the saddle. I had hardly completed my arrangements when a rain-storm, such as Texas only can get up, burst upon me. However, I slept comfortably and dry from above; but the rain soaked in underneath, and I was thoroughly disgusted, and not a little alarmed, next morning to find that my gun, in spite of all precautions, was so wet that I could not discharge it. I had a revolver ; but, having no cartridges to reload, did not try to fire it off, but from appearance judged it to be in the same condition as the gun. I was practically disarmed.

At daylight I started for the Bandera Pass, determined not to waste time in looking for the command, but to make the best possible speed to my station, Fort Lincoln, which was about seventy-five miles off. Soon after sunrise I reached the Guadalupe River, and was travelling quickly and comfortably along a small open prairie, up to the stream, when my attention was attracted by a thin column of smoke, rising apparently from the bed of the river.

Thinking of Indians, I darted at once into the thicket which bordered the prairie, and, keeping well out of sight, skirted around until I got above the smoke. My first impulse was to put as much distance between myself and it, and in as short a time, as possible; but the idea suddenly occurred to me that it might be the camp of my command, and that I had better be dead at once than have it known that I had run away from my own camp. Acting on this I turned my mule, and cautiously made my way back towards the smoke, but still above it, on the river. The thicket was very dense. I suddenly emerged from it to find myself almost in a herd of about twenty horses and mules, which were picketed in a small open space not over thirty yards wide, and just on the bluff bank of the river. To make my position worse, my mule no sooner saw the animals than she lifted her voice and sung out a bray, which I thought might have been heard for miles.

I tumbled off at once, and, thrusting my hand in her mouth, stopped her music, then backed her out of sight in the thicket. After fastening her I returned to the open space. The animals did not belong to my party. The camp was evidently just under the bluff. Crawling most cautiously to the edge, I peeped over the bank, and my scalp felt very loose, as I saw, not forty yards off, seven Indians squatted around a pot eating their breakfast. I got back to the thicket as quickly and cautiously as possible. What to do was the question. My mule, though strong, was very slow in a race. I had two alternatives: either to make off at once on the mule, trusting that the Indians might not find my trail until I had a good start, or to steal a horse and get away on that. I had no compunctions under the circumstances ; but I doubted my ability to select the best horse, and it would take precious moments to change the saddle. I mounted the mule and proceeded cautiously until sure of being out of hearing, when whip and spur were vigorously applied, and that mule never made better time than for the next five or six miles. I crossed the Guadalupe, then the Verde. All this part of the race had been through woods and thickets. From the Verde to the Bandera Pass was a slope of about three miles of bare ground. If I could get over that and through the pass I was pretty safe, as I could on the other side plunge at once into the ravines and thickets of the Medina River, in which I could elude pursuit, at least on foot. When about half way over this bare ground, to my inexpressible delight, I ran into the trail of my command, but had hardly time to congratulate myself before several Indians emerged in full pursuit from the thickets of the Verde. Under whip and spur my mule soon brought me to the summit of the pass, and looking back I found the Indians had stopped on striking the trail of the troops, and were carefully examining it. Feeling pretty safe I also stopped to watch them, and to blow my mule. After consultation they went back as fast as they came, leaving me unmolested to overtake my command, which I soon did.

When travelling without a compass in bad, stormy, or foggy days, when neither the sun nor landmarks can be seen, plainsmen are forced to make devices to keep their course. Sometimes a course may be determined by the way the grass is bent by storms ; and this is not unreliable in the early spring, for the heavy winds of winter being northers, the grass blown down almost invariably points its loose ends to the south.

The direction of heavy winds of any season is pretty constant if not deflected by the vicinity of mountains, and it is not generally difficult to keep a course by the wind. Many times the nature of the country is such that it is impossible to travel on compass courses. Indeed either from hills, ravines, or lack of water, it is extremely rare that an accurate compass course can be maintained for any distance, and a compromise must almost always be made. The general direction is kept with deviations determined by the nature of the ground. Parties travelling from one section of the country to another, a long distance apart, generally keep near some principal stream favourable to the course, or, where the course lies across the general directions of the main streams, the lateral branches are used. The courses of all the larger streams of the plains are so nearly parallel that but little skill is required to keep in a generally correct direction. There is said to be 'cheating in all trades,' and old plainsmen acting as guides frequently take vast credit to themselves for doing what any one could do who simply remembered the parallelism of the plains streams.

Exploring or scouting parties of troops have generally a special section or direction given them, with ample latitude as to all details of marches and camps, to be filled at the discretion of the commanding officer.

Parties on horseback with pack animals can go anywhere; that is, however rugged and broken the country, a skilled plains traveller can, with such an outfit, always find means of arriving very directly at his destination. Waggon trains require much greater care and nicer selection of the line of march; but an uninitiated person is constantly surprised at the ease with which heavily loaded waggons can be taken by a skilful plainsman over what appears to be an impassable country.

One of the great secrets of plains travel is the skilful use of 'divides.' A 'divide' is the portion of upland which separates one ravine from another, whether they be tributaries of the same or of different streams. Level land is either mesa or 'bottom.' The term 'mesa' is applied to a level upland ; ' bottom,' to the level land bordering a stream and enclosed between the sides of the ravine. All land which is not level is ' divide,' though this term is specially and technically applied to the summit or junction of the slopes rising from two contiguous ravines.

The line or ridge separating the waters of two streams not uniting with each other, is called a ' principal divide.'

In very many parts of the plains the sides of the ravines are so extremely precipitous that crossing them is out of the question, and all travel must either be along the ' bottoms' or along the ' divides.' The ' bottom,' though comparatively level, is almost always scored by a ditch which, winding from one precipitous side to the other, necessitates innumerable crossings ; and, as its banks are generally steep, immense labour is required to make a waggon road. Sometimes a ' bottom' is so narrow and broken that it is impossible to follow it. The ' divide,' on the contrary, is nearly always comparatively unbroken level, and offers a good, though sometimes an exceedingly crooked, route.

For the prime necessities of camp life—water, wood, and grass—camps must habitually be made on or near the streams, generally in the ' bottom.' Suppose from such a camp it is desired to go from one main stream to another parallel to it. If some distance apart, a tributary of one may be followed up for water until the party is within a day's march of water on some tributary of the other before taking to the ' divide.' If closer together, or if there be no known tributary with water, the ' divide ' should be taken as soon as possible.

It is not always an easy matter to get out of the ' bottom' into the ' divide.' Fortunately the traveller is restricted in his selection of place for ascent, only by the general direction in which he wishes to travel. Having once mastered the ascent of the side of the ravine, his principal difficulty is overcome.

All ravines take their origin in the general level.
At their heads they have cut but little, and *going up* all
'divides' reach the summit, or 'principal divide.' Here,
however, commences the trouble. 'Going down' is
entirely different from 'going up ;' for while in going up
all the 'divides' lead to one and the same end, 'going
down' is exactly the reverse, and the one surely practicable route or 'divide' must be selected from hundreds
that present themselves, all looking alike, and appearing
at the summit equally practicable. The one 'divide'
selected must be the one that separates the tributary
ravines of two large tributaries of the main stream.
Many times these ravines overlap each other, making
the route extremely crooked.

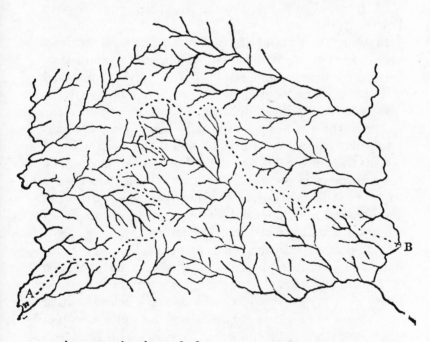

An examination of the accompanying diagram will
show better than any description the advantages and
difficulties of travelling on 'divides.' Suppose each

ravine represented on the map to be a gorge impassable for waggons. To an inexperienced plainsman the difficulties in a journey from A to B would be insurmountable, yet by following the dotted line it will be seen that it is made without a single ravine. In the same way every point on the river B can be reached from any point of the river A without crossing a ravine. The map will also show how easy it is to gain the ' principal divide ' going up from either stream, and how many *cul-de-sacs* constantly threaten the traveller going down from the ' principal divide ' to either. The difficulty, however, is not so great as it appears. A good plainsman can generally tell from the ' lay of the land ' which is the proper ' divide ' to follow.

I received my best lesson in plains craft from a Pawnee Indian, who took a party under my command, with waggons, without delay, or the slightest accident, over a section of ' bad lands ' which, after examination, I believed utterly impassable. The ' divide ' followed was extremely tortuous and narrow ; in one place so very narrow as to require skilful driving for the passage of the waggons, the ravines on each side being generally perpendicular banks from thirty to eighty feet deep.

In the buffalo region the crossing of ' divides ' by waggon trains is greatly simplified. The buffalo always travel on ' divides ' when crossing from one stream to another, and nine times out of ten a waggon can follow wherever a well-marked buffalo trail may lead.

To persons unaccustomed to plains life, who come out on short visits of business or pleasure, the likelihood of getting lost from party or camp is a serious drawback. Every such person should provide himself, before starting on the journey, with a compass and an outline map of the country which he proposes to visit. The most serviceable compass for such use is a not too freely balanced needle, contained in a circular brass box about two inches in diameter, with a spring to unship the needle when not in use. Such a box should be carried in the pocket habitually, so as to preclude any chance of its being forgotten, or left by accident.

The map should show the larger streams and their more prominent tributaries. The position of each camp should be located on the map as accurately as possible, and the line of each day's travel, and the probable position of the evening camp, should be marked in pencil on the map before starting each morning. Where several persons are journeying or hunting together, the maps of each should be a fac-simile of the other, and the person directing operations should see that each day's march is marked on each map before leaving camp, and that all are marked alike.

With these precautions, and the exercise of a little common sense, individuals may wander off with perfect safety on each side of the line of travel, or for miles about the camp, hunting or sight-seeing.

A knowledge of the characteristics of all streams is a very important element in the comfort and pleasure of plains travel. A stream is like a tree pressed flat, except that the branches never cross each other. The tributaries are the branches. Each branch is a perfect tree in itself, and all lead to the parent stem. The camp being on a stream, a hunter may go *up* it or a lateral tributary, and wander for miles on these or their tributaries, knowing that whenever he wishes to return he has but to go down the tributary on which he happens to be to arrive finally at camp. Should his pursuit of game carry him across a 'divide,' he has but to assure himself that the new system of ravines into which he is about to plunge belongs to some principal stream, as those he is leaving. If so, going down any of these ravines will bring him to the same main stream; a little higher or lower, but with the same certainty as to follow the one he went up.

Should the 'divide' crossed lead to a system of ravines

leading to a different principal stream, the novice in plains travel had better be careful. Before entering them he should assure himself of his course, take compass bearings of one or more prominent objects, and must also note all important changes of direction made while travelling in the new system.

Should the camp be located on a tributary of a main stream, and the hunter desire to go *down* for his hunt, he will find the difficulties of his return infinitely increased. In going up he knows that every tributary, every lateral branch, on which he is to hunt, has united each with another and all with the stem on which his camp is, before he arrives there. In going down he passes the mouths of other ravines, many almost like that on which is his camp, and each of which is the outlet of numberless tributaries. On his return he is likely to find no little difficulty in deciding which of the apparently innumerable branches is the one he ought to follow.

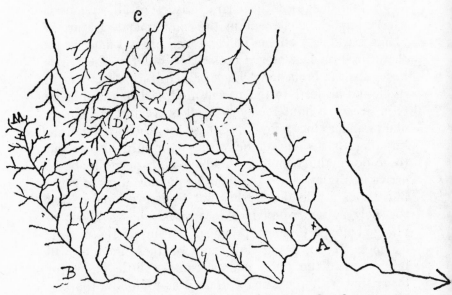

The problem of the 'ravines' is exactly the reverse of the 'divides.' The above map will explain more

clearly. Camp being at A, the hunter may scour the
country on that side of the 'principal divide' as far as D ;
then, crossing the system of ravines which enters the
main stream at B, return certainly and without difficulty
to camp A, simply by always going down the tributary
or stream on which he appears to be. Should, however,
he cross the 'principal divide' going towards C, he will
have much more difficulty in his return. The camp
being at M, should he hunt down stream towards B, he
must, to get back without difficulty, either have a good
'bump of locality,' or be able to follow his own trail on
his return. A camp situated as at D, where the ravines
break away in every direction, is the easiest to get lost
from, unless there be some prominent and distinctive
landmarks.

If, in spite of all precautions, the novice should be
unable to find his camp or party for such time that he
begins to suspect he is lost, there is still no cause for alarm,
provided he be true to himself. I have before said that
the shock of realising that one is lost has a tendency to
unsettle some natures. It is most important, therefore,
that he who suspects he may be lost, make every effort to
keep cool, and to maintain perfect control of himself. The
first thing to do is to get on the highest ground in the
vicinity, and from it make a deliberate and careful survey
of the country, noting the direction of the larger ravines.
Not unfrequently their appearance and direction will
supply the missing link in his consciousness, and enable
him to get back into the system of ravines for which he
is looking. If not, his map should be spread out on the
ground, the compass placed upon it, and both so turned
as to make the north of the map coincide with the direction of the needle. He should then, by going back in
thought over his day's travel, working out his turnings,
&c., try to locate on the map as accurately as possible
the position he occupies. Placing the centre of the compass
over the point so located (its north still coinciding with the

north of the map), he next takes the direction of his camp, and estimates the probable distance.

All this must be done with great care, for it is mere waste of time to attempt it from a second position after having failed from the first. Taking points far ahead on the course decided upon, he goes directly upon them. If the ground is very broken, some prominent point is selected, as far ahead as possible, and on arriving at it the compass should again be consulted to determine another point in the line still in advance. If on travelling over the estimated distance neither camp nor any recognised ground has been discovered, the lost man may try firing his gun several times in rapid succession, and then waiting for an answering shot. If there is no answer, he had better select the highest point in the vicinity, collect fuel and try fire. Indians use smoke for signals; white men fire.

In those portions of the country, however, where there are no Indians, white men use smoke; it being visible at much greater distance.

It would not be safe to make a smoke if the presence of Indians were suspected; but when not in an Indian country, the lost man makes a fire, smothers it occasionally with grass, so as to make as much smoke as possible, and waits for an answering smoke. If night overtakes him, he keeps up as large and bright a flame as possible, until an answering blaze shall appear. If all fail, he should waste no further time in looking for his camp, but, adjusting map and compass as heretofore described, make for the nearest large stream and follow it up or down, as will soonest bring him to settlements.

No man should ever leave his camp or party without his arms and a plentiful supply of ammunition and matches. With these he can always manage to keep himself without suffering, even on a solitary journey of a week or two. In the present condition of the settlements, no man of ordinary intelligence ought to be ' out ' under such circumstances more than two or three days.

In October 1872 I was returning, with three English gentlemen, to Fort Dodge from one of the most delightful and successful hunts I have ever made, and during which our appetites for murder had apparently been fully satiated; for, though travelling through countless throngs of buffalo, we were all together with the waggons, no one caring for a shot. It was our last day; for, though we could not reach the post that night, our next day's travel was to be through a country devoid of game. The prairie was a general level, but much broken by shallow ravines, running apparently to almost every point of the compass. We stopped for lunch, during which thousands of buffalo collected on every side, at 400 or 500 yards' distance, and gazed at us with stupid curiosity.

Desirous of giving my guests one of the most exciting scenes of plains life, and at the same time of securing a quantity of good meat to take into my post, I selected six or eight of the best men of the cavalry escort, and directed them to dash at that part of the herd which was in position to give us the best view of the chase, and to kill as many calves as possible without making a long run. Making ready, they followed a shallow ravine until within 200 yards of the herd, and dashed into it.

Every man was a good rider and pistol shot, and a more brilliant or animating scene of the kind I have never witnessed. In ten minutes the affair was over, and each man had secured from one to four fat six-months' calves.

The chase had roused all the English love of sport, and long before the game was disembowelled and put in the waggons my three friends were off, each for himself, in rapid pursuit of some of the numerous herds. When the meat was loaded, I started with the command and waggons on my proper course, having no fear of these gentlemen getting lost, all of them having displayed during the hunt much more than a natural aptitude for plains travel.

After an hour one joined me, covered with dust, but

rejoicing in trophies of his skill. Shortly after, another came in the same condition ; the third, my most intimate and best loved friend, came not.

We camped at the designated spot, waited dinner until it was nearly spoiled, fired guns, and made smokes, and, when darkness set in, kept huge fires brightly blazing on the highest points far into the night. Still he came not. I had seen him last riding round and shooting at an enormous buffalo bull, that he had wounded and brought to bay. I imagined every mishap and was greatly alarmed, but could do nothing, as it was impossible in the darkness to follow our trail back.

For one, I passed a most anxious and wretched night. At daylight I sent out several parties to search for him, and myself made all possible speed to the post, to send out such a number of parties as would ensure his being found very soon.

As I rode up to my quarters, I was astonished and delighted to see my lost friend standing on the porch waiting for me, as clean, rotund, and smiling as if he had never crossed a horse or given a moment's uneasiness in his life.

His bull had broken his bay, and given him a further sharp chase of two or three miles before being finally despatched. In the chase my friend had lost his reckoning, and, after losing some time in attempts to find the trail, he gave it up, took out his map and compass, struck for the Arkansas River, crossed it, took the road, and arrived at Fort Dodge a little after nightfall, something over thirty miles from the place where he was lost.

While we were lighting fires and bemoaning his fate, he was passing the bottle after a good dinner, and having a jolly time relating his exploits. He displayed in this case good sense and prompt action, very rare in a man new to the plains. It was a bad country to travel in, and, had he wasted time in looking for the trail or camp, he would have assured himself at least one most uncomfortable night on the plains.

The importance of always having a compass cannot be too strongly impressed on all who travel on the plains. ' Old plainsmen,' and so-called ' scouts,' or guides, who desire to be regarded as old plainsmen, frequently profess a great contempt for a man who cannot travel without ' one of them little boxes.' With some this contempt is real, and comes from the entire ignorance of the nature and use of the instrument. Others who profess this contempt are actuated by interested motives. They desire to be employed as guides of scouting or hunting parties, and not unnaturally are very indignant at seeing an officer or civilian, with no guide but his ' box,' plunge unconcernedly into a country the details and difficulties of which it has taken them years to become acquainted with.

Besides this, old plainsmen and guides who ignore the compass, in my experience are not always to be relied on for close or direct travelling. They will lead a party into the wilderness and bring it back ; but for my own part, and with ample opportunity to form an opinion, I would not give up the ' box ' for the best guide on the plains. Of course this is very different in mountainous regions, where the lines of possible travel are very few, and local knowledge almost absolutely necessary.

' Old Bridger,' the most thorough and justly celebrated of all plains guides, was employed by the Government to conduct a heavy waggon train from Fort Fetterman to the Union Pacific Railroad. I was informed by the officer in command of the escort to the train that, on emerging from the foothills of the mountains, Bridger halted the train, and went uneasily now to this hill, now to that, getting on every little prominence, looking at and carefully studying the country. After considerable time spent in this way, he came back to the officer and acknowledged that he did not know where he was. ' Then,' said the officer, ' I think you had better go to the house I see in the valley and inquire.' The house was Medicine Bow Station, on the railroad. Bridger had been in that valley many times before, but, never having happened to come on it in that direction, failed to recognise the landmarks.

Again, these old plainsmen are not restricted as to time. The principal part of their lives is spent wandering from one stream to another, hunting or trapping, and it is of no consequence to them whether the course is direct or roundabout. It is during such journeying that they fill their heads with the memories of ridges, hills, and isolated peaks, landmarks by which their position is to be assured at some future time ; and it is not at all to be wondered at if these memories sometimes become confused, or if the subsequent journeys through the same country should be even more roundabout than the first. This, while all right and pleasant to the old plainsman, becomes a serious matter for a scouting party, which has to do certain work in a specified time, and have rations only for that time, or for a party of gentlemen whose business associations admit of a visit or hunt on the plains of a limited number of days.

A considerable force started from a military post on an important expedition, with a number of the best guides procurable. Though the command made fairly good marches, the men were wakened on the morning of the fifth day by the morning gun at the post, from which they were distant not over twelve miles in a direct line. This result is not, however, entirely attributable to the incapacity of the guides.

I do not mean to intimate that guides are of no value on the plains. On the contrary, their services are at many times really important, especially in a country where water is scarce. I do mean to say, however, that, as a rule, the services of these guides are worth less than a fifth of their own estimation of, and charges for, them. When to their knowledge of country they add a familiarity with Indian languages, or of the sign language of the plains Indians, and also, what is extremely unusual in a white American, are really skilful trailers, their services

with troops become important. The most valuable services rendered by guides is in conducting waggon trains.

Some few of these men have a wonderful capacity,
almost an instinct, for finding road, and, though in a
country entirely unknown to them, can tell almost with
certainty by the ' lay of the land ' where the best route
can be found.

A man possessed of a certain amount of travelling
instinct is very apt, after trusting to it for some time
without accident or difficulty, to fancy that it is all that
is necessary in plains-craft, and tacitly to ignore his compass. The veriest greenhorn is less liable to mishap than
he. He neglects the habit of, I may say, wearing his
compass, and some time or other gets caught in a dilemma
from which he must extricate himself by extraordinary
means, or suffer greatly. I speak from ample experience,
having gotten into numerous scrapes through too much
confidence in my 'instinct.' I have already related one
of these. I will give one more before leaving a subject
of the utmost importance to all who travel on the plains.

I was out with a scouting party. Near the Two
Buttes we were snowed up, and were obliged to remain
in camp on Two Buttes Creek. One morning gave promise of clearing weather, and, taking with me two men,
I went out to get some fresh meat. The country is the
high table land of the second plain, through which the
Two Buttes Creek cuts its way in a narrow and deep gorge.
The Two Buttes, a detached portion of the first plain, is
a single hill of about 500 feet above the plain, the top
of which is broken away in the middle, leaving two
almost conical flat-topped peaks, more than 300 feet apart
at the summits, and each rising probably 200 feet above
their common base.

It is a very prominent and well-known landmark, and
can be seen under favourable conditions for more than
sixty miles. The country is an alternation of nearly level
plain and very broken ground, and would be easy to get

lost in, but for these Buttes. I had wounded an antelope, and was following it slowly on the broad plain,
about four miles from the Buttes, when I saw coming
swiftly down upon me a dense snow-cloud. I felt for
my compass. 1 had left it in camp. Realising the full
danger of a night on that plain in a snow-storm, I at once
took the only means left me of assuring my course. If
I could reach the Buttes I could find my camp. Turning
my horse so that his head pointed directly to the Butte,
I waited the advent of the storm. In a few moments it
struck us, staggering the horses with its force, and shutting out everything beyond a circle of a few feet. Noting
exactly the direction of the wind, with reference to the
position of myself and horse, I started, marching with the
utmost care, in a direct line, and in something over an
hour was rewarded by striking the Butte. My camp was
scarcely a mile away across a spur of the plain, and I felt
certain, as did the men with me, of its direction. But
darkness was coming on, and the cloud of snow was so
dense that I determined to risk nothing to instinct.

Taking a ravine from the Butte, I followed it down to
the creek, then followed the creek up and arrived safely in
camp, where I found all greatly alarmed for our safety.

Next day it was clear, and I went back to the Butte
(being sure of my compass this time) to verify my
instinct. I found, from the horse-tracks, that if we had
taken the course we all thought the correct one from the
Butte, we should have gone directly on to the high plain,
away from our camp, and of course into great danger. I
supplied the need of a compass by travelling 'by the
wind' and 'by ravines;' but, though I came out 'all right,'
our position was so critical, and I felt so keenly the
responsibility of all our lives jeopardised by my negligence, that I have never since been without a compass
when on the plains.

One of the most painful and annoying consequences
of winter travel on the plains is getting 'snow-blind.' Not

unfrequently the days after a snow-storm are bright and beautiful. The sun shines with sufficient warmth to slightly melt the top of the snow, which, when night comes, freezes into a compact mass, the glare of which is simply intolerable. There is nothing to relieve the eye—no woods, no hills, nothing to look at—but one broad interminable sheet of blazing white.

The ordinary plains antidote is to smear the face around the eyes with grease and gunpowder; but this as well as goggles, green veils, broad brimmed hats, and other devices, answering fairly in civilised regions, are al at fault here.

In common with many persons I am simply blind under such circumstances, but suffer no other inconvenience. Many others, however, suffer much more acutely. The face, hands, and every exposed part, blister as if burned by fire. I have known cases of serious illness, the face swollen and extremely sensitive to the touch, the eyes entirely closed, the nose a blister, the lips parched and cracked. Many persons lose the entire skin of the face after such an exposure, and suffer for weeks. After having once been snow-blind, a person is much more liable to subsequent attacks.

There is said to be another plains malady, which, however, I cannot vouch for. It is called 'moon-blind.' The idea is that the full rays of the moon affect the eyes of a man sleeping exposed to them so that he cannot see at night. I have so slept very many times without ill consequences, nor have I ever heard of it affecting a really reliable and responsible man. The malady is confined to 'bull-whackers' or other *employés* of freighters and soldiers, and among the latter I have never known it to attack a really good man.

Indeed, so far as my experience goes, either this malady must have been devised as a special punishment to the worthless, or suspicion must be entertained that it means 'malingering.'

CHAPTER VI.

CAMP.

THE three essentials of a good camp are wood, water, and grass; and, these being present, it would seem a perfectly simple matter to select the proper position.

On this selection, however, depends in a very great degree the pleasure and comfort of a trip on the plains. The most serious mishaps of plains life occur while in camp ; and it requires not only a good eye, but a knowledge of the mishaps to which plains life is subject, to select such a position as is least likely to be affected by them.

Suppose, then, a party has arrived at a stream well wooded, and with plenty of grass. Almost any of a hundred positions might be good under ordinary circumstances ; but the object and duty of the leader is to select that one position which will be best under any of the extraordinary events which may happen. If it is a mere pleasure trip, and the passage of the stream be of no consequence, the relative advantages of every position within reach on either side may be considered ; but if the journey is to be continued beyond the stream next day, he is restricted in the choice of positions to the farther bank, for if not crossed it may rise in the night, and delay him for several days.

The next point is that the animals shall have a grazing ground, where each and every one can be at all times under the eyes of the guards and herders, and where it would be most difficult for Indian or white thieves successfully to stampede and run them off.

The loss of animals being one of the most serious of troubles, the camp should be so situated as to give the greatest possible security to the waggons and picket line against the sneaking attempts of thieves during the darkness. The ground should be sufficiently level to permit the tents being properly pitched ; the sward should be thick, that rain may not render the camp muddy ; the grass short, to secure against accident by fire. A few trees add greatly to the beauty and comfort of a camp; too many shut out the sun's rays and keep the ground damp. The camp should be in close vicinity to water, yet in such a position as to be secure from the sudden rise to which all the lesser plains streams are liable It should, as far as possible, be sheltered from the wind-storms which sweep the higher pláins, and the sand-storms which occasionally render the valleys unbearable.

The smaller the party the more easy it is to find a position to satisfy all these requirements. If it be a small party with pack mules, or but one waggon and few animals, a hundred little nooks can be found, each seeming exactly formed for convenience and comfort. If the party be considerable, with several waggons, more time and care are required to find a suitable camp.

The position being decided upon, the waggons are driven to the spot selected for them, and halted in line at such distance apart that ropes stretched between the hind wheels will give interval sufficient for picketing all the riding animals.[1] The draft animals are fastened to the tongues of the waggons.

The very first thing to be done on going into camp is to send out mounted pickets—one or more, depending on the nature of the ground—to occupy those points in the immediate vicinity which, either from their height or

---

[1] This is the ' picket line,' and should not be confounded with the ' lariat ' or rope by which each animal is fastened while grazing.

position, give the best view of the country around, and all the approaches to the camp.

Every animal should be lariated out for grazing. The best arrangement is a very strong leather head-stall, to the lower part of which, and well down under the chin, is firmly secured a stout iron ring. To this ring is fastened one end of a $\frac{3}{4}$-inch rope thirty feet in length, the other end of which is fastened by a swivel ring to an iron picket-pin. This last is driven home into the ground. In tolerably good soil it is almost impossible for a horse either to break the rope or draw the pin, and an attempt to run is met by a sharp and severe wrench on the lower or weakest part of the head, which, if the horse is going pretty fast, will most likely throw him, and thus put a stop to any foolishness on his part.

This is sufficient for the security of the horses under ordinary circumstances, but when in a country dangerous from white or red thieves additional precautions must be taken. The legs of the horses must be secured. This is done by 'hobbles,' or 'side lines.' Hobbles fasten the forefeet together, side lines the fore and hind foot on the same side. 'Side lines' are most secure, hobbles detracting very little from the speed of a really stampeded animal. Though oftentimes absolutely necessary for his safe keeping, both methods of securing him are cruel to the horse, rendering it difficult and painful for him to feed, and greatly injuring his gait.

During the whole time the animals are grazing they should be surrounded at a convenient distance by a guard, mounted if practicable, and more or less in numbers, depending on the size of the party and the possibility of danger, and with and among the herd should be at least one mounted teamster to every two teams grazing.

The waggons, having been satisfactorily placed and the animals sent out to graze, the tents are pitched or bivouacs made in such positions as will as nearly as possible surround the animals when tied to the waggons at night.

If the weather be bad or threatening, the tents should be placed if possible with their backs to the wind. Whatever may be the state of the weather, there should always be dug a trench around the back and sides, the earth removed, and piled against the tent, and on the flap or loose piece of canvas at the bottom. This will secure the inmates from damp in case of rain, and also, by preventing the wind from getting under the tent, greatly lessen the danger of its getting overturned by windstorms.

I confess to being something of a sybarite. I like to have a good tent, nice mess-kit, plenty of bedding, and everything to make me comfortable. For six or eight years of his youth a man can manage with a couple of blankets for bed, saddle for pillow, hard tack and bacon for provender; but after that, these become a little monotonous, and the ordinary human longs for something more. Especially is this the case in the army, where, after some years of hardships, the result many times more of bravado than of absolute necessity, one begins to realise that this is his life, and the enjoyment of life is simply the aggregation of the enjoyments of each day.

My advice is then to every one, to come to the plains as his means and the amount of his transportation will permit. No superfluities, only necessaries and comforts. His kitchen should have a small sheet-iron cooking-stove (made for plains travel, and can be bought in any frontier town), with a sufficient variety of cooking utensils. His stock of provisions should be as varied as circumstances will permit, including an assortment of canned fruit and vegetables.

There is no reason why his table furniture should not satisfy the eye. He should have a light thin mattress, with ample bedclothes and a bedstead. The simplest, best, and easiest transported consists of three or four thin boards laid lengthwise on a couple of strong but light tressels about twenty inches high. In travelling the boards are put in the bottom or sides of the waggon, and the tressels fastened on the feed-box behind.

These, with pipes and tobacco for smoking, and fluids for those with whom change of water disagrees, give ample means for the full appreciation of what to me is the life most replete with enjoyment and most entirely satisfactory.

In travelling for pleasure, the camp is habitually pitched and ready by 3 o'clock P.M. A comfortable nap of an hour gives vigour for a hunt of a few hours on foot.

The return at sunset is to a good dinner, after which all collected about a camp fire (for the nights of the high plains are always cool) with pipes and bowl and social converse, with songs or stories, spend free, careless, happy hours unknown to formal conventional life, and never vouchsafed to the dull diggers after dimes.

Before sunset all the animals have been brought in, secured in their places, and fed (if there be forage). The pickets are brought in, the old guard is relieved, and the new sentinels posted with care and forethought, for on their positions more than on their vigilance depends the safety of the animals. Nowhere on earth can sleep be so refreshing, so directly sent from heaven.

Up at dawn of day, a plunge in the pure cold brook furnishes an excuse for a breakfast that would founder a hod-carrier. The camp is struck, horses are saddled, mules harnessed, and we are off again to a day of toil, excitement, and adventure, to an evening of similar but ever-varying delight.

Alas for the perfectibility of human happiness! Even camp life is not without its occasional discomforts, even its serious mishaps. The worst of these is the loss of animals. This may occur either by stampede or by stealing from the picket line.

A stampede may be caused intentionally either by Indians or white thieves, or it may come from any accidental and unforeseen cause, which, frightening badly one or more horses, causes them to plunge and snort, communicating the fright to others and others.

A stampede among horses is precisely what a panic is among men. It is the temporary ascendency of an unreasoning fear, during which the instinct of self-preservation seems to usurp the functions of all the other qualities.

Nothing is more senseless and selfish than a panic. A cry of fire in a theatre, the falling of the plastering of the ceiling of a church, is sufficient to change the orderly well-behaved people into a crowd of unreasoning brutes, who, forgetful of every obligation of manhood or duty, rush blindly to the doors, crushing even their own wives and children in the madness each of his own individual selfishness.

Even highly-disciplined soldiers—men who face death as lightly and carelessly as they turn a partner in the dance, men whose courage is so much a matter of habit that the feeling of fear is forgotten, if ever known—become sometimes a blind, headlong, terrified mob, with no more sense or reason than if stricken with madness.

All animals and birds seem liable at times to be afflicted with this malady ; and we have reason to modify our self-glorification of our immense superiority over the brute creation when we reflect that one moment of causeless panic reduces us from our vaunted position, 'just below the angels,' to the level of the poor quail, which, in senseless flight, dashes its life out against a wall.

The stampede is the favourite and most successful ruse of Indian horse-thieves. If the animals are well secured and well guarded, the Indians, though they may be in the immediate vicinity, will make no effort to stampede them ; for, though fond of dash, they take few chances when the stake is life or death. If the animals are not well fastened and guarded, they are likely to be lost at any moment. Gaining unobserved a position close to the grazing herd, a few Indians will suddenly dash among them, yelling like maniacs and shaking buffalo robes or blankets. An American horse, as well as a mule, has an instinctive dread and fear of an Indian, and under such circumstances nothing but absolute physical impossibility will prevent the most gentle animal from going off at the top of his speed. Once fairly started, the best-mounted Indian will gradually get ahead of the stampeded herd and lead them over the best ground in the direction he wishes them to take. When safe from pursuit he lessens his speed, the other Indians keep close to the flanks and rear ; and after a run of ten or twelve miles the whole stampeded band finds itself under control, and is driven wherever the Indians wish.

Sometimes when the marches are hard, grass poor, and short forage scarce, it may become necessary to leave the horses on herd all night. This is an excellent opportunity for the Indian. He will crawl like a snake into a badly guarded herd, while most of the animals are asleep, cut lariats and side lines, and with demoniac yells frighten them into stampede. It is, however, only on rare occasions that he attempts this : first, for reasons arising from his religious beliefs ; and, second. because the stampeded animals will not run well together at night, are unmanageable, and most of them are lost to the stampeders. Sometimes an Indian will crawl on a picket line, cut the halters and get off with an animal or two, but for night a frontier white horse-thief can easily discount any Indian. To small hunting parties these thieves are really much more dangerous than the Indian. Under the guise of hunters they will come into camp in the evening, enter into conversation, give interesting information as to the best hunting-grounds, and make themselves generally agreeable. All the time they are taking mental stock of the position, and when they finally leave it is with perfect knowledge of every locality, the position of the best horses, and the posts of the sentinels. If by morning they have not got off with your best horses, it will be no fault of theirs.

The danger of a stampede is not from thieves alone ; the disposition is inherent, and must be guarded against at all times. The kicking and plunging of a playful horse will excite others to a romp which may end in a stampede. The only stampede by which I ever lost animals was caused by a horse lying down rolling and snorting in a shallow pool of water.

It should always be remembered that the susceptibility of the horse to the force of example to all external influences is so great, that no herd is ever to be regarded as more gentle than its wildest, or more brave than its most timid, member. The stampede of a considerable herd is not only serious, from the probable resultant loss of animals, but as a palpable and imminent danger.

When just getting fairly under the influence of the panic the herd will likely circle round or through the camp. In the headlong rush each animal appears to be perfectly blind to any or all consequences. Crowded together in a compact mass, and moving at top speed, the force is almost irresistible. Tents are thrown down and demolished ; waggons overturned and broken ; and a man caught by the stream would be trampled in a moment to an unrecognisable pulp. Fortunately the front, as a rule, is narrow, and can be avoided by care, quickness, and presence of mind.

I was once sent to investigate the cause of the stampede of a herd of about 600 animals—horses, mules, and asses. I found that the herd had been grazing, under charge of several herders, in a beautiful level valley about a mile long, half-a-mile wide, on one side of which was a deep wooded stream, on the other a range of low rocky hills, much cut and broken by ravines steep and narrow, and their bottoms filled with trees and brush. The main valley was dotted with isolated trees and clumps of bushes. I found that the stampede had been caused by a very large and valuable jack, which, breaking his lariat rope, had gone frisking and roaring through the herd, some of which starting in play had excited or terrified others, so that in a few moments the whole was a mass of plunging madness. From the trail, it was plain that this mass, with a front of about eighty feet, had circled two or three times about the valley. The clumps of bushes and smaller trees within this tract were torn to fragments and scattered to the winds. Near each of the larger trees within the tract were the bodies of one or more dead animals, crushed and trampled out of all semblance.

The front then took to the hills, striking by accident almost its centre against an angular wall of stone, where a lateral ravine had cut its way to the main valley. Against and at the foot of this rock were the bodies of five animals. The rock split the herd into two parts, the larger going up the ravine. I followed this. The ravine was very crooked, while the track of the stampeded herd was as direct as possible. Consequently the front was frequently striking large trees or the jutting mass of rock at the junction of ravines. Each of these obstacles had marked its resistance by one or more dead bodies, and had again split the rapidly diminishing front; and in not one single instance did I find where the two portions so split had come together again. In the main valley and along the route of the stampede were numbers of animals maimed and wounded in every possible way. Following always the trail of the largest numbers, I, at about six miles from the valley, began to come upon small herds— two, three, or more animals, apparently unhurt, but completely exhausted. Still following in the same way, I, at about sixteen miles from the place where the stampede originated, came up with the last herd, about twenty animals; and among them, entirely unhurt and apparently as fresh and frisky as ever, the jack which had caused all the damage.

I returned to my post, leaving the herders to gather

up the animals. It was nearly two weeks before all were accounted for; and I subsequently learned that about 70 had been killed outright, and about 235 more or less wounded, of which nearly 100 were so much injured as to necessitate their abandonment.

Another cause of disaster in camp is carelessness with fire. When the grass is dry it burns like tinder, and if it be long, and there be a brisk wind, the utmost care must be used. Under such circumstances the camp fires should as far as possible be made to the leeward of the camp and grazing ground. If this cannot be done without too much inconvenience, holes should be dug in the ground, large enough to build the fires in, the long grass near should be cut (with a spade in default of a better implement) and carried off, and the earth taken from the holes spread over to leeward.

It is a common custom to burn off a space sufficiently large for the fires, but this is very dangerous if the grass be long and the wind high. Even though men stand around with blankets to whip out the fire when necessary, it sometimes gets beyond the control of the best directed efforts. Early in life I got a serious lesson on the danger of fire, which would have been avoided had any older officer thought it worth while to devote a few moments to my instruction. And here I may remark that this apathy of the older, and more especially of the commanding, officers, is but too common in our service. They expect the youngster to know by intuition, or to learn without instruction, all the details of duty, even under the most unfamiliar circumstances.

I have heard old officers say on this subject, ' Oh, let them learn for themselves! I had to learn for myself, and one's own experience is the only teaching that makes valuable and lasting impression.' Many young men are so imbued with ideas of their own capacity and knowledge that they do not take such instruction kindly, but the large majority would most eagerly accept every hint which might save them from having to purchase the knowledge with unhappy experience.

The neglect to instruct has one most advantageous result, in that it soon teaches the youngster self-reliance ; but many a bitter experience, many an unnecessary hardship, would be spared the young aspirant to plains knowledge did his commanding officer occasionally give him the benefit of an experience earned by his own hardships.

Almost every item of my own knowledge of plains life has been drilled into my memory by the sharp point of bitter experience.

A very little instruction in youth would have saved me many mishaps and annoyances, and it would have been received with much thankfulness.

When a boy, fresh from 'The Point,' new to army life, and perfectly 'green' in frontier service, I was sent on my first scout after Indians, in command of a party of twenty cavalry. I had not the first dawning of an idea of the details of plains life, nor did my commanding officer think it necessary to give me any instruction. The sergeant of the party was an old soldier, well instructed in all the details of scout and camp. When out about a week we went one day into camp, on a piece of ground covered with grass two feet high and very dry. The wind was blowing quite strongly.

After designating the position of the squads and picket line, I saw the horses unsaddled and lariated out, posted the pickets and guards, and, turning over the command to the sergeant, went with my rod to the stream near by to get some fish for dinner.

I had just got interested in fairly good sport, when I was startled by shouts and commotion in camp, not more than sixty yards away. Dropping my rod I ran back to find the whole camp ground in a blaze, and the flames going with great speed towards the grazing horses. Ordering some of the men to the relief of the animals,

I plunged with the others into the flames to save, if possible, the arms and equipments. We had hardly got to work before the carbines (laid across the saddles on the ground) began to go off with the heat; and this fire, added to the other, and an occasional explosion of a cartridge-box, made it so hot that we were all obliged to get out of the camp and take cover. Some of the horses broke their lariat ropes and stampeded; and in five minutes from the first alarm we were reduced from a well-armed, well-mounted aggressive force, to an apparently half-armed, half-mounted, singed, and dilapidated party.

Most fortunately for us the wind was so high that the flames passed with extreme rapidity; and though the heat was intense for a moment, it soon subsided. The wood-work of the arms was scorched and charred, but their utility was not impaired; many of the saddles and equipments were almost ruined, some of the rations destroyed, and all lighter articles of clothing gone completely. I moved camp across the stream. By next evening the guards and pickets had found and brought in all the stampeded animals, the saddles and accoutrements were mended as skilfully as our means permitted, and I was very glad, after such an experience, to continue my scout with only the loss of one day, though I had lost bedding and every article of clothing except what was on my person. Under the circumstances we got off remarkably well, better than we deserved.

The prairie fire of the high plains is a very insignificant affair; but in the cañons, or rich alluvial deposits of the great valleys, where the grass is high and vegetation of all kinds is abundant, to be caught in one is a most serious misadventure, from which it may require the utmost coolness and presence of mind to extricate oneself without injury.

Setting fire to the grass in the vicinity of the camp at night is one of the Indian modes of annoying a party too strong for attack and too vigilant for a successful attempt at theft. Unless proper precautions are taken, horses are almost sure to be lost, for nothing frightens animals so thoroughly as fire.

I have been followed for several days in succession by a party of Indians, who fired the grass to windward of my camp every night, forcing me to burn all round the camp every evening before posting sentinels, and not only to double the ropes securing the animals, but even to keep on side lines to prevent their plunging at the picket line.

I once shot a deer, which, running a little distance, fell dead in a grassy glade, surrounded by a thicket of trees, bushes, and tall grass. Riding near the spot, I dismounted, and, giving the horse to my servant to fasten, I walked to the deer. He was a splendid animal, with, I think, the most magnificent antlers I have ever seen. Admiring his beautiful proportions and meditating how I would have the head 'set up' until the servant joined me, I leaned my rifle against a convenient tree, some little distance off, and we proceeded to disembowel my prize.

Just then I wanted a smoke, filled my pipe, struck a match, got a light, and blowing out the match (as I supposed), threw the extinguished stick behind me, and went on with my work. Scarcely a minute after, the servant (who was holding while I cut the deer) sprang to his feet with an exclamation, and, looking to the rear, I found the grass blazing to the height of three or four feet. We both jumped on the fire and attempted to put it out by trampling with our feet. Finding this impossible and the fire gaining, I directed him to run for the horses. I ran for my gun, and the progress of the flames towards it was so extremely rapid that I barely secured it in time. Running off, and quartering to the wind, I fortunately found under some large trees a spot of half an acre in extent bare of grass and underbrush. Here I remained for nearly half an hour, almost stifled by the smoke and heat, until the fire had passed and the burned ground got cool enough to walk over. I then went back to my deer. He was literally cooked ; not very artistically, as the outside was burned to a cinder, the inside being raw. The antlers and almost the whole head were burned off, and the whole animal lost to me. It was nearly an hour before my servant could find on his, the windward, side of the fire an opening by which to get on to the burnt ground, and even then the heat was so great that the horses were almost frantic.

This was the hottest fire I have ever seen on the plains, the flames sometimes appearing at least thirty feet high.

It has already been stated that the smaller streams of the second or high plain are subject to sudden and extraordinary rises. This comes partly from the fact that the original rains have cut the ground into ravines with such regularity that all pour their waters into the principal stream about the same time; partly that the slopes formed are covered with a thick mat of short sward, which absorbs water so slowly that almost all the rainfall finds its way at once into the ravines ; but principally from the immense quantity of water which falls in an incredibly short time.

Almost all positions of the high plains are occasionally visited ·by most terrific rain-storms, so severe that they have the general name ' waterspouts.' The quantity of water poured from the clouds, and the effect produced, are so apparently incredible, that I would hesitate to describe them but that the facts are perfectly known to every plainsman.

These storms generally occur in the afternoon of a sultry day, and, in gathering and coming up, have all the appearance of an ordinary thunderstorm. The rain, however, does not fall in drops, but in streams, as if poured from the strainer of a shower-bath.

As the myriads of streams are caught by the wind and deflected from their direct course, they present an appearance of sheets or waves of water, and form in the air thousands of mimic cascades of every conceivable variety; now falling in a smooth, unbroken, inclined sheet, now flying into an infinity of jets, down or up, or sideways, as if fretted by opposing rocks.

Nothing can be more beautiful or more disagreeable than these storms; and when the deluge of rain is, as is often the case, accompanied by huge rounded lumps and shapeless chunks of ice, they become really very serious.

Men can generally find means of protecting themselves, though I have seen them pretty badly beaten; but animals are sometimes severely injured, and always rendered frantic, by the pounding.

If the storm overtakes a party on the march, the animals should be unhitched at once and taken to cover, if any be near; or, if there be none, most securely fastened to the waggons. If in camp, every precaution should be taken not only to secure but to protect them. Every approaching storm should be regarded as a possible waterspout, and full preparation made to meet it at its worst.

It has been my misfortune to encounter several of these storms either on the march or in camp, but have never had the means of measuring the rainfall. I have been at military posts where the rainfall was measured. One occurred at Fort Dodge, by no means as severe as several I have encountered, in which two and a half inches of rain fell in less than one hour.

The effect of such a quantity of water poured out upon the high plains and rushing into the ravines can be more easily imagined than described. Depressions in the surface of the ground, scarcely noticeable in dry weather, become in a few moments raging torrents; ravines, ordinarily dry, become impassable rivers; and valleys, even though one or more miles in width, are flooded to the depth of many feet. It took the railroad engineers some time to learn this phenomenon.

A set of grassy slopes of a mile or more in length, debouching into the river bottom by a valley from a quarter of a mile to a mile in width, without a mark of any waterway, appeared so innocent that the embankment across its mouth would be supplied with a culvert of only a couple of feet. A waterspout bursts, the ravines are flooded, the embankment acts as a dam, the water rises over it, cuts it away, and the road is ruined for a mile or more.

I have seen one such instance where the force of the water having broken the connection, the track, ties bound together with the rails, was swung off the break by the power of the current until the loose ends finally rested nearly a quarter of a mile from their proper position.

Fortunately these storms are restricted in area, but unfortunately their disastrous effects are not confined to the vicinity of their occurrence. The flood moves on, carrying trouble, delay, suffering, and loss of life on its surged waters until they are finally lost in some one of the great rivers of the plains.

With the cloud in view, and the storm approaching, it is easy to be on the alert, to arrange, or if necessary to move camp, and to place the party in a position of safety and comparative comfort. But the most careful plainsman cannot always be prepared for ' thunder from a clear sky,' nor arrange for a flood when not a cloud is to be seen. Besides this, these storms are very exceptional. Possibly every portion of the high plains may be visited by one or more each year; but a party may be out for weeks in the worst season—namely, June and July—camping on the streams with perfect impunity, never seeing a cloud or being troubled with the rush of water. This tends to carelessness, which sooner or later will probably meet its reward, if not in actual loss, at least in a thorough ' drowning out.'

I have been in six or eight storms well worthy the name of ' waterspouts,' but in all my plains experience have never yet been 'drowned out' by floods from the upper portions of the stream on which I was encamped. This I attribute to a very large 'bump' of prudence, and also, considering the number of years I have spent on the plains, and the almost innumerable camps I have made, to very extraordinary good luck.

I have witnessed the phenomena several times, the most remarkable of which I will try to describe. My company was encamped for the summer on a bluff bank about twenty-five feet high, at the foot of which was the dry sandy bed of a stream. The bed averaged about 100 feet wide. The opposite bank was low, and from it the ground extended away in a broad bottom, gradually rising to meet a line of low hills. At intervals in the bed were deep permanent waterholes, which, however, except during high water, were not connected by any surface stream. The camp was about twelve miles in a direct line from the mouth of the cañon, by which the stream had cut its way through a high prairie furrowed with innumerable deep ravines, tributary to this principal stream. About eleven o'clock on a clear, bright, beautiful starlight night, I was lying reading in my tent, when I heard a distant roaring, rushing sound, now more now less distinct, but gradually swelling in power.

Guessing at once the cause, I rushed out and placed myself on the edge of the bank overlooking the sand. In a few moments a long creamy wave, beaten into foam, crept swiftly with a hissing sound across the sand. This appeared to be only a few inches in depth. Following with equal speed, and at a distance of about sixty feet behind the advance of this sheet, was a straight, unbroken mass of water of at least four feet in height. The front of this mass was not rounded into a wave, but rose sheer and straight, a perfect wall of water. From this front wall the mass rose gradually to the rear, and was covered with logs and *débris* of all kinds, rolling and plunging in the tremendous current. In ten minutes from the passage of the advance wave, the water at my feet was at least fifteen feet deep, and the stream nearly half a mile wide.

It was three days before this stream was fordable, and fully a month before it returned to its normal condition. This stream drains a section of the second plain, about twenty miles long by ten wide. The rain which furnished all this water was a waterspout of probably an hour's duration. Even supposing that the rainfall extended over the whole section drained by the tributaries of this stream, the quantity of water carried off will give some idea of the fury of the storm.

The portion of the second plain, known as the Guadalupe Mountains of Texas, is peculiarly subject to these waterspouts. The moisture from the Gulf of Mexico, carried inland by the south-westerly winds, is collected in dense clouds about these high lands, and the streams which take their rise in them are notorious for their sudden and tremendous overflows. Just after the close of the Mexican war, and before the army had learned, by sad experience, all the freaks of nature in the plains, the 3rd Regiment of Infantry, then *en route* for New Mexico, was encamped three miles from San Antonio, on the Salado.

This stream is a succession of waterholes, deep, and from fifty to 200 yards long, connected by a thread of water over which it is easy to step. The bed is a very crooked ditch from thirty to eighty feet wide, with precipitous banks of eight or ten feet. Broad level bottoms extend away on each side of this ditch to the bordering hills, generally nearly three miles apart.

The encampment was by the course of the stream, more than fifty miles from the Guadalupe Mountains, in which it takes its rise. One night, or rather morning, for it was in the 'sma' hours ayont the twal,' while the camp was buried in repose, a sentinel on one of the posts nearest the stream found his coat covered with water. The night was perfectly clear, though dark, and for a few moments he sought in vain for the cause. Hearing a rushing sound towards the stream, he finally noticed that its bed, usually a deep, dark ditch, was bright with what appeared to be running water, and on approaching it he found it to be already more than bank-full, and that he was walking in the water of an approaching freshet. Discharging his musket he alarmed the camp. The long roll was beaten, everybody tumbled out of bed and, to their astonishment, into the water. All was alarm and commotion. The water rose steadily but with wonderful rapidity, and began to show a considerable current. The men were directed to make their way to the high lands as best they could; horses were brought, and the ladies, laundresses, and children carried on their bare backs over nearly two miles of water, often up to the horses' bellies, before arriving at the safe high ground.

Not a thing was saved. Nearly all the command— officers, ladies, enlisted men, laundresses, and children— were in their night-clothes. Tents, arms, provisions, clothing, everything was carried down the stream and totally lost. The bottom was so wide that the water was nowhere—except in the channel—more than two or three feet deep, nor was the current so strong as to be dangerous to a man. Only one life was lost.

The next morning the thread of a stream, of only the night before, was a mighty river twice as wide as the Mississippi at Memphis. The most remarkable feature of this storm was, that it occurred late in the fall. I do not recollect the exact date, but I know that it was much talked of, not that it was very unusual or wonderful, but out of season.

In 1873 Company 'F,' 3rd U.S. Cavalry, met with disaster from one of these floods. I append an abstract from the official report of the captain.

'Fort McPherson, Neb.
'June 9, 1873.

'The Assistant Adjutant-General,

'Department of the Platte Omaha, Neb.

'SIR,—I have the honour to report that, in accordance with instructions, I left Fort McPherson, Neb., May 27th, 1873, with one guide, one wagon-master, five teamsters, and fifty-five enlisted men of Company 'F,' 3rd Cavalry, for the purpose of patrolling the Republican Valley, as directed. . . . . May 31st, marched down to Blackwood about twelve miles, and went into camp. About 9 P.M. a terrible freshet, without any apparent cause, swept down the valley, carrying everything before it. Men, horses, tents, army-wagons, were swept along like corks. For five days previous we had no rain, and where this water came from so suddenly I cannot yet understand. The valley of Blackwood is about forty-five miles long, and about one mile to a mile and a half wide. This entire stretch of country was one raging torrent, at least from six to seven feet deep, and how any man or horse escaped is marvellous.

'The only thing that prevented total destruction was the fact that my camp was surrounded by a belt of timber on three sides, and as the men were carried off by the current they were enabled to save themselves by catching the limbs of trees. When day broke on the morning of the 1st June, it showed almost all the men of my company on the tops of the trees, without any covering except remnants of underclothes, and beneath them the torrent still raging. After the lapse of a few hours the water began to fall, and a few men who could swim got to the hills. Afterwards the others, myself among the number, were got off with life-lines and various other means. Up to this time nothing was to be seen of what had been my camp, except the top of an army-wagon, which had stuck to a log on the ground, and on this wagon were collected

eleven men, who were thus saved from a watery grave.
. . . . Six men of my company were drowned and twenty-six horses lost. I remained at the scene of disaster for four days, and recovered five of the bodies of the men.

'I shall not dwell on the details of this calamity further. It can only be understood by each one taking it home to himself and so approaching nearer to a realisation of its import. The men, though almost destitute of clothing and rations, worked laboriously for four days, recovering the bodies and property, without a murmur.'

.   .   .   .

The commanding officer of Fort McPherson, in his endorsement of the foregoing report, remarks :—

'Nothing but the courage and coolness of Captain —— and his non-commissioned officers prevented the loss of the entire command.

'Captain ——'s life was saved by his trumpeter McGowan, whom I respectfully recommend for a medal of honour.'

These are undoubtedly very extraordinary floods, even for a country peculiarly subject to them. Against such no human foresight or precaution can avail anything. Most fortunately such are extremely rare; and, leaving such deluges entirely out of consideration as beyond mortal prevision or precaution, there are yet a thousand gradations of flood, against which care, knowledge, and forethought may fully protect a party.

Wind-storms are the most common of the annoyances of camp life. The ordinary wall tent is, for summer pleasuring, the best that can be had. It should be of strong 'duck' (the 'linen' are of no use, keeping out neither wind nor water) The eyelet-holes for the side ropes should be reinforced, and those at the corners specially protected with stout leather. The string fastenings of the front should be cut off, and their places supplied by stout leather straps and buckles.

Only experience can teach the proper mode of pitching

a tent, so that even in irregular ground the walls shall always be smooth and perpendicular. When the soil is loose, the side and corner pins should be put in the ground inclining to the tent, so that the pin and rope, when fastened to it, shall form one continuous straight line from the tent to the ground. If driven with an inclination from the tent, as is common, the pulling and jerking of the tent by the wind will almost surely loosen the pins in the soil, and the tent may go over when least expected. When much wind is anticipated, or the tent peculiarly exposed, guy-ropes should be fastened to the spike at the top of each upright tent-pole, and the other ends securely pinned to the ground. These precautions will, under almost all circumstances, enable the inmates to sleep in safety and comfort.

I once, however, had my whole tent split and blown away, leaving the poles standing. The latter had been firmly planted in the ground, and securely guyed with double ropes front and back. I must admit, however, that the tent had seen its best days, and deserved honourable retirement after long and faithful service.

In the late fall and winter of the high plains there is no longer any danger of waterspouts, or sudden rises of the streams. Wind, cold, and fire are the only enemies to be guarded against, but these are often amply sufficient to test one's capacity and endurance.

The camp should always at such seasons be nestled in the deepest and cosiest nook, and protected when possible by bluffs and thickets.

One winter I went out from Fort Lyon with a party of officers and soldiers, to procure game for the Christmas holidays. The second day out was delightful, not only the weather being perfect, but buffalo and antelope were very abundant. There was a beautiful camping-place on the bank of the Arkansas, but it was unprotected; and, true to my prudential instincts, I caused the waggons to be drawn through deep sand and ensconced the party on an island in the heart of the deepest and most dense thicket I could find. Tents were pitched, stores put up, and all preparations made for a camp of two or three days.

During the night the weather changed. A furious storm of wind and snow with the most intense cold set in, and we, with all the protection of the thickets, with our 'Sibley' stoves red-hot, were forced to remain under cover of piles of buffalo robes all next day.

Had the camp been on the unprotected bank of the river, we must not only have suffered very considerably, but would undoubtedly have lost a number of animals by freezing. On the third day the storm was over, and we finished with a most delightful and successful hunt.

Only a very few years ago there was in some portions of the plains a danger to camps which unhappily exists no longer. It was of being run over by buffalo. This animal is habitually stupid and sluggish, but under some circumstances evinces a most peculiar nervousness. He is extremely addicted to 'stampedes,' and during this temporary aberration of his mind is as dangerous a beast collectively as can be found in the world. I have heard many stories of 'hair-breadth 'scapes' from buffalo; I have seen railroad and waggon trains stopped to wait his pleasure; and as close a shave as I ever made to 'passing in my checks' was from a buffalo stampede.

I was changing posts in March 1871, and had three or four waggons and a small escort. One night I camped on Big Coon Creek. It was too early for rain, and the weather was cold and blustery. My camp was therefore nearly in the bed of the creek, close under the shelter of the steep, almost bluff hillocks, which border the stream. The nook in which I camped was small, and tents and waggons were unusually crowded together.

It was late at night, and I was in bed. The camp, except one sentinel, was buried in sleep; the fires were out, darkness and silence reigned supreme. A faint and very distant roaring sound struck upon my ear. Thinking of water I rushed out at once, and, running up the side of the hill, peered up the stream into the darkness to discover an approaching line of foam, precursor of the flood.

Just then the wind brought the sound more distinctly. It came from the prairie, not from the stream, and was approaching. I sent the sentinel to wake up the corporal and other two men of the guard, who soon made their appearance with their arms.

Explaining to the men in a few words the nature of the danger, I warned them to keep perfectly cool and to obey orders. By this time the black line of the moving mass of buffalo was distinctly visible. It was bearing directly down upon us with tremendous speed and irresistible force. We were in an excellent position for the protection of the camp, being directly between it and the buffalo, and about fifty yards from it. My only chance was to split the herd. If this could be done, we and the camp would be saved; if not, all would go to destruction together. Waiting until the advance line of buffalo was within thirty yards, the muskets were fired in rapid and continuous succession, and we in unison let out one of the most unearthly yells that ever split the throats of five badly-frightened men. A few of the leading animals fell dead, the others swerved from the fire and noise; the herd was split, and, tumbling in fright and confusion down the bank on each side of the camp, went thundering and roaring into the darkness.

In all my life I have never seen so badly-frightened a lot of people as those in camp, nor do I blame or disparage them in the least. Waked from sound sleep by the rapid firing and hideous yells, they rushed out of their tents to find themselves in the very midst of a plunging, struggling mass of buffalo.

The edge of one portion of the split herd passed within thirty feet of one flank of the camp, while the nearest of the other portion was about seventy feet from the other flank. The members of my little party had the living stream within fifteen or twenty feet on either side. I consider this the most imminent danger that I have ever encountered on the plains.

Had I and the sentinel been asleep nothing could have saved my whole party from a horrible death; for the banks under which we were camped were so steep that, even had they seen and been sensible enough to avoid the camp, the buffalo in front would have been driven upon and over us by the pressure of those in rear. There must have been 4,000 or 5,000 animals in this stampede.

I have already, in speaking of the tent arrangements, recommended a bedstead. In very cold weather it is best and warmest to couch on the ground; but in the pleasant season of summer and fall the ground is too warm, too dirty, and too full of ' things with legs.' The high plains are extremely prolific of insect life, spiders, beetles, &c., and the bed on the ground is apt to be more populous than comfortable.

Except in the vicinity of ' dog towns' (the dwellings of the little marmot, miscalled the prairie dog) there are singularly few snakes on the plains. The only one at all dangerous is the rattlesnake. There is considerable nobility of character about this reptile. Though always ready for battle, he never strikes without fair warning, except when weak, tender, and probably almost blind from just shedding his skin. He is very susceptible to cold, and will at night crawl into the most comfortable place to be found. I have never had a personal experience of his fondness for tent and bedding, but have seen him shaken from a horse-blanket, or found him curled up near the warm ashes of the camp fire.

In Texas rattlesnakes are very plentiful, and I have heard many anecdotes of their fondness for a tent. A brother officer found one coiled under the edge of his pillow. Another, thrusting his foot into his boot, was horrorstricken on feeling it come upon a soft, yielding mass. Dragging the boot off with all possible expedition, out dropped a huge ' rattler.'

A once dear friend, lost sight of since the war of rebellion, was returning with a party from a long and laborious exploring expedition. They camped on the ' Nueces River,' only twelve miles from Fort Inge, then considered the western boundary of civilisation. On the long hard trip my friend had abandoned the habit of changing his dress for the night ; but, being so near to ' white people,' he determined to treat himself to a civilised sleep, and to this end arranged his person in a long night-shirt. He had been asleep some time when he was partially awakened by a cold sensation down his back. Thinking, in his nearly unconscious state, that it was rain, he moved his position and fell asleep. Again he was partially awakened to repeat the process. The third time he was roused more fully. The moon was shining brightly, and he was just wondering where the water could come from, when he felt the cold clammy touch on his back, and a sensation as if a snake were fitting itself against his spine. With a wild yell he sprang to his feet, and rushed from the tent, bursting out the whole front, and was only stopped in his flight by getting his bare feet full of cactus spines. The snake was against the bare skin, and was carried in the folds of the shirt outside the tent, where it fell, and was found and killed by the aroused party.

It was a very large ' rattler,' and appeared stupid, either from cold or fright, and made no attempt at resistance. ' Joe ' used afterwards to declare that no money could tempt him again to sleep when in camp in a night-shirt.

A bedstead is a sure protection against the too intimate nocturnal visits of this reptile, and also of an animal apparently insignificant, but whose attacks are more dreaded by hunters in some portions of the plains than the assault of the most powerful 'grizzly.' This is the skunk—a beautiful little animal, with body about as large as a common house cat. It is covered with long black and white hair. Its tail is disproportionately long and bushy, and, when the animal is roused, it is erected as a banner of defiance. Its legs are very short, and its feet formed for burrowing. A man can easily outrun it; it cannot climb, and it would fall an easy prey to the larger carnivora, but that Nature has supplied it with a weapon of offence and defence in a fetid discharge most horribly obnoxious to everything except panthers and Indians.

The skunk is carnivorous, and his mouth, shaped like that of a racoon, is furnished with a beautiful set of sharp white teeth. He is nocturnal in his habits, and very fearless, penetrating in search of food into camps and tents while the inmates are asleep. In such cases he is greatly to be feared, for, so far from keeping away from selecting men, he will, if he finds nothing more to his taste, deliberately commence devouring the hand, face, or any uncovered part of the sleeper. The bite in itself would be of but little account; but, in all the country between the Republican River and the Indian Territory, it is almost invariably followed up by that most horrible of all horrors, hydrophobia.

I have never had opportunity nor the technical knowledge necessary for a careful investigation; but I am convinced that the terrible disease is the natural result to man of the bite of the skunk (in the territory designated); and that, while inflicting it on the person bitten, it does not follow that the skunk is himself afflicted with the malady.

I judge this to be the case, firstly, from the fact that skunks are very numerous in the valleys of the Arkansas and its tributaries, whilst the number of men bitten each year with fatal result is so great and so widely separated both in location and time as to indicate an epidemic amongst the skunks which, if each were equally rabid, would soon exterminate the whole race. Secondly, from the actions of the biting animals. The bite is not the senseless snap of a rabid animal, but is the result of appetite. The skunk comes into camp in search of food, deliberately sits down on the hand or face of a man, and begins eating. If disturbed, he cocks his tail and stands on the defence ; but if a fire is made, or a candle lit, or he be alarmed by noise and bustle, he scampers off into the darkness, to return again when all is quiet. Thirdly, that, though I have seen many dogs bitten by skunks, I have never known a dog or other lower animal to go mad from such a bite.

The crowds of buffalo hunters that flocked to the plains in 1872-3-4 suffered greatly from skunk-bites. During the years 1872-3, while stationed at Fort Dodge, I knew by report of sixteen cases, every one of which proved fatal.

Assistant Surgeon Jameway, U.S.A., stationed at Fort Hays, in a most interesting article in the *Medical Record*, reports eleven cases of skunk-bite treated by him or coming under his observation, ten of which resulted in hydrophobia, and were fatal.

In 1872, when on a scout, I camped one night on the Cimarron River, near the crossing of the old Santa Fé Road. In the night I was awakened by a noise in the servants' tent next my own. I called out, but receiving no answer, and the disturbance ceasing, I went to sleep again. While dressing in the morning, one of the men came to me with his hand bound up, and asked if there was any cure for a skunk-bite. Though my heart sank within me, I made light of it, and told him that it was no more dangerous than the bite of any other hungry little animal. I examined the wound. The whole ball of the right thumb was torn, lacerated, and gnawed in a fearful manner. I had no caustic or other means of cauterisation except fire, and so many hours had elapsed since the bite, that I thought its application would do more harm mentally than good corporeally.

I therefore had the wound carefully and thoroughly washed with castile soap, cut off the protuberant pieces of mangled flesh, and, binding it up, kept on a simple water-dressing until the wound healed, which was in about ten days. This man was with me for more than a year after the bite. He never experienced any ill effects, except temporary pain from the wound.

He gave me a detailed account of the occurrence. He and another man were sleeping on opposite sides of a common or 'A' tent. He dreamed that he was being eaten up by some animal, but a sort of nightmare prevented his moving. After some time, however, the pain and horror together woke him up to find a skunk eating his hand. With a cry and sudden effort he threw the animal from him. It struck the other side of the tent, and fell upon the other man, who waked up, and, re-cognising the intruder, rushed out of the tent. The bitten man, who had heard of the surely fatal result of skunk-bite, was so paralysed with fear and horror that he made no effort to get up, and, seeing the skunk come towards him again, buried himself in the blankets. The skunk walked all over him, apparently seeking for an opening, and, finding none, began to scratch the blankets as if trying to dig out his victim. The mental position of this poor fellow can be better imagined than described.

In the meantime the other man had loosened the tent pins and lifted up one side of the tent, letting in the moonlight; then pelting the animal with sticks from a distance, at last frightened it so that it ran off into the deep, dark bank of the river. This skunk emitted no odour, and was undoubtedly simply hungry.

This is the only non-fatal case of skunk-bite I have known in the Arkansas country. I have known several cases of skunk-bite in Texas, and some cases in other sec-tions of the country. They were not regarded as at all serious, nor did any ill effect result from them. A surgeon of the United States army for some years stationed at various posts in the Department of the Platte informed me that he had never heard in that section of a fatal case of skunk-bite. I am constrained, therefore, to believe that this singularly fatal result is confined to the section of country heretofore described, the valley of the Arkansas being about its centre.

In many years of frontier life I have never personally known of a single case of rabies in any animal except man. The fondness of soldiers for dogs is proverbial; and many frontier military posts might well, from the number and variety of the canine species, be mistaken for dog-breeding establishments.

Indians say that wolves not unfrequently go mad, rush into their villages, and do great damage. The following most interesting and perfectly authenticated facts are taken from the records of the hospital at Fort Larned, on the Arkansas River:—

' On the 5th August, at 10 P.M., a rabid wolf, of the large grey species, came into the post and charged round most furiously. He entered the hospital and attacked Corporal ——, who was lying sick in bed, biting him severely in the left hand and right arm. The left little finger was nearly taken off. The wolf next dashed into a party of ladies and gentlemen sitting in Colonel ——'s porch, and bit Lieut. —— severely in both legs. Leaving there, he soon after attacked and bit Private —— in two places. This all occurred in an incredibly short space of time; and, although those above-mentioned were the only parties bitten, the animal left the marks of his presence in every quarter of the garrison. He moved with great rapidity, snapping at everything within his reach, tearing tents, window-curtains, bed-clothing, &c., in every direction. The sentinel at the guard-house fired over the animal's back, while he ran between the man's legs. Finally he charged upon a sentinel at the haystack, and was killed by a well-directed and most fortunate shot. He was a very large wolf, and his long jaws and teeth presented a most formidable appearance.[1]

'The wounds were thoroughly cauterised with nitrate of silver, on the plan recommended by Mr. Youatt.'

The Indians are still camped in the vicinity of the post in very large numbers. I have taken particular pains to question them as to their experience with regard to rabid wolves. They say that the appearance of mad wolves in their village is not unfrequent; that the time of year at which they are most often seen is in the months of February and March; that, once having entered a village, the wolf will make no attempt to leave it, but will rush furiously from place to place until he is disabled; and that in no instance have any of them ever known a person to recover after having received the smallest scratch from the teeth of the rabid animal. They make no attempt at treatment; and one or two instances were related where an Indian, on being affected with the hydrophobial spasms, threw himself into the water and was drowned.

'September 9th.—Corporal —— showed signs of commencing hydrophobia on the evening of the 6th instant. The symptoms were as usually described, were well marked and very characteristic. He died on the morning of the 9th. No treatment was attempted after the symptoms commenced. The wounds had been well cauterised with lunar caustic from time to time, and washed with alkali washes, and had he allowed the finger to be removed at first there would have been a greater probability of his recovery. A large Newfoundland dog, which had been seen fighting with the wolf, has also just died with marked symptoms of hydrophobia.

'The wounds have healed in the other two persons, and they appear to be in perfect health.'

[1] This is the large grey or buffalo wolf.

The officer bitten is now (1875) in perfect health, having never experienced any ill effects beyond the ordinary pain of the wounds.

The evidence as to frequency of rabies in wolves comes entirely from Indians, and, with all due respect and consideration for their veracity, I doubt it.

For nearly thirty years the army has been as constantly a resident of the plains as the Indians themselves, and with equal opportunity for witnessing all the phenomena of plains life; yet the instance given above is the only one on record. Rabies is not a plains malady.

No description of life on the plains can now be given which will be more than a special record of a particular time and place. But a few years ago the journey across the plains was the work of a whole summer. From the time of leaving the Missouri River the party was lost to the world, and lived only in and for itself: no mails, no news, no communication of any kind with civilisation. Surrounded on all sides by treacherous savages, by danger of every kind, each man became a host in himself.

To a fascination of a life of perfect freedom from all conventional restraints, of constraint and adventure, was added that other fascination, far stronger to many natives —the desire to penetrate the unknown.

Now all is changed. There is no longer an unknown. Railroads have bared the silent mysteries of the plains to the inspection of every shopboy. Civilisation, like a huge cuttlefish, has passed its arms of settlements up almost every stream, grasping the land, killing the game, driving out the Indian, crushing the romance, the poetry, the very life and soul out of the 'plains,' and leaving only the bare and monotonous carcass.

PART II.

GAME.

'Merry it is in the good greenwood,
    When the mavis and merle are singing,
When the deer sweeps by, and the hounds are in cry,
    And the hunter's horn is ringing.'   SCOTT.

CHAPTER VII.

To the sportsman the most prominent fascination of plains life is the abundance and variety of game. I use the term abundance in its sportsmanlike sense, meaning the sufficiency.

Leaving out the buffalo (which plainsmen scarcely consider game) there is little to be had without skill and knowledge.

Nowhere on the plains that I know of can one slaughter such numbers of beasts as are bagged, we are told, by sportsmen in either Abyssinia, Southern Africa, or India. The plains hunter must *work*, and he must know how to work, or his bag will be of the lightest. There are no villages of natives to be subsidised to drive dangerous animals to where the hunter sits securely ensconced in a tree; no hundreds of peasants to make a line of miles, and force the game to a battue; no battalion of keepers to drive birds to the sportsman sitting comfortably in his box, with two or three breech-loaders and a man to load them, a bottle of Roederer and a box of cigars to keep the time from hanging heavily. On the plains it is a fair fight between human sagacity and brute instinct, and even with the most approved arms the odds are by no means always in favour of the human.

I have said that the buffalo is scarcely considered game by the plainsman. It is for the reason that this animal, less than any other, requires an exercise of that skill and sagacity in which the true sportsman finds his pleasure and the reward for all his toils.

The man who kills his two or three pound trout with an eight-ounce rod, correspondingly light tackle, and delicate fly, has a half-hour of exquisite enjoyment of which the ground-bait man can form no conception, though the latter may get more fish ; and the successful stalking of a black-tailed buck, even though it involves hours of severe labour, is more full of pure satisfaction to the thorough sportsman than the murder of an acre of buffaloes.

The first necessity to a successful sportsman is a good equipment. For all large animal game he must have a good breech-loading rifle, of calibre not less than forty-five, and plenty of the best ammunition.

The arrangement of sights and triggers is a matter of taste and habit, but it is of the gravest importance that the sight, however arranged, should be exquisitely fine.

Personally, I most decidedly object to elevating sights for the rifle. Out of ten deer or other animals missed, at least nine are over-shot. Either from excitement, or because the game appears dwarfed in the wide expanse of prairie, even the most experienced sportsmen habitually overestimate distance, and the tendency to put up the elevating sights is so irresistible that nearly every successful sportsman of my acquaintance has discarded this sight entirely. Besides this, the use of the elevating sight does not in the least solve the problem. It does very well for shooting at a target where the distance is accurately measured ; and if the sportsman could only induce the deer to stand still at 500, 600, or 800 yards, he might estimate the distance and hit it. But the deer fails to be so accommodating, and will insist on stopping at 650, and 737 yards, or some irregular distance of which the sight takes no account. Moreover, as the trajectory of these high ranges must necessarily be greatly curved, the chances are infinitely against the sportsman. He must first guess at the distance, then put up the elevating sight nearest that distance ; then guess again as to whether a fine or coarse sight ought to be taken through the sight as now arranged.

The very best sight, and the one almost universally in use by sportsmen and professional hunters on the plains, is the plain 'buck-horn,' a description of which is unnecessary, as every gunsmith knows it.

The very large mass of game 'bagged' is killed inside of 200 yards.. A good gun will carry a ball to that distance with almost a flat trajectory.

Of the best gun I have ever owned, the line of fire never cut the line of sight at all, but was tangent to or coincident with it; in other words, the gun did not shoot too high at any distance, and I took precisely the same sight at an object at ten feet as at 100 or 200 yards off. This is very unusual, but a gun is good as it approximates to this extreme accuracy. After 200 yards, however, the curve of the trajectory of even the best gun increases with great rapidity, and it is only by constant practice that the sportsman can keep himself up to the mark at long ranges. Sportsmen who use the 'buck-horn' must learn to sight 'on the barrel.' With practice there is no reason why this should not become second nature; and a sportsman soon learns to take his sight at a distant object and elevate his gun to the proper angle, just as the trombone player learns by practice to stop his hand at the exact spot to give the correct note.

The greatest difficulty of this kind of shooting is that when the barrel is elevated it shuts out the sight of the game. This difficulty I obviate by shooting with both eyes open. With the right I keep the line of sight and estimate the distance ' on the barrel ; ' with the other I have a clear view of the game and its surroundings. This is very easy to learn ; and, though I have never known any other sportsman to shoot a rifle in this way, it has been of such invaluable use to me, especially in antelope shooting and at running game, that I recommend every young sportsman to learn and practise it.

The trigger is of importance, though this, even more than the sight, is a matter of habit. In common with nearly all plains sportsmen and hunters, I use a hair trigger, and can shoot accurately with no other. My preference is for the old-fashioned Kentucky double-set trigger. Some sportsmen use the single-set, and some few the French double-set trigger. With this latter the gun can only be brought to full cock after the trigger is set, which peculiarity gives occasion for numerous accidents and much bad language. I do not like either of these triggers.

There are among the soldiers some few successful hunters and good shots; and this is a constant marvel to me, since they are obliged to use the rifle-musket provided by the Ordnance Department, on which the sights are so coarse that without moving the gun a man may take apparently accurate sight on any object within a horizontal radius of ten or fifteen feet, and which is so hard on trigger that few men can pull it off with the first joint of one finger. I have frequently cocked a United States rifle-musket, turned it muzzle downwards and dandled it, the whole weight of the gun being on the trigger resting on my finger, without pulling it off. With such a weapon and great economy in the expenditure of cartridges, it is little wonder that the majority of the army are as poor shots as can be found. The system on which even the little practice that soldiers have is conducted is as absurd as can well be imagined. To put a recruit to firing off-hand at a target 300 yards away, when he cannot, with a rest, hit a cracker box at twenty paces, is as ridiculous a performance as could well be devised by even the most unpractical men.

There is no sort of excuse for such sights as are put on the rifle-musket. The apology for the hard trigger is, that men would be more likely to shoot each other if the triggers were easy—a most weak and frivolous pretence when taken in connection with the facts that a breechloader is never charged until wanted for use, and that when not actually at the 'ready' the gun stands at the half-cock notch, which may be as hard as they please to make it. Old men are nearly always opposed to innovation. 'The old way is the best way.' What was best in the active, practical days of a man's life, is very apt to be best to him in his last days. It is extremely rare that a man progresses with the age in which he lives. As he grows old, or drops out of active life, his place is taken by the young and pushing. It is not necessary that a man grows old in years. Any occupation, or lack of it, that takes him out of active life produces the same effect.

It is not, therefore, at all to be wondered at if some of our staff officers are as complete fossils as can be found in the tertiary deposits of the Bad Lands. They are out of life; their future is assured. Their occupation becomes a matter of routine, in which the correctness of a form is of more importance than the establishment of a fact.

The practical men of the line have had a hard fight with the 'inertia' of their masters of the staff, and have no reason to be disheartened at the result. We have an excellent rifle; we have the bronze barrel, and may hope in time to secure proper sights and triggers.

The rifle shooting now becoming so fashionable is destined to work great improvement in the use of arms. It is, however, only a step in the right direction. The trials, as at present conducted, are rather tests of the rifles than of the men. When these trials have progressed until men begin to compete at distances unknown to and estimated by themselves, without elevating sights, off-hand and necessarily with light triggers, then the maximum of efficiency and skill is not far off. Then must the soldier put in practice such shooting as he must necessarily use against an enemy.

I have never seen a really ardent sportsman, however experienced, who did not become more or less excited when in the actual presence of game. This excitement is the culmination of the pleasure of the pursuit. With the novice it is ' buck fever,' and leads to all sorts of absurd situations. I remember, when a boy, following the first black squirrel I ever saw for a quarter of a mile, my gun pointed, my finger on the trigger, pulling with all my might; and it was only when the squirrel was safe in his den in a hollow tree, that I discovered that my gun was not cocked.

With every new animal encountered, in a pretty long experience, I have had a recurrence of the malady, though not frequently to the extent of interfering with my success. The best shot at game I ever saw was so nervous in its presence, that he could hardly hold his rifle; but let him get within range, and a rock could scarcely be steadier than his rifle barrel, as it blazed out almost certain death.

When I first went to Texas, soon after entering the service, I had never killed a deer. My first post was at Fort Lincoln (long since abandoned), in the vicinity of which deer were almost as abundant as rabbits in a North Carolina 'old field.' In spite of their numbers and indefatigable hunting, I could not bag a deer, though I fired at them ten or fifteen times every week. When this had continued for a month, I in despair laid away my rifle, and took to my shot-gun to go after turkeys and quail. Some time after I was sent on a scout in the Guadalupe Mountains; black bear were very plentiful, and I bagged a good many. One day, taking a carbine from one of the men, I went into a cañon, looking for Bruin. When about three miles from camp, a herd of at least fifty deer sprung up from the bottom of the valley, and ran a little way up the side of the opposite hill. I could not resist such an opportunity, and, dismounting, fired at a splendid animal near the foot of the hill and about eighty yards off. At the report my deer threw up its flag and went off, as did the herd. While looking at them with thorough disgust I noticed one acting in a strange manner, and in a moment a huge buck came tumbling down the steep side of the hill. I lost no time in securing him. He was shot through the head, though his position on the hill was at least thirty feet above the one I aimed at.

Thus I bagged my first deer. The charm was broken. Next day I bagged two, and since then have never had any difficulty in killing deer.

We will suppose the sportsman well fitted out, and ready to take the field against the denizens of the plains. If he has no knowledge of the habits of game, and intends only a short hunt, he had best hire a good hunter to go with him and find the game for him.

In this case he must stipulate that the hired hunter is not to shoot at game unless specially ordered, otherwise very little game will fall to his bag. The desire to kill in the professional plains hunter is so much stronger than his regard for the truth, that, when his rifle goes off unexpectedly and a deer falls, he will turn, with ample apology, to his employer to declare that the animal was just starting to run when he first saw it, and there was no time to point it out.

Each animal has to be hunted differently, and no amount of previous oral instructions can supply to the novice the place of actual experience. A few general rules are all that can be given :—

1. Always hunt against or across the wind. If the wind will permit, it is preferable to hunt across small valleys, ravines, or rolling ground.

2. Approach the top of each elevation as slowly and carefully as if you knew that game was just beyond, keeping your body well concealed ; and be sure, before exposing yourself on the top, that you have carefully scanned every portion of ground in view.

3. Recollect that to kill game you must see it before it sees you.

4. If game is seen, reconnoitre all the ground and decide how you can best approach, keeping always out of sight, and constantly having the wind in your favour.

5. When within shot, do not show yourself until perfectly cool.

6. Never fire when panting or blown with exertion, unless it is a desperate case.

7. Play all the advantages, and always take a rest for your rifle when you can get it.

8. If a long shot, be sure not to overestimate. A shot too high is utterly wasted. No one ever heard of an animal being killed by an over shot. I myself have killed numbers by the *ricochet*, the aim having been too low.

9. When the game is down approach cautiously, and not until reloaded.

10. If the game should become alarmed and run off, do not try to follow it, unless you should be in a wild country where it is very tame from not having been hunted. Continue your hunt in some other direction than that taken by it, as the running game will alarm all other animals near which it passes, or, at least, put them on the alert.

There is great difference of opinion among sportsmen as to whether game is best and most successfully hunted on foot or on horseback. When game is very plentiful, and the cover at all thick, the footman has a most decided advantage; but under all ordinary circumstances I most unhesitatingly give my vote in favour of hunting on horseback.

The increase in bulk and greater noise render the sportsman more liable to be seen and heard; but these disadvantages are more than counterbalanced by the increased range of his vision, and the very much larger extent of country he can hunt over in a specified time.

Besides this, when he does find the game undisturbed he can approach coolly and fire deliberately, unfatigued by a previous long tramp. Moreover, his having a horse does not in the least prevent his hunting on foot when occasion requires; and if, during his hunt, he finds a cosy dell likely to be the home of a red deer, or a cedar thicket into which leads a recent trail of black-tails, he can dismount, steal into these places noiselessly on foot, and, if nothing is found, remount and go in search of better fortune. When a sportsman of only ordinary pedestrian powers hunts on foot he is constantly trammelled by the thought of the return tramp, and is apt to cut short his hunt. Should his enthusiasm carry him far from his camp, the fatiguing return march will very likely unfit him for work next day, especially if he has to pack in much game. The sportsman should never permit his ardour to convert sport into mere labour.

Whether on foot or on horseback, I cannot too urgently recommend to the sportsman that he never hunt alone. Two hunters should not go together, but each hunter should be accompanied by a servant or other person.

If on horseback, this person holds the sportsman's horse when he dismounts, and follows at a long distance when he is beating-up cover. If on foot, he assists in carrying the game. In either case the presence of this person is a guarantee against an ordinary mishap becoming a serious casualty. A thousand accidents may happen to a sportsman which are serious only when he is alone. He may turn his ankle by a miss-step, or slip down a bank and break his leg. The same accident is not likely to occur to two men; and, if one should get hurt in any way, the other may not only make him comparatively comfortable at once, but can go for assistance. I have known of several instances where men went out hunting alone, and were never afterwards heard of. One of these cases occurred in the Black Hills, within six weeks previously to the time that this is written. I knew an estimable man who went out alone after buffalo. Three weeks afterwards his remains were found in the bottom of a deep chasm, into which he had fallen and broken his leg, and where he had perished miserably by starvation.

I have known very many instances of accidents, not very serious in themselves, but which would probably have been fatal had the individuals been alone when they happened. I speak from ample experience. Do not go hunting on the plains alone.

A well-trained dog is most invaluable to the sportsman; for, whatever his skill as a marksman or a trailer, he will lose more or less game unless he has the assistance of man's best friend. All plains animals have extraordinary vitality; and nothing but the breaking of the backbone, or a shot through the brain, will certainly bring one down 'in his tracks.' Any one of these animals is liable to run for a quarter of a mile, though his heart be split as with a knife.

The red deer loves the cover of thick jungle of willow, or quaking asp (a species of aspen, or cottonwood, which grows profusely in mountain gorges). The black-tail prefers the thickets of pine or cedar, which grow on rocky crags and ledges. In many cases the trail of the wounded animals through such thickets defies the skill of any but an Indian; and the animal is likely to be lost, though he expend his strength and latest breath in going but a hundred yards. It is on such occasions as these that the value of a good dog is best appreciated. To be of value, however, he must be thoroughly under control. He must be trained to remain at heel until sent forward, then to find and take the trail of the wounded animal. Should he run after one unhurt, he expends his strength, and is liable to be lost. He-should be taught, when he has found or pulled down the wounded game, to bark loudly and continuously until his master come to him.

This training is very simple, and easy to give. For such work I very greatly prefer the pointer. His nose is as good as the best; he has sufficient speed, strength, and endurance, and is more easily taught. Greyhounds, bloodhounds, foxhounds, setters, and even the common cur, are used as above indicated. The first two lack intelligence; the third and last are difficult to train; while the setter, though otherwise a fine animal for such hunting, cannot stand the heat and aridity of the dry plains.

It is difficult, and fortunately unnecessary, to decide upon the relative merits of the rifle and shot-gun.

The lover of the shot-gun has a quicker and more frequent return for his expenditure of time and effort. He has, moreover, the companionship and opportunity to admire the wonderful instinct—nay, more, the human sagacity—of his dog, without which shot-gun work is no sport.

I have known many keen, indomitable sportsmen who expressed the utmost contempt for the rifle and its returns; men who would work all day for a dozen quail, but not an hour for the chance of a deer. I love both arms, and always take both with me for a hunt on the plains, but, to my thinking, the rifle is the noblest of weapons.

The man who succeeds with it must have patience, endurance, a quick eye, and a steady nerve. His opportunities are more rare, but their results infinitely more satisfactory. The one is dilettante work, delightful coquetry, with many pleasing objects changeable at pleasure; the other, ' grande passion,' faithful to one aim, and culminating in supreme satisfaction, intelligible only to the initiated.

In the Eastern States, where the hunter is put on a stand at a runway, and the deer driven by him at full speed by the hounds, the shot-gun is in almost universal use, and is undoubtedly for such hunting the best arm. To my taste this is, at best, a mean kind of hunting only exceeded in meanness, indeed, by the boat-hunting of the Adirondacks. This last is simply despicable. On my first visit to that celebrated region I committed a murder, which has since lain heavily on my conscience.

Preliminaries having been arranged, I was sent with

my boatman to a distant lake across a three-mile portage, over which I was expected to carry everything—guns, oars, seats—except the empty shell of the boat. Arrived at the lake I awaited for two hours, with some interest, the development of this new style of hunting. Far off I faintly heard the bay of hounds, and some moments afterwards my boatman evinced the greatest excitement ; he sprung into the boat, calling upon me, and at his best speed made for the opposite shore. After a few moments I saw the head of a noble buck coming directly for us, swimming easily and freely ; he scarcely noticed the boat until we were within shot, then turned and attempted to retrace his way. With a fine sweep of his oars the boatman threw the boat directly in his path, and called upon me to fire. The noble head, proudly erect, with half-defiant, half-frightened bearing, was scarcely six feet from the boat.

‘ Have I got to shoot that poor animal, without giving him any show ? ’ I asked. ‘ Pshaw ! ’ answered the boatman, ‘ that ain't nothin’. You arter come here when ther'n the red coat ; then they'll sink when they'r shot ; so afore lettin’ the gentlemen fire I allers gets a good grip of their tails so as to save ’em, you see.’ I wanted venison, and I wanted the magnificent head, so I fired. I have always regretted that shot ; and though I have made two subsequent trips to the Adirondacks, I have never been seduced into shooting another deer in the water. If such be sport, I don't want it.

But this is digression, and fortunately it is not plains hunting.

On the prairie the combat is at equal wits between man and animal, and the fire must usually be delivered at such a distance that the shot gun is of little use.

For some unknown reason, there are many ardent sportsmen successful with shot-guns who cannot acquire the art of rifle shooting. To these, much that is most pleasurable in plains hunting must always remain a sealed book. Against buffalo, elk, and mountain sheep, the shot-gun is not nearly so effective as a bow and arrow in the hands of an Indian. Against deer in thickets where the hunter often finds himself within a few paces and with only the most momentary glimpse of the game, a shot-gun may be very effective, though, to be successful in his bag, the hunter must always have a well-trained dog.

I have frequently killed deer with a shot-gun, which I could not possibly have bagged with a rifle. A captain of cavalry, almost in my presence, bagged a buffalo-bull of eighteen months old with a single charge of No. 4 shot; and there is a well-authenticated story of an old hunter in the ' nine-mile bottom ' of the Purgatory River bagging seven antelope and a fine dog, with one discharge of a huge weapon which he called a shot-gun.

These are all exceptional cases. Under ordinary circumstances the rifle is the weapon for plains shooting; and if the choice of the hunter is limited to one arm he should take the rifle, if he knows how to use it.

It is a very singular fact that even the best rifle shot varies very greatly in his shooting at different marks. One of the very best target marksmen I ever knew could not hit a living animal at fifty yards, and some of the most successful hunters are very poor shots at a target. I know a good hunter who has killed an immense quantity of nearly all kinds of large game, who cannot bag a black-tail deer though he has been shooting at them for years. I rarely miss a decent shot at a deer or an antelope, yet I find it almost impossible to hit a wolf or a hawk; and though I have, I am sure, fired at least 500 shots at wolves, I have killed with the rifle less than twenty in all my life. It is impossible to account for this; but almost every good hunter with whom I have compared notes on this subject, confirms my own experience. However skilful and successful each may be, there is yet something at which he shoots, with no confidence in his ability to hit.

Dead game should be butchered at once; all large

animals very soon becoming unfit for food unless the viscera are removed immediately after death.

Once needing fresh meat for my command I sent out some soldiers to shoot buffalo. They killed four or five just at dark, and hurried to camp. I sent a waggon out before daylight next morning, and, though the night had been cool, the flesh was found to be so offensive that it could not be used. The hunters had neglected to remove the intestines.

It is a curious fact, and an admirable example of the universal providence of nature, that the young of game animals have no scent. In some mysterious way, the dam communicates her instructions to the newly-born offspring, which, in quiet obedience, lies motionless in the hiding place selected for it, never moving except to escape the most imminent danger.

A hungry cougar or half-famished wolf may pass and repass within a few feet of the little one, which, had it the slightest scent, would at once fall a victim to these keen-nosed gluttons. That great numbers do fall victims is evidenced by the fact that at this season all the carnivora are fatter than at any other. But for the admirable provision of nature in withholding scent from the young of game animals, the races would soon be extinct.

It is sad to reflect that there is another enemy against which nature has made no provision, and from whose ravages there is no escape, and that in a very few years all the larger animals of the plains must inevitably be extinct.

This enemy is man. There are no game laws. There can be none—at least none that can be executed. An army of officials could not now protect the game. Within the last few years hundreds of men, too lazy or shiftless to make a living in civilisation, have found a congenial mode of life on the plains.

A tent or hut far in the wilderness is the home of two or three of these men, who have solved the problems how

little a man can do with and be healthy, how little he
may have and be contented. These are professional
hunters.

In season or out of season they kill everything that
comes in their way. If the animal is unfit for food its
skin may bring a dime or two. Once in two or three
months they will go to the nearest railroad town, sell off
the peltries they have accumulated, buy a little flour and
bacon, a bag of salt, and a few beans. The balance of
the money is either lost at a faro bank or spent in a
roaring spree, after which they return to the wilderness.
These men think only of to-day. The game have no
respite or opportunity for recuperation, and must soon
disappear.

Every sportsman can appreciate the feeling, even
though he may not imitate the action, of the old fisher-
man who, going out to catch cat-fish, threw back into
the water all other fish caught, even though better than
cat-fish, saying in explanation, ' When I go a-catting, I go
a-catting.' There is great gratification in feeling that one
has so educated himself to a knowledge of the habits of
game as to say with certainty, ' I shall kill such game
to-day.' This feeling is not confined to hunters of large
game. I know an Eastern sportsman who will not fire at
a quail when out after woodcock or snipe; but the most
successful plains hunters, when after bear or elk, will
fire at nothing smaller. This is really necessary to
success with these large animals, which are so timid that
even a distant sound of the rifle will at once send them
to close cover.

However satisfying to one's vanity this kind of hunting
may be, I confess that my taste for sport is rather of the
vagabond order. I like to bag these large animals; but
I like better to ride through a country where game is in
great variety, rifle and shot-gun both ready for use, bagging now a deer or an antelope, now getting into a flock
of turkeys; at one time banging into a flock of ducks, at

another beating a marsh for snipe, or quartering the grass for grouse or quail in true Eastern style. One gets less large game in this kind of hunting, but he has a vast deal more enjoyment.

The most delightful hunting of this kind I have ever had was in the country south-east of Fort Dodge, on the small tributaries of the Cimarron River. I append the record of a hunt of twenty days in this section, in October 1872, in which one officer besides myself and three English gentlemen participated. Everything bagged was counted as one, and an idea of the sport can be formed from this list:—

127	buffalo.	6	cranes.
2	deer (red).	187	quail.
11	antelope.	32	grouse.
154	turkeys.	84	field-plover.
5	geese.	33	yellow legs (snipe).
223	teal.	12	jack snipe.
45	mallard.	1	pigeon.
49	shovel-bill.	9	hawks.
57	widgeon.	3	owls.
38	butter-ducks.	2	badgers.
3	shell-ducks.	7	racoons.
17	herons.	11	rattlesnakes.
143	meadow larks, doves, robins, &c.		
1	blue bird, for his sweetheart's hat.		

Total head bagged, 1,262.

The next year nearly the same party, diminished by *one*, went over nearly the same ground with a bag of like variety, numbering 1,141.

I think that the whole world can safely be challenged to offer a greater variety of game to the sportsman.

BUFFALO ON THE PLAINS.

CHAPTER VIII.

BUFFALO.

Bos Americanos (*American Bison.*)

I SUPPOSE I ought to call this animal the ' bison ;' but, though naturalists may insist that ' bison ' is his true name, I, as a plainsman, also insist that his name is buffalo.

As buffalo he is known everywhere, not only on the plains but throughout the sporting world ; as buffalo ' he lives and moves and has his being ;' as buffalo he will die ; and when, as must soon happen, his race has vanished from earth, as buffalo he will live in tradition and story.

The general appearance of this animal is well known to all. His enormous bulk, shaggy mane, vicious eye, and sullen demeanour give him an appearance of ferocity very foreign to his true nature. Dangerous as he looks, he is in truth a very mild, inoffensive beast, timid and fearful, and rarely attacking but in the last hopeless effort of self-defence.

The domestic cattle of Texas, miscalled tame, are fifty times more dangerous to footmen than the fiercest buffalo. He is the most unwieldy, sluggish, and stupid of all plains animals. Endowed with the smallest possible amount of instinct, the little he has seems adapted rather for getting him into difficulties than out of them.

If not alarmed at sight or smell of a foe, he will stand stupidly gazing at his companions in their death throes until the whole herd is shot down. He will walk unconcernedly into a quicksand or quagmire already choked with struggling, dying victims. Having made up his mind to go a certain way it is almost impossible to divret him from his purpose. He is as timid about his flanks and rear as a new recruit. When travelling, nothing in his front stops him, but an unusual object in his rear will send him to the right-about at the top of his speed.

In May 1871 I drove in a light waggon from Old Fort Zara to Fort Larned, on the Arkansas, thirty-four miles. At least twenty-five miles of this distance was through one immense herd, composed of countless smaller herds, of buffalo then on their journey north. The road ran along the broad level ' bottom,' or valley, of the river.

Some few miles from Zara a low line of hills rise from the plain on the right, gradually increasing in height, and approaching the road and river, until they culminate in Pawnee Rock, when they again recede.

The whole country appeared one mass of buffalo, moving slowly to the northward; and it was only when actually among them that it could be ascertained that the apparently solid mass was an agglomeration of innumerable small herds, of from fifty to two hundred animals, separated from the surrounding herds by greater or less space, but still separated. The herds in the valley sullenly got out of my way, and, turning, stared stupidly at me, sometimes at only a few yards' distance. When I had reached a point where the hills were no longer more than a mile from the road, the buffalo on the hills, seeing an unusual object in their rear, turned, stared an instant, then started at full speed directly towards me, stampeding and bringing with them the numberless herds through which they passed, and pouring down upon me all the herds, no longer separated, but one immense compact mass of plunging animals, mad with fright, and as irresistible as an avalanche. The situation was by no means pleasant. Reining up my horse (which was fortunately a quiet old beast that had been in at the death of many a buffalo, so that their wildest, maddest rush only caused him to cock his ears in wonder at their unnecessary excitement), I waited until the front of the mass was within fifty yards, when a few well-directed shots from my rifle split the herd, and sent it pouring off in two streams, to my right and left. When all had passed me they stopped, apparently perfectly satisfied, though thousands were yet within reach of my rifle, and many within less than one hundred yards. Disdaining to fire again I sent my servant to cut out the tongues of the fallen. This occurred so frequently within the next ten miles, that when I arrived at Fort Larned I had twenty-six tongues in my waggon, representing the greatest number of buffalo that my conscience can reproach me for having murdered on any single day. I was not hunting, wanted no meat, and would not voluntarily have fired at these herds. I killed only in self-preservation, and fired almost every shot from the waggon.

The winter of 1871-2 was unusually severe on the Arkansas. The ponds and smaller streams to the north were all frozen solid, and the buffalo were forced to the river for water. Their retreat was to the northward. The Atchison, Topeka, and Santa Fé Railroad was then in process of construction, and nowhere could the peculiarity of the buffalo of which I am speaking be better studied than from its trains. If a herd was on the north side of the track, it would stand stupidly gazing, and without a symptom of alarm, although the locomotive passed within a hundred yards. If on the south side of the track, even though at a distance of one or two miles from it, the passage of a train set the whole herd in the wildest commotion. At full speed, and utterly regardless of the consequences, it would make for the track on its line of retreat. If the train happened not to be in its path it crossed the track and stopped satisfied. If the train was in its way, each individual buffalo went at it with the desperation of despair, plunging against or between locomotive and cars, just as its blind madness chanced to direct it. Numbers were killed, but numbers still pressed on, to stop and stare as soon as the obstacle had passed. After having trains thrown off the track twice in one week, conductors learned to have a very decided respect for the idiosyncrasies of the buffalo, and when there was a possibility of striking a herd ' on the rampage ' for the north side of the track, the train was slowed up and sometimes stopped entirely.

Late in the summer of 1867 a herd of probably 4,000 buffalo attempted to cross the South Platte, near Plum Creek. The water was rapidly subsiding, being nowhere over a foot or two in depth, and the channels in the bed were filled or filling with loose quicksands. The buffalo in front were soon hopelessly stuck. Those immediately behind, urged on by the horns and pressure of those yet farther in rear, trampled over their struggling companions, to be themselves engulfed in the devouring sand. This was continued until the bed of the river, nearly half-a-mile broad, was covered with dead or dying buffalo. Only a comparatively few actually crossed the river, and these were soon driven back by hunters. It was estimated that considerably over half the herd, or more than 2,000 buffalo, paid for this attempt with their lives.

When travelling unmolested the buffalo is extremely careful in his choice of grades by which to pass from one creek to another; so much so indeed that, though a well-defined buffalo trail may not be a good waggon road, one may rest well assured that it is the best route to be had. He seems to have a natural antipathy to the exertion of going up or down steep places. In crossing streams his instinct deserts him. He plunges in anywhere, without fear or care, and shows less sense in extricating himself from the difficulties incident to such action than any other animal, wild or tame.

His indisposition to travel over bad ground is by no means to be taken as inability to do so. When frightened he will, with perfect impunity, climb banks or plunge down precipices where it would be impossible, or certain death, to a horse to follow. I have elsewhere spoken of his liability to stampede; but, even when impelled by the madness which overpowers the stampeded animals, such is his strength and power of resistance, that he is rarely seriously injured by tumbles which would disable if not kill any other animal.

The habits of the buffalo are almost identical with those of the domestic cattle. Owing either to a more pacific disposition, or to the greater number of bulls, there is very little fighting, even at the season when it might be expected. I have been among them for days, have watched their conduct for hours at a time, and with the very best opportunities for observation, but have never seen a regular combat between bulls. They frequently strike each other with their horns, but this seems to be a mere expression of impatience at being crowded.

The small herds, of which I have spoken as comprising the great herd, have each generally more bulls than cows, seemingly all on the very best terms with each other.

The old bulls do undoubtedly leave the herd and wander off as advance or rear guards and flankers; but I am disposed to believe this to be due to a misanthropic abnegation of society on the part of these old fellows, to whom female companionship no longer possesses its charm, rather than to their being driven out by the younger bulls, as is generally believed.

The habitual separation of the large herd into numerous smaller herds seems to be an instinctive act, probably for perfect mutual protection. It has been thought, said, and written by many persons that each small herd is a sort of community, the harem and retainers of some specially powerful bull who keeps proper order and subjection among them. Nothing is farther from the truth. The association is not only purely instinctive, voluntary, free from the domination of power, of sexual appetite, or individual preferences, but is most undoubtedly entirely accidental as to its individual components.

I have, unobserved, carefully watched herds while feeding. I have seen two or more small herds merge into one, or one larger herd separate into two or more. This is done quietly, gradually, and as it were accidentally, in the act of feeding, each buffalo seeming only intent on getting his full share of the best grass. The cows and calves are always in the centre, the bulls on the outside. When two feeding herds approach each other and merge into one, the only perceptible change—and this is so gradual as scarcely to be noticeable—is that the bulls on the sides of contact work themselves out towards a new circumference, which is to enclose the whole ; and when a larger herd breaks by the same gradual process into smaller ones, the bulls instinctively place themselves on the outside of each.

When pursued the herds rush together in one compact plunging mass. As soon as the pursuit is over, and the buffalo are sufficiently recovered from their fright to begin feeding, those on the outside of the mass gradually detach themselves by breaking into small herds, until the whole large herd is in the normal condition. If each dominant bull had on such occasions to run through the whole great herd to look up his lost wives, children, and dependents, his life would not only be a very unhappy but a very busy one.

There is one very marked and curious difference between buffalo and domestic cattle. The cow seems to possess scarcely a trace of maternal instinct, and, when frightened, will abandon and run away from her calf without the slightest hesitation. The duty of protecting the calves devolves almost entirely on the bulls. I have seen evidences of this many times, but the most remarkable instance I have ever heard of was related to me by an army surgeon, who was an eye-witness.

He was one evening returning to camp after a day's hunt, when his attention was attracted by the curious action of a little knot of six or eight buffalo. Approaching sufficiently near to see clearly, he discovered that this little knot were all bulls, standing in a close circle with their heads outwards, while in a concentric circle at some twelve or fifteen paces distance sat, licking their chaps in impatient expectancy, at least a dozen large grey wolves (excepting man, the most dangerous enemy of the buffalo).

The doctor determined to watch the performances. After a few moments the knot broke up, and, still keeping in a compact mass, started on a trot for the main herd, some half a mile off. To his very great astonishment, the doctor now saw that the central and controlling figure of this mass was a poor little calf so newly born as scarcely to be able to walk. After going fifty or a hundred paces the calf laid down, the bulls disposed themselves in a circle as before, and the wolves, who had trotted along on each side of their retreating supper, sat down and licked their chaps again; and though the doctor did not see the finale, it being late and the camp distant, he had no doubt but that the noble fathers did their whole duty by their offspring, and carried it safely to the herd.

When the calves are young they are kept always in the centre of each small herd, while the bulls dispose themselves on the outside. When feeding, the herd is more or less scattered; but on the approach of danger it closes and rounds into a tolerably compact circular mass.

Although there is not a particle of danger in approaching such a herd, it requires in a novice an extraordinary amount of nerve. When he gets within 300 yards, the bulls on that side, with heads erect, tails cocked in air, nostrils expanded, and eyes that seem to flash fire, even at that distance, walk uneasily to and fro, menacing the intruder by pawing the earth and tossings of their huge heads.

The enemy still approaching, some bull will face him, lower his head, and start on a most furious charge. But alas for brute courage! When he has gone twenty or thirty yards Mr. Bull thinks better of it, stops, stares an instant, and then trots back to the herd. Another and another will try the same game, with the same result; and if, in spite of these ferocious demonstrations, the hunter still approaches, the whole herd will incontinently take to its heels.

This bullying proclivity, combined with his natural indisposition to get out of the way, has been the cause of the death of thousands at the hands of men to whom buffalo killing was no novelty, who needed no meat, and who would not have gone fifty yards out of their way to kill, but in whom opportunity so roused that spirit of murder which is inherent in every sportsman's breast, that the temptation was too strong to be resisted.

I should be doing injustice to this animal, and be wide of the facts, did I assert that there is no difficulty or excitement in its pursuit. What I have said refers to buffalo hunting on foot, the natural and approved method of approaching almost all game which is to be taken with firearms.

Buffalo hunting on horseback is a very different thing, and, to a novice, full of excitement. A buffalo can run only about two-thirds as fast as a good horse; but what he lacks in speed he makes up in bottom or endurance, in tenacity of purpose, and in most extraordinary vitality.

A herd will stand staring at an approaching horseman until he is within about 300 yards. It will then begin to move off slowly, and, when he is within about

250 yards, it will probably break into a gallop. This is the sportsman's moment. A good horse ridden by a man who knows his business will be among them before they have gone 200 yards, to shoot and slaughter at his pleasure. A poor horse, or careful rider, and the hunter will find to his sorrow that ' a stern chase is a long chase.' If a herd is not overtaken in 500 or 600 yards the chase had better be abandoned, if any regard is to be had for the horse. The difficulty in this hunting is that the herd is enveloped in a cloud of dust, which prevents very careful aim ; the explosion of the pistol creates a turmoil, confusion, and change of places among the flying animals, rendering it almost impossible to shoot at any individual buffalo more than once ; and their vitality is so great, that it is an exceedingly rare exception when one is brought down by a single shot.

The danger is not so much from the buffalo, which rarely makes an effort to injure his pursuer, as from the fact that neither man nor horse can see the ground, which may be rough and broken or perforated with prairie dog or gopher holes. This danger is so imminent that a man who runs into a herd of buffalo may be said to take his life in his hand.

I have never known a man hurt by a buffalo in such a chase. I have known of at least six killed, and a very great many more or less injured, some very severely, by their horses falling with them.

The knowledge of the danger, the rush of the horse, the thundering tread of the flying brutes, the turmoil, the dust, the uncertainty, and, above all, the near proximity and ferocious aspect of the lumbering throng, furnish excitement enough to set wild the man who is new to it. There is, however, a sameness about it which soon palls, and an old buffalo hunter rarely runs buffalo. It is very good for an occasional ' flyer,' but frequent repetition is like eating quail on toast every day for a month—monotonous. However ardent the sportsman, however ardent

for this especial sport while new to it, two or three seasons
will dull the edge of the keenest appetite.

The running is very different under different circumstances. A single buffalo offers very little sport even to
an enthusiastic novice. He is generally an old fellow
whom solitary life has rendered self-reliant. He has little
disposition to run from any enemy ; and, when he does
start, he runs so slowly and wastes so much time in
'gibing and filling' to watch his pursuer, that he is
generally a prey so easy that, after the killing. the murderer's conscience smites him, and his self-respect is gone.

'I'd as lief shoot an ox,' has often been the report, in
a lachrymose, self-abashed tone, of a beginner whom I
had sent off in a fury of excitement after a solitary old
bull.

The pursuit of a small herd of bulls is equally unsatisfactory. A race after a small herd of twenty or thirty
cows and six months' calves gives to the hunter a much
more ample compensation for his time and trouble. When
from three to six months old, the calves run like the wind ;
and to dash into such a herd, single out a calf, pursue
and bring it to bay, is a feat worthy of record for the
novice. This selection of the animal is the beauty and
perfection of buffalo hunting. On account of the confusion of numbers and the dust, it can scarcely be done
in a large herd, except by first splitting it up into small
herds.

This is much more easy than would appear. When
a hunter rushes into a large herd, the buffalo on each
side of his horse push from him laterally. As he gets
farther into it the buffalo passed do not close in his
rear, but being now able to see him more clearly, press
farther and farther away. The consequence is that the
hunter finds himself riding in a V, the point of which is
only a little in advance of his horse's head. By going
completely through the herd it is not only split, but the
leading buffalo on each side, now clearly seeing the

CHARGE OF A BUFFALO BULL.

position of the foe, immediately diverge from him, and consequently from each other.

The herd is now two herds, which run off in different directions. Pursuing one of these it is split again and again, until the hunter is enabled to select his animal from the diminished numbers.

All this requires an excellent horse, a cool and skilful rider, and, what is difficult to find on the plains, good ground and plenty of it. Among steep ravines or very broken ground the buffalo can travel better than the best horse.

Once when on a hunt I came upon two Mexican buffalo hunters, one of whom possessed the finest and most perfectly trained buffalo horse I have ever seen. They were encamped near a water hole to which the buffalo came to drink. On the approach of a herd the horses were saddled, the fine horse and rider dashed into it, split it up as I have described, singled out a victim, always a fat two-year-old, separated it entirely from its companions, and headed it towards his camp, all at tremendous speed. They were soon met by the other hunter, and the two, placing themselves on the flanks of the now tired animal, drove it to their camp, when a pistol shot finished the race. They had a fine lot of meat and a goodly pile of skins, and they said that every buffalo had been driven into camp and killed as the one I saw. 'It saves a heap of trouble, packing the meat to camp,' said one of them, naively.

Forty years ago the buffalo ranged from the plains of Texas to beyond the British line; from the Missouri and Upper Mississippi to the eastern slopes of the Rocky Mountains. Every portion of this immense area was either the permanent home of great numbers of buffalo, or might be expected to have each year one or more visits from migratory thousands.

Hunters' tradition says that the first great break in his regular irregularity occurred about the winter of

1844-5, in that portion of country now known as Laramie Plains. That whole section was visited by a most extraordinary snow-storm. Contrary to all precedent, there was no wind, and the snow covered the surface evenly to the depth of nearly four feet. Immediately after the storm a bright sun softened the surface, which at night froze into a crust so firm that it was weeks before any heavy animal could make headway through it.

The Laramie Plains, being entirely surrounded by mountains, had always been a favourite wintering place for buffalo. Thousands were caught in this storm and perished miserably. Since that time not a single buffalo has ever visited the Laramie Plains.

When I first crossed these plains in 1848, the whole country was dotted with skulls of buffalo, and all apparently of the same age, giving some foundation for the tradition. Indeed, it was in answer to my request for explanation of the numbers, appearance, and identity of age of these skulls, that the tradition was related to me by an old hunter, who, however, could not himself vouch for the facts.

The next great break occurred at a comparatively recent date. The great composite tribe of Sioux, driven by encroaching civilisation from their homes in Iowa, Wisconsin, and Minnesota, had crossed the Missouri and thrust themselves between the Pawnees on the east and south, and the Crows on the north and west.

A long-continued war between these tribes taught at least mutual respect ; and an immense area, embracing the Black Hills and the vast plains watered by the Niobara and White Rivers, became a debateable ground into which none but war parties ever penetrated. Hunted more or less by the surrounding tribes, immense numbers of buffalo took refuge in this debateable ground, where they were comparatively unmolested, remaining there summer and winter in security. When the Pawnees were finally overthrown and forced on to a reservation, the Sioux poured into this country, just suited to their tastes, and finding buffalo very plentiful, and a ready sale for their robes, made such a furious onslaught on the poor beasts, that in a few years scarcely a buffalo could be found in all the wide area south of the Cheyenne and north and east of the North Platte.

This area, in which the buffalo had thus become practically extinct, joined on the south-west the Laramie Plains country, and there resulted a broad east and west belt from the Missouri to the mountains which contained no buffalo.

In 1870 the original great buffalo range had become permanently divided into two ranges. The Southern buffalo ranged from Northern Texas to about lat. 41° 30′. The Northern ranged from about lat. 43°, through what is known as the Powder River country, into the British possessions. Of the numbers and position of the Northern buffalo but little is known.

We will see what has come to the Southern.

Their range was as described above, but their most prized feeding ground was the section of country between the South Platte and Arkansas Rivers, watered by the Republican, Smoky, Walmit, Pawnee, and other parallel or tributary streams, and generally known as the Republican country. Hundreds of thousands went south from here each winter, but hundreds of thousands remained. It was the chosen home of the buffalo.

In 1872 some enemy of the buffalo race discovered that their hides were merchantable, and could be sold in the market for a goodly sum. The Union Pacific, Kansas Pacific, and Atchison Topeka and Santa Fé Railroads soon swarmed with ' hard cases ' from the East, each excited with the prospect of having a buffalo hunt that would pay. By waggon, on horseback, and a-foot, the pot-hunters poured in, and soon the unfortunate buffalo was without a moment's peace or rest. Though hundreds of thousands of skins were sent to market, they scarcely indicated the slaughter that, from want of skill in shooting, and want of knowledge in preserving the hides of those slain, on the part of these green hunters, one hide sent to market represented three, four, or even five dead buffalo.

The merchants of the small towns along the railroads were not slow to take advantage of this new opening. They furnished outfits, arms, ammunition, &c., to needy parties, and established great trades, by which many now ride in their carriages.

The buffalo melted away like snow before a summer's sun. Congress talked of interfering, but only talked. Winter and summer, in season and out of season, the slaughter went on.

The fall of 1873 saw an immense accession of hunters; but by this time the local merchants, recognising its importance, had got the trade pretty well into their own hands. Most of the hunting parties were sent out by them, and were organised for even a greater destruction of buffalo, and with more care for the proper preservation of the hides and meat. Central depôts were established in localities where buffalo were plentiful. Parties were sent out from these which every few days brought back their spoil. Houses were built for smoking and corning the meat, and, though the waste was still incalculable, the results would be incredible but that the figures are taken from official statistics.

In 1871–2 there was apparently no limit to the numbers of buffalo.

In 1872 I was stationed at Fort Dodge, on the Arkansas, and was not on many hunting excursions. Except that one or two would be shot, as occasion required, for beef, no attention whatever was paid to buffalo, though our march led through countless throngs, unless there were strangers with us. In the fall of that year three English gentlemen went out with me for a short hunt, and in their excitement bagged more buffalo than would have supplied a brigade. From within a few miles of the post our pleasure was actually marred by their numbers, as they interfered with our pursuit of other game.

In the fall of 1873 I went with some of the same gentlemen over the same ground.

Where there were myriads of buffalo the year before, there were now myriads of carcasses. The air was foul with sickening stench, and the vast plain, which only a short twelvemonth before teemed with animal life, was a dead, solitary, putrid desert. We were obliged to travel south-east to the Cimarron, a distance of nearly ninety miles, before we found a respectable herd. Even there we found the inevitable hunter, the southern line of the State of Kansas being picketed by them. They were wary of going into Indian territory, where they might be arrested; but an unfortunate herd no sooner crossed the line going north than it was destroyed. The butchery still goes on. Comparatively few buffalo are now killed, for there are comparatively few to kill. In October 1874 I was on a short trip to the buffalo region south of Sidney Barracks. A few buffalo were encountered, but there seemed to be more hunters than buffalo. The country south of the South Platte is without water for many miles, and the buffalo must satisfy their thirst at the river. Every approach of the herd to water was met by rifle bullets, and one or more buffalo bit the dust. Care was taken not to permit the others to drink, for then they would not return. Tortured with thirst the poor brutes approach again, always to be met by bullets, always to lose some of their number.

But for the favouring protection of night, the race would before now have been exterminated. In places favourable to such action as the south bank of the Platte, a herd of buffalo has, by shooting at it by day, and by lighting fires and firing guns at night, been kept from water for four days, or until it has been entirely destroyed. In many places the valley was offensive from the stench of putrefying carcasses.

At the present time the Southern buffalo can hardly be said to have a range; the term expresses a voluntary act, while the unfortunate animals have no volition left. They are driven from one water hole to meet death at another. No sooner do they stop to feed than the sharp crack of a rifle warns them to change position. Every drink of water, every mouthful of grass, is at the expense of life ; and the miserable animals, continually harassed, are driven into localities far from their natural haunts, any-where to avoid the unceasing pursuit.

A few, probably some thousands, still linger about their beloved pastures of the Republican ; a few still hide in the deep cañons of the Cimarron country ; but the mass of Southern buffalo now living are to be found far away from the dreaded hunter, on a belt of country extending south-west across the upper tributaries of the Canadian, across the northern end of the Llano Estacado, or Staked Plain, to the Pecos River.

The difficulty of getting the hides to market from these remote and Indian-infested regions is some guarantee that the buffalo will not be extinct for a few years.

In the beginning of the hide business, the hunting parties organised themselves on any haphazard basis. Every man wanted to shoot ; no man wanted to do the other work. Buffalo were slaughtered without sense or discretion, and oftentimes left to rot with the hides on. This did not pay, and these self-organised parties soon broke up. When the merchants got the business into their hands they organised parties for work. The most approved party consisted of four men—one shooter, two skinners, and one man to cook, stretch hides, and take care of camp. Where buffalo were very plentiful, the number of skinners was increased. A light waggon, drawn by two horses or mules, takes the outfit into the wilderness, and brings into camp the skins taken each day. The outfit is most meagre : a sack of flour, a side of bacon, five pounds of coffee, ten of sugar, a little salt, and possibly a few beans, is a month's supply. A common, or 'A,' tent furnishes shelter ; a couple of blankets for each man is bed. One or more of Sharp's or Remington's heaviest sporting rifles, and an unlimited supply of ammunition, is the armament ; while a coffee-pot, Dutch oven, frying-pan, four tin plates, and four tin cups, constitute the kitchen and table furniture.

The skinning knives do duty at the platter, and 'fingers were made before forks.' Nor must be forgotten one or more ten-gallon kegs for water, as the camp may of necessity be far away from a stream. The supplies are generally furnished by the merchant for whom the party is working, who, in addition, pays each of the party a specified percentage of the value of the skins delivered. The shooter is carefully selected for his skill and knowledge of the habits of the buffalo. He is captain and leader of the party. When all is ready he plunges into the wilderness, going to the centre of the best buffalo region known to him, not already occupied (for there are unwritten regulations recognised as laws, giving to each hunter certain rights of discovery and occupancy). Arrived at the position he makes his camp in some hidden ravine or thicket, and makes all ready for work.

Early next morning, rifle in hand, and belt well supplied with ammunition, he sallies forth. His object is not only to kill, but to avoid frightening the living. Keeping the wind, peeping over hills, creeping along ravines, now bagging a solitary victim, now screened by a bank, putting bullets into three or four before they can get away. Occasionally he may find a herd in an exceptionally favourable position. Crawling like a snake along the bottom of a ravine, he may approach unsuspected to within thirty or forty feet of the nearest.

Hiding his every movement, the heavy rifle is brought to bear, and a bullet sent into the heart of the nearest buffalo. The animal makes a plunge forward, walks a few steps, and stops with the blood streaming from his nostrils. The other buffalo, startled at the report, rush together, but, neither seeing nor smelling danger, stare in uneasy wonder. Attracted by the blood they collect about the wounded buffalo. Another bullet is now sent in; another buffalo plunges, stops, and bleeds. The others will stare, and, seeming to think the wounded animals responsible for the unusual noise, concentrate their attention on them. Again and again the rifle cracks. Buffalo after buffalo bleeds, totters, and falls. The survivors stare in imbecile amazement.

The game is so near, and the shooter so well understands his business, that but one shot is necessary for each life. The wounded animal may walk off some distance, but is sure to come down.

When the shooter has killed or mortally wounded as many as his party can skin, he crawls off as cautiously as he approached, and returns, well satisfied, to camp.

This is called in hunters' language 'getting a stand;' and the number killed by the hunter, under such circumstances, is only limited by the number of animals in the herd, or the capacity of the hunting party to skin.

I have myself counted 112 carcasses inside of a semicircle of 200 yards radius, all of which were killed by one man from the same spot, and in less than three-quarters of an hour.

Sometimes the buffalo will stand even when they see their enemy. Two such instances have occurred to me. Once returning down the Arkansas River from an exploring expedition, I had arrived within a day's journey of my post, and wished to take in a quantity of meat. A herd of some seventy-five finding itself on the wrong, or river, side of me, dashed past at full speed. I fired. The herd disappeared on to a table land to my left. I

followed, and, on reaching the top of the hill, found it
standing around a cow dying on the ground. As I
approached all stared at me, but did not offer to run.
I sat down on the ground in plain view, within fifty
yards of the nearest, and deliberately shot down every
calf in the herd—twelve—and killed another cow, a
bullet passing through a calf into her. By this time
my waggons were up. Going to the edge of the bank
I called up the men, and when we went to butcher our
game we were obliged to drive the uninjured buffalo
away by waving our hats, shouting, and throwing stones.
The other 'stand' was very similar, but, needing less
meat, I killed but four or five calves.

The skinners with the waggon follow the shooter at
a distance, taking care to keep out of sight of the
buffalo.

The skins of the victims are whipped off with marvellous dexterity and rapidity, and the tongues cut out.

If preparations have been made for smoking, corning,
or otherwise saving meat, the hind quarters are cut off,
and loaded with the skin and tongue upon the waggon.
The loin, the ribs, the hump, all the best and most
savoury parts of the animal, are left to rot, or are eaten
by wolves. In the very large majority of cases the
whole carcass is left to rot where it fell.

In the height of the furor of slaughter (1872-3),
when buffalo were so plentiful that skinning was the
only work, the ordinary process was found to be much
too slow for the 'great American buffalo-skinner,' so he
devised a plan of his own. An incision was made
across the back of the head, just in front of the ears
and around the throat. This thick skin, ears included,
was started by skinning down some six or eight inches.
Connecting incisions were made from the throat down
the belly, and from this down each leg to the knee as is
usual. A stout rope was fastened about the thick skin
on the back of the head, the ears preventing its slipping

off when pulled. A strong iron spike about three feet long was then driven through the head of the buffalo into the ground, pinning it fast. The waggon was then brought up, and the other end of the rope made fast to the hind axle. The horses were whipped up, and the skin torn from the carcass at one pull. I have seen a skin taken off in this way in, I think, less than five minutes (though I did not time it by the watch). Sometimes the skin was badly torn, and always, more or less, flesh adhered to it, giving additional work to the stretcher. When, therefore, the careful preparation of each skin began to be of greater importance than time, this process was abandoned, and the skinner returned to his usual greasy, filthy, and legitimate work.

When the skins are brought to camp the work of the stretcher begins. This is of no little importance, for, if not done properly, the value of the skin is diminished, if not destroyed. A smooth piece of ground, exposed all day to the rays of the sun, is selected. Small slits are cut in the edges of the skin all around its whole circumference at intervals of about a foot. The skin, flesh side up, is stretched as tightly as possible, and pinned fast by wooden pegs driven through the slits into the ground. Every particle of flesh or fatty matter is then carefully removed from the exposed surface, which is left to dry and harden in the sun. Should a rainfall occur during this process the skin is lost, as, in drying, it contracts so as to draw the pegs or tear loose from them, shrivels up, and is worthless as a merchantable article. In from two to five days, according to the season and heat of the sun, the skin is cured and stacked with others ready for transportation to market.

At the present time such is the care bestowed on killing, skinning, and curing, that with the most successful parties 100 skins delivered in market represent only about 125 dead buffalo.

It was my desire and intention to have furnished com-

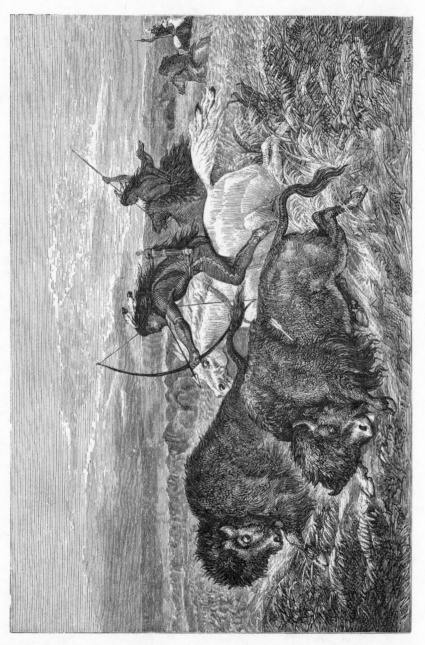

INDIANS HUNTING BUFFALO.

plete and authentic official statistics of the number of
hides of buffalo transported over the different railroad
routes, and thus obtain a pretty accurate knowledge of the
numbers actually killed. To that end, I made application,
either direct or through friends, to the officers of the
various railroads which bring this product to market.

To my very great surprise I soon found I was tread-
ing on most delicate ground ; the authorities of but one
prominent road giving me the information desired.

The refusals, couched in most polite language, were
grounded on the alleged impossibility of giving the information without going over all the loose bills of lading of
those years, involving time and a large amount of clerical
labour.

It is impossible to conceive that two great railroads
like the Union Pacific and Kansas Pacific, with an enormous carrying trade, should do their business without
books, and that the officers are really unable to give,
without such labour, the amount of any kind of freight
carried in any specified time. I am, therefore, constrained
to believe that the refusal is prompted by fears that
publicity in this matter might result in some legislation
which would interfere with profits.

Such fears are without foundation. The buffalo are
virtually exterminated. No legislation, however stringent
or active, could now do anything either for or against
the trade in the ' buffalo product.'

Most fortunately this general reticence found exceptions. The Atchison, Topeka, and Santa Fé Railroad gave
me a prompt, full, and clear statement, from which, and
from personal knowledge of the business of other roads,
I am enabled to make a very satisfactory estimate of the
numbers of buffalo slaughtered for their hides since the
winter of 1871-2.

The three great railroads mentioned—the Union
Pacific, Kansas Pacific, and Atchison, Topeka, and Santa
Fé—have done most of the carrying trade, and have

divided the lion's share very equally between them. The
last-mentioned road penetrates the very heart of the
great Southern buffalo range.

The Union Pacific has done less; but it and the
smaller roads which touch the buffalo region, taken together, have carried about as much as either of the two
principal buffalo roads.

Careful inquiry convinces me that the Atchison,
Topeka, and Santa Fé Railroad has carried about one-
third of the entire buffalo product (exclusive of robes).
On this I found my estimate.

BUFFALO PRODUCT.

Year	Atchison, Topeka, and Santa Fé	Union Pacific, Kansas Pacific, and all other Railroads	Total
	Hides—No.	Hides—No.	
1872	165,721	331,442	497,163
1873	251,443	502,886	754,329
1874	42,289	84,578	126,867
	459,453	918,906	1,378,359
	Meat—lbs.	Meat—lbs.	
1872	None	None	
1873	1,617,600	8,235,200	4,852,800
1874	632,800	1,265,600	1,898,400
	2,250,400	4,500,800	6,751,200
	Bones—lbs.	Bones—lbs.	
1872	1,135,300	2,270,600	3,405,900
1873	2,743,100	5,486,200	8,229,300
1874	6,914,950	13,829,900	20,744,850
	10,793,350	21,586,700	32,380,050

In the transportation of Indian tanned hides or robes,
the Atchison, Topeka, and Santa Fé Railroad has but one
rival, and that not a dangerous one, in this trade.

It is even more difficult to get at the statistics in this
trade than of the other, much of it being clandestine.

Persons who, by trading illegally with the Indians, have accumulated many robes, are too careful to be caught in so gross an error as shipping their goods as freight on railroads.

They evade publicity by hiring freight cars and loading them themselves. The railroad is not solicitous, except as to the number of pounds carried.

The exact amount of the robe trade is known to but one or two firms in the United States, and they are extremely careful that outsiders shall not have the details.

The Atchison, Topeka, and Santa Fé Railroad carries a freight of about 19,000 robes each year. The Union Pacific about 10,000. Probably an average of about 5,000 are put upon the market clandestinely. An average of about 55,000 comes down the Missouri from the Northern Indians. The robe 'crop' is therefore in the neighbourhood of 90,000 yearly.

I have already spoken of the immense waste of hides incident to the first great rush of green hunters into the masses of buffalo. My own estimates are confirmed by well-informed persons 'in the trade,' who were in the heart of the buffalo region at that time. The mass of these hunters were such poor shots that they wounded two or three buffalo for every one bagged, and most of which subsequently died or were killed by wolves. The skinners and curers knew so little of the proper mode of curing hides, that at least half were lost of those actually taken. In the summer and fall of 1872 one hide sent to market represented at least *three* dead buffalo. This condition of affairs rapidly improved; but such was the furor for slaughter and the ignorance of all concerned, that every hide sent to market in 1872 represented no less than five dead buffalo.

Early in 1873 the organisation of hunting parties had been properly effected.

The 'hunter' had learnt his work, and dead buffalo

were now so plentiful that skinning became arduous labour. Little care was taken ; the skins, jerked off in any way, were frequently torn. The curer left flesh on, or failed to stretch them properly, and they spoiled. In the crop of 1873 one hide delivered represents two dead buffalo.

As the game became scarce, more attention was paid to all details ; and in 1874, and up to this time, so much care is taken by the best hunting parties, that 100 skins delivered in market during that and the last year represent 125 dead buffalo. No parties have ever got the proportion lower than this, and it is therefore not a fair average. To avoid overestimating, I have in every case taken the lowest figures :—

Years	Hides delivered	Dead buffalo
1872	497,163	1,491,489
1873	754,329	1,508,658
1874	126,867	158,583
	1,378,359	3,158,730

It is much more difficult to estimate the number of dead buffalo represented by the Indian tanned skins, or robes, sent to market. This number varies with the different tribes, and their greater or less contact with the whites.

Thus the Cheyennes, Arrapahoes, and Kiowas of the Southern plains, having less contact with whites, use skins for their lodges, clothing, bedding, par-fléches, saddles, lariats, for almost everything. The number of robes sent to market represents only what we may call the foreign exchange of these tribes, and is really not more than one-tenth of the skins taken. To be well within bounds I will assume that one robe sent to market by these Indians represents only six dead buffalo.

Those bands of Sioux who live at the Agencies, and whose peltries are taken to market by the Union Pacific

SLAUGHTER OF BUFFALO ON THE KANSAS PACIFIC RAILROAD.

Railroad, live in lodges of cotton cloth furnished by the Indian Bureau. They use much civilised clothing, bedding, boxes, ropes, &c. For these luxuries they pay in robes ; and as the buffalo range is far from wide, and their yearly ' crop ' small, more than half of it goes to market.

The wilder Indians of the Upper Missouri yet use many skins, though their contact with whites has given them a taste for civilised luxuries for which robes must be paid.

I have no personal knowledge of the proportion, but am informed, by persons who profess to know, that about one robe is sent to market for every five skins.

The yearly crop of robes already estimated represents their dead buffalo as follows :—

	Sent to market	Represent dead buffalo
Kiowas, Comanches, Cheyennes, Arrapahoes, Indians whose crop goes over A. T. and S Fé R. . .	19,000	114,000
Sioux at Agencies Union Pacific Railroad . .	10,000	16,000
Indians of Upper Missouri	55,000	275,000
		405,000
In three years, 1872-73-74		1,215,000
Add total killed by whites in those years . . .		3,158,730
Total . .		4,373.730

Making the enormous, almost incredible, number of nearly four and a half millions of buffalo killed in the short space of three years. Nor is this all. No account has been taken of the immense number of buffalo killed by hunters, who came into the range from the wide frontier, and took their skins out by waggons ; of the immense numbers killed every year by hunters from New Mexico, Colorado, Texas, and the Indian territory ; of the numbers killed by the Uetes, Bannocks, and other mountain tribes, who make every year their fall hunt on the plains.

Nothing has been said of the numbers sent from the Indian territory, by other railroads than the Atchison,

Topeka, and Santa Fé, to St. Louis, Memphis, and elsewhere; of the immense numbers of robes which go to
California, Montana, Idaho, and the Great West; nor of
the still greater numbers taken each year from the territory of the United States by the Hudson Bay Company.

All these will add another million to the already
almost incredible mortuary list of the nearly extinct
buffalo.

MOUNTAIN OR WOOD BUFFALO.

In various portions of the Rocky Mountains, especially
in the region of the parks, is found an animal which old
mountaineers call the ' bison.' This animal bears about
the same relation to the plains buffalo as a sturdy mountain pony does to a well-built American horse. His body
is lighter, whilst his legs are shorter, but much thicker
and stronger, than the plains animal, thus enabling him to
perform feats of climbing and tumbling almost incredible
in such a huge and apparently unwieldy beast.

These animals are by no means plentiful, and are
moreover excessively shy, inhabiting the deepest, darkest
defiles, or the craggy, almost precipitous, sides of mountains, inaccessible to any but the most practised mountaineers.

From the tops of the mountains which rim the parks,
the rains of ages have cut deep gorges, which plunge
with brusque abruptness, but nevertheless with great
regularity, hundreds or even thousands of feet to the
valley below. Down the bottom of each such gorge
gurgles a clear, cold stream of the purest water, fertilising
a narrow belt of a few feet of alluvial, and giving birth
and growth to a dense jungle of spruce, quaking asp, and
other mountain trees. One side of the gorge is generally
a thick forest of pine, while the other side is a meadow-
like park covered with splendid grass. Such gorges are
the favourite haunt of the mountain buffalo. Early in the

morning he enjoys a bountiful breakfast of the rich nutritious grasses, quenches his thirst with the finest water, and retiring just within the line of jungle, where, himself unseen, he can scan the open, he couches himself in the long grass and reposes in comfort and security until appetite calls him to his dinner late in the evening. Unlike their plains relatives, there is no stupid staring at an intruder. At the first symptom of danger they disappear like magic in the thicket, and never stop until far removed from even the apprehension of pursuit. I have many times come upon their fresh tracks, upon the beds from which they had first sprung in alarm, but I have never even seen one.

I have wasted much time and a great deal of wind in vain endeavours to add one of these animals to my bag. My figure is no longer adapted to mountain climbing, and the possession of a bison's head of my own killing is one of my blighted hopes.

Several of my friends have been more fortunate, but I know of no sportsman who has bagged more than one.[1]

Old mountaineers and trappers have given me wonderful accounts of the numbers of these animals in all the mountain region 'many years ago;' and I have been informed by them that their present rarity is due to the great snow-storm of 1844-5, of which I have already spoken as destroying the plains buffalo in the Laramie country.

I ought to say here, however, that experience has taught me that the stories of these worthies must be taken with many grains of allowance. As a rule they regard every man who does not lead their life, who is not as unkempt, greasy, and filthy as themselves, as a 'greenhorn' whom it is their privilege and their duty to 'stuff'

[1] The author is in error here, as, in a point on the Tarryall range of mountains, between Pike's Peak and the South Park, in the autumn of 1871, two mountain buffalo were killed in one afternoon. The skin of the finer was presented to Dr. Frank Buckland.—W.B.

with as many impossible stories as they can. One may find out from them a good many valuable facts, by listening, apparently uninterested, to their talk with each other; but show any interest or ask a direct question, and a hundred to one that the answer is the hugest lie that the spokesman can invent for the occasion. Under the most favourable circumstances at least half of what these old fellows tell is downright fabrication, and as it and any thread of truth that there may be are told with the same grave face and apparent sincerity, one can never tell which half to believe.

One of my friends, a most ardent and pertinacious sportsman, determined on the possession of a bison's head, and, hiring a guide, plunged into the mountain wilds which separated the middle from the South Park. After several days, fresh tracks were discovered. Turning their horses loose on a little gorge-park, such as described, they started on foot on the trail; for all that day they toiled and scrambled, with the utmost caution, now up, now down, through deep and narrow gorges and pine thickets, over bare and rocky crags; sleeping where night overtook them. Betimes next morning they pushed on the trail, and about 11 o'clock, when both were exhausted and well-nigh disheartened, their route was intercepted by a precipice. Looking over they descried, on a projecting ledge, several hundred feet below, a herd of about twenty bison, lying down. The ledge was about 300 feet at widest, by probably 1,000 feet long. Its inner boundary was the wall of rock on the top of which they stood ; its outer appeared to be a sheer precipice of at least 200 feet. This ledge was connected with the slope of the mountain by a narrow neck. The wind being right, the hunters succeeded in reaching this neck unobserved. My friend selected a magnificent head, that of a fine bull, young but full grown, and both fired. At the report the bisons all ran to the far end of the ledge and plunged over.

Terribly disappointed, the hunters ran to the spot and found that they had gone down a declivity, not actually a precipice, but so steep that the hunters could not follow them.

At the foot lay a bison. A long, a fatiguing detour brought them to the spot, and in the animal lying dead before him my friend recognised his bull—his first and last mountain buffalo. None but a true sportsman can appreciate his feelings.

The remainder of the herd were never seen after the grand plunge, down which it is doubtful if even a dog could have followed unharmed.

CHAPTER IX.

WILD CATTLE.

I SHOULD be doing injustice to a cousin-german of the buffalo, did I fail to mention as game the wild cattle of Texas. It is the domestic animal run wild, changed in some of his habits and characteristics by many generations of freedom and self-care. I have already spoken of the ferocious disposition of some of the so-called tame cattle of Texas. A footman is never safe when a herd is in his vicinity; and every sportsman who has hunted quail in Texas will have experienced the uneasiness natural to any man around whom a crowd of long-horned beasts are pawing the earth and tossing their heads in anger at his appearance.

I admit some very decided frights, and on more than one occasion have felt exceedingly relieved when an aggressive young bull has gone off bellowing and shaking his head, his face and eyes full of No. 8 shot, and taking the herd with him. I speak, I am sorry to say, of an experience now more than twenty years old. Texas was a new country then, and certainly an aggressive country. Every bush had its thorn; every animal, reptile, or insect had its horn, tooth, or sting; every male human his revolver; and each was ready to use his weapon of defence on any unfortunate sojourner, on the smallest, or even without the smallest, provocation.

I doubt if time has ameliorated the qualities of the bush, the reptile, or the insect.

The cattle which are brought north seem to be somewhat gentled, either by the 'softening influence of a higher civilisation,' or by hard driving; and, judging from newspaper items, the real or homicidal Texan, who killed his man every few days just to keep his hand in, is less plentiful now than in the 'good old times.'

The tame cow is nearly as dangerous as the bull; while in its wild state, the cow, except in defence of her calf, is as timid as a deer. The wild bull is 'on his muscle' at all times; and though he will generally get out of the way if unmolested, the slightest provocation will convert him into a most aggressive and dangerous enemy.

The wild cattle are not found in herds. A few calves and their cows may associate together for mutual protection, but the bulls are almost always found alone. Should two meet, a most desperate combat determines the mastery then and there, very frequently with the life of one of the combatants.

He who would enjoy the favours of a cow must win his way to them by a series of victories. The result of this is that the number of bulls is greatly disproportioned to the number of cows; and this disproportion is increased by the fact that it seems impossible for the bull to keep his mouth shut, and when not actually eating he is bellowing, or moaning, or making some hideous noise which indicates his whereabouts to the hunter.

Among buffalo there are more bulls than cows; among wild cattle there is probably one bull to thirty cows.

The buffalo and domestic cattle will cross,[1] successfully, however, only when the buffalo cow is the mother of the mule. The domestic cow will receive the attentions

---

[1] This has been denied. I am, however, positively assured by officers who have seen the animals that there were several specimens of the cross to be seen in 1874, on the farms on the Republican and its tributaries. I am also informed that several authentic instances are recorded in the United States Patent Office Reports.

of the buffalo bull, but invariably dies, being unable to bring forth the calf.

It is somewhat singular that two animals, sufficiently similar to cross in breed, should be so entirely dissimilar in all traits of character. The buffalo bull, as we have seen, is gregarious, inoffensive, seldom or never fighting, and truly fatherly in his care for his progeny. The wild bull, on the contrary, is sullen, morose, solitary, pugnacious, and, except on occasions, associates with neither wife nor offspring.

The buffalo cow has little or no natural instinct, runs away from her calf on any fright, and leaves its protection to the bulls.

The wild cow takes the most anxious care of her calf, and is transformed by maternal affection from one of the most timid of animals to a most daring and desperate combatant, attacking the cougar, leopard, or even her own lord and master, should they come too near its hiding place.

The buffalo loves to roam at large over the treeless plains, taking long journeys every year and having no fixed abiding place.

The wild cattle bury themselves in the closest recesses of the most dense chapparal, and rarely stray even in a lifetime beyond a few miles from their chosen haunts.

Wild cattle hunting is a sport either too exciting or not sufficiently so. There is no mean. The Mexicans ordinarily kill them by lying in wait, hidden in the thick branches of a tree at a water hole to which they resort. This is a slow, unsatisfactory, and cowardly way of taking game, but it is the only method by which these animals can be successfully and safely got at.

As I have said, the whereabouts of a bull can be readily discovered by his bellowing.

This would seem to give the hunter an easy success. Not always so, however. He is probably at that moment ensconced in the darkest recesses of a dense thicket of ' wait-a-bit' trees. This bush generally puts a prompt quietus on the most sanguine temperament. It stands ' thick as hair on a dog's back,' about twelve feet high, the straight stems from the size of a pipe-stem to two inches in diameter. Lateral branches spring out from every stem so thickly as to make a jungle almost impenetrable even of themselves; and when each is armed with innumerable thorns bent like fish-hooks, sharp as needles, and strong and tough as steel, it will readily be seen that hunting in such a thicket is no sport. His broad horns, thick hide, and immense strength enable the bull to make his way through such a thicket with ease and immunity.

Suppose that, under cover of the noise made by the bull, a hunter has overcome the natural difficulties of the approach. Moving with the greatest care he finds himself within twenty feet of the unconscious animal. He plainly sees the outline of his quarry; but when he raises his rifle he finds a thousand tough twigs and branches between him and his aim, either of which is sufficient to deflect the bullet from a vital part. Suppose, however, that an accidental opening gives him a good shot. He knows that the chances are a thousand to one against his bringing the animal down with one shot, and that the explosion of the gun will bring the bull upon him in full charge; and this in a thicket through which the bull moves easily and quickly, while he can scarcely move at all, and where there is not a tree behind which he can take cover, or in the branches of which he may find refuge. A man must be endowed with more than the ordinary disposition for getting into scrapes who would attack under such circumstances.

Sometimes a bull may be caught feeding in an opening of the chapparal. In such case, as he will not run away, he becomes an easy prey, provided the hunter has the wind, keeps perfectly quiet after his shots, and is so covered by the thicket that the bull can see neither him nor the smoke of his piece. The bull seems to have little faculty of judging the position of an enemy by sound, unless the sound is very close.

The cows are extremely difficult to bay, being excessively timid, and hiding in the densest thicket at the first symptom of danger. If caught feeding and mortally wounded, a cow will generally manage to get into the thicket and elude her pursuer. Nothing but his approach to the hiding place of her very young calf will cause the mother to stand and show fight to her arch enemy—man.

There is an old army story to the effect that, when General Taylor's little army was on the march from Corpus Christi to Matamoras, a soldier on the flank of the column came upon and fired at a bull. The bull immediately charged, and the soldier, taking to his heels, ran into the column. The bull, undaunted by the numbers of enemies, charged headlong, scattering several regiments like chaff, and finally escaped unhurt, having demoralised and put to flight an army which a few days after covered itself with glory by victoriously encountering five times its numbers of human enemies.

Twenty-five years ago a friend and classmate (long since gone to 'that bourne') was stationed at a post in Texas. He was a bright, intelligent, rollicking, roystering blade, full of kindly feeling, and honourable in all his instincts ; but so given to practical jokes, or 'fun,' as he called it, that he was cordially hated by many of his associates, and was a terror even to the friends who appreciated the worth hidden under all his curious foolishness.

This officer was visited by a cousin of his, a young gentleman of good presence and manners, who was not only a graduate of an institution of learning in the 'Mother of Presidents,' but had received his diploma as a M.D. from a medical college in Philadelphia. In spite of his education, the young gentleman, though an

ardent sportsman, was not only profoundly ignorant of
what game ought to be found in Texas, but was the
'greenest' man in all practical affairs of frontier life that
ever fell into the hands of such a joker. He was made
to believe the most improbable stories, and to attempt
the most impracticable things. One morning the host
gravely proposed an elephant hunt. 'What?' said the
doctor in the greatest excitement, 'do you have elephants out here?' 'Plenty of them,' said the host.
Preparations were at once commenced, and by 9 A.M.
a party of youngsters, ripe for the fun, were after
elephants.

The doctor was fed with all sorts of stories, given
every kind of advice, and in the course of the morning
sent into every impossible place in search of elephants,
until he was well-nigh frantic with eagerness and disap-
pointment.

When some five or six miles from the post, the
doctor was sent through a thicket of 'wait-a-bit' thorns,
of which he knew nothing. Anticipating rare sport at
his plight on his return, the host sat on his horse waiting,
when he heard a shot, and was soon after startled with
loud cries for help.

Galloping through the glades he arrived at a small
prairie opening of an acre or two in extent, around
which the doctor was frantically urging his pony, while
only a few yards behind was a huge wild bull in full
charge. All the manliness of the host was aroused by
this real and unexpected danger of his friend, and without
a moment's hesitation he dashed in and fired a pistol
shot. In an instant the bull turned upon him. His
large American horse was unequal to the emergency,
and in turning was met full in the side by the horns of
the beast. Both horse and rider were lifted for one
instant into the air, and then came down in a heap together. The horse was dead without a struggle, one horn
being completely through his body, the other caught in

the bones of the chest. One leg of the rider was between the horns of the bull, pinned fast between his head and the body of the horse. When heaped together the horse's body was on the bull's head, fastening it to the ground, and most fortunately preventing any movement; and the rider, his leg fast, was lying on the bull's back. The whole hunting party was soon assembled. They were afraid to shoot the bull, lest his struggles might further injure the man pinned to him. At last his jugular vein was opened, and he slowly bled to death. His horns were then cut off, the horse lifted off, and the now nearly dead man carried on a litter back to the post. Though no bones were broken, he paid the full penalty of his 'joke,' not only in the loss of a fine horse, but by several weeks of severe suffering. It was his last 'elephant' hunt.

I was once a party in a fight with a wild bull, which we caught by accident on a small prairie dotted with mesquite trees. Two of the party crept behind trees and fired with rifles, while two others besides myself attacked on horseback with pistols. For half an hour we had a most lively fight, the bull charging first one then the other with the greatest fury, never stopping for an instant. When finally brought down he was covered with wounds, over twenty of which must eventually have proved mortal.

CHAPTER X.

ELK.

(*Cervus Strongyloceros.*)

Of all American game the elk is justly entitled to stand first in the estimation of the sportsman.

His size, splendid form, noble presence, and magnificent antlers, excite the most hopeful enthusiasm in the breast of the sportsman, while his quickness of eye, keenness of ear, and wonderful delicacy of scent, render his successful pursuit a feat to test the skill of the hunter. The average elk will weigh about 500 pounds. I was some years since presented by a friend with a pair of antlers of a noble buck of his own killing, which he said weighed as he fell 800 pounds. I can readily believe it, since the antlers attached only to the frontal bone weighed of themselves sixty-one pounds.

The range of the elk seems originally to have been commensurate with the territory of the United States, from the Atlantic to the Pacific, from Michigan to (Florida, I was going to say, having no evidence of an elk ever having been seen in that State, I will substitute) Texas. They are now found on the plains, in greater or less numbers, from the British line on the north, to the Red River on the south, from the Missouri on the east, far beyond the plains through the Rocky Mountains to the Pacific coast.

They are not prolific, and, though cautious and difficult to approach by the novice, are easily killed by the skilled hunter. Moreover, they have many foolish traits, which oftentimes puts it in the power of a hunter to kill a great many at one time; and, as I have said in the same case in reference to buffalo, few sportsmen can resist the desire to kill when the opportunity presents itself. Besides this, the Pacific railroads having opened the eastern markets to western game, the country in their vicinity is overrun each winter by pot-hunters, who kill as many as possible for shipment.

All these cases combined rapidly diminish the number of elk. They do not long survive the settlement or occupation of a country, or the constant and murderous attacks made upon them by the pot-hunters.

One must go, at the present time, to the wild and unknown parts of the country to find elk in any great abundance.

Elk vary in their habits with the locality and season of the year. The following is descriptive of the habits of those frequenting the Laramie Plains. In May, June, and July, it is rare to find two together. The female is secluded in some close thicket or rocky fastness, preparing for, or taking care of, her calf. The buck is also in trouble. The immense antlers which he so proudly tossed last autumn dropped off in February, and he is undergoing the tedious, painful, and wearing process of growing another pair. He is weak, languid, and rather thin in flesh, for, although food is good and abundant, most of the blood he makes goes to the building-up of his magnificent horns. These start from the same base from which the old ones fell, and, at starting, are about the size or a little larger than the old base. The horn starts like an asparagus shoot, and from the commencement grows full size in diameter. The upper surface of the old base gets soft and bulbous. A thin skin covered with short downy hair stretches over this bulb, which contains apparently only thick black blood, and grows at the rate of nearly half an inch in twenty-four hours. Soon after fairly getting started, a deposit commences at the centre of what is to be the future horn, a bony substance which gradually increases in size and strength, until, when the embryo horn is a foot in length, the portion near the base is of full size, of tolerably strong compact bone, and surrounded on the outside by a network of innumerable blood vessels, more or less separated from each other by layers of bone. These layers form the corrugations and knobby protuberances which appear on or near the lower portion of the perfect antler. The growing horn is exceedingly tender, and liable to be injured in a thousand ways.

I have been told that an elk will sometimes bleed to death should a horn be knocked off at certain stages of its growth. During this time, therefore, the buck elk is exceedingly careful of himself, retires to the most solitary spot known to him, as near the snow line as convenient in order to get rid of flies, and spends all the time not necessary to obtain food and water in lying in the high grass or small bushes, which he utilises in keeping the flies off without danger of hurting his horns.

By about the 10th of August the horns have attained their full growth. The blood vessels gradually dry up, commencing at the tips of the spikes, after which the whole horn, though yet covered with ' velvet,' arrives at its perfect hardness. The ' velvet' now begins to crack, and evidently to itch in an intolerable way; for the buck spends most of his time in rubbing his horns against small trees, or weaving them, as it were, up and down in a thick bush. This, in hunters' language, is called ' shaking,' probably because the bush is shaken backwards and for-wards. During this time the buck is very easily killed. He is generally alone. The hunter from a high point surveys the slopes and higher valleys, and sees a bush being shaken violently. He has no need to be more careful than to assure himself that he has the wind right. The buck, sawing his head up and down in the bush, can see nothing, and himself makes too much noise to hear anything, and so falls an easy victim. By about the 1st of September the antlers are entirely clear of velvet, and the buck elk, fat, sleek, and proudly tossing his new-grown weapons, is the most magnificent, noble-looking animal on the continent. And now in splendid condition, and looking each 'the monarch of the glen,' the bucks come down to the valleys ready to try their fascinations on the does, who, on their part, having about completed their maternal duties, are ready to be fascinated, and come with their calves to swell the numbers of the herds, which at this season congregate together.

All are now in the very best condition, and this is the true time for the sportsman who shoots for pleasure. He will not kill so easily as when the bucks are 'shaking,' but every one he does get is in its absolute prime, and, fortunately for him, the pot-hunters are not yet out. They must wait for freezing weather or their harvest is spoiled. It is impossible for the eastern gourmand to realise how delicious elk or venison is in September. The game sent east in mid-winter is of the poorest. The bucks through the remaining season are thick-necked, poor, stringy, and tough. The does are all with young, though fatter and far better eating than the bucks.

About the 15th of September the running season commences. I have heard so many stories about duels between buck elk at this season that I suppose the fighting must be conceded, though I have met but one person who claimed to be an eye-witness to such a combat. I must say on my own part that with several years' experience among these animals I have never seen a fight, or any wound, scar, or other evidence of a fight on a buck elk, and I have seen twenty or thirty bucks in a herd, with probably twice as many does, all apparently on the very best terms with each other, though more or less ' running' was going on. Certainly there was no fighting or offering to fight, or interference in any way of one buck with another. These may have been exceptional ' community' arrangements, but my opinion is that fights are exceptional.

The buck has a deep bellow as call for the doe. In defiance or as warning of danger his note is a low whistle, very much prolonged, and capable of being heard at incredible distances. A musical friend tells me that the note is the soft natural ' E ' of the organ. It is by no means combative or warlike, and I think indicates the true character of the elk.

It is somewhat singular that while endowed by nature with splendid proportions, wonderful strength, and the most formidable weapons of offence, the elk is one of the most timid of animals. I have never seen even a wounded elk evince the slightest disposition to defend himself. In a close encounter with either man or dog he is not to be compared for a moment as a dangerous animal with either the black-tail or the common red deer. His size, strength, and horns seem to be utterly useless to him.

An exception to this general rule occurred in the experience of an army officer, who related to me the following anecdote : He was, with one soldier, crossing a section of country about half of which was covered with timber. Their attention was attracted by a loud and singular noise proceeding from a thicket on one side of their route. Approaching cautiously, they found a small park-like opening of about a couple of acres in extent, in which two immense buck elks were having a mortal combat. They did not push with their horns, as would appear natural ; but, backing from each other for about twenty feet, would, with blazing eyes, hair turned the wrong way, and heads lowered, rush together like knights in the tournay, with tremendous speed and force, meeting with a fearful crash of horns, and each emitting at the moment of contact a shrill snort of anger and defiance. Each would then back off for a new start. Many courses were thus run, without advantage on either side, when the officers, getting tired of the sameness of the affair, fired at one, when both ran off together. There were no does in the vicinity, and the 'running' season was over. It is presumable, therefore, that these 'gentlemen' elk, having some private quarrel, had retired to this sequestered spot to settle their personal difficulty in accordance with the rules of honour.

From September to the next May or June the elk are in herds of generally from five to seventy-five animals, although I have seen a herd which I verily believe contained more than 500 head. This was, however, in the days of good hunting, before the Union Pacific Railroad had rendered the haunts accessible to all the world.

When feeding unmolested the habits of the elk are almost identical with those of domestic cattle, except that they generally feed in one direction, and pass much more quickly over the ground.

Elk are very great travellers, passing over great distances. A herd found feeding in one spot in the afternoon may be twenty miles away the next morning. They travel mostly at night, and rarely spend even forty-eight hours in the same vicinity.

When travelling unmolested they always walk in single file, or one after the other, no matter how many there may be. In this way a herd strings out to a great distance, and makes a marked trail very easily followed.

When disturbed, either while feeding or travelling, they run together for an instant like a flock of sheep, and huddle up in a close clump, their long necks stretched out, and their eyes staring with a scared, helpless look. Soon an individual starts off, all the others following, not now in single file, but in a widening wedge, the leader being the point.

If the leader is knocked down by a bullet all stop and huddle again, seeming to hold a silent consultation. After a moment another leader starts, and all follow. Should the hunter get very near before disturbing the herd by a shot, this peculiarity of always having to stop, seemingly to select a leader, gives him, if a good marks-

man, the means of killing several, if not many. If, as
soon as the leader gets fairly started, he is dropped, all
stop, and by the time another is selected and starts the
hunter can have reloaded and possibly gained many
paces nearer. Another start, another knock down, and
so on. I have myself killed five from one herd in this
way, knocking down one after another two leaders, and
being much nearer to the herd when I shot the last than
when the first fell.

The gravest objection to this style of shooting is that,
in my experience, nine times out of ten the leader is a
doe. Unlike the buffalo, the buck elk rarely takes the
lead, and if he brings up the rear it is only because his
fat prevents him from running faster. His favourite
position is in the middle of the herd, surrounded by
admiring females, any one or all of whom he is as willing
to sacrifice to his own safety as was Artemus Ward to
let his wife's cousins go to the war. The larger, fatter,
and more tempting he is to the sportsman, the more
timid does he appear and the more pains does he take to
keep himself well surrounded by the herd.

To bay this 'monarch' is no easy matter, and so, by
all rules, he is the special one the sportsman most desires
to bay. It is not like murdering him when his head is
in the bush and he has nothing but his nose to depend
on. Now he has not only his own eyes, but a score of
other eyes are watching for him; not only his own ears,
but a score of feminine ears are specially sharpened for
his protection. But the eyes and ears of a whole herd
may be successfully eluded; noses never. The very
first necessity to a successful stalk is to have the wind
right. It is best to approach directly up the wind, but
this cannot always be done without exposing one's self to
the eyes and ears. Across the wind, if it be strong, is
equally good; but if it blows in flaws it is dangerous.
The elk may hear the hunter, and turn and stare in the
direction of the sound; but, if the alarm is not confirmed

by other senses, they will commence feeding again. If, however, they either see or smell him, they are off at once, travelling with such speed and to such distance that pursuit is generally useless. If, therefore, the sportsman finds that he cannot approach without exposing himself to discovery by one of these senses, he had better lie still and wait patiently until the herd has moved to such a position that he can approach with every advantage. Even when he has succeeded in approaching sufficiently near to the herd he may have to wait a long time before he gets a fair chance at the bearer of the special pair of antlers on which he has set his heart. This is very trying to the nerves, and if the sportsman does not get 'buck fever' under such circumstances he may regard himself as proof against the malady. The moment arrives at last. If the ground is fairly open and favourable for tracking wounded game, a steady sight close behind the shoulder, and three inches above the brisket, gives the most deadly wound. It is not, however, sure to drop the elk at once, for, even though shot through the heart, it may run half a mile. If, therefore, the ground is much broken, and there be ravines and thickets in which the wounded animal may conceal himself, the best shot is through the shoulder-blade, about six inches from the top of the withers. This is a risky shot, as the sportsman has nothing but his eye to guide him in the selection of the exact spot; and if the bullet is put too high, or too low, or too far forward, or too far back, the animal, though mortally wounded, may run for miles.

If, however, the sportsman is near enough and marksman enough to put his ball just right, the game is sure to drop in its tracks. In nearly all my elk hunting I have had the advantage of good dogs; and how inestimable that advantage is may be judged from the following experience :—

I had succeeded in crawling up to within forty yards of the nearest of a herd of about thirty elk. My dog,

a fine large pointer, was flat on the ground behind me.
After some waiting my chosen buck gave me a fair shot;
but, whether from 'buck fever' or from allowing too
much for his movement in walking, I put the bullet too
far forward. I had time to see this when the herd rushed
together, looking in all directions for the danger. Slipping
another cartridge into my gun, I took most careful aim
at a splendid doe that was nearest me, and fired. To my
intense disgust the doe did not fall, and the whole herd
pitched over a bank and disappeared. Reloading, I ran
to the edge of the bank, and found the herd again huddled
together, about 125 yards off. Again I fired after a most
careful aim, and at the report the whole herd went away
at a great rate towards some high bluffs about a mile off.
I now sent the dog after them and yelled frantically to
my servant to bring up my horse. Mounting in all haste,
I dashed furiously after the retreating game, which, however, reached and climbed the bluffs far ahead of me.
When, with great difficulty, I succeeded in gaining the top,
I found the herd again crowded together about 600 yards
off, and my dog just entering the compact mass. Again
they started. I had great fears for the dog, but presently
saw him bounding pertinaciously against apparently one
animal, which after some moments turned out of the herd
and came to bay. Galloping up I recognised my wounded
buck. A bullet dropped him, and, sending the dog on, I
followed at my best speed. The herd was by this time
out of sight. The dog, too, soon disappeared, and I
followed only by the dust which was kicked up by the
retreating herd. I was riding a well-built and most
powerful Canadian pony, and never before or since have
I ridden at such speed over such rough ground. True
to their instinct the elk had taken the worst ground they
could find. It was the soil of the 'bad lands,' through
which water cuts its way in ravines with perpendicular
sides. These were small, only a foot or two in depth and
from six to twelve inches wide; but the ground was thickly

scored by them, and, to make matters worse, was covered
with sage bush from one to two feet high, completely
concealing them from the view of either myself or horse.
One moment the pony's fore feet would go down, the
next his hind feet.   I rode him from his ears to his tail,
sometimes in front, sometimes in rear of the saddle.   How
I stuck on I do not know, but after a mile of such riding
(if it could be called riding) I was rewarded by seeing my
dog holding one elk at bay while another was lying down
a few yards off.   I got them both.   All three elk had
been mortally wounded, yet I should have bagged neither
had it not been for the dog.

Singular as it may appear, plains hunters are equally
divided in opinion as to the gait of the elk when at his
best speed.   Some old hunters who have bagged their
hundreds of elk, stoutly maintain that the elk only trots,
even when at his best pace; while others, equally good
authorities, insist that he runs like a deer.   The truth is
that both are somewhat right and both wrong.   The
elk trots with great speed, and this seems to be his
easiest and most natural gait.   He, however, can and
does run much faster than he can trot, but it is a
laboured effort and soon tires him out.   A hunter
on foot in August, September, and October might
well declare that an elk only trots, for at this season he is very fat, easily blown, and nothing short of
being absolutely forced to do so will induce him to break
his trot.   When thin he runs much more easily and
readily, and a hunter seeing him in February might with
equal truth declare that he did not trot at all.   I believe
an elk will trot across ordinary prairie at the rate of
about a mile in 3 min. 30 secs.

His run will lessen the time by thirty seconds at least.
The peculiarity of the animal is that his gait is about as
good on the worst as on the best ground.   In going up
and down bad places he is only excelled by the mountain
sheep, and no heavy plains animal can compare with him

in crossing a bog. He has a faculty of spreading out his hoofs and false toes, and getting down on his legs, so that his track in the soft mud is of the most nondescript character, at least eighteen inches long and of no shape.

In going through bush or timber, he sticks his nose in the air, throwing back the points of his huge antlers on each side of his body, and makes about as good time as if in the open.

For doubling, dodging, and hiding, this huge animal is, considering his bulk, far superior to the hare, or even the fox; and the facility with which he will squat and conceal himself in the slightest possible cover, is really most remarkable.

It is this peculiarity which makes him so difficult to bag in thickets and wooded countries. The hunter may have the wind and be ever so cautious. The cracking of a dry twig or the rustling of withered leaves will put the elk on the alert and send him noiselessly out of danger. If, however, he finds his enemy very near, he relies on his skill in hiding, and will remain motionless, though the hunter pass within a few yards of him. Two hunters of my command, in September 1875, followed a trail of elk into a little valley filled with a jungle of quaking asp. All at once one of the hunters found himself so close to a huge buck that he could almost have touched him with his gun. The animal was perfectly motionless, had his head down, but was watching the hunter steadily, and with so fierce an aspect, that the man was, though an excellent shot, actually frightened into a miss at that distance. At the report of the rifle the whole valley suddenly became alive with elk. The men were in the very midst of a herd of at least a hundred, many of them within a few yards.

Nothing is more provoking than to trail an elk into a beaver dam thicket, to know he is in there, within a few feet of you, whilst you can neither see nor get him out. In such a case a well broken dog is invaluable.

The most exciting of sport is an elk chase on horse-back; but, unless the country be particularly favourable, it is not likely to be very successful. When pursued, the elk takes instinctively to the very worst ground. He will go easily in and out of the almost perpendicular ' bar-rancas' of the ' bad lands,' where no horse can possibly follow. He will go at full speed across a morass, in which a horse must inevitably stick at the first bound. He will dash without a moment's delay or hesitation through a thicket so dense that horse and rider are forced to go at a walk. Though, therefore, he cannot cope with a good horse in speed, he has the most decided advantage in a country which is at all difficult.

The first necessity in the race is to force him to break his trot. It is said that an elk will trot at an equal speed, without stopping or even flagging, for twenty miles. If, therefore, the horse is too slow or the ground too difficult to force a break, the race may as well be abandoned at once.

Suppose, however, the ground good and the horse fleet. A tremendous burst of speed brings the horse and rider on the haunches of the elk, who until now has been going at an even trot but at tremendous speed, throwing his legs easily and holding his head proudly in the air. The pursuer gets very near, sometimes within a few paces. The speed must be increased, and the elk is at the best of his trot, so reluctantly he breaks into a run, thus increasing his speed very considerably. But in taking the run he gains in speed at the expense of all his ease, grace, and beauty of movement. His run is an awk-ward, lumbering, rolling gallop. His head is carried low and thrust forward. A few hundred yards of this gait tells. His mouth is open, his tongue out, his eyes glazed with fear. A few moments more and he must surrender, unless some ruse can be hit upon to outwit the pursuer. He doubles at the most unexpected moment, dodges into every ravine, runs around points of hills, pushes into every place where there appears a chance for cover, and, finally, when all have failed, he squats in some bunch of grass or sage bush and receives the *coup de grace* without resistance or struggle.

I have had a number of such chases, and, though several times I have been near enough to be by courtesy 'in at the death,' I am obliged to admit that I have never run an elk down and killed it.

In 1867 I went with several gentlemen on an elk hunt in the Loup country. I had with me six Pawnee Indians, and, as the Sioux were at this time very hostile, a small force of infantry. We had several days of fair sport, and bagged all the meat needed by the party.

We camped one night on one of the head tributaries of Wood River. This stream is hardly a stream, there being but little running water; but it has cut through the deep alluvial of the 'bottom' a most crooked channel, about thirty feet wide by at least twenty feet deep. This chasm is filled with trees and underbush, forming an almost impenetrable jungle. Next morning, just as we had finished breakfast, an Indian informed me that a large buck elk had gone into the channel some half a mile below. We determined on a chase. The north side of the stream being most favourable, I sent the Indians below the elk, with instructions to drive him by us on the north side.

I was mounted on an excellent, powerful, and long-winded horse, but not, however, remarkable for speed. One of the party was riding a regular 'quarter horse,' exceedingly fleet for a short distance, and he was selected to break the elk's trot.

We had but fairly crossed the chasm and settled all preliminaries, when there came trotting by with free and easy grace one of the most magnificent bucks I have ever seen. He passed within twenty-five yards of us; and, with a shout that made the welkin ring again, we dashed after the game.

Within 300 yards the 'quarter horse' ran almost against the buck, who, turning his head in surprise, broke into his lumbering run. Some accident stopped the fast horse, but I was near enough to take up the running. In a mile the elk was nearly pumped, and showed every symptom of the greatest distress. Looking back I saw all the party strung out for half a mile; none were near enough to be my rival in the chase. I therefore husbanded my forces, and let my horse only run fast enough to keep the elk at the very top of his speed. The race was up to the creek bottom. I kept on the left of the elk, between him and the ravine, and so near that I could easily have killed him with a boar spear had I had one. I was admiring my prize and enjoying every moment, running easily, horse perfectly in hand, when, without a single preliminary look or act, the elk turned sharp to the left, frightening my horse into a momentary swerve, passed in front so near that I could have touched him with my hand, and, without a moment's hesitation, plunged off a perpendicular bank of twenty feet into the chasm, and disappeared in the jungle.

The whole line of pursuers saw the act, and turned short to the ravine, but it was at least fifteen minutes before we could hunt the elk from his hiding place. As it was he broke cover 500 yards from me, on the other side of the ravine, and, before I could find a place to cross, I was hopelessly out of the race. Galloping from one hill top to another, I saw the finish. Like myself, the whole party was thrown out except two Indians, one mounted on a poor pony, the other on a mule. Though terribly blown the elk led them a long chase, and, getting into some broken ground, would have escaped any pursuer similarly mounted but an Indian. From my vantage ground I could see all his manœuvres, and he worked hard and well for his life. Though now scarcely able to trot he was full of ruses. He would dodge around the point of a hill, get out of sight of his pursuers, double his track, turn to one side, and squat in a little ravine or clump of sage bush. When they lost sight of him the Indians would dismount, take the trail, follow it up, jump the game, now slightly refreshed by the rest, and off all would go again. This was done several times, until finally, completely exhausted, the elk squatted in some high grass, and one of the Indians, walking up, finished him with a pistol shot.

An old army friend, who was stationed many years ago in the Indian territory, has told many stories of splendid and successful runs in that open and beautiful country. He even yet, however, bears a grudge against one especial buck, which outwitted him.

He was out hunting alone, and had got nothing. To make matters worse, a cold rain set in, drenching him to the skin. On his way homeward he came upon a magnificent buck elk alone. Dismounting, he crept up, took good aim, and 'snapped.' Powder was pricked into the tube of his old-fashioned muzzle-loader, but all to no purpose. The gun snapped again and again. The powder in the barrel was hopelessly wet, and would not burn. Returning to his horse, he mounted, and after a splendid dash came alongside of the buck, who, however, would not break his trot, even although the horse ran against him. Lifting with one hand his rifle high above his head, he brought the heavy barrel with full force across the elk's back, without apparently producing the slightest effect. Again and again the blows fell, until, after receiving about a dozen, the elk made up his mind he had had enough, and, when the heavy barrel again descended, he by a quick motion to the right avoided it. The blow fell with terrific force against the horse's ribs, almost breaking them in, and nearly dislocating my friend's arm. The chase was continued, however, for some distance farther, when, coming to a small lake or pond of water, the elk plunged in, and only stopped when the water was over his back. The lakelet was out

of the hunter's depth in the centre; and, even had he
followed, the pursuer could have done nothing but pound
the elk on the antlers, which would have produced no
effect. Besides, if the elk had mustered courage enough
to show fight, both horse and rider would have been
helpless. The lakelet was not over fifty yards across;
but after pelting the elk with sticks and stones, and
failing to dislodge him from his retreat, my friend was
fain to return home discomfited, wet, sore, disappointed,
and miserable. He has not forgiven that elk to this
day.

Next to the buffalo the elk is the animal on which
the Indian depends for food. The plains Indians usually
stalk them, and are very successful. Not being biassed
by such puerile considerations as size, appearance, or
wealth of antlers, the Red hunter fires at that animal
which he is most sure to hit, and, having wounded, is
almost sure to bag it, as he will follow its trail for miles,
if necessary, with indomitable patience, and the instinct
of a hound.

The Utes, Bannocks, and other Indians living on the
slopes of the mountains, sometimes make a wholesale
slaughter in winter. A herd being discovered, a surround is made, and the elk are driven into a deep snow-
drift, where they are butchered at leisure. It is the
principal food of these Indians, there being no buffalo
in the country.

I have been told that the remnant of a plains tribe
(now living in the Indian territory, but the name of
which I have forgotten) is very successful in killing elk
from horseback. Each hunter is armed with a long
pole, light but strong, the small end of which is split
and forced open for about a foot, forming a **Y**. About
six inches from the open end is fastened a knife blade,
sharpened to the finest edge, and set diagonally in the
Y; that is, one end is farther forward than the other.
The whole is firmly secured by thongs of raw hide.

A herd being discovered, the hunters make a surround, and dash upon the frightened beasts, which,
confused by the sudden onslaught, and having no leader,
crowd together. Running up behind the elk, the hunter
sets the crotch of his pole against the hind leg, just above
the knee ; a sharp push severs the hamstring. The
other leg is served in the same way. So quick and
noiseless is this work, that it is said not to be unusual
for each hunter to secure two or three victims before the
herd finally breaks away.

Although the elk generally shows himself possessed
of the instinct of self-preservation to a degree which
makes him a fair match for any sportsman, he sometimes
becomes so paralysed with fear as to be apparently unable
to move. At other times he seems entirely to lose his
senses, and will rush into a snow-drift, or over a precipice
to certain death, under circumstances of danger from
which a deer or an antelope would easily extricate himself.

A pot-hunter came one day, not far from Fort Fred
Steele, upon a band of twenty-eight elk, feeding in a
cañon, the sides and upper end of which were perpendicular rock. Entering the cañon from below he walked
directly up the centre to within fifty yards of the herd,
which were crowded together at the upper end. He then
opened fire, and shot down, one after the other, the whole
herd, not one making an attempt to escape, though the
cañon was more than 100 yards wide, and they could
have passed the hunter on either side without approaching nearer to him.

The Big Horn River breaks its way through the
mountains by one of the most magnificent cañons on the
continent, the sheer descent of the gorge being in many
places not less than 2,000 feet. Three army officers,
hunting elk one day along the edge of this chasm, came
upon a herd of some thirty elk, which took refuge in a
small growth of pine timber. One hunter took position
on each side, while the third went into the timber.

He soon found the herd, fired, but missed, and the elk disappeared. After searching from one side of the timber to the other he joined one of his companions, who told him that the elk had not passed out by him. The two then went to the other, who made the same report. Their positions covered all the ground, and, it being certain that the elk were in the timber, all three went in. After a long search, the herd was found standing on a ledge, from one to three yards wide and scarcely thirty long. To get on this ledge, they had made a clear jump down a precipice of not less than fourteen feet. Their position was apparently without remedy. On one side a perpendicular wall of fourteen feet, on the other a sheer descent of 2,000 feet into the depth of the chasm.

In the excitement of finding the game, one of the officers fired. An elk fell, struggled an instant, toppled over the brink, and, after what appeared an age of anxious waiting, a faint thud announced the arrival of the carcass at the bottom of the gorge. Another was shot with the same result, and the firing stopped. The officers remained on the ground for an hour, so near that they could almost touch the elk, and yet unable to bag one. They looked in vain for some means of releasing the elk from their voluntary prison, and, finding none, returned to their camp, leaving the poor beasts to their fate.

In a very few years this most splendid animal will have shared the fate of the buffalo.

The presence of the Indians was, a few years ago, a protection to the game of the plains. Their general removal to reservations has made it safe for worthless whites, too lazy to work, to penetrate almost every portion of the country. These men butcher the game for their hides in season and out of season.

CHAPTER XI.

BLACK-TAILED DEER.

(*Cervus Macrotis.*)

THE black-tailed deer is the largest of the deer proper in this country. He is a magnificent animal, surpassed by the elk in size, but not in beauty of outline or grace of movement.

When in good condition and on the alert, just startled by an unusual sight or sound, he combines all the beauty that the most exacting imagination could desire. His splendidly proportioned body is set lightly but firmly upon the most delicately tapering legs. A glorious neck supports the most perfect head, crowned with antlers, magnificent, not from size, but from regularity and grace of curve. He steps as if walking on air, and with head proudly aloft, flashing eyes, dilated nostrils, attitude half of timidity, half of defiance ; even a Landseer must despair and must fail to do justice to the perfections of his noble proportions. I once saw a small herd frightened by a train of cars on the Union Pacific Railroad, near Sherman. They made off at speed, but in such a direction that by a sharp curve the train emerged from the rocks directly across their line of flight, and within thirty yards. The frightened does scattered in every direction. Not so a magnificent buck, startled by the sudden appearance and close vicinity of the snorting monster ; but, disdaining to fly, he drew up and back his form, as if expecting but defying attack, and stood stockstill until the train passed, the most perfect picture of animal life it has ever been my good fortune to see.

I may be a little enthusiastic; but the black-tail is to me the finest of plains animals, and its pursuit possesses a fascination which I find in no other hunting.

The black-tailed deer is considerably larger than the red deer, the bucks in good season not unfrequently weighing over 250 pounds, and I have heard of one killed by an army officer which kicked the beam at 280.

In colour it is very dark grey or mouse colour, though for some time after shedding in the spring the coat consists of a thin covering of coarse reddish hair. Its tail, unlike the broad white flag of the red deer, is rather thinly haired, and the end is tipped for two or three inches with a thick tuft of short black hair, which gives the name to the animal. Its tail is not lifted in running as with the red deer. Its ears are rather long and heavy, from which circumstance it is in some parts of the country called the 'mule deer.'

The ease and grace of motion of this animal are confined to his slower movements. In running, other deer project themselves forward by a great muscular effort of the hind legs, alighting on the fore feet, but using the fore legs only as support until the hind legs can be brought into position for another effort.

The black-tail uses all four of his legs in making his spring. All his feet strike the ground at the same time and are in the air at the same time. This gait appears very awkward, and these 'buck jumps' would seem to promise but little speed. On the contrary, however, he is extremely fleet on any ground, and he gets over rocks and ravines with almost as much ease and certainly with as much speed as that king of climbers, the mountain sheep. His habits are very similar to those of the elk, except that he rarely trusts himself on the plains except when migrating.

The buck loses his horns in February; and in April and May he retires to the fastnesses of the mountains, as near the snow line as possible, to grow another pair. This process is evidently as painful and sickening to him as to the elk, for from May to July it is only by penetrating to and rousing him from his lair that he can be seen at all.

During these months the does, unlike cow elk, assemble in herds, probably for mutual protection of the fawns; but they also, though never seen with or near the bucks at this season, keep well up on the sides of the highest mountains within reach.

While the horns are yet in the velvet, the bucks collect in herds, but it is not until October that both sexes congregate together again. The velvet is rubbed off at the proper time, against trees and bushes, as with the elk.

During the running season the bucks are exceedingly pugnacious, the friends and companions of only a few days before fighting desperate battles for the 'favours of the fair.' They rarely kill each other, however, the weakest or most timid betaking himself to flight before any serious injury is done. Frequent and large scars show, however, that these encounters are no child's play.

A herd of black-tails in the height of the running season resembles a well-ordered family of barn-yard fowls. Each buck has by actual experiment ascertained which of the other bucks he can whip and which can whip him; and while tyrannical to the last degree, and permitting no familiar approach of the former, he takes most excellent care to keep well out of the way of the latter.

The buck's life at this season is a very busy one. Twenty or thirty may be in one herd, with as many does, but his love-making is beset with innumerable difficulties. One moment he is charging a buck that he can thrash; the next, getting promptly out of the way of one that can thrash him. He sees a young Lothario making love to a doe, and ' goes for ' him straightway, but has hardly time to congratulate himself on his acquisition before he in his turn has to get away as fast as his legs will carry him. The herd is a scene of turmoil and confusion. The does are jostled and driven without ceasing.

There is no ' selection ' allowed her, and so that she gets a lover she seems perfectly indifferent as to the individual. This season lasts but a short time; and soon after it is over, the bucks, their animosity having departed with their love, separate from the does, and again set up their bachelor establishments. They are terribly run down, are poor and unfit for food; but they very soon recuperate, and I have seen almost as fine fat black-tailed bucks in December as in September, when, however, they are at their very best. In August and September the black-tails come down from their mountain fastnesses, and spread themselves over the country, wherever they find a locality suited to their tastes. This is the migratory season, and these animals not unfrequently make journeys of more than a hundred miles. The places selected are to be their homes until the next April or May, and they are very choice in the selection.

The ground must be broken by deep and crooked chasms, the tops and sides of which must be covered with thickets of cedar or pine. The black-tail must have long slopes dotted with cedar and covered with rich grass for his feeding grounds, and, if possible, a contiguous pine forest in whose sombre depths he can hide himself from enemies or the too ardent rays of the sun. He is exceedingly wary and difficult to bag, unless his habits are thoroughly understood; so much so, indeed, that I have known sportsmen, excellent at other game, who had never bagged a black-tail; and I take no shame in confessing that I hunted them occasionally for many years before arriving at the secret of success. He feeds a great deal at night, but in the very early morning he may generally be found feeding on the cedar-dotted slopes on his way to his lair. He may then be stalked as a red deer; with more caution, however, as his senses are more delicate and he is more ready to take alarm. By 7 A.M. he has usually satisfied his appetite, and, after going to water, lies down in some position where he is least likely to be seen. The deep cañons, in the neighbourhood of which he makes his haunt, have generally the upper edges rounded off by water, so that the plain or mesa above is joined to the precipice below by an inclination longer or shorter and more or less steep. The black-tail's favourite position for rumination and siesta is on the lower edge of this slope, just where it begins to be precipitous. From this point he can see all that passes below, whilst he is undistinguishable from the rocks, bushes, and grass around him. He cannot be seen from the plain above, and nothing can approach down the slope without starting fragments or loose stones which give him warning. When in this position the hunter can hope to bag him only by the help of another man. When alarmed he will not quit the slope unless forced to do so. The sportsman, having discovered the game from below, must make an ample detour, and station himself on the slope to the leeward of the deer. When he is in position another man must approach on the slope from the windward. As soon as the deer scents the intruder he will get up and walk quietly down the wind, and, of course, directly upon the sportsman waiting for him.

The black-tailed deer has one fatal quality—curiosity. He is never quite satisfied with the evidence of any one sense, except his nose; and if an enemy approach against the wind, and yet close enough to be heard, he will spring to his feet, make a few bounds away from the noise, then

stop and look around for the cause. This is the sportsman's opportunity, and nine-tenths of the black-tails
bagged are killed in that pause. If not fired at or if
missed during that pause, and he starts again, no further
effort need be made to bag that deer, for, after fully
satisfying himself what the danger is, he never stops until
safe in the thickest cover which is known to him.

Once in a while they seem to become almost paralysed
with curiosity, and will stand staring until several shots
have been fired. I have had frequent experience of this.
Once a friend and myself came suddenly on a herd in a
dense, dark cedar thicket. They broke up the side of a
steep hill—or rather mountain—stopped and stared until
we had dropped two in 'their tracks' and mortally
wounded three more.

On the 16th of August 1875 I came within long shot of
a herd of four—as fine bucks as I ever saw—and knocked
down all. Three I bagged; but the fourth, though mortally
wounded, hid in a thicket and was lost. On this occasion,
and the only time in my life, I bagged two noble bucks
with one rifle-ball.

If there be no convenient cañon for his noonday
siesta, the black-tail betakes himself for his nap to some
ridge or point surrounded by cedars as dense as possible.
This is my favourite stalk; and when the ground is soft
enough to show the tracks, and the wind is right, I always
consider such a deer as 'my meat.' A trail leading to
such a thicket being found, it should be followed with the
greatest caution if the wind will permit. If the wind
should be unfavourable a careful survey of the thicket
must be taken, and a detour made sufficiently wide to be
sure of bringing the sportsman to leeward of the game.
The difficulty of this approach is that the thicket may be
so extensive that the sportsman may be obliged to trust to
chance. He may pass within a few feet of the crouched
animal, give him the wind, and lose him. This cannot
occur if he has the trail. All at once a scramble and a

bound indicate the presence of the game sometimes only a few paces off. An outline is visible through the thick branches. A quick sight, a sharp report, and another is added to the bag.

In such hunting, an old-fashioned round bullet propelled from a muzzle-loader, even 'Hawkins's best,' is worth absolutely nothing. Each twig—and they are innumerable between the gun and the game—would serve to deflect the ball. The 'old hunters' killed very few black-tails, and those were usually stalked when feeding. I have never seen a black-tail feeding in the evening, and am inclined to believe that they remain crouched until nightfall.

When suddenly surprised by the very close vicinity of an enemy, the black-tail seems sometimes to make up his mind that the best policy is to remain concealed. Under such circumstances he will crouch close to the ground, with his head down, and allow a man almost to step on him without moving. I was once hunting in Elk Mountain. My route led through a little vale, in which thickets and open sports or parks irregularly alternated. Passing in the open but close to a thicket, my orderly called to me in a low tone, and on my halting pointed out something in the bush which he said was a deer. I scouted the idea. We were too near, and I could see nothing unusual, but he insisted that he had seen it move. I dismounted and walked quite near, when I could see through the bush a grey patch as large as my hand, apparently on or very near the ground. I was about to fire at it, when it flashed across my mind that there were many men, tie-cutters, at work about the mountain, and that this might be some sleeping or drunken man. I approached still nearer and called out in a loud voice, warning whoever was there that I was about to fire. I did this two or three times, still advancing, until I was scarcely twelve feet from the object, when, giving a last loud warning, I fired, and bagged a splendid black-tail.

An army surgeon, a keen and successful sportsman, informed me that once he was marching across country with a command of several companies. One afternoon they had encamped in a small mountain valley, meadow-like in its evenness and the luxuriance of the grass.

Near his tent was a small clump or thicket of bushes scarcely ten feet in diameter. Having occasion to go into the clump, he was startled to find himself within six feet of a splendid pair of antlers, and, looking closely, he saw the form of a magnificent buck, crouched close, his head on the ground, perfectly motionless, but watching the intruder from the corners of his eyes. Returning to his tent, the doctor got his rifle, and, going again to the thicket, violated the order against firing in camp, but secured full pardon for the offence by bagging the largest and fattest black-tail buck that ever fell to his lot before or since.

The reader will recollect that in the earlier part of this work I separated 'the plains' into three plains, each of which has its characteristics; and the lines of demarcation between which are generally indicated with much precision.

The great 'divide,' on a slope of which Denver stands, and which is itself a portion of the great second plain, extends eastward in a direction from a little north of west to south of east, crosses diagonally the Arkansas and Purgatory Rivers, and pushes its way far into the Indian territory.

The Purgatory cuts through this second plain by a most magnificent cañon; while the Chaquaque, Rule Creek, and many other streams, take their rise in the grand step by which the descent from second to third plain is accomplished. The step is very marked. For at least 200 miles the second plain terminates in a wall, generally precipitous, and varying in height from 500 to 2,000 feet. From the foot of this wall the third plain stretches eastward to the alluvial.

This wall is not built by the plumb or square of the human mason, but is cut by the Great Architect into myriads of fantastic shapes, and furrowed by seams and chasms innumerable, from five to thirty miles in length, and of every conceivable pattern, and running at times to every point of the compass, all, however, to pour their waters at last in the direction of the Arkansas River. The sides of these cañons, and the upper and lower plains in their vicinity, are more or less thickly covered with cedar. Sometimes the gorges are filled with a small though thick growth of pines.

These cañons, of all places I have ever seen, are much frequented by the black-tails; and from the latter part of August until the next April, they are here to be found in abundance amply satisfactory to the keenest sportsman.

The line of the grand wall was at its nearest point only about twenty-five miles from Fort Lyon, at which post it was my fortunate privilege to be stationed for two hunting seasons.

Every respite from my legitimate duties found me in these cañons, and I habitually bagged from fifteen to thirty-one splendid animals in a week's hunt, the latter being my highest number.

I am informed that there are now many sheep in that lovely hunting ground. If so, there are no deer. The black-tail has the strongest antipathy to sheep, and, when a herd is driven into any locality, the deer leave with as much precipitation as if the sheep were hounds; nor will they return until all scent or indication of the sheep's presence is obliterated by time. This may appear a curious statement; but I have had such ample opportunities of demonstrating its correctness, that I give it as a positive fact.

I once spent a week at a fine spring in the heart of a series of cañons, which more abounded in black-tails than any locality I have ever seen. It was on this occasion that I bagged thirty-one. The constant presence of men, horses, and dogs had no effect to frighten away the deer, and one or more were bagged early each morning, sometimes within a few hundred yards of camp. About a month after, wishing to show special attention to a favoured guest, I took him to the same place. There was a slight fall of snow on the ground, and, as we came within a couple of miles of the spring, I noticed trails of deer, which became more frequent as we neared the spring. All the trails indicated that the deer were at full speed, bounding as if badly frightened away from the neighbourhood. My curiosity being excited, I followed some of these trails, and discovered that the deer had entirely left the system of cañons which I came to hunt, had crossed a portion of the second plain, and taken refuge in the almost inaccessible rocks and ravines of the 'Mesa de Maio,' at least fifteen miles away. As far as I followed these trails, they showed that the deer never stopped or even flagged. This, and their taking to the open plain, indicated their action to be based on terrible fright, or other equally strong motive. Returning to the spring, we encountered a herd of sheep which were being driven across country through these cañons. We went into camp, and next day commenced hunting in earnest, but with such poor success that after some days we moved to another locality, through which the sheep had not passed. This experience has been repeated so often, that I am perfectly confident in the assertion that black-tails will not live in the same neighbourhood with sheep. I have seen a few apparent exceptions, as Cariso Creek, the valley of which is a favourite sheep-range, while on the tops of its adjacent mountains black-tails are to be found. In every such case, however, it will be found that the sheep never go up the mountain, nor the deer down into the valley, and that the deer is separated from his antipathy by 1,500 to 2,500 feet of altitude.

The black-tail has wonderful strength and vitality,

and is exceedingly tenacious of life. One morning, after a long and trying stalk, I had approached sufficiently near to three splendid bucks for a shot, but was so situated that I could not see them from where I stood, nor change my position to where I could see them, without danger of giving them the wind. After some hesitation and careful study of the ground, I decided to risk the wind. I had not progressed fifty paces, when I saw all three dash into a small clump of cedars in full view and at short range. This clump was separated from a dense and contiguous thicket of small pines by a little glade of less than ten feet in width. I sat down on the ground and pointed my rifle at this glade. I was hardly ready when a buck sprung into the glade, paused scarcely an instant, and plunged into the thicket. I 'drew a bead' on the spot where he had been, and a moment after another sprung directly in front of my rifle, and as he turned to gain the thicket I fired. He went off. Slipping in another cartridge, I looked up to see the head of the last deer, as he peeped through the branches to see the cause of the unusual noise. A bullet through his head dropped him ' in his tracks.' After securing him I went into the glade and found a trail of blood, showing that the second deer had been hit. I followed this trail most carefully, through an unusually dark, dense, and tangled thicket, for more than 400 yards, and was finally rewarded by finding my buck dead. My bullet had struck him, as he turned, just on the rearmost rib, very near the spine, and ranged forward. Five ribs had been cut as completely as though the blow had been struck with a heavy axe. The bullet had then passed inwards through the lungs, and came out well up in the chest. Scarcely any other animal but would have fallen at once; yet this buck ran for a quarter of a mile through a thicket, every step of my progress through which was attended with unusual exertion.

The capacity of the black-tail for scrambling over

rocks and escaping from a pursuer after receiving a wound entirely disabling to most animals, is exemplified in the following anecdote, which I relate at the risk of becoming tedious: I was hunting near Red Rocks, on the Purgatory River, with a dear friend who lives in St. Louis, Missouri. As I approached the brink of a chasm, a deer sprung to his feet on the opposite brink, and stood facing directly towards me. It was a very long shot; but estimating the distance as well as I could, and taking careful aim, I fired. I saw the bullet strike the sloping rock below and in front of the deer, which, however, fell, but immediately got up again and made off. I lost some time in finding a place where the chasm could be crossed, but finally got over, took the trail of the deer, and followed it for about 200 yards, when the animal sprung up from a little cover, and attempted to make off, but fell ' all in a heap ' in the top of a small fallen tree. I was within six feet of my game, when I saw another deer at some distance, went after, wounded, followed a long distance, but finally lost it. I then returned to bag my first. To my very great surprise it was not to be found. My servant came up with the horses, and aided me in the search, but to no purpose. There was no blood anywhere to be discovered, and the ground was so marked with tracks that it was impossible to follow those of any one deer. Close by was a sharp ravine, not over eight or ten feet deep, across which was a game trail: so steep, however, that I could scarcely believe that a wounded deer would make the passage. However, as one side had been thoroughly searched, I crossed it, and had gone scarcely twenty paces, when the deer jumped up and made directly for me. I was about to fire at it again when I noticed that a hind leg was broken and that his gait was otherwise most unsteady. I therefore ran after, thinking to catch him. He soon slipped on a rock and fell. Getting close to him I noticed that the bone of his fore leg was protruding through the skin of the shoulder.

Here was something more extraordinary than my experience had before shown me. Anxious to secure and, examine this curiosity I shot him through the head, and, placing him on my horse, took him into the camp to my friend. Together we dissected out the course of the bullet. From the *ricochet* it had struck the deer on the fore arm, passing through and breaking the bone. It had then gone into the chest, striking a rib which deflected it outward, so that it passed just under the skin to the paunch, where it came out and struck the hind leg just above the knee, breaking the bone. The deer had a fore leg and hind leg broken on the same side; yet it managed to change its position for a distance of 300 yards, and to cross the ravine—easy enough for an unwounded animal, but which I should have pronounced entirely impossible for one with such a wound as I have described.

CHAPTER XII.

RED DEER, OR WHITE-TAILED DEER.

(*Cervus Lencurus.*)

Of all the animals that inhabit the plains, the red deer is the most generally and widely known.

Some of the others are exclusively plains animals, while he seems to be indigenous to all climes and places alike. He is found almost everywhere on the continent, from the gloomy pine forests of Maine to the brush-covered islands of the Pacific Coast; from the icy plains of British America to the ever sweltering glades of Florida.

He is a splendid deer, yielding the palm in size and majestic appearance to the black-tail, but in beauty and grace to no living animal. His gait and speed are the perfection of motion. His magnificent bounds, in which strength, speed, ease, and lightness are combined, his gallant carriage, the flaunting defiance of his white flag of a tail elevated high in air, all combine to render him, to a student of nature, one of the most beautiful and interesting of animals.

These, together with his natural capacity for taking care of himself, and thus calling into play all the best points of the sportsman, make him an object of the keenest interest and desire to every lover of the chase, while the delicacy and exquisite flavour of his flesh render him an object of at least equal interest to the gourmand.

The most widely disseminated, he is also, except the

antelope, the most prolific of large game animals ; and, while comparatively few have enjoyed the pleasure of bringing him to bay, there are not many persons in all the length and breadth of the country who have not at some time enjoyed the pleasure of bringing him to table.

While always the same animal in general appearance, red deer vary in size and habits in so remarkable a degree that it is not to be wondered at that plainsmen divide them into several groups or branches of the same family. Their habits are always adapted to their safety and preservation in the particular locality of which they are denizens.

On almost all plain streams that are fringed with cotton-wood the red deer is found, a very independent animal, feeding by day or night as it suits him, going out on the plain as fearlessly though not so far as an antelope, and living a twofold life—now a prairie animal, now an inhabitant of the jungle. When danger threatens him on the prairie, he flies to the cover of his cotton-wood thickets. Should they be invaded, he seeks the solitude and safety of the high plains. The sand hills, which in some places border the great rivers, harbour numbers of red deer; and, but that the soft and yielding sand renders stalking difficult and most tiresome, the results of hunting in these localities are generally most satisfactory.

The willow-covered islands of the Platte and Arkansas are favourite homes for the red deer; and here he becomes a rabbit in his habits, feeding only at night and remaining crouched in his lair by day. Here he loses his freedom and elasticity of movement. When disturbed, instead of going off with high springy bounds, as is his wont in other places, he steals away, ears back and tail down, to crouch again in the grass as soon as he is out of immediate danger. The islands below the junction of the two Plattes were, in the winter of 1867-8, plentifully supplied with these animals; yet the oldest and best hunters, whether white or Indian, were unable to bag them. It was useless to hunt on foot, as the high grass and bushes completely concealed the movements of the deer, which would lie so close, and sneak away so silently, that the hunter was never aware of the near vicinity of his game. Hunting on horseback with rifle was equally out of the question; for though a deer was occasionally seen, it was but the most momentary glance.

After repeated failures I struck upon a means of out-witting them. Seated in a light, strong waggon, and with another person to drive, I passed slowly, shot-gun in hand, through the long grass and willows. From my elevated position I could occasionally see a brown form, sneaking swiftly and silently away, sometimes only a few feet from the horse's head. A charge of buckshot deve-loped this form into a deer, and during the winter I was enabled to add to my bag several fine animals which I could have got in no other way.

As a rule, the red deer, wherever found, is a lover and frequenter of thickets, and I have never met him very far away from cover of some kind.

The variation in size is not easily accounted for, but it exists in quite as remarkable a degree as in mankind. In the Black Hills of Dakota this inequality in size is more marked than in any other locality in which I have hunted. In the same day's hunt a sportsman may bag a mammoth buck of over 200 pounds, and another buck, equally old, equally fat, which will scarcely weigh seventy-five pounds. On Rapid Creek I bagged two bucks which, closely dressed, neck and legs cut off, yet weighed about 130 pounds each. On Box Elder, the next stream, and only ten miles north, was killed a little buck, well antlered and very fat, which, dressed in the same way as the others, scarcely weighed forty pounds. Yet these are undoubtedly the very same animals. Deer precisely similar in every particular, except size, are to be found filling all the intervals from the largest to the smallest, and all seem to run together as amicably as would people who differ only in size.

The red deer, like the elk and black-tail, loses his horns in February, but he undoubtedly suffers very little from their renewal. He does not seek solitude or mountain fastnesses during their growth, but remains about his usual haunts, and in company with others of his kind.

The rapid growth of this huge frontlet seems to have no effect either on his disposition or his habits, except that, while it is hardening, he betakes himself on hot days to some sunny spot, ' drying his horns,' as hunters term it. This is remarkable, as he naturally loves damp, shady places, and except at this particular season, or in winter, I have never seen a red deer lie down in the sun.

The red deer is not migratory, and can generally be found all the year round in the vicinity of his chosen haunt. When located in the neighbourhood of mountains, or on ground likely to be affected by the black-tail, he has to give way to the larger, more powerful, and more pugnacious animal. In August, therefore, as the black-tails come down to select their fall and winter residences, the red deer (or white-tail, as he is commonly called wherever there are black-tails) moves down in lower country and away from the immediate neighbourhood of the black-tails. The habits of the animals are so dissimilar, however, that they rarely come in contact; the black-tail preferring the tops of cañons and high rocky ridges, while the white-tail is better satisfied in the dark, shady dells at the bottoms of the cañons. If the country is very broken, it is not unusual to bag black and white-tails in the same day's hunt, and sometimes even near each other, on the tops and at the bottoms of the same ravines. Such cases are evidence that there is plenty of food on the summits; for when the black-tails come into the valleys to feed, as they do in the late fall and winter, the white-tails decamp and abandon that vicinity.

The white-tail is much more gregarious and domestic than either the elk or the black-tail, the bucks and does being found together at all seasons. However, all the does found with bucks between May and September are barren, those that have produced fawns keeping apart, and each one by herself until the fawn is weaned, when both join the herd. The running season commences in October and lasts a much longer time than with the black-tails, sometimes as long as two months. There is not that constant fighting which marks this season with the black-tails, but they do fight, and most furiously. The whipped buck is generally run out of the herd. It is of course impossible to say exactly how these domestic details are managed; but it has always seemed to me that a portion of the bucks form a conbination which, while not interfering with its own individual members, drives out of the herd all not belonging to 'the ring.' In the earlier part of ' the season' there is much fighting. About half the bucks are soundly whipped and run out, after which the others seem to get along peaceably, though there may be only one buck to every two or three does. The whipped bucks sulk off alone or in bands of three or four, never going near the herds where the does are. They are to be pitied; for they are not only deprived of female companionship, but, possibly from being spared the cares of domestic relations, become extremely fat, and are eagerly sought after by hunters; while those bucks which have been favoured by the sex are thin, tough, unfit for food, and are not worth the pulling of a trigger.

Though generally producing one fawn each season, the does are very irregular in breeding. Many are barren, while many others bring forth two fawns at a birth. There is a well-authenticated instance of a doe with three fawns; but it is a question whether all were hers, or whether she may not have adopted a little one which had lost its own dam—an habitual occurrence with antelope.

On the average red deer are prolific; and, as the does not unfrequently commence breeding when only a year old, they soon stock a country suited to them when not hunted by men or other carnivora.

Though my fortune has taken me over a great portion of one widely extended country and into many uninhabited regions, I have never seen any section which could compare in numbers of red deer with Southern Texas. In the winter of 1848 the plains at the back of Port La Vaca were alive with them, and I believe that I am well within the mark when I say that I have seen 1,000 in a herd. When collected together in this way it was exceedingly difficult to approach sufficiently near for a successful shot, at least with the muzzle-loading round-bullet rifle of that day.

I have elsewhere spoken of a lovely valley in the Guadalupe Mountains in which I discovered an Indian camp, long since abandoned except by the dead. A month after that discovery I obtained permission to go on a hunt, and arrived in that valley about noon one day, hunted that afternoon, all next, and until noon the third day. My bag to my own hand was five black bear and twenty-three deer, which altogether being as much as my pack mules could possibly carry, I was forced to return to my post before my hunt was half out. This was an exceptional oasis. The foot of white man had probably never before trod it. The Indians being debarred by superstition from entering it, the game for several years had been entirely undisturbed, and knew nothing of the danger of the presence of man. Deer would stand and look at me within fifty paces, and but that I was young and ardent the sport would soon have degenerated into murder.

While red deer are not so wary or acute of sense as the elk or black tail, and are, therefore, much more easily bagged, they are not afflicted with the stupidity of the former nor the curiosity of the latter. No panics of fright or of curiosity interfere with their instinct of self-preservation; and, though on a few very rare and exceptional occasions I have bagged several red deer from the same herd with successive rifle shots, it was because I had every advantage of position and wind. Being unable to see or smell anything unusual, the shots only produced a momentary alarm.

This deer has less vitality than any other of the large plains animals, and more readily succumbs to a well-directed bullet. Unless the back is broken, however, he rarely falls at once, and being generally found near thickets, and instinctively taking to them when wounded, he is very frequently lost unless the hunter has a good dog. Even with his heart split he may run 100 or 200 yards—ample space in which to conceal himself, should the thickets be dense. I once, on a specially unlucky day, mortally wounded four splendid bucks without bagging either. On the next day I went over the same ground with my dog (which had been sick the day before), and found all the bodies, unfortunately spoiled from remaining so long after death without disembowelling. The best sportsman, unless he has a good dog, may calculate on losing one out of every three actually killed.

CHAPTER XIII.

(*Antelope furcifer.*)

THIS is peculiarly a plains animal, loving the high, dry prairie, and being frequently found so far from water as to raise a doubt in the minds of many plainsmen whether he may not be able to live without drinking. Absurd as this is, the hypothesis has more of plausibility than would at first appear. There is scarcely a desert so barren and arid that the antelope cannot find means of existence, and apparently a very comfortable existence, as, wherever found, he is invariably at the proper season in splendid condition.

He, however, drinks with as much regularity as the deer; and however parched and dry the desert may be to man, if antelope are found on it, their keen noses have shown them where to find a spring, or pool of rain water in the cavity of a rock, and to which they resort at least once a day to slake their thirst.

Should a man suffering from want of water on a desert, where none is known to exist, come on a herd of antelope, and exercise due care in watching their movements without alarming them, his patience will within twenty-four hours meet its reward in the discovery of their hidden store of the precious fluid.

The antelope is the smallest of the larger game animals of the plains, averaging, when dressed, scarcely fifty pounds. The head of the male is armed with horns from eight to fourteen inches in length, and, though very considerably larger, are of the same character as the horns of the chamois. At about two-thirds of its length, measured from the base, the horn becomes somewhat palmated, and a short prong branches off, giving to the animal its name 'prong-horn.' The tips are bent inward—a fortunate provision, as these little animals are very pugnacious, and, were the horns straight, their combats would frequently result in death. As it is they cannot seriously hurt each other, and the fight consists in a simple trial of pushing. They do not butt like sheep, nor strike like goats, but, putting their heads together, each combatant pushes with all his might. The weaker gradually gives ground until, finding himself overmatched, he attempts to escape, generally receiving such a punch in the side or buttocks as most decidedly accelerates his speed and puts an end to the combat.

Though these horns are apparently of the same growth as those of cattle or goats, the antelope nevertheless sheds them every year. The horn has a pith, and is not wholly shed, as the elk or deer horn, but the hard horny shell comes off the pith just as the shell comes off the body of a crab. In May the outside shell begins to get loose ; the antelope retires to some solitude, the shell drops off, leaving a spongy, white, fleshy substance, sparsely covered with short, stiff, black bristles, pointing towards the end, and the growth of which evidently aids in pushing off the shell. This pith grows with wonderful rapidity, becomes somewhat larger than the old horn, and the outside hardens into a horny shell. The whole process takes but two or three days.

Many plainsmen, who ought to know better, insist that antelope do not shed their horns. I know they do. I have killed an antelope with the shell already off one horn ; the other loose and nearly off. I have killed many with the shell loose, and several times have had a shell come off in my hand. I have bagged antelope when the point of the horn, though already turning black, was so soft that it might be bent backwards and forwards between the fingers; and at the proper season and in favourable localities I have found the dropped horns in greater profusion than I ever saw those of elk or deer. Although I hear it frequently disputed, there is no fact connected with the habits or characteristics of any game animal more certainly within my personal knowledge than that the antelope sheds his horns.

The coat of the antelope can only be called ' hair' by courtesy. Each fibre is less like hair than like the separate delicate plumes which go to make up each feather of a large bird. This hair is very thick, brittle, nearly two inches long, and of a reddish colour, inclining to yellow on the sides and white on the belly. Around the root of the tail and extending well up and down on the buttocks, the hair is perfectly white, and longer than elsewhere. Under ordinary circumstances this is scarcely noticeable ; but, when the animal is frightened or otherwise excited, he possesses the faculty of erecting this white hair, spreading it out like a fan, and, as it were, intensifying its whiteness.

This peculiarity, with the ease and lightness of his movements, and his graceful carriage, make him a most beautiful animal, attractive alike to the lover of nature and to the lover of sport. He loves the treeless plains, and is rarely found in wooded or mountainous countries, although the cedar wooded slopes through which the black-tailed deer so loves to roam, seems to possess equal fascination for the antelope. The two animals seem to get along together much better than the two deer. In the Rule Creek cañons I have frequently seen black-tails and antelope browsing in close vicinity ; and during my hunts in that, my favourite hunting ground, I usually bagged about an equal number of the two animals, and not unfrequently two or three of each in the same day's hunt. Even in these cañons, however, there is but a small space of common ground, and the habits of the two animals are so entirely dissimilar that the hunter has only to vary the direction of his hunt to change the game. A close hugging of the higher portions of the cañon ensured an encounter with black-tails, while a circle in the plains beyond the foot of the slopes was equally sure of antelope. This peculiarity was one of the great charms of that hunting ground. The morning was devoted to the deer; the return trip in the afternoon to antelope. When caught in the common ground, each instinctively made for what to him was the safest place. The black-tail disappeared with magical celerity in the cedar jungle or pine thickets of the upper cañons; while the antelope gained with all possible despatch the wide plain, where he had ample space for watchfulness. The black-tail relies on concealing himself from the sight of his enemy; the antelope on keeping the hunter in view and himself beyond range of possible danger. The determination to see is carried to such an extent that, having once been seen by antelope too far off for a shot, the hunter can have but the barest hope of getting nearer. However favourable the ground, the result is the same. The moment he disappears from view in his effort to approach, the antelope also disappears, or at least changes his position; and, when the hunter arrives at the point from which he expected to get a shot, he finds nothing to shoot at. When several persons are together, if those in view stop and remain stationary, the antelope may also stand and watch, giving opportunity to one in rear to slip into a position for a shot. Should, however, any of those seen attempt to slip to one side for a like effort, the animal is off like a rocket. Much has been said and written of the curiosity of the antelope, and of the modes of taking advantage of this peculiarity by flagging, waving hats, &c. It is undoubtedly their most fatal defect of character, though, from lack of skill or patience, I have rarely been able to profit by it.

There is a phase of curiosity peculiar to this animal, which is in itself more remarkable than that ordinary curiosity which it has in common with all plains animals, the black-tail especially ; and this has added more antelope to my bag than any other of its characteristics. It is a panic produced by a combination of curiosity and terror. In a country where antelope have not been much hunted, they become, as it were, beside themselves at the appearance of any object very unusual and strange.

Thus a waggon train crossing such a country will attract every herd within the range of vision. They will rush at it with every indication of extreme terror, and, passing within a few yards, will sometimes make a complete circuit of the train, going off at last in the direction from whence they came. I have known a few instances where the panic was so great that the herd passed between the waggons, although the whole wide plain was open to them.

On one occasion, when scouting in the ' Two Butte' country, then very little known, I crossed three or four miles of very high table land, during the passage of which at least half a dozen herds charged desperately at my two waggons, made in some instances complete circuits, and went off, leaving one or more of each herd to pay the penalty of their temerity.

On another occasion, when passing in a 'spring waggon' over a broad, barren, and apparently lifeless plain, three specks appeared on the far horizon, and, making directly for us, soon developed into antelope. The waggon was stopped. A companion and myself seized our rifles, sprang out, and made all ready to give them a warm reception. The antelope came on, passed completely round us, within fifty yards, and went off in the direction they came, unhurt, though we each fired eight or ten shots at them. I do not like to record such an instance of bad shooting ; but, as the sportsman as a rule remembers only his remarkably successful shots, it is

well occasionally to recollect that he may do very badly.[1]
And here, by-the-bye, on behalf of sportsmen, I protest
against the .general disposition to take hunting stories
cum grano salis, and to laugh at that trait of the
sportsman which induces him to relate only the most
remarkable of his experiences. This is the most natural
thing in the world, and is true not only of the sportsman
but of all men. The most hum-drum business man would
not be likely to speak of the daily recurring details of
his business; but let him make a specially good bargain, or
have a counterfeit bill passed on him, and his confidant
will assuredly have the story in all its details. When the
sportsman has bagged his thousands or even hundreds of
heads of game, the adding of another is of little consequence, and not likely to be remembered unless its acquisition was accompained by an experience out of the
common. It is not the every-day experiences which
make an impression. Memory refuses to take note of
the commonplace, and records only those experiences
which are marked by something unusual, of good or ill,
of fortune or of misfortune.

Another peculiarity of the antelope is his apparent
inability to connect sound with danger. The striking of
a bullet on the hard, dry prairie always knocks up more
or less dust; and the antelope, instead of running away
from the sound of the gun, runs from the dust made by
the bullet. I have frequently taken advantage of this
trait, and when a herd, entrenched in an expanse of level
prairie, was too far off for anything but the merest chance
shot, I have, by causing my bullets to strike the ground
beyond, driven them in a panic to within fair distance
for a shot, and have bagged one or more. On one
occasion I stalked a large herd feeding in an open glade,
surrounded by rocks and cedar thickets. Unable to

---

[1] The author is an admirable shot at antelope and other game. I have
seen him kill with right and left shots two antelopes running in opposite
directions, at a distance of 300 yards.

locate the sound of the rifle, or to see any dust, they rushed round and round the glade, and only escaped after I had knocked down seven of their number.

Another trait he has in common with the domestic sheep, namely, that where the leader goes the rest will follow at all hazards; and if the leader. in his fright, or from having been hit, should bound in the air, all the others bound likewise in the most ridiculous manner. A knowledge of this peculiarity enables the hunter frequently to bag antelope which would otherwise escape him.

Sometimes a herd will start in a diagonal direction which the sportsman can cut by rapid riding. Provided he does not interfere with the course of the leader, he need not fear that the others will change their direction. As he nears them they increase their speed, but keep in the track of the leader, and the hunter may get near enough for several good shots. I one afternoon bagged three antelope by successive shots from my hunting waggon, in which, by a rapid dash across the prairie, I had cut their line of flight.

I have already spoken of the antipathy of the antelope to woods and close cañons, and their disposition always to take refuge on the open prairie. This I have frequently taken advantage of. A herd being discovered in a cañon, a circuit is made, and the hunter suddenly shows himself at the mouth of the cañon. Without a moment's hesitation the whole herd will rush for the open, even though they have to pass within twenty feet of the sportsman. A friend and myself one day bagged five in such a rush, the herd passing within thirty yards of us.

The antelope is the most fleet of all the plains animals, though he may be pulled down by greyhounds, and on a few occasions I have run into a herd on a good horse. His run is remarkably even and regular, so that he is nearly as good a mark running as when standing. Indeed, I think I have bagged more antelope on the run than when perfectly still; and, contrary to the usual rule in killing game, I am quite sure that I have bagged more over 200 yards than within that distance. Their habit of collecting in large herds in the late autumn, and the knocking up of dust from the dry prairie by the bullet, very greatly assists the sportsman in this kind of shooting.

Unless it strikes an antelope, each bullet indicates its position on the ground, and the sportsman has an opportunity to rectify a previous error. The long-range rifle of the present day will kill at incredible distances if it hits, and is so quickly loaded that, after stalking a herd of antelope, and getting one fair standing shot, the sportsman has still the chances that six or eight running shots may give him.

I have already spoken of knocking over seven from one herd. This was by no means a fair criterion, as the animals were panic-stricken, and did not run away; but I have frequently bagged two, and many times three, even when the herd went directly away from me at full speed. On one occasion, after missing a fair standing shot at 150 yards, I yet bagged three antelope as they went off.

Except the buffalo, the antelope is the most gregarious of the plains animals; yet in April they are scattered singly in twos and threes. The does are alone, preparing for their fawns, and can generally be found not far from water and some little cover in which they can hide their little ones for a few days, or until they are old enough to escape their enemies by flight. The bucks go off alone when shedding their horns; but, as this process requires but a short time, they soon collect again in groups. Unlike the deer, the female antelope, after parturition, leaves her fawns hid, and consorts during the greater part of the day with the herd; and, when they are strong enough to keep up with the herd in running, she permanently joins the herd with her little ones.

As a rule, and for the whole year round, antelope are in herds; but in September and October these herds increase in number, until sometimes hundreds are collected in one band. The does are very motherly, and will give suck to other young besides their own; consequently very few of the fawns die, even although their dams may have been killed.

The seasons for running and for parturition are the same as for other deer. Antelope are very prolific, the female generally producing two fawns at a birth, whilst barren does are unknown. In all my experience I have never seen one, while among red deer in some locations at least half the does are barren.

In September and October the flesh of the antelope is no better for food than that of the black or white-tailed deer, nor so good as that of the mountain sheep, but it has the unusual advantage of being most excellent all the year round. At the season when the other large game animals are poor, tough, stringy, and unfit for food, antelope meat, however poor, is always tender, juicy, and most delicious.

In the late fall, when the antelope congregate in great herds, the Utes and other Indians of the foot hills make surrounds and kill great numbers of the panic-stricken herds.

Antelope possess very great vitality, and will carry off more lead in proportion to their size than any other animal. They possess, too, remarkable courage, and, under ordinary circumstances, do not trouble themselves to get out of the way even of the large buffalo wolves. A single antelope will bravely face a single wolf, and successfully beat off his attack, and a herd does not fear the attack of any number of wolves. Wherever the antelope are numerous there will generally be found plenty of wolves, who lie around the herd at a little distance, watchful and ready to take advantage of any accident in their favour; now pouncing upon one which has strayed from the protection of the herd, and making a prompt meal of any one which should happen to be sick, or get injured in any way.

I once wounded a large doe from a herd which ran past me. I saw she was badly hurt, shot through the body, and wished to give her time to lie down. Mounting my horse, I rode slowly in the direction taken by the herd. After proceeding half a mile I saw her standing with her face partly towards me, and very much on the alert, and in a moment discovered that she was in the heat of a combat with a large wolf. The wolf circled round, trying to get at her flanks and rear, and made many feints of springing upon her, but, in spite of the advantage of his sharp teeth, he was too cowardly to come to close quarters. The little antelope bravely faced her foe, and continually charged, striking viciously with her fore feet, and would certainly have beaten off her assailant, but that the smell of blood made him unusually pertinacious. I watched the fight for more than five minutes with the greatest interest. At last the antelope in making a charge slipped, probably from weakness. In an instant the wolf had her by the throat, threw her on the ground, and worried her like a dog. I wanted the wolf to kill her, and waited for some time until she was perfectly quiet, and I believed dead. I then rode up slowly. The wolf took to his heels on my approach, and to my very great surprise the antelope sprung to her feet and went off in another direction at as great a rate of speed as before. I ran her with my horse for a long distance, and finally brought her to bay with another shot. The wolf, though a large one, had only scarified her throat ; and, though he would eventually have killed and eaten her, he had done her no serious injury, although he had had her unresisting in his jaws, and had been worrying her for several minutes.

Very different was the result when a pack of wolves got after a wounded antelope. On the same hunt as in the last case (and during which I saw more wolves than ever before or since in the same time) a friend and I had got several shots at a herd, bagging four or five, several of which, though mortally wounded, ran off to greater or less distances. Leaving the dead we went at once after the wounded, securing, after some little time and trouble, all but one. When we got near the place where he had been last seen we started a pack of six or eight wolves, and, going to the spot, found our antelope, its throat lacerated, its hamstrings cut, its flanks torn open, and half the viscera already devoured.

With a good pack of greyhounds, and in a good running country, where antelope are not too numerous, splendid sport may be had in coursing them. Many portions of the plains, apparently good running ground, are covered with beds of cactus, growing low, but very thick, which are scarcely noticeable until one is among them. The antelope instinctively takes to these when pursued by dogs, passing over them unscathed, while the hounds, if not stopped at once, as is frequently the case, are sure to be lame, possibly for weeks. If there are many antelope the hounds become scattered in pursuit and are liable to be lost, the effort is a failure, and the game escapes.

I have never yet seen a single greyhound pull down an unwounded antelope. I have heard of plenty of owners of such dogs say that this dog could and would do it ; but, when I have gone out to see, something has always happened to prevent the dog's execution of the feat on that particular occasion.

A very fleet, powerful, favourite pointer of mine once caught and killed an unwounded antelope. There was a little snow on the ground, and the weather was very cold. I have always believed that the antelope slipped and strained himself on the icy ground, so that he could not do justice to his natural fleetness. As it was, that one success nearly ruined the finest antelope dog I ever saw. He ever after believed himself able to catch antelope, even though unwounded, and was constantly 'trying it on' in spite of repeated and severe thrashings. He never succeeded again.

Unlike those of deer, which are so useful in thousands of ways, the skins of antelope are thin, porous, and weak. They are of little value, and are rarely preserved, except by the poorest of the pot-hunters, who, after taking the hair off, sometimes attempt to sell them as buckskins. The Indians make use of them for fringes and ornamental work.

CHAPTER XIV.

MOUNTAIN SHEEP—BIG-HORN.

(*Ovis montana.*)

THIS splendid animal, which among the horned beasts of the Great West ranks next in size to the elk, can scarcely be called a native of the plains. His home is among crags and broken rocks, generally at an elevation above tide-water of not less than 5,000 feet.

It must be remembered, however, that the plains proper rise to an altitude of 8,000 or 9,000 feet above the sea level, and their surface is cut with many huge cañons and deep barrancas, and torn and broken into confused and tumbling crags, forming congenial homes for many animals usually inhabitants of only mountainous regions.

I have designated as ' the plains ' all the non-primary country between the Mississippi and the Rocky Mountains. Many portions of this section would be considered grandly mountainous were they not overshadowed and dwarfed by the real mountains in the background.

The mountain sheep appears to care very little whether he lives among primary or secondary rocks, provided they be sufficiently elevated and torn and jagged enough to suit his fastidious taste.

In 1868, when the position now known as ' Fort Fred Steele ' was first occupied by troops, the adjacent country more abounded in game than any I have ever seen. Elk, black-tail deer, and antelope were to be had at any time, and mountain sheep were far more plentiful than in any locality I have ever visited. I have frequently encountered two or three herds in a day's hunt, some containing not less than fifty animals. They are, however, exceedingly difficult to kill, especially by a hunter on horseback. Though they come down from their rocky fastnesses for water and occasionally for food, they must do so at night. I have many times seen their tracks about a water hole or spring in a valley, but in all my experience have only found the animals themselves in the valleys some three or four times. They are usually to be found high up on the mountain side where the precipitous rocks rise from the natural slope of the mountain.

The sportsman who wishes to bag mountain sheep must be a good mountaineer, patient, and careful, with a keen eye and noiseless tread. He must always have the wind, for the sheep's nose is as keen and accurate as that of the elk.

With these advantages, and wind and pluck enough for a mountain scramble of fifteen or twenty miles a day, the sportsman may in many portions of the plains very surely count on finding ' big-horn,' and if he does find him, and is cool, he may bag several from one herd. When surprised in his rocky home, the action of the mountain sheep is greatly dependent on the sense which notifies him of the vicinity of his enemy. If he smells the hunter he is off at once, and without taking the trouble to notify his pursuer that he has been near. If he hears him he will run about, prying inquisitively with eyes and nose to discover the nature of the approaching danger. If the hunter succeeds in approaching near enough for a shot without being either smelt, seen, or heard, he may count on a splendid opportunity.

The animals, on the report of the rifle, will rush together and stand gazing at the smoke of the piece, until time and repeated explosions have convinced them of the necessity for a retreat. In this way I have known four or five to be bagged before they decided to leave. I am a very poor mountaineer, and have had less personal experience with this animal, and have bagged fewer, than any other of the game animals of the plains. These few have been generally from lucky shots at the herds as they scampered among the rocks far above me. I have, however, been with parties when many were killed by sportsmen more enamoured of mountain climbing than I am ; and, though I know but little of the habits of the animal, I am consoled by the fact that the oldest mountaineers know scarcely more.

The mountain sheep is a curious combination. His body is that of a very large deer; his head that of a domestic sheep, except that no domestic sheep could possibly carry the enormous horns with which his mountain cousin is provided. These horns are often more than twenty inches in circumference at the base, and, starting out at the rear, make more than a complete circle, the points projecting below and in front of the eyes. I have been told that head and horns will often weigh sixty pounds. He sheds his winter covering very late, whilst, after shedding, his coat is thick with short, greyish hair. By fall this has changed to a dun, almost the colour of the elk. The outer hair has become more than an inch long, rather wiry ; and in winter he puts on an additional jacket in the shape of a coating of exceedingly fine wool, which, though sometimes quite three inches long, never shows outside the other hair, but lies curled up close to the skin.

As with all animals whose habits are not positively known, there are many fables as to his mode of life ; among others, the habit, when pursued, of throwing himself down immense precipices and alighting unscathed on his huge horns. As he is a beast of heavy body, the first attempt at such a feat would most undoubtedly result in a broken neck. The truth is that his feet, though protected with the horny toes of other animals of this class, are soft, spongy cushions, almost erectile, and clinging almost with the tenacity of a fly to any projection, however slight, on which it may strike.

I have seen mountain sheep run up the face of a rock—
slightly inclined it is true, but apparently offering not the
slightest foothold for man or beast—for a distance of
nearly thirty feet. I have known them go down an
apparently sheer precipice, at least an equal distance, and
over which it would seem that only a rock squirrel might
pass unharmed. In these cases a careful examination has
shown me little crevices and narrow ledges furnishing
foothold sufficient for such a climber, and by springing
from one to the other of which he undoubtedly made the
descent.

Of their domestic habits scarcely anything is positively
known, though, from what I have seen of the animals, I
judge that in these they are very similar to sheep. The
lambs begin to be seen in June, generally stowed away
on some shelf of rock inaccessible to man or dangerous
animal.

The little fellow takes to climbing very naturally, and
soon follows its dam and the herd wherever they please
to journey.

What becomes of the mountain sheep when man
invades his stronghold it is impossible to say. Hundreds
may be in a locality. Man appears: a few, possibly ten,
are killed; the others disappear, and leave no sign.

From about the middle of August until the 1st of
November the flesh of the mountain sheep is the most
delicious *bonne bouche* that ever tickled the palate of
the gourmand. It is impossible to describe it; but if one
can imagine a saddle of most delicious 'Southdown,'
flavoured with the richest and most gamy juices of the
black-tail, he will form some idea of the treat in store for
him when he shall sit down to a feast of mountain sheep
in season and properly cooked. Except when 'in season,'
the mountain sheep is thin, tough, and the poorest food
that the plains furnish to man.

CHAPTER XV.

WOLVES, JACK RABBIT, ROCK RABBIT, AND PRAIRIE DOG.

(*Canis Lupus, Occidentalis.*)

THERE is scarcely a portion of the prairie that can be traversed by the hunter on which he will not see wolves. These are of two kinds—

The buffalo wolf, as tall as an ordinary greyhound, lean, gaunt, and hungry-looking; the prairie wolf (miscalled coyote on the middle and northern plains), about half-way in size between the fox and the buffalo wolf. The coyote proper I have never seen except in Texas and Mexico. It is a miserable little cur of an animal, scarcely larger than a fox.

All of these wolves are exceedingly cowardly, one alone not possessing courage enough to attack even a sheep. When in packs, and very hungry, they have been known to muster up resolution enough to attack an ox or cow, if the latter be entirely alone. Writers of all ages have linked the name of the wolf with hypocrisy, with famine, and with ferocity, until we have come to regard the animal as the incarnation of all that is mean, treacherous, bloodthirsty, and dangerous. What American boy but has felt the glow of enthusiasm or tremor of terror on reading the exploit of the heroic young Putnam? It is not a grateful office to divest the imagination of ideas imbibed from childish story-books; but truth compels me to assert that, of all the carnivorous animals of equal size and strength, he is the most harmless to beast and the least dangerous to man. He will not even attack when wounded; and, though he will snap at attacking dogs in self-defence, he never follows up the advantage which his sharp teeth and powerful jaws give him, but takes to flight the moment he can do so.

The wolf is marvellously acute in all his senses, so that it is only in places remote from hunters that a good shot can be had at him. He furnishes splendid sport when hunted with hounds, though he is so fleet and long-winded that no ordinary pack can overtake him. It is usual to have in each pack one or more greyhounds to overrun and bring him to bay, and thus enable the slower hounds to come up.

THE JACK RABBIT.

(*Lepus Americanus.*)

This animal is, I am told, almost identical with the English hare.

He is found in greater or less numbers in all the length and breadth of the plains. He is very easily bagged by the shot-gun sportsman. Though a fine large animal, he is, to my taste, very poor food, and I have therefore killed comparatively few of them.

To the hunter who owns a pack, he is an object of the greatest interest, and to an ardent follower of the hounds presents as perfect sport as can be had on the plains.

He runs with great ease and amazing swiftness, and will give even the very best pack of hounds all the work they want.

He usually runs very straight, only resorting to doubles when nearly tired out, or when pursued by greyhounds.

When the plains have become settled and civilised, and the large game killed off, he will furnish to the sportsman an unfailing source of pleasure, and I doubt not the time will come when coursing this animal will be as common here as coursing the hare in England.

ROCK RABBIT.

This is a pretty little animal, not so large as the eastern rabbit, living generally in clefts and holes in rocks. He is delicious eating and furnishes good sport. The hunter rarely finds him far from his hole, and must bag him with a quick shot as he scuttles away to that safe refuge.

PRAIRIE DOG.

This well-known animal is badly named, having no more of the dog about him than an ordinary grey squirrel. He is a species of marmot, and burrows in the ground as do wolves, foxes, racoons, skunks, and all the smaller animals on the treeless plains. He lives on grass and roots, and is exceedingly prolific, each female bringing forth several sets of young each year. He is not excellent eating; but the young are as good as the common squirrel, and, when other fresh meat is not to be had, they make no unwelcome addition to the bill of fare.

I regard the prairie dog as a machine designed by nature to convert grass into flesh, and thus furnish proper food to the carnivora of the plains, which would undoubtedly soon starve but for the presence in such numbers of this little animal. He is found in almost every section of the open prairie, though he prefers dry and arid to moist and rich localities. He requires no moisture and no variety of food. The scanty grass of the barest prairie appears to furnish all that is requisite for his comfortable existence. Though not in a strict sense gregarious, prairie dogs yet are fond of each other's company and dig their holes in close vicinity. Such a collection is called a town, and they sometimes extend over immense areas. The numbers of inhabitants are incalculable.

Cougars, panthers, wild cats, wolves, foxes, skunks, and rattlesnakes, all prey upon them without causing any perceptible diminution of their immense numbers.

CHAPTER XVI.

OTHER ANIMALS:

INCLUDING GRIZZLY, CINNAMON, AND BLACK BEARS—COUGAR, OR PUMA—PANTHER, AND WILD CAT.

IN the foregoing pages I have endeavoured to give the reader a correct idea of the nature and habits of such animals as the plains hunter will be sure to encounter if he goes to the right places. There are other animals which he may come across, but which no length of hunt or selection of locality can beforehand guarantee even a sight of; and, unless specially fitted out for their pursuit, his hunting for them will meet with no success, except by the merest accident.

This special fitting out consists in providing himself with a pack of first-rate dogs, trained to hunt the animals of which he is in search. If intending a long hunt, he should have dogs specially to hunt each kind of wild beast. These should be carried in waggons when not wanted for hunting, otherwise they will soon disable themselves in crossing the cactus-covered prairies. Of course this kind of hunting costs money. If he can afford the expense it is for the sportsman himself to decide whether he had better hunt, say for bear, for several reasons, without a dog, on the very slim chance of catching one on the open; or spend money in the purchase of one or more good bear-dogs, with the assurance of bagging his bear on the first hunt.

Of all animals to be hunted with dogs the most important in size, and formidable in character, is the

GRIZZLY BEAR.

(*Ursus ferox.*)

This is the largest of the carnivora of America. His home is in the mountains; but in the fall of the year he comes down to the plains for plums, berries, grapes, and other wild fruit, of which he is inordinately fond. These animals are scarce and shy, keeping as much as possible in thickets, whence, without dogs specially trained, it is impossible to dislodge them. If feeding in the open the slightest sound or suspicious circumstance will cause him to take to the nearest cover, where he will lie concealed though the hunter pass within a few feet of him. If too closely approached, he rises suddenly with ' hough, hough,' a hideous noise, half grunt, half roar, which causes the stoutest heart to stand still, and the bravest man promptly to find business in some other locality.

A grizzly will always run away if he can, and never attacks except when wounded, or when he thinks himself cornered. The female will occasionally attack in defence of her young, but more generally runs away and leaves it to its fate. When wounded a grizzly attacks with the utmost ferocity, regardless of the nature or number of his assailants; and then his great size and strength, his immense teeth and claws, his tenacity of life, and, above all, his determination to do injury, render him without doubt the most formidable and dangerous of wild beasts.

My personal knowledge of this animal is of the slightest. In many years of plains and mountain experience I have never encountered but one grizzly. He ran like a deer. I pursued on horseback; but, after an exciting chase, he escaped into a beaver dam thicket, from which it was impossible to dislodge him.

I have known several men to be killed by grizzlies; and one of the most complete wrecks of humanity I ever saw was a man whom a grizzly, in the last moments of his life, had gotten into his embrace. The man told me his story. He was huntsman for a party of miners in California. One day, when out alone, he ascended a steep and high mountain, and, just as he arrived at the top, met face to face a huge grizzly just starting down the trail by which the man went up. Neither could retreat without giving great advantage to the other. The bear raised himself on his hind legs, and, thus erect, approached the man, who, presenting his rifle and getting his knife ready, awaited the attack. The bear slowly advanced and took the muzzle of the rifle in his mouth. Depressing the butt of the piece so as to direct the ball through the bear's brain, the man fired. Before he had time to use his knife, or even to think, he found himself in the bear's clutches. ' It was all over in a second,' said he. ' I didn't feel pain, and I remember thinking I was about like a mouse in a cat's jaws, and what a fool I was to think I might hurt a grizzly with my knife, when everything went away, and I didn't know any more 'til I come to the next day in camp.'

His companions had found him and the grizzly apparently dead in a heap together. The bear was dead, shot through the brain. The man showed signs of life and was taken to camp, restoratives were applied, and his wounds examined and dressed. The bear in his last throes had apparently given but one rake with each of his terribly armed paws. One fore claw passed over the man's right shoulder, had hooked under the right shoulder-blade and torn it out entirely. The other fore claw had torn all the flesh from the right side. One hind claw had torn open the lower abdomen, letting out the bowels and badly scarifying the left leg, while the other hind claw had torn every particle of muscle from the right thigh from groin to knee. In spite of these terrible injuries, the man, after many months, recovered. When I saw him he was apparently in good health, but could not use or even move his right arm or either leg. He gave me

the particulars of his fight and described his wounds with
great animation and gusto, smoking his pipe the while,
and wound up with the remark, ' Anybody can fight bear
that wants to ; I've had enough grizzly in mine.' I thought
he had.

A year or two ago two soldiers from Fort Wingate
foolishly attacked a grizzly on foot. Both were terribly
torn, and I believe both died. Only a year ago a soldier
of the 3rd Cavalry died from injuries received from a
wounded bear, which he rashly followed into a thicket.

In 1870 a small party of citizens were going up the
Chaquaque cañon. The trail led along a bench high
above the bottom, in which were trees and thickets. The
piping of young turkeys was heard in the thicket, and
one of the citizens who carried a shot-gun proposed to
go down and kill some for supper. The party waited for
him. He had hardly disappeared in the thicket before
he reappeared in full flight, while close at his heels followed a huge she-grizzly with two cubs. In a few seconds
she overtook and struck him a powerful blow with her
fore paw, knocking him senseless. She then deliberately
smelt over the prostrate body, and, apparently satisfied
that he was dead, went slowly back to the thicket. The
party above had been unable to do anything. As soon
as the bear left they hastily consulted together, and some
of the boldest were about to go down when the body
sprang to its feet, and made the best possible time to the
top of the hill. An examination disclosed the fact that
the bear's claws had struck the man's body behind, just
below the waistband of his trousers ; and though every
particle of clothing, upper and under, had been torn from
that part of the person, the skin was not broken nor the
man injured beyond some slight bruises. He explained
that the blow, throwing him forward on his stomach, had
knocked the breath and consciousness out of him. When
he recovered his senses the bear was smelling at him, and,
knowing the consequence of moving, he laid still. I have

never heard a more striking instance of presence of mind and nerve.

The female grizzly bears from one to three cubs each year, producing them early in the spring. She has great maternal affection (though sometimes her fears get the better of it), and the young remain with her until they separate to go into winter quarters.

All bears are, I believe, omnivorous; yet it is difficult to understand how so huge an animal can become so enormously fat on the scanty supply of food to be found in the regions in which he prefers to live. He is an indefatigable worker, turning over the logs and stones for the larvæ of beetles and other insects, tearing open ant hills, and digging for roots, whilst he will travel long distances for acorns, plums, cherries, and other wild fruits.

THE CINNAMON BEAR

is the compeer of the grizzly in ferocity, in tenacity of life, and in everything but size, and the remarks on one apply equally well to the other.

THE BLACK BEAR.

(*Ursus Americanus.*)

This animal is well known, being found in almost all portions of North America suited to his taste. He is by no means a plains animal, but delights in mountains, rocks, thickets, and damp, cool jungles, scarcely trusting himself on the open prairie even to cross from one ravine to another. He is not large, his weight at the very best rarely exceeding 300 pounds. He is very shy and timid, avoiding sight and pursuit in every way; and, though when approached closely, he makes great bluster and show of fight, he is really not more dangerous to the hunter than would be a hog of the same size. It is difficult to find him without dogs, though in the berry season, many years ago, I bagged without a dog no less than five in one day, catching them in little patches of plum or hackberry bushes, dashing up on horseback and shooting them with a revolver as they ran. This, however, was in the valleys of the Guadalupe Mountains of Texas, where they were in greater plenty than I have ever seen elsewhere.

When hunted with dogs they give excellent sport, running fairly for some time, with much more speed than one would give them credit for, and then taking to a tree. Unless the country is exceedingly unfavourable, one is rarely started that is not brought to bay. The general habits and characteristics of all the bear family are nearly the same.

COUGAR, OR PUMA.

This animal, called variously the ' Mexican lion,' 'Californian lion,' and ' mountain lion,' is an habitual resident of many rough and broken parts of the plains. He is shy, spending his days in thick cover, and prowling like a huge cat at night. His senses are very acute, and it is exceedingly rare that one is seen ; and the hunter might easily be forgiven for disbelieving the existence of such an animal, were it not that the prints of his footsteps in the vicinity of camp show plainly when and where he has been prowling.

Except by the rarest accident the hunter cannot hope to bag him except by the aid of dogs. Although, when pressed by hunger in the winter, he will seize, carry off, and eat the most powerful mastiff, yet at other times he will fly from the baying of the tiniest cur. When pursued by a pack, he runs well for a little distance, but soon tires, and will then take to a tree, selecting one that leans well to one side, for he is not a good climber. Out of reach of the dogs he stands upright on a horizontal branch, and calmly surveys his vociferous and baffled pursuers. Should a man appear on the scene, he ceases to watch the dogs, and, dropping in a crouching position on the branch, prepares for a spring. Under such circumstances I would advise no one to approach within thirty or even forty feet. He is now, of course, easily bagged ; but no bungler with the rifle should be allowed to shoot at him, as, when wounded, he is a desperate and most formidable antagonist, dangerous to the hunter, and sure to kill some and lacerate others of the dogs. A bullet through the brain is the only perfect safety, and none should fire except the rifleman sure of his aim.

A pair generally live together, selecting for their home a cave or overhanging rock. In default of these a den is not unfrequently constructed in some dense thicket, leaves and bough being so piled together as not only to make a bed, but the sides and even the top are somewhat protected from the winds and weather. I once found such a den in a thicket on the bank of the Laramie River. Near it were lying the skeletons of a large elk, of a fine black-tailed deer, and of a huge buffalo wolf. The latter had evidently been attracted by the scent of the fresh meat, and, prowling near in the hope of a meal, had himself served as dinner for his more powerful and voracious conquerors.

The female gives birth to a pair of young, with which it is by no means safe to meddle, even when found alone. One or other of the parents is sure to be not far off, and a cry of the young one will bring on the intruder an encounter by no means agreeable.

PANTHER.

This is nearly the same animal on a smaller scale. The cougar is almost a lion. The panther is but a huge cat. It is much more plentiful than the cougar. It lies in the thickets by day, and prowls at night. It is equally difficult to bag without dogs, and even more easy with them. It is a good climber, and, when pursued by dogs, runs up the first tree, however straight, and lies like a squirrel close to the trunk, with its head in a crotch, watching the dogs. It takes no notice whatever of the approach of a man, who might even pull its tail, with no more effect than to make it go higher up the tree. It is not at all dangerous to man, never attacking him even when wounded, though a poor shot may cause sad havoc among the dogs.

One becomes accustomed, as he grows older, to having the illusions of his youth dispelled; but after having killed fifty or more panthers, under a variety of circumstances, without ever seeing one show fight, it is difficult to account for the respect, even the terror, with which eastern professional hunters surround the ' painter' as they call it. In listening to the soul-stirring recitals of the Adirondack hunters, of their 'deeds of high emprise' and 'hair-breadth 'scapes,' in encounters with the ' painter,' one would never suppose that the animal is really very harmless to the hunter, and bagged with less danger than any other of the larger carnivora.

In many years of panther hunting I have never known a person to be hurt by one ; and I have myself seen a Mexican boy lay hold of the tail of a panther which had taken refuge from dogs in a small mesquite tree, and hold on lustily, while his brother shot the animal through the head.

I was once on a most glorious hunt with a large party of officers, all of whom, save one other and myself, have gone to ' that bourne.' The dogs started a panther, which, taking refuge in a tree, was bunglingly shot by one of the party with a revolver. Springing from the tree the panther fled to a narrow-mouthed cave on the side of a steep hill, into which it was followed by five or six of the dogs. Among the party of hunters which soon collected around the mouth of the cave was a Mexican guide, called Policarpio, much liked and petted by the officers, by whom he was called Polly for short. Polly was devoted to the dogs, and came up with tears in his eyes, and many reproaches to the officer who fired the unlucky shot. We could hear the fight going on in the bowels of the earth. ' Some of the dogs 'ill be killed,' said Polly to the officer, ' and it 'ill be all your fault.' Still the fight went on, the growls of the combatants being interspersed with an occasional yell of pain as some dog got into the jaws of the enemy. Polly became more and more excited, yelling, swearing, and crying by turns or together. At last a piteous yelp was heard as from a dog in its last agony. ' He's a killin' Lucy, by ——,' screamed Polly, with a ferocious glare at the offending officer; and, throwing off his coat, he, without a word of notice, pushed himself into the hole, which at the entrance was barely large enough for him to crawl in on his belly. He disappeared all but the soles of his boots, but in an instant was seen to work himself backward. We seized his feet and helped him all we could, and in a moment or two got him out dragging a dog by the hind leg. Again and again he went in, each time bringing out a dog, until only the favourite bitch, Lucy, remained in the den. The cave widened out and became considerably larger inside than at the entrance; the fighting animals were constantly changing positions; there was not a particle of light when Polly was in the entrance, and he had to get hold of each dog by feeling, at the risk of a bite from panther or dog. It was too dangerous; and we tried to prevent his going in for the last dog, preferring to leave her to her fate, and had almost persuaded him when a most piteous wail from Lucy sent him in again. After what seemed an age of waiting, his feet were seen struggling towards the entrance. Seizing them, we dragged him out with some difficulty; but, though he held firmly by the leg of the dog, he could not get her out. Quick as thought he drew his pistol, and, placing it within the mouth of the cave, fired. The dog, released suddenly, was thrown down the hill, and a few moments afterwards we dragged out the dead panther. It had seized the bitch by the throat. Polly's keen eyes saw the situation, saved the dog, and settled the affair by a shot in the panther's brains.

I have been told that the panther is more prolific than the cougar, the female producing as many as four at a birth. I think it probable, as they are more plentiful than the cougar, but I am not able to state it as a fact.

WILD CAT.

This animal is widely diffused through almost all portions of the territory of the United States. On the plains, however, it attains a size unknown to its relations in the eastern States. I once killed one in the Rule Creek cañons south of the Arkansas, which, without the viscera, removed at the time of killing, weighed a week afterwards, when it had become thoroughly dry, fifty-four pounds. This is nearly three times larger than any I have ever seen in the mountains of North Carolina, where they are thought to attain their maximum proportions.

The wild cat is more common and more easily killed without dogs than any of the larger carnivora of the plains, yet it cannot be relied on for sport unless the hunter has one or more dogs especially educated for its pursuit. Of all the carnivora, it yields the best sport when hunted with dogs, running with great speed and endurance, taking refuge in a tree when tired, but on the approach of the hunter bounding off again, leading hunter and pack a merry race over rocks and through thickets for many a mile before yielding up his life. It is no more dangerous than a house cat except that it inflicts a severer wound.

It is the most destructive of plains animals, except, possibly, the skunk, feeding by day or night; now destroying a brood of young grouse or quail, now climbing a tree to a turkey roost, and carrying off the unsuspecting bird. It generally prefers bird diet; but, if this fails, it takes up its residence near a prairie dog town, and lives a comfortable and happy life, being able to pursue these animals into their holes, where it dines at pleasure.

The wild cat makes its den in a hole in the rocks, in a hollow tree, or in summer time contents itself with a deserted hawk's nest, or, if that becomes too warm, with a bed on the soft grass in some dark thicket.

The female produces from three to six kittens at a birth, and, unlike the house cat, only one litter a year. The male takes no part in the provision or care for the young.

Besides the before-mentioned animals, the hunter may find—and will find if he has dogs—foxes, badgers, and racoons, all of which give some sport. None of these animals run well, all taking to holes when closely pursued.

The true sportsman owes it to the brotherhood to do what he can to preserve the game birds of the country by destroying, whenever he has an opportunity, all the above-named animals, as well as skunks, opossums, hawks, and snakes.

CHAPTER XVII.

THE GAME BIRDS OF THE PLAINS, VIZ.:

THE 'COCK OF THE PLAINS'—DUSKY GROUSE—SHARP-TAILED GROUSE—RUFFED GROUSE—PINNATED GROUSE—WILD TURKEY—ROCK PARTRIDGE—QUAIL, AND OTHER BIRDS.

IT is not to the rifleman alone that the plains offer facilities for glorious sport. The lover of the shot-gun can find his opportunities. Almost everywhere at the proper season can small game be found in greater or less numbers. Among these, the first, not in size but in the sport they yield, is the grouse. There are on the plains or foot hills of the mountains no less than five varieties of the grouse:—

1. 'Cock of the Plains'—*Tetrao* (*centrocercus*) *urophasianus.*
2. Dusky Grouse—*Tetrao obscurus.*
3. Sharp-tailed Grouse — *Tetrao* (*centrocercus*) *Phasianellus.*
4. Ruff Grouse—*Tetrao umbellus.*
5. Pinnated Grouse.

I do not propose to enter into a detailed description of these birds. This can be obtained from any recent standard work on ornithology. I shall confine my remarks to such peculiarities of each as I think are not generally known.

' COCK OF THE PLAINS.'

Tetrao (centrocercus) urophasianus.

This noble bird has been doubly unfortunate in its name. Audubon, in giving it the above name, intended, doubtless, to signify his appreciation of the size and beauty of the bird. It was, however, a most unfortunate selection of title in that it did not catch the popular taste (which no sportsman can wonder at). Had he called it the 'grey cock,' or ' sage cock,' or even the ' plains cock,' his name would probably have been adopted; but the frontiersman is too economical of speech to adopt any such nomenclature as that bestowed, and the consequence is that the finest grouse in America is commonly, almost universally, known as the ' sage hen.'

As the Pacific Railroad has put these grouse within reach of sportsmen, I propose to do a favour to them by proposing a change of name. ' Sage grouse ' is most appropriate. While in no sense a mountain bird, this grouse is a lover of high altitudes, being, I think, never found below 3,000 feet above the sea level, and flourishing most abundantly on the very high mesas and slopes on the first plain, 8,000 or 10,000 feet above tide water, where he gains his greatest preponderance in size and beauty of plumage.

He varies very greatly in size in different localities, the best cocks of some sections being but three or four pound birds, while in other sections they will weigh eight, ten, or even more pounds.

The habits of this grouse are almost identical with those of the common barn-yard fowl. They go in packs at all seasons of the year. In the early spring, in April or May, depending on altitude, the hen makes her nest in the same way and in some such cover as the domestic hen would select, and steals away daily to deposit an egg.

When she has twelve or fifteen she commences sitting. The period of incubation is said to be twenty-one days. The chicks gain strength very rapidly, and, in a day or two from her first pip, the mother walks forth with her brood. Until the little ones are well able to take care of themselves she keeps them near thick cover, where they are comparatively secure from the attacks of hawks, but all join the pack while the young are yet small. I have seen packs numbering not less than several hundred birds, of all ages and sizes, from huge old cocks of apparently ten or twelve pounds, to chicks not larger than quails.

In spite of the identity of habits of this grouse with those of the barn-yard fowl, it appears to be impossible either to cross the two, or to domesticate the grouse. Several persons have told me of the utter failure of persistent and well-directed efforts. They have set the eggs under the common hen, but as soon as hatched the little ones desert their foster mother, and run into cover. If hatched and kept in a coop, they refuse food, wear themselves out in continued efforts to escape, and soon die.

There is a common prejudice against this grouse, on the ground that its flesh is said to taste strongly of the sage which is its principal food in winter. My experience is that this is simply imagination. I have never been able to discover such a taste, and I have eaten them at all seasons of the year. I must admit, however, that when I have shot them in winter I have so far yielded to the prejudice as to remove the crop at once. At all other seasons of the year they feed, as other birds do, on insects, principally grasshoppers, and I have frequently opened crops which were distended to the utmost with these plagues. To my taste, there is no bird (except the field plover) so perfectly delicious as the young sage grouse during the month of August. It is as juicy, tender, and delicate as a spring chicken, besides having the richest game flavour.

Early in the season this grouse affords most admirable sport. They lie well to the dog, and, if approached cautiously, get up very irregularly, sometimes almost one at a time. Once, although using a muzzle-loader, I had sixteen birds down before one was retrieved. The flight is short, and the pack scatter as they settle. Although apparently very strong and swift on the wing, a charge of No. 6 shot is amply sufficient to stop the flight, and the bird is so large, and flies so fairly, that the merest tyro finds it no difficult matter to make a bag.

In September and later the hunting is a different thing. The pack rises as one bird, the flight is long, and it settles together ready for another flight. It does not lie to the dog unless thoroughly tired, and, after settling, runs with great celerity. Besides all this, they have a way of disappearing entirely, baffling the dog, and exasperating the hunter. On many occasions I have seen a pack marked down by experienced hunters; yet on proceeding to the spot neither dog nor hunter was able to get one up again, or even to find a trace of them. At this season. therefore, the pursuit of the sage grouse requires much more labour and skill than in August. Yet, at any time in the hunting season, when found in sufficient abundance, it yields better sport and a greater return for the labour bestowed than any bird on the plains.

This grouse is very fastidious in his choice of abode, and must have everything to suit him. The sage bush may be regarded as his home. In it he shelters himself from storms and from the attacks of his enemies. Under it he sleeps in security and comfort. He must have convenient to him one or more grassy glades where he procures his supply of grasshoppers, and he must be within easy reach of the purest water.

Fort Fred Steele is a sort of centre of the very best hunting ground for this grouse that I know of. In 1868 I took a small party of gentlemen on a short excursion to the 'heads of the Muddy.' We remained but two days. Each morning, before 9 o'clock breakfast, we had killed an ordinary horse-bucket full of trout, and between breakfast and dinner bagged so many grouse that, although we mustered, including hunters and escort, some thirty persons, and all ate what they wanted, we yet carried into the post nearly 200 birds, of a weight of almost 1,000 pounds.

THE DUSKY GROUSE.

(*Tetrao obscurus.*)

This bird has a variety of names, being called in different parts of the country the 'blue grouse,' the 'black grouse,' and the 'mountain grouse.' He is found almost everywhere in the mountainous regions of the Great West, between an altitude of about 6,000 feet and the snow line. As many portions of the plains attain an elevation of from 6,000 to 10.000 feet, and are otherwise suited to his habits, he not unfrequently comes in the way of the plains hunter.

Though a fine large bird, second only to the sage grouse, and most delicious as food, he affords less sport to the hunter than any other of the grouse family. In his habits he differs entirely from other grouse. He is solitary, never being found in packs after the brood has been weaned by the mother bird. He frequents jungles and pine or quaking-asp thickets, will not lie to the dog, nor fly from the hunter. He is usually found on the ground, but when disturbed takes refuge on a branch of the nearest tree, and will sit still though the hunter approach within a few feet. He gives no opportunity for wing shooting, for, if driven from his perch, he seeks another a few feet off, or darts off among the thick branches of the pine in a rapid and tortuous flight sufficient to baffle the quickest aim.

While the brood is yet with the mother they are to be

found on the margins of thickets of shrubs and bushes that dot the surface of otherwise open grassy glades. When driven from these a few may be killed on the wing; but the larger number fly into the branches, whence they may be shot one after another. Though this pot-shooting is repugnant to the true sportsman, it keeps the larder well supplied with most delicious food, and when other game is scarce great numbers of these birds fall victims to this peculiar habit.

I have frequently known a bird to sit quietly on a branch while a bungler with a rifle fired half a dozen or more shots at him from a distance of only a few feet.

Of his domestic habits but little is known. I have never seen two fully-grown birds together at any season. The female makes her nest generally on some dry bank close to a stream, and where the ground is so steep that it is comparatively safe from the tread of heavy animals. She lays from ten to fifteen eggs, about the size of those of a guinea fowl. When hatched, the brood is taken to the nearest shrub-dotted glade, where it remains until weaned, when it separates, and each bird betakes himself to a solitary life among the pines.

SHARP-TAILED GROUSE.

Tetrao (centrocercus) Phasianellus.

This bird is commonly and erroneously called the ' willow grouse.' It is said to be a native of British America, and that it is gradually working its way south and east, as the pinnated grouse is pushing its way to the west. Whether this be true or not, certain it is that the bird is now much more plentiful on the plains than it was only a few years ago, and that it is now found in great abundance even as far east as the Missouri River, where less than ten years ago it was unknown.

It takes its name from the fact that the two middle

feathers of its tail project an inch or more beyond, and are somewhat stiffer than, the others, forming a sort of spike. It is also somewhat lighter in colour than its cousin, the pinnated grouse, though marked much in the same way.

In its habits and general characteristics it is almost identical with the more common bird, with the exceptions that it loves the thickets of willow and cotton-wood along the margins of streams, and that it is much more of a percher, frequently alighting in trees, especially in cold weather.

In spite of these peculiarities this grouse furnishes splendid sport, though its pursuit is attended with more labour than that of the pinnated grouse. Early in the season it lies to the dog almost too well, requires close hunting, and its flights are very short. Later on it be-comes more wild, often getting up beyond the reach of the hunter, and, flying to a great distance, alights in thick cover, from which it is dislodged with great difficulty. However, the hunter who has the assistance of a good dog may count on a fair proportion of every pack he en-counters.

This grouse is now found in greater or less numbers on all the streams in the west from the British line to the Canadian River, and from the Pacific Ocean to the Missouri River. It is a very great accession to the game of this vast region, to which the pinnated grouse has not yet penetrated, and adds much to the pleasure of the plains hunter.

It is very prolific, each hen bringing up yearly one or more fine broods of from fifteen to twenty young, which are so well cared for that comparatively few fail to reach maturity in spite of hawks and other enemies. She makes her nest on the ground, like the pinnated grouse, in the most secluded spot she can find. I think she must have the power of withholding her scent during the period of incubation, otherwise it would seem to be impossible for the eggs at least to escape the search of prowling wolves and foxes, or the more patient and penetrating skunk, all of which abound in the wild regions which she inhabits. Not unfrequently the nest is broken up; the hen seeks another locality and makes another and another nest, rarely failing of success in the end.

THE RUFF GROUSE.

(*Tetrao umbellus*)

This bird, so well known to eastern sportsmen, scarcely deserves a place in a list of plains game birds. A few may be found in the timber along the foot hills; a large number were killed by my command in the Black Hills, but it delights in timber, in thick cover, and is in no sense a plains bird. It exists in certain favourable localities on the plains, but cannot be relied on for sport by the plains hunter.

PINNATED GROUSE.

The appearance and habits of the pinnated grouse are almost as well known as those of domestic fowls. I have therefore but little to say of them, except to enter my protest against the name ' prairie chicken.'

Probably no name that could be adopted would take the place of the name by which the farmers and non-sportsmen of the west know this bird; but I confess that after working hard, and getting a fine bag of grouse, my gorge rises like Mr. Podsnap's when some one says, ' You have a fine lot of chickens.' This game is spreading west with advancing civilisation. This apparently curious problem is easily solved. It being a purely prairie bird, and going to cover only when forced to do so, it cannot protect its young from the attacks of hawks, and the broods are either entirely destroyed, or but few arrive at maturity. The settlers shoot the hawks for the protection of their domestic fowls, and the grouse, thus indirectly protected, increase with wonderful rapidity. It is found in great numbers far up the Arkansas.

There is nothing to warrant the belief that this grouse will cross with the sharp-tailed ; but they are not only found in the same localities, but I am assured by a keen and observing sportsman that he has bagged the two birds from the same pack at Omaha, Nebraska.

MIGRATORY BIRDS.

In spring and fall almost all kinds of migratory birds pay a visit of greater or less duration to the plains. I propose, however, to notice in detail only those birds which breed upon the plains. These may be divided into ' game birds,' or those which lie to the dog; and ' other birds ' which, though called ' game ' when killed, are not so in this sportsmanlike sense. Of ' game birds ' proper there are, besides the grouse, but three which are indigenous to the plains. These are the turkey, the rock partridge, and the quail.

THE WILD TURKEY.

Of all the game birds of the world the wild turkey is undoubtedly the finest, not in splendour of plumage, but in his magnificent proportions, and the sport he affords the hunter. In size the wild turkey is simply magnificent, the full-grown cock, when fat, not unfrequently weighing from twenty to twenty-five pounds.

His domestic habits are identical with those of the tame turkey. They go in large flocks, are polygamous, and the cocks are exceedingly pugnacious in the laying season. The hen makes her nest on the ground, and is

extremely ingenious in selecting its hiding place. She
leaves the flock daily to deposit an egg, until she has
twelve or fifteen. Then commences the work of incubation. As soon as the hen commences to sit, the cocks
cease their quarrels and collect together in amicable
companionship.

It is said that the cocks will kill the young; at any
rate, the hen keeps the brood away from them until the
young birds are nearly grown. In the fall all collect
together, sometimes in incredible numbers. I have seen
flocks which I am quite sure contained several hundred
birds.

They frequent the valleys of streams along which
is a fringe of heavy trees, on the branches of which they
roost at night. They are very choice in their selection
of a roosting place, preferring a dense mass of trees not
far from a bluff bank, from the top of which they can
easily pitch into the branches. The turkey flies strongly
and well, but his great weight makes it difficult for him
to rise from the ground; consequently, he takes the
wing very reluctantly. I have known a flock remain for
several hours on the bank of a stream fifty or sixty yards
wide, and which it wished to cross, running up and down
the bank, piping loudly, and making constant feints of
efforts. When one dares to fly over, all the others follow
rapidly and easily. Every one who has kept tame
turkeys must have noticed the dilatory and ridiculous
performances attendant on getting to roost each night.

Though each has roosted on the same branch for
months and knows exactly the best way to get to it, he
will go round and round the tree, noting each branch and
favourable alighting place with critical eye, and seemingly
intent on finding some new way to arrive at the old end.
Now he thinks he has found it, squats and almost stretches
out his wings, when he thinks better of it, and walks on to
do the same thing over and over again. The wild turkey
has the same peculiarity and makes as much ' to-do '

about getting to bed as a spoiled child. The wild turkey runs with great celerity, and, when much hunted, learns to put as much space as possible between himself and his pursuer in as short time and with as little noise as can be.

All his senses are exquisite, and in sense of smell he is scarcely excelled by the elk. When, therefore, this game is wild it requires no little skill to bag him without a dog specially trained. The hunter must work on foot against the wind, cautiously pushing his way without noise. If he is discovered either by hearing, sight, or smell, the turkeys silently disappear in the cover, and the hunter only knows of their vicinity by seeing their tracks. If, however, he succeeds in approaching, undiscovered, near enough for a shot, the explosion of the gun throws them into a panic, of which the knowing hunter will take the fullest advantage. Some will fly up and alight in the branches of the nearest trees; some will squat where they are in any little cover that promises protection; others, again, will fly to a distance, alight, and squat in the grass or bushes. The hunter marks these latter carefully, certain that they will not stir from their hiding places until they think all danger is over. Those in the trees first claim his attention, as they are likely to fly at any moment, and, having now seen him and realised the nature of the danger, will probably go a long distance. One or at most two shots is all he can hope for at these. The ground should then be carefully gone over to find any which may have squatted on the first alarm, and finally he proceeds to pick up those which have taken to cover, and from which he has the right to expect his best return. A flock of twenty or thirty birds under such circumstances ought to yield six or eight to a good hunter; early in the season, and with young birds, even more. When a flock is caught on the prairie and frightened, they will run to the nearest ravine, in the breaks of which many will squat, hiding so closely as almost to allow themselves to be stepped upon before taking wing.

In October 1873 I bagged twenty-two turkeys from one flock, shooting from my horse. I discovered the flock in a small ravine, fired into it and drove it out into a prairie on which there was but little cover. Galloping up to within good range of the closely running birds, I discharged both barrels. The turkeys flew up, but settled immediately and continued to run, crowding together as if for mutual protection. When nearly all had been killed, the remnant ran into some high grass and squatted. I kicked them up and bagged them like quail, getting all but two or three of the flock.

In Texas, many years ago, I used occasionally to kill them with a stick from horseback. A flock being discovered on the edge of an open prairie two or three miles across, a detour was made, and the horsemen, coming up from the wood, rushed with a yell at the birds, frightening them so badly that some would fly to the open prairie. The first flight was from 400 to 600 yards, depending on the weight and fatness of the bird. Alighting, he ran at full speed. At the end of his first flight he would probably be 200 or 300 yards ahead of the horseman, but this distance was soon lessened after he alighted. On the near approach of his pursuer, he would essay another flight, this time scarcely 100 or 200 yards. A third flight generally finished all wing business, and his further efforts at escape were confined to running and dodging. A stick four feet long and as large as one's finger was carried by the hunter, and, as the turkey turned to avoid the horse, a smart blow on the head finished its life and the race. Of course, such hunting is only possible on ground especially favourable. In this way I one day killed two, and a brother officer three, turkeys from one flock and in one race.

Some days after, another officer from the same post

went out riding with his wife. Coming on a flock of turkeys in a favourable position, he proposed they should catch one. After a beautiful and exciting chase, a fine large cock was run down so that he could scarcely move, and confined himself solely to avoiding the feet of the horses. The officer had no stick to kill with, and in his excitement, thinking he could easily catch a bird so exhausted, he sprang from his horse and took after the turkey on foot. He ran his best, but the bird ran just fast enough to avoid his clutch, and finally, when utterly blown and exhausted he gave up the chase, he turned to see his horse disappearing in the distance, and his wife on her horse in full pursuit of the runaway. He had to walk about eight miles to the post, and for some months after it was not quite safe to say 'turkey' to him.

A well-trained dog is almost invaluable in all hunting. He is less indispensable in turkey shooting than with other small game, although when the birds are scarce and wild he is of the greatest assistance.

The most effective dog for turkey shooting is one trained to rush into the flock, barking loudly and continuously. The birds fly into the trees and bushes, or into high grass, where they squat. Those in the trees watch the barking dog, paying no attention to the hunter, who can approach and shoot them at leisure. Those in the grass lie as close as quails, and furnish the most perfect shooting. In less than an hour one morning I bagged fourteen fine birds from a small patch of grass scarcely two acres in extent.

One of the most common and effective methods of killing turkeys is by shooting them upon their roosts at night. This is taking a rather unsportsmanlike advantage of the bird, but is good sport, and, as numbers can be more easily and certainly bagged by this method than any other, it is the best when numbers are required. It can only be used successfully when the leaves are off the trees. A clear starlight night is better for this

hunting than any one made brilliant by the moon, as
in this latter case the birds are much more apt to fly
away after a shot or two. The roosts are easily found
by day from the marks under the trees. Sometimes only
two or three birds will roost in one clump of trees; at
other times a roost of twenty or thirty birds may extend
in a thin line for half a mile along a stream; and, again,
a small wood favourably situated may be the roosting
place of hundreds of birds, forty or fifty being occasionally found on one tree. The hunter should approach
with caution. He will necessarily make some noise in
pushing through the thicket in the dark, but this will not
generally disturb the birds so as to cause them to fly.
There must be no talking; the sound of the human voice
will send the birds off more rapidly than the noise of a
dozen guns.

Arrived at a favourable spot under the trees, from
which he may shoot at several without changing position,
he selects the bird nearest the ground, takes careful aim,
and fires, keeping perfectly quiet after the shot. It is
desirable to kill dead each bird fired at, for if only
wounded it may flounder from branch to branch, making
a great disturbance, and frightening away many birds,
besides the chance of its flying off into the thicket and
being lost. If a bird high up in the tree be shot first, it
will, even though killed dead, probably frighten away all
the birds below it and near which it passes in its fall.
The hunter should use, therefore, a good charge of
powder and heavy shot, and always fire first at the
lowest bird within reach. If the hunter is careful, and
the turkeys have not previously been much shot at while
roosting, he may get as many as he wishes.

In 1872 I shot twelve from one tree, on the Cimarron
River. Many years ago a soldier in Texas bagged twenty-
six from one tree without changing his position. On one
occasion in Texas I had been sent out with a small party
of cavalry to procure game for the post at which I was

stationed.   One night we encamped near an immense
turkey roost.   Four or five of the men went into the
roost after dark, and, though armed only with the mus-
quetoon, a most miserable weapon, bagged eighty-two
birds in a couple of hours.   This was in earlier times,
before hunting had become a trade with so many persons.
At the present time there is scarcely a portion of the
country in which the turkeys have not had experience of
the danger of having white men near their roosts, and,
unless the birds be much scattered, there is, even in the
most unfrequented localities, little hope of getting more
than six or ten shots before all have taken to flight.   In
places where they are much shot at on the roost, they
become extremely shy and difficult to approach, flying
off to the hills at the first sound of the hunter in the
thicket.   Under these circumstances they become much
more difficult to kill by night than by day.

For some few years past a very considerable number
of wild turkeys have been sent from the plains to the
eastern markets alive.   These are caught in pens by a
process too old and well known to need description, and
taken in coops to the nearest railroad station.   By the
time these birds reach their destination they are, through
fright and starvation, the mere shadows of their former
selves.   I have, within the last few years, met several
gentlemen, whose highest ambition was to be thought
epicurean, whose verdict was unanimous that the western
wild turkey was unfit for human food.   They had evidently been dining upon some of these unfortunate
anatomical specimens.   If they will make a trip west
and try the bird in its natural condition, I think I can
guarantee an entire change of opinion.

Wherever civilisation has not exterminated them,
wild turkeys are to be found from the Atlantic to the
Rocky Mountains, and from the Gulf of Mexico to
about latitude 44° N.   They have even crossed the
southern range of the Rocky Mountains, some of the

largest and finest specimens I have ever seen being found
in North-Eastern Arizona.   It is a prolific bird, and
most Indian tribes are debarred by superstition from
eating it.   The consequence is, that, in spite of the unremitting attacks of white hunters, they are yet found in
almost incredible numbers on many portions of the plains.
Near the railroads and along the confines of advancing
civilisation they are comparatively scarce; but there are
still immense sections of country in which the hunter has
only himself to blame if these most delicious birds fail to
furnish at least a portion of his daily fare.

ROCK PARTRIDGE.

This bird is not described in any work on ornithology
I have yet seen.   It weighs about a pound, being two or
three times larger than the ' Bob White' of the Eastern
States, and forms an intermediate link between it and the
sharp-tailed grouse, which it resembles somewhat in
habits.   In shape and colour it is usually like the ' Bob
White;' but in the laying season the cock changes its
plumage almost entirely, and becomes the most beautiful
game bird of the country.   His back remains the same
sober brown; but the white and black lines about his
eyes increase in intensity of colour, his breast becomes a
dark red, while his legs down to the knee are jet black.

They go in coveys, like the quail, but in entirely
different ground.   They love the bare rocky sides of hills
or bare mountains, and take readily to the cover of cedar
thickets.   Their favourite resort, however, is the grassy
tops of limestone mesas through which the waters have
cut yawning chasms and cañons.

Disturbed from these, a flutter and a plunge places
500 or 1,000 feet of precipice between him and
his pursuer.   While scarcely grown, they lie well to
the dog, and very early in the season, when found in
fairly good ground, this bird affords splendid sport.

Later they lie very close until flushed once, then scatter and run in every direction, so that even with the best dog the hunter rarely gets more than two or three shots at a covey.

In North-Western Texas and South-Eastern New Mexico this bird is abundant; that is, three or four coveys may sometimes be found in a day's hunt. I have, however, never seen it except in the portion of country specified, and the plains hunter cannot rely on it for sport.

QUAIL.

The western quail, though sufficiently like its eastern cousin, 'Bob White,' to be constantly confounded with it even by observing sportsmen, is yet a different bird. The general appearance and characteristics of the two birds are the same; but the western is smaller, has less white, and the white is not so pure. He does not lie so well to the dog, and is more fond of brush and thickets. His flight is swifter and more erratic, and to bag him requires harder work and better shooting.

Transport him to the rich grain fields of the east, remove from him the constant apprehension of the attacks of hawks, skunks, and foxes, and he might in a few generations become the same bird. The richer food would probably increase his bulk, the comparative safety induce him to live in the open fields rather than in thickets, and thus getting more sun he might lighten in colour.

This quail is found in immense numbers on nearly all the streams which water the plains from the Arkansas River to the Gulf of Mexico, and the wilder and more unsettled country the more decidedly does he differ from the 'Bob White.'

Except when found in or driven into grass he will, in the wild countries, scarcely lie to a dog at all. He delights in thickets of wild plum, rose, or sunflower, and can be driven from these only with the greatest difficulty, running from side to side, and, when forced to fly, hopping up with a whirr to dart down again, sometimes within a few feet of where he got up. The hunting is hard work, and the hunter gets only snap shots. It is rare shooting either for practice or to the hunter who wishes to test his skill. It is no sport for a beginner.

If, however, this bird can be forced from his favourite cover and takes refuge in grass, he yields the same sport as the eastern bird, although under the most favourable circumstances even the very best shot will be surprised at the number of misses he makes. As food he is as delicate and delicious as the eastern bird. So far as I have been able to discover, his domestic habits are identical with those of 'Bob White.' The birds pair, take turns in sitting on the nest, and together care for the young brood. The male has the same call, though not so distinct or loud, and in spring may be seen sitting on a log or stump of a tree repeating his monotonous note.

OTHER BIRDS.

Other birds than the birds already mentioned, there is, to my knowledge, but one single bird which makes its home the year round on the plains. This is a pretty little bird with a light brown back, lighter belly, and a black and white ring round its neck. In some sections of the plains it is called the 'skylark,' from the habit of the male poising himself in the air over its nest and mate on the ground, and twittering his little song. In other sections it is called the 'snow bird' from its being present in great numbers when the whole wide waste is covered with snow, and all other birds have sought a warmer climate. It collects in immense flocks in the fall and winter, and, being very fat, is equally tempting to the palate as the 'rice bird.'

There are a very considerable number of birds which

come to the plains in the early spring, rear broods, and return in the fall to a more congenial clime.

Of these the 'Brandt goose' is the largest. They prefer the more northerly of the plains streams, never breeding, so far as I know, south of about latitude 42° N.

Beaver dams are seldom found on streams which are subject to high water, and are always in muddy places, the beaver not 'founding his home upon a rock.' The black water saturates the adjacent soil, making all approach exceedingly difficult, except to webbed feet, and giving rise to dense thickets of willow and other water-loving bushes.

Along streams thus secure from freshets and prowling animals the Brandt makes a nest of small sticks, grass, leaves, and feathers, on some secluded point only a few inches above the water. On streams liable to spring rises and otherwise unprotected, she builds a huge structure of sticks, some of them apparently too large for her to carry, in some convenient fork of a tree, twenty, thirty, or even more feet above the ground, and not unfrequently a hundred feet from the water. This outwardly rough affair is nicely lined with leaves, grass, and feathers, making a superb bed for the eggs.

The North Platte River was in 1868 a favourite resort of these birds, and in the vicinity of what is now Fort Fred Steele there were numbers of such nests, some of them high up in the lofty cotton-woods quite forty feet above the ground. I one day found a nest in the hollow upper end of a huge cotton-wood, the top of which had been broken off by the wind. It was just such a cavity (only larger) as would have been selected by a wood duck. There were eight eggs. I broke one to test their freshness, but the little goose was already formed. The eggs are not quite so large as those of the domestic goose, but when fresh are more delicate and of a richer flavour. They are eagerly sought after as a most welcome and delicious addition to the ordinary breakfast fare of the plains.

The young grow very rapidly; but it is some months, and they are almost if not quite fully grown, before their wings can lift their heavy bodies from the ground. For a month or more the young are covered with a yellowish down. From the time they commence feathering they are delicious food, and their hunting is good sport, though there is, of course, no wing shooting.

The mallard duck also breeds in great numbers on the beaver-dammed or sedgy streams of the plains, as far south as the Arkansas. Its habits are those of the common puddle duck, except that they pair.

The teal also pairs, but prefers to make its nest in the bottom lands adjoining such swift-running streams as the Arkansas or Platte. The young of both these birds are fine eating, and in August and early September, being then unable to fly, are easily bagged.

In the early spring, soon after the 1st of May, the plains are enlivened with immense flocks of curlew. These soon break up into pairs, and, scattering over the high, dry prairie, commence making preparations for 'raising' a family. The nest is a most crude affair, a mere circular depression of an inch or two hollowed in the ground. It is scarcely lined, a few feathers and a very scanty supply of grass alone keeping the eggs from the soil. Scarce an effort at concealment is made, the bird evidently relying for its safety upon its sober, un-attractive light brown, hardly distinguishable from the brown earth and grass.

When the female is sitting, a person may pass within a few feet without disturbing her. She has the habit, common to many birds, of pretending to be wounded when disturbed, and I have several times been startled to see a large bird fluttering and tumbling along the ground from almost under my feet. She lays from eight to ten eggs. They are about the size of those of a guinea fowl, but more nearly oval in shape. The young brood leaves the nest in a day or two, and follows the mother bird.

They are most comical little fellows, with their long legs
and bills, and their disproportionately small bodies, covered
with soft, yellowish down. They are wonderful adepts
at hiding; and a brood suddenly come upon, when on an
apparently bare prairie, will disappear as if they went
into the ground. Only the sharpest eyes may, after careful search, be able to discover one or two. The young,
when newly fledged, give tolerably good sport to the
hunter. They will not lie to the dog, nor do I think
they possess any game scent; at this time, however, their
flights are short, and they do not run, but walk deliberately off after alighting, giving the sportsman opportunity
again to get within shot. Many persons esteem the curlew
very highly as food. To my taste he is a poor bird—dry,
and without flavour.

With, or soon after, the curlew come myriads of field
plover which, pairing and scattering in a somewhat similar
manner, occupy in incredible numbers the highest and
driest slopes of the third plain. I have said that they
pair. I am led to the belief by frequently seeing them
by twos in the nesting season, but I am by no means
positive of the fact. They come in flocks, and remain in
flocks throughout their stay on the plains. Some specially
favourable locality will be the nesting place of numbers;
and in that vicinity numbers may always be found together, not in coveys like quail, or flocks like ducks, but
scattered, each independently seeking his food in his own
way, but keeping within call of his neighbours. If they
pair the females go off alone during the process of incubation, while the males remain together. I have never
seen two old birds with the young, and therefore conclude
that the female has its sole charge and responsibility.

The nest is made like that of the curlew. But two
eggs are laid, and the young follow the mother soon after
hatching. I have seen them running after her while yet
scarcely dry. Their appearance is most curious. A little
ball of soft white down, not larger than a pigeon's egg,

mounted on a pair of long stilts of legs, causing the
beholder to wonder how they could possibly have been
disposed inside of an egg-shell, much too short for either
joint to have been developed when straight. The period
of incubation is very short, and they arrive at maturity
with wonderful rapidity, so that early in July the young
birds are ready for the sportsman. At this time they
furnish excellent sport, and are to my taste the most
delicious bird that ever tickled the palate of a gourmand.
In July and August all, old and young, are mere lumps
of fat of most exquisite flavour, far surpassing canvas-
back, reed bird, or the most delicate tit-bit of any bird
that flies or swims.

Some few years ago I went on a short exploring expedition, accompanied by an officer very appreciative of
all the good things of life. It was in August, and our
table was daily loaded with most delicious birds—young
turkeys, ducks, goose, quail, and plover. The officer was
devoted to quail; and when I urged him to try plover,
extolling its superior excellence, he invariably replied,
'No, I thank you; quail is good enough for me.' One
day it happened that we had no quail, and he concluded
to try plover, which he had never yet tasted. Pulling
off the little lump of fat which served the bird as a leg,
he placed it in his mouth. In a moment he looked at
me earnestly and rather reproachfully, and said, with
emotion, 'I wish some one would kick me.' 'Why?' I
asked. 'Because,' he replied, in despondent tones, 'I
have for a week past been eating quail, when I might
have had plover every day.'

The plover is not, properly speaking, a game bird,
though it has the game scent. It does not lie to the dog,
nor squat, nor attempt to hide. It runs well, and, when
approached too nearly, takes to flight. Immediately on
alighting it has a pretty and graceful manner of
stretching its wings upward and together until they
almost touch, before settling them in their places.

In August it is difficult to bag on the wing, as it will not permit a footman to come within shot. It, however, seems to have no fear of a horseman or a vehicle, and is easily bagged on the ground, the sportsman riding or driving as near as he pleases. About the middle of August they leave the high lands and collect in immense numbers in the low lands of the streams, more or less constantly flying back and forth, and the sportsman can have splendid wing shooting. By the end of August all, or nearly all, have disappeared as silently and mysteriously as they came.

On almost every part of the plains where running streams are bordered by grassy meads, the Bobolink may be found in early spring—the same light-hearted, merry creature that he is in the east. He spends this portion of his life in tumbling in short eccentric flights through the air, pouring forth almost incessantly his ecstatic song. They arrive in immense flocks, but pair very soon after, and under a cover of a thick bush or bunch of grass they make on the ground a round, well-built, softly-lined nest, in which they rear four little ones, feeding them in the nest until fully fledged. When the young are grown, the birds collect in flocks almost innumerable, and many may be bagged by a single charge of No. 10 shot. Though very fat and excellent, they are not, I think, quite so delicate in flavour as later in the season when, after migration, they have become reed or rice birds. When they arrive in spring the male has already donned his brilliant coat. By the time he is ready to leave before the 1st of September he has exchanged this for the sober dark brown, almost black, and the sexes are indistinguishable.

Beside the birds above mentioned, the prairie furnishes nesting places for a great variety of smaller birds, songsters and others, which, however, furnish neither good sport to the hunter nor fine food for the table.

About the middle of September the great Arctic

breeding places begin to pour upon the plains migrating millions of water fowl of every variety, from the uncouth pelican to the smallest of sand pipers, geese of several kinds, ducks in wonderful variety, plover in half a dozen varieties, snipe, &c. Some of these stop for longer or shorter periods on every stream, and it is not until the ' icy hand ' of winter has closed the water-courses that all disappear.

These add immensely to the pleasure of the sports-man, and make the months of September and October the choicest of all periods of the year to the plains hunter.

CHAPTER XVIII.

FISH AND FISHING.

Ask an old frontiersman about fish and fishing, and the chances are a hundred to one that he will answer, ' Oh, there are no fish in the plains streams.' If you want fish you must go to the ' Big Horn,' or Bear Lake, or the Timpanogos, or the Middle Park, or some other mountain locality of which he has specially pleasing reminiscences.

This is easily accounted for. After a man has taken his one, two, and even five and six pound trout ' as fast as he could throw his hook in,' the ordinary plains fishing is tame even to monotony. Nevertheless, there is scarcely a stream on the plains which will not furnish fair sport to one not so enamoured of ' game' fish as to disdain any that will not rise to a ' fly.'

Many of the streams which take their rise in the gorges of the great first plain are filled with trout near their heads. These disappear as soon as the streams fairly reach the second plain, their place being filled by other and more common fish.

The Purgatory, a tributary of the Arkansas, and the Muddy, a tributary of the Green River, are notable examples of this.

There are said to be trout in some of the streams which take their rise in the second plain, as the Bijou and some of the tributaries of the Republican. This is not well authenticated, and I doubt it. It is a most curious fact, well known to plainsmen, that there is not a trout in any tributary of the North Platte River, while every tributary of the South Platte in the mountains furnishes an abundance of this noble fish.

The head waters of the Cache-le-Pondre and Laramie are in many places but a few yards apart, rising on different slopes of the same mountain. One set of tributaries is full of trout; the other set has not one. The same peculiarity occurs in many places—for example, in the rim of mountains which separates the North and Middle Parks, and the range separating the waters of the Papo-agie and the North Platte. North, south, and west it is the same : no single tributary of the thousands that finally find their way to the North Platte has trout.

From the facts that the head waters of these tributaries are so pure, and that they rise in the same strata and under precisely the same circumstances as the trout streams, it was for a long time supposed that there was something injurious in the main stream of the North Platte preventing the trout from passing up.

A gentleman much interested in these matters determined to test this. The small stream on which Fort Sanders is situated is extremely pure and clear—a model trout stream, but containing no trout. In 1868 this gentleman sent east for eggs, and went to some trouble and expense in arranging a proper hatching box in the very head spring of the brook. The eggs were hatched, and the young trout, apparently perfectly healthy, were, when large enough, turned into the brook to take care of themselves. I am informed (in 1875) by an officer stationed at Fort Sanders that not a single one of those trout has ever been seen or heard of since.

However pure the head waters of streams, their impurity lower down has a most decided effect in keeping trout from those heads. Thus the waters of the Black Hills of Dakota are pure, cool, and delicious enough to satisfy the most fastidious trout, yet there is not one in all this splendid mass of mountains. Nor is there a trout to be found in any stream, however pure, whose waters lower down pass through the great tertiary beds called the 'Bad Lands.'

The 'speckled' or brook trout of the west, though not the same fish, is very like his brother of the Eastern States—so like, indeed, that many sportsmen insist that they are identical. The western fish grows to much greater size; the spots are not so brilliant; and the back and sides, just in front of the tail, are covered with small, short, black marks, or 'hatchings,' as if made with the point of a pen. It takes the fly well, but not so greedily as the eastern fish. The reason is, that they are from early spring gorged with food in the myriads of young grasshoppers which fall into the stream before getting their wings. I have seen the whole bottom of a small stream literally covered with grasshoppers for miles. Later in the season this supply becomes less plentiful, and the fish bite better. On an August morning, before breakfast, I once took from some beaver dams on the 'heads of the Muddy' 116 trout from four ounces to half a pound in weight. I used three 'flies,' and several times took three fish at a single cast.

The best months for trout fishing on the first plain, or in the Rocky Mountains, are August and September, though good sport can be had in July and October. In every section of country the 'gamest' fish found is almost invariably trout. Thus, in some portions of the Southern States the 'trout' is a black perch. In Texas and in the Indian territory, as far north as the Canadian, the 'trout' is a magnificent bass, very like the striped sea bass in appearance. His usual maximum weight is from three to six pounds; although I have taken a ten-pounder from the Medina River of Texas, and have seen a glorious fellow which weighed thirteen pounds taken from the Guadalupe River.

They are very game, and the smaller take a gaudy 'fly' readily. The 'big fellows' can only be seduced by

live bait. In the Rio Azul of Western New Mexico, and
in many other pure streams where the real fish does not
exist, the 'trout' is a dace. In size from a mere minnow
to half a pound, he is very 'game,' taking the fly as
greedily and well as any trout.

In almost all the plains streams is found a fish of the
herring family, and most generally called the 'white fish.'
It has large, coarse, white scales, is very thin and flat for
its length and depth, is quite bony, and not very delicate
food. It is, however, exceedingly voracious, seizes any
kind of bait with tremendous vigour, and makes a most
interesting fight, especially as, his mouth being bony and
easily torn, he must be handled delicately. His maximum
weight is about three pounds.

In Walnut Creek, a tributary of the Arkansas, I have
taken a fish which I have never seen elsewhere. I call it
the 'white bass.' It is almost the exact counterpart of
the black bass in size, shape, and manner of biting, but
it is pure white and has large staring eyes.

In the purer streams of the plains is found a beautiful
species of cat fish, called in some parts the 'lady' cat,
and in others the 'channel' cat. Its maximum weight
is about three pounds. The spines on the pectoral fins
are unusually developed and inflict a most painful wound.
The body is long and tapering, covered at irregular
intervals with small black spots, like trout; its head is
narrow, and mouth very small for a cat fish; it has few
bones, and is most delicate and delicious food. The best
bait is a small piece of the white fish before mentioned.
Unlike other cats, it is very dilatory in its biting, nibbling a
long time before taking a good hold. It is very strong and
active, and, when hooked, makes almost as good a fight as
a bass or trout of equal weight. It is the trout of cat fish.

The blue cat is also common in all the plains streams,
attaining sometimes a weight of fifteen to twenty-five
pounds. These large fish are coarse, but the smaller are
fine eating. No special skill is required for taking them,

as they swallow the bait and make off at once. A large hook and a strong line are indispensable, however, as they pull like oxen.

In the deep, sluggish streams of the lower third plain is found the great mud cat of the Mississippi. They attain an enormous size, and to my thinking are unfit for food, being very coarse and tasting of mud. At Fort Larned, in 1871, several were taken in a seine by some of the soldiers. One of these weighed fifty-four pounds, and an ordinary striped-head fresh-water turtle, eight inches long, was found in his maw.

Streams whose beds contain no running water, but in which there are large and deep permanent pools, even ponds, and lakelets which have no apparent outlet, are frequently crowded with fish. These are usually sun fish or perch, cat fish, suckers, and chub.

It is his own fault if the plains traveller does not have good sport and all the ' brain food ' he requires from the plains streams.

PART III.

INDIANS.

SONG OF THE WILD BUSHMAN.

'Let the proud white man boast his flocks
  And fields of food-full grain,
My home is 'mid the mountain rocks,
  The Desert my domain.'

THOMAS PRINGLE.

CHAPTER XIX.

IT is doubtful if there be a people on earth concerning whom there is so wide a difference of opinion as the North American Indians.

Eastern people, educated, by reading Cooper's and other similar novels, to a romantic admiration for the 'red man;' misled by the travellers' tales of enthusiastic missionaries, or the more interested statements of agents and professional humanitarians ; and indulging in a philanthropy, safe because distant, and sincere because ignorant, are ready to believe all impossible good, and nothing bad, of the 'noble savage.'

The western frontier people who come in contact with him, who suffer from his depredations, and whose life is made a nightmare by his vicinity, have no words to express their detestation of his duplicity, cruelty, and barbarism. No amount of reason, no statement of facts, will ever change the opinion of either eastern or western people on this subject.

In the east, Christian charity and sentimental humanitarianism form good 'paying leads,' which the professional philanthropist will not fail to work to his own best advantage by statements of 'facts' and an array of statistics satisfactory to the most sceptical ; while the western man, who has lost his horses, had his house burned, or his wife violated and murdered, finds a whole life of hatred and revenge too little to devote to his side of the question.

The conception of Indian character is almost impossible to a man who has passed the greater portion of his life surrounded by the influences of a cultivated, refined, and moral society. As well undertake to give to a pure and innocent maiden a realising sense of the depths of degradation to which some of her sex have fallen. The truth is simply too shocking, and the revolted mind takes refuge in disbelief as the less painful horn of the dilemma.

As a first step towards an understanding of his character, we must get at his standpoint of morality. As a child, he is not brought up. Like Topsy, ' he growed.' From the dawn of intelligence his own will is his law. There is no right and no wrong to him. No softening stories of good little boys are poured into his attentive ears at a mother's knee. No dread of punishment restrains him from any act that boyish fun or fury may prompt. No lessons, inculcating the beauty and sure reward of goodness, or the hideousness and certain punishment of vice, are ever wasted on him.

The men by whom he is surrounded, and to whom he looks as models for his future life, are great and renowned just in proportion to their ferocity, to the scalps they have taken, or the thefts they have committed. His earliest boyish memory is probably a dance of rejoicing over the scalps of strangers, all of whom he is taught to regard as enemies. The lessons of his mother awaken only a desire to take his place as soon as possible in fight and foray. The instruction of his father is only such as is calculated to fit him best to act a prominent part in the chase, in theft, and in murder.

Imagine a white boy growing up with such surroundings. The most humane of Christian gentlemen will exclaim, ' There is a fit subject for the penitentiary or the gallows ; ' and yet that same Christian gentleman believes the Indian boy to grow up and develope into the ' noble red man,' endowed with all the virtues.

BOYHOOD.

At twelve or thirteen the boy begins to be a man, and yearns for some opportunity of signalising his courage or his craft. Banded together, the youths of from twelve to sixteen years roam over the country (restricted only as will hereafter appear), and some of the most daring and desperate attacks have been made by these children, in pursuit of Indian fame.

These excursions teach the boy all that is necessary to his savage life. Privation teaches endurance. When he has food, he eats to repletion; when none, he hunts for it. If he has clothing, he wears it; if not, he is happy and contented in breech-clout and paint.

He is patient, for time is nothing to him; never homesick, because all places are equally his home. His eye becomes keen for every mark on earth, or tree, or blade of grass; and he puts in practice all he has heard from the elders around the camp fires, as to how to conceal his trail, or hide his camp, or of the best method of approach to, or attack upon, an unsuspecting enemy. Virtue, morality, generosity, honour, are words not only absolutely without significance to him, but are not accurately translatable into the Indian language of the plains.

THE ORDEAL.

From each of these excursions return, with crest erect, and backbone stiffened, one, two, or more youngsters, whose airs and style proclaim that each has made his *coup*, and is henceforth candidate for the distinction of warrior.

The chiefs and warriors assemble in general council, and with the utmost gravity listen to the claims of the candidates. Each in turn, frenzied with excitement, with bounds and yells, and frantic gestures, pours forth in almost incoherent language a recital of the deeds on which he bases his claim.

When conflicting claims are made by the candidates, their companions on the excursion are called on for their statements; and when all the testimony is in, the candidates, their friends, and spectators are turned out of the council, which then proceeds to deliberate. After a lapse of time the names of the happy few deemed worthy of initiation as warriors are formally and loudly announced from the door of the council lodge.

The initiation is a religious as well as a military ceremony, and varies with the different tribes, the ordeal, as a rule, being more trying as the tribe is more warlike.

The process here described is that of the Southern Cheyennes, a tribe numbering less than 3,000 souls, but powerful in the skill and daring of its warriors.

When it has been formally announced by the general council that a youth has earned his right of initiation as a warrior, he is taken by his father (or, in case of the father's death, by his nearest relative), himself a warrior, to some spot outside the Indian camp. After some religious ceremonies have been first transacted the youth is stripped to the skin. A broad-bladed knife is then passed through the pectoral muscles, so as to make two vertical incisions, about two inches from each other, and each about three inches long, in each breast. The portion of the muscle between these incisions is then lifted from the bone, and the ends of horse-hair ropes, about three-fourths of an inch in diameter, passed through the opening and tied in a knot. A stout post, of some twenty feet in height, has already been set in the ground, and to the top of this are tied the other ends of the ropes.

Having fastened the ropes so as to give the boy a play of ten or twelve feet from the post, the father takes leave of him, and he is left to fight his battle of endurance, of pain, and terrible suffering. Here he remains alone without food, water, or sympathy; denied even

the poor consolation of showing to others how bravely
he can bear his sufferings, until his own vigorous efforts,
or the softening of the tissues through partial mortification, enable him to tear out the incised muscles and
escape from his bondage. Having freed himself, he
makes his way to his family lodge, where he is carefully
examined, and, if it is found that he has fairly torn the
muscle, his wounds are washed, and dressed with herbs,
rudely, but with so much skill that they are in a few
weeks entirely healed. Singular as it may appear, an
instance of fatal result, even in the hottest weather, is
almost unknown.

Sometimes the incisions are made in the muscles of
the shoulder-blade or of the back. In this case the
ropes are attached to some movable object. Two
American gentlemen, visiting a Cheyenne camp in the
fall of 1873, came one day upon a poor boy of not
more than fourteen years, dragging after him, by long
ropes, three buffalo skulls; one from a cut on each
shoulder-blade, and the other from an incision beside
the back-bone. It is terrible to see these poor boys
tugging and pulling, with whoops and yells, at their iron
flesh; but each understands that it is best for him to
tear loose as soon as possible; best, not only physically as
a quicker ending of his torture, but also best in a religious point of view. It is 'good medicine' to tear
loose at once—bad medicine to be several days about it.

Let it not be supposed that the father's affection
stays the knife, even one line, to spare his boy from
suffering. His religion would deter him from any, even
the slightest, modification or lessening of the pains of the
ordeal, even if his pride in his son's endurance were not
stronger than his sympathy as a parent.

Few white men have witnessed this ordeal; and even
the Indian, who comes by accident upon a boy in the
throes of his agony, is required by religion and etiquette
to 'pass on the other side.'

Should the candidate cry out, or even flinch, under the knife, the ceremony is over, and he is taken back to the lodge to be brought up with the women, and made to perform woman's drudgery and menial offices.

He cannot marry, or hold property, and is held in extreme contempt by the warriors. Though generally treated with indignity by the women, one occasionally manages to make himself a favourite with the sex, not a little to the discomfort of the warrior husbands, who cannot, however, demean themselves by showing jealousy of such a party.

Should the courage or endurance of the candidate fail him after being tied, he can at any time untie himself, or, in case the incisions are in the back, can go to the camp and ask to be untied. In each case the result is the same as that given. He can never be a warrior of the tribe. It speaks highly for the endurance of the Southern Cheyennes, when it is stated on good authority that there are not over six of these men-squaws in the whole tribe.

From the initiatory ordeal the candidate steps at once into manhood, with all its rights and duties, privileges and immunities. He is no longer under the control of his father, holds property if he can beg or steal it; can marry if he has the wherewith to pay for his wife; and his associates are the warriors of the tribe.[1]

---

[1] It is proper to state that *this* initiatory ordeal is not a condition of manhood, except among the Cheyenne tribe. These Indians have as far as possible kept themselves from the demoralising influence of whisky sellers, and are probably, at this moment, more nearly aboriginal than any tribe in the territory of the United States. They have kept nearly clear of intermarriages with the whites, and from contact with other tribes and Mexicans.

These sketches nearly all relate to the Cheyennes. Where the habits and customs of other tribes are noted, it will be so specially stated.

THE WARRIOR.

Behold him now a warrior!

And here let us stop a moment to take an inventory of his peculiarities and capabilities.

He is enduring, self-reliant, patient, and cunning—a magnificent rider, a fair shot with bow, pistol, or rifle, and a thorough plainsman.

His eye is prompt in detecting either the slightest mark on the ground, or object at the farthest verge of the horizon. A lazy loafer about his camp one day, he is a swooping demon the next—an abject beggar, or daring thief, as circumstances warrant. Lying is to him one of the fine arts, and his tongue is active to ' conceal his thoughts.'

Licentious without generosity, treacherous in all his acts and dealings, most cold-blooded, and full of invention in the refinements of his cruelty, he is a most dangerous and terrible animal, and would be tenfold more so did he possess courage, as the white man understands the term. Bravery he undoubtedly possesses. He makes rattling dashes, in which whoops, and yells, and shaking of buffalo robes are expected to do almost as much as his shots (and woe betide the unfortunate enemy who trusts his safety to flight). He springs to his arms from soundest sleep at the first symptom of alarm, and is ready to fight or fly, as may seem best to him. He fights to the death when cornered; but it is as the wolf fights, who neither gives nor expects mercy.

His fighting is either the excitement of the charge or the desperation of despair ; and, giving him every credit for physical prowess and personal bravery, there is yet in every Indian a total lack of that courage which prompts men to fight from a sense of duty.

His charge is magnificent when sure that his numbers,

or the completeness of the surprise of his enemy, give him an easy success ; but two or three cool whites, seated on the ground and remaining quiet and ready, will, by simply bringing to their shoulders the deadly rifle, change the most headlong charge of a dozen Indians to a retreat.

For this there are two reasons : first, the Indian's lack of discipline, and that shoulder-to-shoulder courage which comes of discipline ; and, secondly, he is taught to risk life as seldom as possible, and that, in all his exploits, craft is better than courage.

The grandest of exploits and the noblest of virtues to the Indian are comprehended in the English words—theft, pillage, rapine, and murder. He can expect no honour from man, or love from woman, until he has taken a scalp, or at least stolen a horse ; and he who crawls upon a sleeping enemy, and kills him before he can awaken, is a better warrior and entitled to more praise than he who kills his enemy in fair fight.

The securing of a scalp is an affair for tribal rejoicing. A scalp dance, council meetings, general commotion, and unlimited adulation, lift the happy taker to the seventh heaven of gratified vanity. To this end, a scalp is a scalp. The tender cuticle which covered the skull of an infant, and the ' long, fair hair' of a helpless woman, are as eagerly taken and as dearly prized as the grizzled scalp lock of the veteran of a hundred fights.

CHAPTER XX.

NOTHING is more difficult to understand than the government of an Indian tribe, and for the good reason that it is a very curious compound of despotism, oligarchy, and democracy.

The office of chief or ruler of each tribe was originally hereditary. This has been greatly modified of late years, the United States Government having in some instances deposed refractory chiefs, and substituted in their place others supposed to be more manageable.

Their own very peculiar and eccentric ideas on the subject of government have also a material bearing on the virtual deposition or advancement of a chief. The head chief is supposed to be the principal man of the tribe. Whether he is so or not is a matter of accident or good management.

Each tribe is more or less divided into bands, each under the control of a sub-chief (generally an ambitious, aspiring man, envious of the head chief, and jealous of the other sub-chiefs), whose great anxiety is to make himself popular, and get as many lodges as possible under his command. Each sub-chief, as a rule, keeps his band as much as possible away from other bands. This is done in order to ensure its safer and more perfect control, and is desirable on account of the greater facility for procuring food.

So long as the head of a lodge is under his actual control, the sub-chief has unlimited power over him and his, extending even to life and death. An abortive attempt to change his allegiance to another sub-chief may involve him in the most disastrous consequences. But, should the deserter succeed in reaching the other band, he is not only absolved from blame, but may meet his former chief and master without ill consequences and on good terms.

In 1867 the Cheyennes were at war with the United States. A portion of the Brulé band of Sioux were very desirous of joining and assisting them in spite of the orders and influence of Spotted Tail, then, as now, chief of the Brulé band. One morning it was discovered that twenty or more lodges of the malcontents had decamped during the night. Assembling his guards Spotted Tail pursued the fugitives, overtook and captured them. Every deserting warrior and many of their women were soundly beaten, the horses killed, the arms broken or confiscated; all the lodges, provisions, robes, property, and finery of all kinds ruthlessly destroyed, and the miserable band driven back to camp, beggars, and powerless for good or evil. While under Indian ruling, this was a perfectly just and proper thing to do; the deserters themselves would have been right and free from blame or danger had they succeeded in reaching the Cheyenne camp.

This is an exceptional instance; and the severity of punishment was justified by the facts that the intended desertion was to a different tribe, and that the action of the deserters was likely to compromise the whole Brulé band, and possibly involve it in a war with the United States.

The change of allegiance from one sub-chief to another of the same tribe is a common occurrence, and little notice is taken of it; but the rule seems to be that, while the sub-chief's word is law to his band, any member of that band may change his allegiance at will, at his own risk, while making the change.

A prominent part of tribal government is the council,

PEACE OR WAR?—INDIAN COUNCIL.

but what the functions of this council are, what its duties
or powers, and how far these latter are concurrent with
those of the chief, are questions about which I could
never get a satisfactory answer from even the most
intelligent Indian. It is certain, however, that it is regarded by the Indians themselves as a most important
feature in their governmental affairs.

A council lodge is provided for every band, and the
council is summoned to meet on any and every occasion.
There seem to be no regular members of the council.
On the contrary, it seems to be composed of any and all
warriors who may choose to assemble or call. The chiefs
and prominent warriors do, however, most of the talking,
the younger warriors keeping in the background.

The conclusion is not arrived at by vote, but by
acclamation; hence eloquence, or the power of swaying
by words the opinions or passions of hearers, is an important lever in Indian governments.

It may not be out of place here to remark upon the
peculiar and unnatural style of speech-making which
obtains whenever whites and Indians meet in council,
and in which there is always much twaddle about the
Great Spirit, Great Father, &c. It is not a natural way
of speaking for white men, and, from careful inquiry, I
am convinced that it is equally foreign to the Indian.
It is not fairly accounted for by the paucity of words in
Indian languages, and must have originated with our
'Pilgrim,' 'Pennsylvania,' and other 'Fathers,' in whom
a strong desire to convert the savage was constantly
struggling with a painful lack of knowledge of his language,
which would, of course, force them to recur over and
over again to the same set of words. This peculiarity
being accepted by the Indian as the white man's manner
of speaking, he (being an imitative animal) adopted it;
and so we go on, year after year, making and listening to
speeches which are as absurd to the Indians as to ourselves.

Whatever the power or influence of chief and council,

there is another power to which both have to yield on all matters which it assumes the right of deciding. The first two may be said to represent the brains of the tribe or band; the latter represents its stomach. As brains are only occasionally called into requisition, while the demands of the stomach are incessant, the tribe is habitually under the control of this 'third estate.' This power is composed of all the hunters of the tribe, who form a sort of guild, from the decisions of which, in its own peculiar province, there is no appeal. Among the Cheyennes these men are called 'dog-soldiers.' The younger and more active chiefs are always enrolled among these 'dog-soldiers,' but do not necessarily command. The 'soldiers' themselves command by *viva voce* determination on general matters, the details being left to the most renowned and sagacious hunters selected by them. Among these 'dog-soldiers' are many boys who have not yet passed the initiatory ordeal as warriors.

In short, this 'guild' comprises the whole working force of the band. It is the power which protects and supplies the women and children. A war party is under the command of the chief. The home, or main camp, with its women and children, horses, lodges, and property of every kind is under the control and protection of the 'dog-soldiers.' From them emanate all orders for marches. By them the encampments are selected. They supply the guards for the camp, designate the hunting parties and the ground they are to work over, and, when buffalo are sought, they select the keen-eyed hunters who are to go in advance and make all the arrangements for the surround.

One of the most important functions of the 'dog-soldiers' is the protection of the game. Except when laying in the supply of meat for winter, only sufficient buffalo is killed for the current supply of the camp. Great care is taken not to alarm the herds, which will feed for days in the vicinity of an Indian camp of a thousand souls, while a camp of half a dozen white men would have driven them all away in a day. Only designated parties or individuals are permitted to shoot at herds, or even at solitary buffalo ; and an Indian not so designated will take as much precaution to avoid a herd as, under other circumstances, he would take to approach it. The boy parties spoken of heretofore are never permitted in any way to molest herds within one, two, or more days' march from the main camp.

Punishment is not often resorted to, but, when decided upon, is prompt and severe. Crimes against the body politic, or violations of the orders of the chief, are punished severely ; sometimes by death, at other times by beating and destruction of property. In these cases the chief acts ; but he must have at least the tacit consent of the council, and the active assistance of the 'dog-soldiers.' Nearly all crimes against individuals are compounded by the payment of damages, the amount of which is assessed generally by the chief, assisted in important cases by two or more prominent men. A violation of the ' dog-soldiers' ' rules is at once met by a sound beating.

I cannot say exactly how the powers and duties of these three governmental forms blend and concur, or where they become antagonistic, and I have never met an Indian or white man who could satisfactorily explain them. The result, however, is fairly good, and seems well suited to the character, necessities, and peculiarities of the life of the plains Indian.

When Texas was annexed to the United States the Comanches, by far the most powerful Texan tribe of Indians, were governed by *San-ta-na*, a chief distinguished above all others by his eloquence and wisdom in council, and his daring, skill, and success in the field. His word was law, and such his popularity with his tribe that sub-chiefs and warriors vied with each other in anticipating his wishes. When the United States troops were sent to occupy and defend Texas it was found that scarcely a

place in all the length and breadth of this immense new
State was safe from the incursions of this tribe of daring
warriors. Whites were killed and scalped on the very
outskirts of San Antonio, then the most populous town in
the State ; and a very considerable village, New Braunfels,
was sacked, the men massacred, and the women and
children carried into captivity.

The scanty force of regular troops, though well-nigh
ubiquitous (as it is always expected to be), failed
necessarily to protect so immense an extent of
territory from the inroads of the most dashing and
venturesome of all Indian raiders. At this juncture a
successful effort was made to bring San-ta-na into council
with the whites. He was loaded with presents, and
induced to make a visit to Washington city. The effect
of such a journey on this utterly 'untutored savage' may
be imagined. The immense distances traversed, through
country entirely occupied by white men, the numbers of
people, the great cities, the quantities of arms and warlike
appliances of all kinds, convinced him of the utter futility
and certainly disastrous consequences of further warfare
with the whites.

On his return to his tribe he explained, as far as he
was able, what he had seen, and attempted to impress on
his people the necessity of keeping the peace. They at
once attributed his change of mind to bribery, and his
account of his journeyings and the wonders of the white
man's country were set down as fabulous tales 'got up'
for a purpose. He was looked upon with suspicion, as a
traitor to the interests of his people, and regarded as a
remorseless and criminal liar. His influence declined, his
people fell away from him, and ambitious sub-chiefs
seized the opportunity of increasing their own power and
influence. A few years and this once-powerful leader,
heart-broken, deserted by all except two faithful wives,
paid the last debt to nature. In a little cañon, near the
Bandera Pass, was, twenty years ago, a small mound of

stones. It marked the final resting place of the greatest Indian warrior of his time. Such was the fate of an hereditary chief who dared to go against the prejudices of his tribe.

The history of Red Cloud, the head chief of the Ogallalla Sioux now living, almost reverses the picture. Not an hereditary chief, he owes his prominence to his persistent hostility to the whites. The United States Government determined to open a road to Montana by way of Powder River. It must necessarily pass through a favourite hunting ground of the Sioux. Treaties were made with prominent hereditary chiefs of the Sioux bands, by whom the right of way was granted. So great was the dissatisfaction among the Indians that Red Cloud saw his opportunity and denounced the treaties and their makers ; he declared war to the knife against every white man who came over that road, or ventured into that country. Clouds of warriors, the ambitious and the disaffected of all the tribes and bands of that country, flocked to his standard. The hereditary chiefs found themselves deserted and powerless, and in some instances were only too glad to preserve their control over their bands by acknowledging Red Cloud as master. A long and tedious war ensued, in which Red Cloud made a great reputation, and constantly received accessions to his power, at the expense of the hereditary chiefs.

Avoiding any general or even serious engagement, he so harassed all trains and expeditions that the few troops then in his country could scarcely be said to hold even the ground they actually stood upon. Several forts were established, but they protected only what was inside the palisades. A load of wood for fuel could not be cut outside without a conflict. This at last culminated in the terrible massacre of Fort Phil Kearney, in which half the garrison (gallantly, though unwisely, meeting the enemy outside) perished to a man. Instead of sending more troops, and promptly and terribly punishing the Indians, a 'humane' commission was appointed to treat with them. The garrisons were withdrawn, the road abandoned, and in their own opinions the Indians are unconquerable, and Red Cloud the greatest warrior in the world.

Spotted Tail, another Sioux chief (already mentioned), also rose from the ranks. When a boy of nineteen or twenty years, he incurred the implacable enmity of a sub-chief, already noted for his daring and ferocity, by aspiring to a girl on whom the chief had set his eye. One day, meeting accidentally a short distance from the camp, the chief peremptorily demanded of Spotted Tail a renunciation of the girl under penalty of instant death. Drawing his knife, Spotted Tail defied him to do his worst. A long and bloody conflict ensued. Some hours after a straggler from camp found the two bodies locked in a death grip, and each gaping with innumerable wounds. The chief was dead. Spotted Tail recovered, to step at once into prominence ; and when, a few years after, the hereditary chief died, he was almost unanimously selected as principal chief, in spite of the most determined opposition of the sub-chief, who by regular succession should have obtained the position. Spotted Tail has proved an able and judicious ruler, and has well justified the choice of his tribe. One instance of what may be termed a political execution, and I have done with the subject of Indian government.

Big Mouth, another chief of the Brulé Sioux, was the peer of Spotted Tail in most manly and warlike qualities. In the constant complications arising of late years from the more direct contact of Indian and white, Big Mouth steadily gained in power and influence. A few years ago Spotted Tail made a visit to Washington, New York, and other eastern cities, and was much fêted. On his return, with changed views and 'new-fangled' notions as to the policy of the Indians, Big Mouth eagerly seized the opportunity of increasing his power

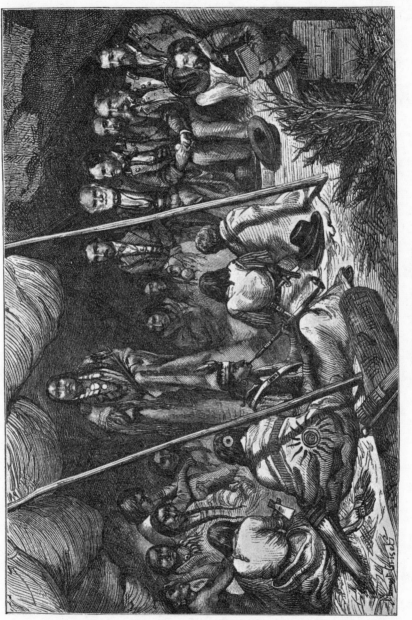

THE PEACE COMMISSION AT WORK.

Indian Council on Medicine Lodge Creek in October, 1867.—Treaties made by General Sherman, Harney, Terry and Augur, with Kiowa, Comanche, Arrapahoe, and Cheyenne Indians.

by disparaging the honesty and good sense of his superior in position.   Finding matters inclined to go against him, Spotted Tail one day called at the door of Big Mouth's lodge and asked to speak with him.   On Big Mouth's appearance, he was seized by two warriors, who held him fast, while Spotted Tail drew a pistol, placed it against his body, and shot him dead.

Nothing was ever said or done about the murder, and, as may be well supposed, there has not since been much political 'log rolling' or 'wire pulling' in that Indian tribe.

CHAPTER XXI.

RELIGION.

No Christian, Moslem, or Bhudhist is more devoted to his religion, no High Churchman a greater stickler for form, than the Cheyenne Indian. His religion is mingled and interwoven with every phase of his life ; and no project of any kind, governmental, social or individual, is ever undertaken without first obtaining the sense or disposition of the deities on the subject.

In common with the best of the plains Indians, the Cheyenne believes in two gods, equals in wisdom and power.

One is the ' *good god*,' aiding the Indian, to the best of his ability, in all his undertakings, whether good or bad, and (without reference to abstract right or morality, of which the Indian has no conception) always and under all circumstances his friend and assistant. From him comes all the pleasurable things of life : warmth, food, joy, success alike in the chase, love, and war.

The other is the '*bad god*,' always his enemy, and injuring him at all times and places, when not restrained by the power of the good god. From the bad god comes all pain, suffering, and disaster. He brings the cold, he drives away the game, and through his power the Indian is tortured with wounds or writhes in death.

Constant conflict, of which the Indian is the subject, is going on between the two gods, with constantly varying results. Having no inward sense of right or wrong, and no idea of any moral accountability, either present or future, the Indian attributes to the direct action of one great power all the good, and to the other great power all the bad, that may happen to him. For his devoted and unremitting services on behalf of the Indian the good god demands nothing in return—no adulation, no prayers, not even thanks. He is the Indian's friend, as the bad god is his enemy, for some inscrutable reason of his own, which the Indian does not undertake to divine.

While the Indian believes in another life after death, the power of the two gods does not extend to it, but is restricted entirely to benefits or injuries in this world; and his status after death does not in any way depend either on his own conduct while living, or on the will of either of the two gods.

It must be understood that the Indian can do no wrong; in other words, he has no moral sense whatever. Murder and theft are his means of livelihood. Greed, incontinence, and other traits, which we call vices, are as natural to him as to any other animal, and under no greater restraint than brute instinct or fear. He may be punished corporally for a crime against his chief or tribe. He may have to pay ponies for stabbing another Indian, or for taking away his wife; but all crimes and peccadilloes bring, or do not bring, their punishment in this life. Whatever his character, whatever the actual deeds done in the flesh, the Indian, when dead, goes at once to the Happy Hunting Grounds, unless debarred by accident.

There are two ways by which the Indian soul can be kept out of the Happy Hunting Grounds. The first by scalping the head of the dead body. No scalped Indian can ever inherit their kingdom of heaven. Hence the eagerness of each tribe to scalp all their enemies, and the care they take to prevent being themselves scalped. This superstition is the occasion for the display of the very best traits of Indian character. Most reckless charges are made, and desperate chances taken, by warriors to carry off unscalped the body of a chief or of a

dear friend.   Instances have occurred where many
Indians were killed in vain efforts to recover the bodies
of slain warriors.   An Indian Homer might find an
Indian hero as worthy of immortal fame as Achilles for
his efforts to save the body of his friend; and no Christian missionary ever evinced a more noble indifference to
danger than the savage displays in his efforts to save (as
he thinks) his friend's soul.   Let the scalp be torn off, and
the body becomes mere carrion, not even worthy of a burial.

The other method by which an Indian is cut off from
his heaven is by hanging.   The Indian believes that the
soul escapes from the body by the mouth, which at the
moment of dissolution opens by itself to allow a free
passage.   Should death ensue by hanging or strangulation, the soul can never escape, but must always remain
with the body, even after complete decay.   This death
has, therefore, more terrors than any other to an Indian,
and he will rather submit to a thousand deaths at the
stake, with all the tortures that ingenuity can devise, than
die by hanging.

There is no hell or purgatory for the Indian.   The
souls of all the dead reach the same place, except those
annihilated by scalping, or those condemned to live for
all time and eternity with the putrid or decomposed
bodies which die by strangulation.   Believing that no
line of conduct of his own can avail him for good or
evil, feeling his helplessness and entire dependence, or
the relative powers of the two great beings who fight
continually for or against him, the Indian's first and most
important concern is to find some sure means of discovering which of the gods has the ascendency for him at
any particular time.   This is by divination.

The word 'medicine' is of universal application
among the Indians.   Everything supposed lucky, or
healthful, or indicative in any way of the presence or
pleasure of the good god, is a 'good medicine.'   Everything the reverse, 'bad medicine.'

Being, like all primitive people, extremely superstitious, there is scarcely anything that does not partake of one or the other character. The flight of a bird through the air, the course of a snake in the grass, the yelping of a fox, all sights and sounds of every-day life, have to the Indian a spiritual significance and meaning. But for a more intimate knowledge of the immediate future he depends on a process of ' making medicine,' thoroughly known only to the Indians themselves.

Different coloured earths or sands, ashes of certain plants, or of particular bones of birds, animals or reptiles, and other ingredients, which are kept sacredly secret, are mixed together in a shallow dish or other receptacle, and gently stirred with a stick (as one might compound a dressing for a salad). From the combination of colours, or some other peculiarity developed during this process, the Indian believes that he can infallibly divine which god is to him in the ascendant at that time. Should the ' medicine ' be ' good,' a small quantity is put in little pouches of dressed deer skin, and tied in the hair of the warrior, and around the necks of the women and children. What is left over is carefully burned on the lodge fire. Should the process develope ' bad medicine,' the mixture is taken outside of the camp, and is carefully buried, no one touching it.

No Indian will undertake a hunt or trivial journey of a few days without first ' making medicine.' If 'good,' he goes off happy and contented; if ' bad,' he remains at home. In summer, when the Indian life is active, scarcely a week passes that ' medicine' is not made in every lodge.[1] This may be called private devotion; Each band occasionally ' makes medicine ' in common, and at least once a year the whole tribe is assembled, and spends even weeks in a ceremony as interesting, and sometimes as tragic, as can be well conceived.

[1] Many of the old trappers of the plains have firm faith in their power of ' making medicine,' and in their religion are as good Indians as any.

While each warrior head of a lodge is the priest for himself and family, there is in each tribe a 'medicine chief,' who may be called the bishop of the diocese. He is usually a man of strongly marked character, with brains, *savoir faire*, and knowledge of men sufficient to enable him to sustain his rather difficult *rôle*. He is necessarily the head of a band, though his spiritual duties in no way debar him from temporal command, or even from service in the field. As a rule, however, he is content with the ease and dignity of his position, and relies upon his influence with the head chief for prompt punishment of any contempt or violation of his orders by any individual of the tribe.

The Indian, not being a worker, has no need of a Sabbath day. No regular time is set apart for the ordinary duties of religion. The priest is not, therefore, expected to perform any ceremonies; and his duties seem to consist principally in taking care of himself and family in all distributions of game killed, in maintaining his precedence and superior sanctity by a studied non-intercourse with the commons of the tribe, and by an occasional visit to a sick man, for which he is paid if the patient recovers. To his priestly office he unites the professional duties of physician and surgeon. These require no special knowledge of the healing art; for as all disease is only the presence of the bad god, if 'he' can be exorcised by the spiritual power of the priest the patient will get well at once. This exorcism is supposed to be accomplished by incantation—the performance of mysterious ceremonies to the music of most doleful wails and lugubrious howls, sufficient, one might suppose, to drive out the most obstinate of devils.

Almost all Indians have some knowledge of simples and of the treatment of wounds, so that the medicine chief is only called in in extreme cases.

In winter, when cold and snow proclaim the presence of the bad god, the Indian, his camp snugly ensconced

in some sheltered nook, is content to doze or gamble
away the hours and days, satisfied to escape hunger. But
when the good god smiles in genial warmth and bursting buds, when the green grass shoots up, and the half-
starved ponies begin to fatten, the Indian blood warms,
and he begins to plan expeditions of foray for scalps and
horses. Now is the opportunity of the medicine chief.
Selecting some eligible situation, he sends runners to the
various bands, directing them to meet at that point at a
specified time to ' make medicine.'

This is not always a pleasant summons; and, when
there is no imminent or serious question of war, the
bands oftentimes prove refractory, sometimes escaping to
such a distance as to defy pursuit. A vigorous medicine
chief, backed by the power of a strong head chief, will,
however, as a rule, bring all in time to the appointed
rendezvous.

In 1872 a band of the Cheyenne tribe positively
refused to obey the summons. Some days after, the band
was suddenly pounced upon by an overwhelming force of
dog-soldiers. The new comers made no attack on or
remonstrance with the refractory warriors; but, having
made the proper military dispositions against armed
resistance, a number of warriors were detached, who, going
to the lodges, ordered the squaws to pack up at once. If
this order was not obeyed with proper alacrity, the squaw
was most soundly beaten with a rod quite as thick as her
thumb. From begging and crying the squaws soon fell
to working, and in a very little while the lodges were
struck, and women, children, and household goods
marched away, escorted by the whole force of soldiers.
Of course the lovers, husbands, and fathers could do
nothing but sullenly follow.

CHAPTER XXII.

ALL being collected at the rendezvous, preparations are at once commenced for the 'medicine dance.' The squaws are set to work patching the old, or making a new, medicine lodge—a huge structure of dressed skins, capable of holding some hundreds of people. All is bustle and excitement; for not only does the policy for the year depend upon the result of this dance, but somebody is likely to die during its performance, and the selection of dancers is not yet announced.

The medicine lodge is completed. A joss, or image, rudely cut from a plant or split log, with the profile of a man, one side painted white, the other black, is suspended from the centre and near the top of the lodge. A circular space of some twenty feet in diameter is roped off for the dancers. A concentric space of a few feet is for the guard; all the outer portion of the lodge is for the spectators.

In accordance with his right and duty the 'medicine chief' now announces his selection of the warriors who are to make the dance. The number varies; but is, on an average, one for every hundred persons in the bands represented.

The head chief also announces his selection of the guard, whose duty it is to see that the dancers are in no way interfered with, and that they perform their duty in accordance with the instructions of the medicine chief.

CELEBRATING VICTORY.—THE SCALP DANCE.

The number of guards is about equal to that of the dancers. The announcement of the names of dancers and guards, and of the hour when the dance is to commence, is made in a loud voice from the door of the medicine lodge. Each and all named are warned that disgrace and death will be the portion of any warrior who fails to appear at the time appointed.

A few moments before the specified time, the guard, fully armed and under its appointed captain, files into the lodge and takes its place just outside the ropes of the inner circle. At the appointed instant the dancers are escorted by the medicine chief to the inner circle. Each is stripped to the breech clout (sometimes entirely naked), and holds in his mouth a small whistle of wood or bone, in the lower end of which is fastened a single tail feather of the medicine bird.[1]

The medicine chief arranges the dancers in a circle facing to the centre, whilst he himself, having got out of the way, gives the signal to commence. At once every dancer fixes his eye on the suspended image, blows shrilly and continuously on his whistle, and begins the monotonous and graceless Indian dance, the whole line of dancers moving slowly round the circle. Some of the young ones, carried away by religious enthusiasm, bound vigorously into the air; but the older and more experienced expend only a bare sufficiency of force, for this is a dance of endurance. The will of the gods is to be known by the effect of the dance on the dancers, and, until the high priest shall announce himself satisfied, the dancers must continue their weary round, without sleep, food, drink, or obedience to any call of nature.

For the first eight or ten hours the dance is uninter-

---

[1] The Road Runner, or Chapparal Cock. This bird is believed by all the plains Indians to be wonderfully ' good medicine.' The skin, or even some feathers, are as efficacious in keeping evil from the lodge as was the horse-shoe to our ancestors. The poor bird pays dearly for this favourable opinion. It is incessantly hunted by the Indians, and is now exceedingly rare on the plains north of Texas.

esting enough ; but by that time fatigue, the slow rotary
motion, the constant keeping the eyes on one spot, and the
expenditure of breath in unceasing whistling, begin to tell.
By this time every foot of space inside the lodge is crowded
with eager and intensely interested spectators. Relatives
and friends watch every movement of the dancers, rouse
up the flagging by yells and shouts, by words of encouragement or terms of endearment. The lodge is a fright-
ful babel of sounds, which culminate in shrieks and a
rush of women, as some dancer totters, reels, and falls to
the ground. The rush is sternly met, and the body
dragged by the guard out of the dancers' into the guards'
circle. There it is laid on its back, and the high priest
proceeds to paint symbols and hieroglyphics on the face
and person with 'medicine paint' of varied colours. If
consciousness is not restored by this treatment, the body
is taken into the open air and buckets of water thrown
over it. This, as a rule, soon revives the inanimate form,
at sight of which the women set up yells of delight, and
surround the priest with prayers and entreaties that this
dancer may be spared further effort.

Throughout all the ceremony the word of the medicine chief is law, which no power may question. He may
now order the revived dancer back to the circle, to dance
until he again falls, or he may excuse him. Influenced
by the women, or by the promise of one, two, or half a
dozen ponies (according to the wealth of the dancer), the
priest generally accedes to the request, and the overcome
dancer is carried off to his lodge by his women, to be
petted and condoled with until fully recovered. In the
meantime the dance goes on. One by one the dancers
fall, to be revived by the same process, and excused by the
same persuasion, or sternly ordered back to their work.
As the death of a dancer is indicative of 'bad medicine,'
this forcing one back after falling is only done in rare
and important cases, or when the priest has an object
to gain.

If the dance progresses to the end of the appropriate time (from one to three days, or until all the dancers have fallen at least once) without a resulting death, the priest proclaims 'good medicine.' The dance ceases, the dancers are fêted and caressed, the medicine lodge is taken down. Happiness and congratulation are expressed in every face. The chiefs and warriors, assured of the power and pro tection of the good god, meet in council to decide upon the programme for the year, which, after ' good medicine,' is always war.

But it may happen that one or more bodies are brought from the dance which neither paint nor water will revive. There is no need to announce ' bad medicine,' for no sooner is death assured than the whole camp becomes a pandemonium. The howls of the men mingle with the shrieks and wails of the women. The dance is broken up. Horses are killed for the use of the dead in the Happy Hunting Grounds. Their widows inflict ghastly wounds on their arms and breasts. The whole camp is a turmoil of consternation and mourning. As soon as the last rites for the dead are completed, the bands separate, and each in its own way seeks to escape or avert the wrath of the bad god.

The power of endurance developed during these dances is simply wonderful. I am assured by persons who claim to know that it is not unusual for some of the warriors to continue the dance for three days and nights without a moment's intermission or particle of nourishment. No warrior is ever required to make the medicine dance the second time.

The last few years, which have been so full of troubles in the Christian world, have not spared the religion of the Indian. More frequent intercourse with the whites has lessened the power of superstitious belief, and in many of the plains tribes the medicine dance is getting into disrepute. The Cheyennes and Kiowas, however, either from their stronger natures or from less contact with the whites, abide by their ancient faith, and each year celebrate the medicine dance in all its original rigour.

A chief of the Arrapahoe Indians once gave me his reasons for not believing in the medicine dance. A medicine chief of the Arrapahoes was an ambitious man, and aspired to the temporal command of the tribe. However much the views of the other chiefs on the temporal affairs of the tribe differed from his, it was always found that the result of the medicine dance was in accordance with and furtherance of his wishes.

If he wanted war, the strongest warriors available were selected to make the dance, and they were, besides, allowed indulgences, intermissions, and resting spells. The result was, of course, ' good medicine.' If he wanted peace, some weak warriors were selected for the dance, which was, moreover, conducted with such rigour that even the strongest failed. He was rich, because he always selected a number either themselves rich, or the sons of rich men, who were made to pay roundly for being let off after falling. In other words, he used his priestly office in a way to advance his temporal interests, and if the ' good ' or ' bad ' god allowed him to do this without punishment, the medicine dance was no test of the power or wishes of either.

However different it may be among intelligent, educated people, it is very certain that priestcraft is a trade among the ignorant savages.

CHAPTER XXIII.

THE HAPPY HUNTING GROUNDS OF THE INDIAN.

THE Indian's idea of the future life in the Happy Hunting Grounds is as vague, confused, indefinite, and inconsistent, as can well be imagined. He believes that he will be happy—perfectly happy; but of the how, why, or wherefore, he pretends to know nothing.

His creed is a wide one; for all persons, of all ages, sexes, colours, or beliefs, who die unscalped or unstrangled, will meet in that final heaven of bliss. He goes there just as he was here, with the same passions, feelings, wishes, and needs. His favourite pony is killed at his burying place, to enjoy an eternity of beautiful pasture and to bear his master in war or in the chase.

He will need arms to defend himself against enemies (man or beast) : his rifle, pistol, bow, and quiver are buried with him. He will need fire : so flint and steel or a box of matches go towards the outfit for his final journey.

There is no death in that life ; but wounds and pain, hunger and thirst, love, revenge, ambition, all the passions, or incentives to action, are there. The Indian knows no happiness in this life, except in the gratification of his natural appetites. His future life will develope greater capacity and wider opportunity for the enjoyment of the appetites.

He will meet enemies, whom, however, he strives to make as few as possible in that world, by scalping as many as possible in this. He will encounter dangerous beasts; for the spirits or phantoms of all animals, reptiles, birds, insects, and fishes go also to the Happy Hunting Grounds. In short, the next world is to be simply an intensified continuation of this—death alone overcome.

How an unhappy disposition here can be happy there, he does not try to explain. He has no conception of, or belief in, any special divinity presiding over the future state; consequently he cannot conceive of a special miracle in each case fitted to the necessities of the beneficiary.

The conception of the abolition of death in the future state seems to be attended with a doubt or modification. He expects to kill and eat all the game he wishes; to clothe himself with the skins of animals; to fight with, and even to take the scalps of, his enemies; but what becomes of the slain phantoms of animals, or the spirits of scalped ghosts of men, is a problem which he wisely leaves for future solution.

From what has been said it will be truly inferred that not only animals but inanimate nature is represented in the future state. All things which the Indian can make for himself in this life he can make in the next; consequently there is no need to take that class of things along with him. He can there procure skins for his clothing and for his lodge, robes for his bed, &c. But articles beyond his skill in manufacture—gun, powder, lead, caps, knife, blankets, and an iron pot for cooking—must all be carried into the next world by the dead man, who is, moreover, buried in shirt, pants, and coat of civilised manufacture (or as many of those articles as the owner possessed during life).

The Indian understands perfectly well that the dead does not actually take with him into the next world the material articles buried with him in this, for some of them are hung round the burial place exposed to view. He believes, however, that, if the articles are allowed to remain with or near the body until decomposition is completed, the spirit of the dead man will have in the next world the use of the phantoms of those articles.

The most touching trait of Indian character is the universal desire that the dead shall enter the Happy Hunting Grounds with as complete an outfit as possible. Any article supposed necessary in a future state which the dead man did not possess in life, is at once supplied by relatives or friends, often at considerable sacrifice. Whatever the absolute needs of an Indian life, there is no known instance of his despoiling, to satisfy them, the grave or burial place of another Indian of his own tribe. He will go hungry from lack of means to kill game, though he knows a dozen trees containing graves in each of which are gun, powder, and lead.

The personal misfortunes and peculiarities which an Indian has in life stick to him beyond the grave. A one-legged man in life is one-legged to all eternity. One who loses his sight here gropes blind through the Happy Hunting Grounds. Time is no more. There is no growing older there, consequently every one remains for ever at exactly the age at which he entered the new life. The puling infant, the decrepid hag, the young virgin, or the stalwart warrior, as each dies, so shall he or she remain to all eternity. A body emaciated and distorted by pain and disease sends on the long journey a soul which shall suffer in the same way.

As the surroundings of the final scene of this life make their impress on the whole future of the soul, it is but natural in the Indian to desire to be taken off the stage as suddenly as possible, and while in the full power and vigour of man or womanhood.

I have heard a story connected with the death of Major Elliott, a gallant officer of cavalry, who three years ago fell in an encounter with the plains Indians. It smacks too much of sentiment to be genuine; but I give it for what it is worth, premising, however, that, if true, it is the solitary instance I have ever known of an Indian showing any generosity to, or favourable appreciation of the gallantry of, a foe.

Major Elliott, with some sixteen men, got separated during the battle from the main body of troops. They were surrounded, and all perished, gallantly fighting to the last. Some time after a party was sent out to discover and bury the remains. All were found where they died, the soldiers scalped and terribly mutilated; Major Elliott unscalped, but with his right hand and foot cut off. Months after, when the war had ceased, a chief who was known to have been in the fight was asked how it happened that Major Elliott was not scalped. His reply was, that he and the other Indians were so impressed with admiration at the gallant conduct and unyielding courage of Major Elliott that they did not wish to prevent his getting to the Happy Hunting Grounds, but that in order to deprive him of the power of injuring them there they had cut off his hand and foot.

Another well-known superstition of the plains Indians is, that a man killed in the dark will dwell in darkness throughout eternity. This, for the white man, is a most fortunate belief, and materially lessens the dangers and labours of the troops. With their stealth, craft, patience, and knowledge of country, the Indians would be truly terrible in night attacks. As it is, such an attack is very rare, and, when decided upon, is invariably made by moonlight. They will crawl into a camp and steal horses, and may sometimes fire a few shots into it from a distance. But on a dark night there is little danger to be apprehended, even though surrounded by the most hostile Indians.

In common with the ancients of history, the Indians believe that the manes or shades of the departed slain in battle require to be appeased by the death of the slayer, if possible; or, failing his, by that of some one of the slayer's nation or tribe.

In the spring of 1873 a band of Cheyennes on a

marauding expedition to New Mexico were surprised by troops, and some six or eight killed. When the survivors reached home with the news, the most fearful excitement prevailed throughout the Indian camp, and a party was at once made up to go to the settlements to obtain white victims in retaliation. Fortunately for the unprepared settlers, but most unfortunately for themselves, a small party of surveyors were at work on the route of the Indian march. They were set upon by the Indians, who, when they had killed a number sufficient to appease the shades of their slain friends, returned satisfied to their encampment without molesting the settlers.

Two or more warriors of contiguous tribes have a collision in which one is killed. His relations and friends seek every opportunity to retaliate by killing one or more of the relatives of the slayer. The shades appeal in turn to their friends for appeasement, and in course of time what may have arisen in a mere broil between two half-drunken bucks has widened and deepened until almost every family of each tribe has a blood feud with one or more families of the other.

No mercy is ever shown in Indian warfare ; and when ambition is stimulated by superstition, and hatred and revenge by religious duty, the conflict becomes more personal, more and more bitter, bloody, and barbarous, until each individual of each tribe will only be satisfied with the complete extermination of the other. The Sioux and Pawnees are perfect exemplifications of this feeling.

It has already been stated that the plains Indians regard all pain and suffering as direct manifestation of the power of the bad god.

During the last thirty years they have been visited by small pox and cholera. To describe the superstitious terror, the consternation and abject fear, of these ignorant savages at such times is almost beyond the power of words. When the epidemic is sufficiently pronounced

for sure recognition, a universal cry of despair ascends
to heaven, for the bad god has them in his power, in
his most terrible and dreaded form. Camp and lodges
are abandoned ; the dead and dying left alone and uncared
for ; and those not yet afflicted, breaking up into families,
fly in every direction from the scene of suffering. They
hope by the rapidity and secrecy of their movements to
baffle the pursuit of the bad god.   An unfortunate
seized with the disease *en route*, is forced to leave the
party, to live or die, solitary and alone in the wilderness.
Husbands abandon their wives, children their aged parents,
mothers their nursing infants; and this terrible race for life
continues until the disease has worn itself out, either from
want of contact or lack of victims. The places at which
these visitations have overtaken the Indians are for ever
regarded with superstitious terror, and no persuasion or
bribe could induce an Indian knowingly to visit them.

More than twenty-five years ago the writer, with a
small force, was scouting in the Guadalupe Mountains in
Texas, then a favourite hunting ground of the Indians. In
going from one mountain pass to another, an old Indian
trail was discovered. It was deep and wide, showed
plain evidence of much and frequent usage, but no sign
of recent travel. It evidently led to some spot which
had been a favourite place of resort, but which, for some
reasons, had for several years been abandoned. Curious
to know more, the trail was followed. After winding
along ridges for three or four miles, it led by a long and
steep descent to a most charming valley, nestled and
hidden in the very bosom of the mountains. This valley
was about twelve miles long by an average of three-fourths
of a mile in width. A beautiful stream wound in graceful
curves from mountain to mountain as if seeking to leave
no spot of the valley untouched by its invigorating
influence. Tall, shapely trees clustered along the margins
of the stream ; smooth lawns of the greenest grass, dotted
with clumps of shrubbery, and covered with lovely

flowers of every hue, made a picture as fair as the eye of man could wish it.

Descending the stream for some two miles, we came, in one of the loveliest of the many lovely nooks, upon the remains of an Indian camp. Many of the old lodge poles were still standing, though the lodges themselves had long since gone to decay. Scattered about, rusted and rotten, were cooking utensils, arms, saddles, all the paraphernalia that go to make Indian wealth and Indian comfort. In the midst of these, and in every direction in and around the camp, were innumerable bones—the dislocated skeletons of the Indian inhabitants : some, almost entire, lying where the breath had left the bodies ; others scattered and broken as they had been dragged, and gnawed, and left by the wolves. To all appearance not a thing had been touched by man ; not a living soul had entered that camp since the day of its awful visitation by the bad god.

CHAPTER XXIV.

BURIAL OF THE DEAD.

THE final disposition of the body of a dead Indian may or may not be a religious ceremony. In some cases the most elaborate care is taken, and every form religiously observed. In other cases the body may be thrown into a ravine or hole, and carelessly covered with grass or leaves, or it may be left to rot on the ground. The favourite burying place of the plains Indians is in a tree. From the care taken in its selection, and the more or less elaborate construction of what may be termed the casket, or burial case, a very fair estimate may be formed of the rank and standing of the dead.

If a chief, or a son of a chief, is to be buried, the country for miles around the camp will be scouted over, and several eligible burial sites selected, the relative merits of which form a subject of discussion worthy the consideration of a general council. A position is finally decided upon. It must be in a sound, strong tree, well sheltered from the wind, and apparently safe from any chance of being uprooted by the violent wind-storms which sweep with terrific violence over the plains. The branches must be so situated that the final resting place shall be as nearly horizontal as possible.

Poles are cut for the construction of a platform, and the whole is firmly bound together and to the branches by thongs of raw hide. It is from six to ten feet long, and from three to five feet wide. Upon it are spread rushes, grass, or the leaves and small boughs of trees, and

'OKOLOHAMA, THE LAST HOME OF THE INDIANS.

Burial-ground in Trees on Medicine Lodge Creek, Indian Territory.

over these is laid one or more buffalo robes. On this bed the corpse is disposed, sometimes in a sitting posture, but generally lying on the back in a natural position.

The body is dressed in the most gorgeous appare obtainable; for the spirit will appear so dressed in the Happy Hunting Grounds, and as good a first impression as possible is greatly desirable. An old uniform coat which has rendered faithful service to some lieutenant of the army, a pair of tarnished epaulettes, and a hat from some military post, are greatly prized portions of the burial dress.

As has before been stated, such articles of civilised manufacture owned by the dead in life or furnished by the generosity and piety of friends, as are considered necessary to his comfort or his appearance in the future world, are buried with him. His hair is combed carefully, parted in the middle, and plaited (with buffalo hair to increase the length) in a long tail on each side of the head, each ornamented with large circular silver or plated buckles. Around his neck is suspended the medicine bag, containing his ' totem,' and the bones, ashes, earths, &c. used in his private devotions. At his girdle (or on his lance, or shield among the more southern plains Indian) are hung all the scalps he has taken in life. His face is painted in the most splendid style of Indian art.

All being completed, light but strong branches are attached to the sides of the platform, and bent over the body like the bows of a waggon. The enclosure for a body buried in a horizontal position is not over two feet high. Over these are stretched buffalo hides (green if they can be obtained), with the hair out, and securely fastened to the platform and to the boughs with thongs of raw hide. Every aperture is closed as tightly as possible. Such necessary articles as pots, kettles, &c., as might be in the way inside, are securely fastened to the platform or the neighbouring branches; and over all are hung streamers of red and white cloth, to frighten away any animals or birds which might venture to disturb the remains.

Such a tomb in the dry climate of the plains will last for several years. Whether it does or does not appears not to concern the Indians in the least. They never rebuild or repair; and when time, decay, or accident has destroyed the platform and scattered the bones on the ground, they are left as they fall, no further care or notice being given to them.

The elaborate arrangements described above are only made when the Indians are in a winter encampment, and have plenty of time to devote to the excitement and luxury of grief. At other seasons, or when on a journey, or pressed for time, caves are used for chiefs; holes or small ravines for the common warriors. Scalped warriors are never buried, but left where they fell. Occasionally a favourite wife of a chief is buried in a tree; but, as a rule, dead women are hustled into the first convenient hole in rock or prairie without ceremony or special manifestation of grief.

The country in the vicinity of the Cimarron River, south of Fort Dodge, is almost exclusively a gypsum formation. Instead of wearing channels on the surface of the ground and forming ravines, the rains have penetrated the soil, dissolved the gypsum, and formed for watercourses long intricate tunnels and caverns innumerable. These are favourite burying places. During a visit to this locality with a party of soldiers, a cave elaborately walled up was discovered and broken into by the men, and a great quantity of useful and curious articles, trinkets, and Indian finery taken from it. I was little disposed to scold them for the desecration when they brought me a string of at least a dozen white scalps, some of infants, and one of long, fair, and most beautiful silky hair, which had undoubtedly adorned the head of some woman at least sufficiently cultured to appreciate and take excellent care of the lovely ornament.

Even chiefs are not always buried with religious care and attention. Once, on a scout, I came upon an Indian encampment very recently abandoned, and which, from the dead horses, broken arms, cut-up lodges, and signs of blood, I at first supposed had been harried by a hostile band. A more critical examination soon convinced me that these were only evidences of the death of some prominent man. I found where a heavy body had been dragged over the ground. Following this trail for about 200 yards, I came to a small mound of dry leaves. Pushing them aside I was astonished to recognise the body of the *war chief of the Comanches*, a man greatly loved and feared by his tribe. He was dressed in a uniform coat; his head was adorned with a hat and feather; his face was painted; his gun and equipment, complete, were beside him, and in his hand he held a box of matches. A closer examination disclosed the fact that one end of a rope had been tied around his ankles, the other evidently attached to the pommel of a saddle, and the body, thus dragged naked from camp, was afterwards dressed for the grave. All the skin was torn from the back, sides, and loins, and the body otherwise greatly mutilated by this rough treatment. It was not until some months after that I learned that this chief had died of *delirium tremens*. The tribe had gone into all the usual mourning ecstasies, and had given him a good outfit for the Happy Hunting Grounds, but had shown its appreciation of the mode of his death by treating his body with indignity.

CHAPTER XXV.

LOVE, COURTSHIP, AND MARRIAGE.

'Love rules the court, the camp, the grove.'

THERE is a vast amount of love making in an Indian encampment. No sooner has the boy passed his ordeal and become a warrior than he begins to look for a wife. Although the only real essential in the affair is that he has ponies to pay for her, yet, for reasons which will hereafter appear, it is always better to win, if possible, the love of the girl. His first approaches are very like those of a bashful backwoods lover. He frequents the lodge of his charmer, does much 'heavy standing around,' showing only by *looks* the feelings which agitate his breast. Not meeting with rebuff he takes to serenades, 'vexes the drowsy ear of night,' and sets all the dogs and old women in camp frantic with 'most doleful strains' on a wretched substitute for a flute. Now he begins to hope, and for hours each night lies in wait near the door of her lodge, watching for the appearance of his beloved, but carefully concealing himself from the observation of any other person.

There being an average of eight or ten people living in the one room of the lodge, his opportunities for private converse with his mistress would be of the fewest, but for her assistance. In case his addresses are not distasteful to her, nor unfavourably regarded by the father, she, after lark, leaves the lodge, and is immediately pounced upon the lover. If she resists or cries out he is obliged

A DAKOTA OR SIOUX BELLE.

immediately to quit her. If she does neither, he carries her to a little distance, just out of hearing of the lodge. There they seat themselves side by side on the ground, and, throwing a blanket over the heads and forms of both, make love to their hearts' content.

Couples so engaged are never disturbed. It is one of the social fictions of Indian life, that the lover is supposed to be entirely unknown to any but his mistress (love in a man being regarded as a weakness). It not unfrequently happens that two or more lovers are paying addresses to the same girl at the same time. All are lying flat on the ground, as well concealed as possible, but within a short distance of the lodge door. The girl appears. A rush is made. A lover seizes her. If the right one, she yields passively and is borne off, the others disappearing at once. If a wrong one, a slight resistance or exclamation and she is at once released, to repeat the process until satisfied with her captor.

Slight as is the opportunity, no little coquetry can be and is displayed by the Indian maiden in these momentary love passages. The girl is finally won. And now a curious scene ensues between the lover and the cruel parent of his beloved. 'I think of taking your daughter for my wife,' says the lover. 'She is an ugly thing, lazy as a bear, does not know how to cook or to work, and is of no sort of account; but as I am sure you must want to get rid of her, I came to tell you that, as a favour to you, I will take her off your hands.'

'Oh,' answers the father, 'you want my darling girl, the best and most loving daughter man ever had; the best cook and dresser of buffalo skins, the finest bead maker, the hardest and most willing worker in the whole tribe. I cannot spare my darling. I will not part with her to any one, much less to you, who are young, who have taken only one scalp, who have stolen not over two ponies. You, indeed! No; you cannot have my daughter, unless you give me twenty ponies for her.'

' Twenty ponies!' cries the lover, with great contempt; ' twenty ponies for an ugly girl not worth one buffalo robe ; I can buy a dozen better girls at the price.'

With many hard words and much personal vituperation the war goes on, the father praising, the lover disparaging, the girl, until after a stormy altercation, running sometimes into weeks (if the old man sees any lover-like weakness or impatience in the younger), a bargain is struck at something like the fair market value of the girl, which is usually from one to four ponies. There is no marriage ceremony. The price being paid, the man conducts his new purchase to the lodge of his father, there to remain until the increase in his family, or his wealth and consequence in the tribe, force or enable him to set up a lodge for himself.

CHAPTER XXVI.

SOCIAL LIFE.

THE life of an Indian woman is a round of wearisome labour. Her marriage is only an exchange of masters. The pride of a good wife is in permitting her husband to do nothing for himself. She cooks his food, makes or mends his clothing, dresses skins, dries meat, goes after and saddles his horse. When making a journey, she strikes the lodge, packs the animals, and superintends the march. On arriving at the camping place she unpacks the animals, pitches the lodge, makes the beds, brings wood and water, and does everything that ought to be done, hardly permitting her lord and master to unsaddle his own horse.

What she gets in exchange for all this devotion it is impossible to say. Whether from ignorance of any better fate, or from constant occupation, certain it is that a happier or more contented woman cannot be found. And yet she is more absolutely a slave than any negro before the war of the rebellion, for not only may her person, but her virtue ,be sold by her husband to any one who will buy it.

Polygamy seems to ·be natural ; at least it is a custom of all primitive or natural people. Each red man has as many wives as his inclination prompts or his wealth allows. Indeed, his wives are like gamblers' diamonds, to be accumulated in times of prosperity, as a sure revenue when disaster shall overtake him. In spite of all this, the women are not without their weight and influence in all the affairs of the tribe, and, though not permitted even to enter the council lodge, they are very frequently the 'power behind the throne,' directing and guiding almost without knowing it themselves.

The husband owns his wife entirely. He may abuse her, beat her, even kill her without question. But if moderately good-looking, or having a fair reputation as a worker, she has a sure remedy against all conjugal ills in being able to leave him for any other man who will take her and pay for her. The transfer of devotion and allegiance of women to other men than their rightful owners is not at all an unusual occurrence among the plains Indians. It may come from ill-treatment on the part of the husband, or from what would be termed in civilised society a regular elopement or seduction.

A man takes a fancy to another man's wife. He makes his advances, is met by encouragement, and, after a siege more or less protracted, wins her. The husband wakes up some morning to find his wife gone. He searches for her through the encampment, and finds her in another man's lodge, going about her avocations as if at home, and he is informed that she has become the wife of that other man. The bereaved husband goes at once to the chief and states his grievance. One or two prominent warriors are called in. They examine into the case and assess the damage, somewhat in accordance with the circumstances, but more usually with reference to the ability of the new husband to pay. Whatever forfeit is decided upon by the chief and his advisers must be paid at once. This being done the affair is over. There is seldom any wrangling or fighting, and in every case, forfeit or none, the woman is permitted to remain with the man of her choice.

Few persons have been in the Indian territory who have not heard of 'Romeo,' a Mexican Cheyenne half-breed, an excellent guide and interpreter. His mother was a Cheyenne Indian. He was brought up with that tribe, has a Cheyenne wife, and lives among them. He is fluent in several Indian languages, has the sign language at his fingers' ends, and besides speaks very excellent English.

He was employed as guide and interpreter for my command for one season, and I was glad to while away the time on the monotonous prairie marches by inducing him to talk of himself and his people. One day he told me of a love affair. He had a year before fallen in love with the wife of an Indian in the same camp. She was beautiful, charming, fascinating, all that was lovely. Her husband was poor and rather worthless. Romeo laid violent siege to her heart. For two months all that devotion and presents could do was done, and finally she crowned his happiness by coming to his lodge. Next morning the husband came and found her. He went to the chief. 'The chief and some of the old men came to me,' said Romeo, 'and we went down to the herd to select the animals to pay for my new wife. After a long talk they took five ponies and two mules (five of my best ponies and a splendid pair of mules). It was very hard ; but then she was so beautiful, and I loved her so much, I would have given all I had for her ; I was in heaven with her, she was so good and pretty. Three mornings after I woke up and found her gone. I was wild. I rushed out to look for her, and found her in the lodge of her other husband. She told me that she had gone back to him. I went to the chief. He came with some old men to the lodge. I demanded my wife or the return of my ponies and mules. The other husband said, "That is your wife ; I did not bring her here ; I do not want her ; I have the ponies and mules paid me for the wife you took from me. You cannot have them. Take your wife if you want her." The wife refused to go with me. She said she loved her first husband best, and wanted to live with him, and would not live with me. After a long talk, the chief and old men decided that the woman should take her choice of us, but that, as the other husband haa not seduced or stolen her back, he was entitled to keep the ponies and the mules. So,' added Romeo, 'I lost my wife, my ponies, and my mules. I did not care for the ponies and the mules, but I did for my wife. She was *so* beautiful and so good.' After some moments of silence, in which he struggled manfully with his emotions, Romeo turned to me with the tears forced back in his eyes, and said, in a choked voice, Colonel, I think that was a put-up job.'

Should the wife of a chief be seduced from her allegiance, nothing, as a rule, is said about it. The chief is too great a man, too high and mighty, far too removed from the feelings of common humanity, to waste a moment's thought on so insignificant a thing as a woman. His runaway wife may be in the same camp, in the very next lodge, and he may pass her every day without even deigning to bestow a word or a look upon her.

The unmarried women have a similar right of seu-protection against their arbitrary sale by their fathers. The girl may be sold. She goes with her purchaser to his lodge, but resists, with all her power and strength, his efforts to consummate the marriage. If in two or three days and nights his entreaties or passions have failed to make her his, she has a right to go back to her father's lodge, who, however, in this case is obliged to pay back to the purchaser the price he received for her.

An American had been for a long time with the Brulé Sioux. He had already one Sioux wife, but, taking a fancy to a girl, he, without any previous courtship, bought her of her father for one pony. She remained in his lodge three days and nights, resisting all his entreaties, protestations, and promises. At the end of that time she went back to her father, and the marriage became null and void. The purchaser got his pony back, but this was the only satisfaction he received from his conjugal investment.

Another American bought a Sioux girl (without court-ship) and took her home. Towards bed-time the husband attempted some little familiarity, whereupon the new wife drew a huge knife and attacked him with the utmost ferocity. Taken by surprise, he avoided her repeated lunges with great difficulty, and very nearly paid for his venture with his life. By good luck he at last got in a blow with his fist, which knocked her down. Disarming her and seizing his riding-whip, he proceeded to give her a tremendous thrashing; after which recreation he went to bed, leaving the wife crying bitterly on the floor. Half an hour after she dried her tears, got up, undressed, and went to bed, and has been since not only a good, but most affectionate wife.

The Indian has not the first dawning idea of moral obligation. His views on chastity might well have been derived from a close study of the ancient Hebrew records.

For the man there is no such word, no such idea, as continence. He has as little control over his passions as any wild beast, and is held to as little accountability for their indiscriminate gratification. Women are expected to be chaste, not from any moral sense or obligation; but, being the absolute property of their husbands, they are required to keep themselves entirely for their husbands.

Unmarried girls are generally more virtuous than the married women. Unchastity not only injures their chances for a good husband, but is likely to be severely punished by the father, as it considerably depreciates their market value, to the loss of the latter.

Indian *men* of all tribes (that I know of) are the same in their entire abandonment to the gratification of their passions at any time and in any way.

There is no single point in which tribes differ so greatly as in the average chastity of their women. The Cheyenne and Arrapahoe tribes occupy the same territory, live together in the same camps, and are closely and constantly associated. The men of the two tribes are identical in their habits of personal chastity, but entirely different in their ideas of family government and the virtue of their women.

Among the Arrapahoes infidelities are not specially regarded, even by the husband. Among the Cheyennes a discovery would result in serious consequences, possibly death, to the woman. The result is remarkable.

The Cheyenne women are retiring and modest, and for chastity will compare favourably with the women of any nation or people. The Arrapahoe women are loose almost without exception. The females of the one tribe are almost models of purity and chastity; those of the other tribe almost exactly the reverse.

The exchange of husbands spoken of heretofore is in no sense a violation of the rules of the strictest chastity. It is legitimate and proper. It is the woman's protection against tyranny. The Cheyenne woman, being of a spirited, high-strung race, is very quick to resent any ill-treatment of one husband by taking another.

No tribe visits any punishment on the lover. The man's right is always to importune, to win if possible, and the attempt of one on the virtue of another's wife is not at all incompatible with the closest friendship between the men. There is no such thing as 'seduction,' as understood by the whites. The woman is expected to protect her virtue or take the consequences. The object of all attention is understood, and a Cheyenne belle cannot receive the secret addresses of an admirer under the convenient civilised form of an innocent flirtation. The blame of a *liaison* falls on the woman entirely. She is expected not only always to say 'No,' but to keep herself out of the way of temptation. A Cheyenne woman is never seen alone. Two or three women sitting at the door of a lodge will get up and go inside on the approach of a man not of their own family, even though he be an intimate friend. When the husband is absent from home at night, the wife, before retiring, ties a lariat, or rope, about her waist, and wraps it tightly around her legs to the ankles. Custom has made this a perfect protection. With it she may sleep alone in a lodge unmolested ; without it half the bucks in the band would visit her before morning, even though her children and other persons were in the lodge with her.

The woman is required to be virtuous, and to protect herself. Custom gives her certain means and assistants to that preservation. If she conforms to these she is safe ; if not, it is her own fault, and she is likely to be punished as for a wilful crime. Thus, a man forcing a woman who had tied her legs would be killed. The woman neglecting that precaution can be violated by all the bucks, and she alone has the blame.

There are other customs equally arbitrary and equally to the disadvantage of the women. Imagine a village of 500 people, in which there are 100 bucks of all ages, from thirteen to sixty, entirely irresponsible to any power, human or divine, and restrained from the indiscriminate gratification of their passions only by certain customs which from long usage have attained the force of laws ; imagine 100 females of all ages above puberty, required to keep themselves virtuous, yet protected from violence at any time and place only by their observance of certain arbitrary rules, unnatural and uncomfortable ; imagine these bucks constantly on the alert for some neglect of these rules, with the right to enter any lodge when the husband is absent at night to see if the wife has tied herself, and the absolute right to force her if she has not ; imagine all this and more, and some idea may be formed of the morals of a Cheyenne Indian village.

The plains tribes vary greatly in the punishment meted out to unfaithful wives. By unfaithful wives is meant not only those who willingly enter into a *liaison*, but those who, by neglect of some rule, have subjected

themselves to violation.[1]   The Cheyennes are the most
severe, not unfrequently inflicting death.   A young girl
had become the third or fourth wife of a man at least
fifty years old.   As was, perhaps, natural, she became
enamoured of a young buck, who, not having the means
to buy her, persuaded her to run away with him.   The
elopement was successfully accomplished, and the young
couple arrived at the village of another band of the
same tribe, where they 'set up' housekeeping as man
and wife.   Some five or six months after the whole tribe
was called together for the 'medicine dance.'   The
husband found his runaway wife, and demanded that she
be returned over to him for punishment.   Had the
young lover possessed any means to pay for her
abduction the affair would probably have been settled in
that way; but, having nothing, the girl was, by order of
the chief, delivered to her husband.   Seating her on the
ground, he crossed her feet so that the instep of the one
was over that of the other, and deliberately fired a rifle
ball through the two.   He then formally presented her
to the young man, grimly remarking, ' You need not fear
that she will run away with any other man.'

The Comanches split the noses of unfaithful wives;
and I have seen one unlucky woman with five separate
gashes in her nasal organ, entirely destroying both its
usefulness and its beauty.   These public marks have a tendency to lessen the value of a woman should the husband
desire to sell, and are, therefore, not always resorted to.

In all the plains tribes the husband has the entire
disposal of his wife's person, and may sell or lend her at
his discretion.   I spent one winter at North Platte
Station on the Union Pacific Railroad in charge of
Spotted Tail's band of Brulé Sioux.   There was considerable trouble from drunken Indians; and, when I

---

[1] These remarks apply to married women only. A buck forcing an
unmarried girl or widow would be required to take her as his wife, and pay
for her. The tying is a custom of the Cheyennes only.

came to inquire closely as to where they obtained liquor, I found that almost any common warrior of the band would sell his wife for a night for a bottle of whisky, and that citizens and soldiers were in the habit almost nightly of paying this price.

In this band one of the duties of hospitality was to furnish a wife to a guest whom the host wished specially to honour. A citizen physician, employed by the Government to act as assistant surgeon, was stationed at a military post at which the Sioux frequently visit. The doctor had a charming and lovely wife, without the slightest disposition to flirt; but he, being a gay individual, extremely devoted to the sex, was correspondingly jealous lest his wife might imitate his example. Spotted Tail came on a visit to the post, and the doctor was specially attentive and hospitable to the Indian chief. One night, the doctor and Spotted Tail came into a room in which were assembled several officers. The doctor was jocose, full of fun, rallying the Indian on their manners and customs, on his having several wives, &c. Spotted Tail stood it for some time. At last he said, 'Doctor, you come to my camp, I give you plenty to eat, good bed, and wife to sleep with. I have been in your camp three days, and you no say wife to me once.' It is impossible to describe the horror depicted in the doctor's face. He soon made an excuse to leave, and his close intimacy with Spotted Tail was at least suspended.

The sale of a wife is not unusual. The Indians are very fond of children, and anxious to have as many as possible. Should the wife not bear a child within a reasonable time she is almost sure to be sold; and if she remains barren she is not unlikely to be passed from hand to hand by sale and purchase, until she either has a child or is too old for further sale. In transferring a wife by sale the husband generally keeps the children, if there be any (though I have heard of cases where the wife and children were sold together). The possibility of separation helps to keep the wife in proper subjection, though neither her sale nor her voluntary abandonment of her husband and children (by exchange of husbands) prevents her visiting, when she pleases, the lodge of her first husband, and seeing her children at her pleasure.

In times gone by the Sioux had a very peculiar ceremony, which I have never heard of as practised in any other tribe. At a certain season of the year the whole band was assembled. All the males who had arrived at the age of puberty were formed in two lines, about four feet apart, facing inwards. All the females of and above the same age were required to pass in single file between the ranks. Any man in the ranks who had within the year had sexual intimacy with any woman was obliged by his honour and his religion to put his hand upon her as she passed. So sacred was this obligation that, it is said, if a man failed to touch a woman he should have touched she turned upon him, slapped his face, and proclaimed him a coward; on which he was publicly disgraced and forced to leave the band. The touch of the man bore no ill consequences to him, nor was the woman punished nor discarded by her husband. Though still living as before with her husband and children, she became an outcast. If found alone away from the camp, she could be ravished with impunity by any man or men. This fate she could avoid by never going away from her lodge unless accompanied by some one. When the next yearly ceremony took place, if she passed through the lines without being touched the curse went off, and she was restored to her original purity and standing.

Civilisation and Christianity, which punish one sin by cursing a whole life, might take a lesson in charity from these ignorant savages. White men came to live and intermarry with the Sioux, and were placed in the lines; they not only did not touch, but they persuaded their paramour beforehand that there was no honourable or religious necessity for exposing themselves. These soon taught their other lovers and the other women. Women were also sometimes suspected of denouncing and disgracing, for the gratification of malice or revenge, men who really had not been guilty with them. The ceremony fell into disrepute, then into disuse, and is now, I believe, entirely discontinued.

It is regarded as effeminate in a man to show any affection for his wife, or attention to any other woman (where he may be seen). A very noticeable exception is Powder Face, a prominent chief of the Arrapahoes, a desperate and dangerous fighter, covered with scars, and celebrated for the many scalps he has taken, and risks he has run. His wife is a rather pretty woman of about twenty-five. They have been married some years, and have no children. In spite of this no two people could be more devoted and apparently happy. She goes with him everywhere, his most willing slave. He will sit for hours before his lodge door combing her hair, painting her face, petting and fondling her—conduct which would disgrace a less determined or well-known warrior.

Children are highly prized. The father feels pride in his sons, who keep alive his ambition. They also help to feed the family, and take care of the stock. He feels interest in his daughters as a sure revenue when marriageable. The little children are much petted and spoiled, tumbling and climbing unreproved over the father and his visitors in the lodge, and seem never to be an annoyance, or in the way. The boys grow up, as it happens, without restraint in anything. The girls are early taught the lesson of subordination, and begin to labour almost as soon as they can walk.

Indians are gregarious. Even the chief prefers to have one or more families beside his own in his lodge. Each lodge of the common people contains from three to five families (rather crowded for a single room not over twenty feet in diameter).

There are no regular hours for meals, nor is there, as

a rule, more than one meal a day. A huge pot or kettle full of meat is put on the fire. When done it is placed in the middle of the lodge, and each person helps himself with his fingers. When they have no flour, dried buffalo meat is used for bread. When all are satisfied the kettle is set aside, and those who get hungry oftener than once a day go and help themselves.

They are hospitable to each other and to strangers, always offering something to eat to visitors. If it is known that there is anything specially good to eat in any lodge, and wherever more than an ordinary smoke indicates cooking, there is sure to be a lot of loafers drop in. They always have the first chance at the pot, the occupants of the lodge contenting themselves with what is left. Tea, coffee, and sugar are exceptions, and are only given to distinguished guests.

A great deal has been said and written about the stoicism of the Indians. Years of intercourse with them has convinced me that this stoicism is only manner, the result of a life of watchfulness and comparative solitude. Of their wonderful endurance of pain and want I have already spoken. But the Indian is really of a very nervous and excitable temperament, easily acted upon. No people who fight at all, fight so badly when surprised. No people are more easily and thoroughly ' stampeded,' or rendered senseless by fear. The Indian will talk himself wild with excitement, vaunting his exploits in love, war, or the chase, and will commit all sorts of extravagances, when telling or listening to an exciting story. In their everyday life Indians are vivacious, chatty, fond of telling and hearing stories, indulge in broad wit, and are specially fond of practical jokes.

The nights are spent in song, and dance, and revelry, and, for the number of people engaged, a permanent Indian camp (safe from all danger of enemies) is at night the noisiest place that can be found.

Uneducated people of our own race feel no surprise

at the rising of the sun, the change of season, the flash of lightning, or the roll of thunder. They accept them as facts, without explanation, and, though beyond their comprehension, without surprise. One shows surprise at something out of the ordinary line of his experience. It is an act of comparison.

The Indian has actual and common experience of many articles of civilised manufacture, the simplest of which is as entirely beyond his comprehension as the most complicated. He would be a simple exclamation point did he show surprise at everything new to him, or which he does not understand. He goes to the other extreme, and rarely shows or feels surprise at anything. He visits the States, looks unmoved at the steamboat and locomotive. People call it stoicism. They forget that to his ignorance the production of a glass bottle is as inscrutable as the sound of the thunder. A piece of gaudy calico is a marvel; a common mirror, a miracle. He knows nothing of the comparative difficulties of invention and manufacture, and to him the mechanism of a locomotive is not in any way more matter of surprise than that of the wheelbarrow.

When things in their own daily experience are performed in what to them is a remarkable way they do express the most profound astonishment. I have seen several hundreds of Indians, eager and excited, following from one telegraph pole to another a repairer, whose legs were encased in climbing boots. Where he walked easily, foot over foot, up the pole their surprise and delight found vent in the most vociferous expressions of applause and admiration. A white lady mounted on a side-saddle, in what to the Indian woman would be almost an impossible position, would excite more surprise and admiration than would a Howe's printing press in full operation.

Twenty years ago, when Indians knew comparatively little of the wonders of civilisation, Lieutenant (now

General) P—— was sent with a small force to treat with
a band disposed to be troublesome. He took with him as
guide and interpreter a Delaware chief, Black Beaver, a
warrior celebrated throughout the length and breadth of
the plains. Beaver was semi-civilised, had been to Washington, owned a farm, and was a person of social consequence in his country. The refractory Indians were
assembled in council, and the difficulties adjusted. Lieut.
P—— then proceeded to descant upon the numbers and
power of the whites, and the folly of the Indians making
war upon them. As a peroration, he directed Beaver to
tell the Indians about steamboats. Beaver had seen
steamboats, and gave a glowing description. At its conclusion a murmur ran through the council. 'What do
they say, Beaver?' asked P——. ' He say he don't
b'lieve that d——d lie,' said Beaver. ' Tell them about
railroads, then.' Beaver had travelled on railroads, so
proceeded to give his ideas and experiences on that subject. Again a murmur passed through the assembly.
'What do they say now, Beaver?' asked P——. ' He
say he don't b'lieve that d——d lie either.' Somewhat
nonplussed for a wonderful thing which they *might*
believe, P—— at last said, 'Tell them about the telegraph.' 'I don't know what that is,' answered Beaver.
P—— explained that by the aid of a little wire he could
stand where he was and talk to the Great Father at
Washington, &c., &c. Beaver listened attentively, but
with a grave face, and made no attempt to translate.
'Why don't you tell them?' said P——, impatiently.
' 'Cause,' said Beaver, nodding his head slowly and
emphatically, ' 'Cause I don't b'lieve that d——d lie
myself.' [1]

---

[1] This story was told me in 1867 by the officer to whom it is accredited.
After I had written it out as above, I came across it in General Marcy's
excellent work on frontier life. The story illustrates my point, and, whoever
may be the author, it is too good a one to lose. If I am poaching on the
General's manor, I apologise.

The home or lodge of the plains Indian is a comical covering of dressed buffalo hides, supported on a framework of light peeled poles, crossed near the top and spread out at the bottom. It is from twelve to twenty feet in diameter, and about fifteen feet high. The fire is built in the centre, and the smoke escapes through an aperture at the top. This aperture is guarded by a sort of winged cap, capable of being turned in any direction, and which prevents the wind from blowing directly down into the lodge. The draught is, however, very defective, and the lodge is usually in cold weather too full of smoke to be bearable to any one but an Indian. It is, however, admirably adapted to their necessities. Its shape secures it from the danger of being overturned by wind-storms, and with very little fuel it can be kept warm and comfortable even in the coldest weather.

The beds are piles of buffalo robes and blankets, spread on the ground as close to the outer circumference as possible. They serve the double purpose of sleeping places by night, of seats and lounges by day. They are not 'made up,' though on fine days bedding is taken out of the lodge, shaken, and spread in the sun. In this small space are oftentimes crowded eight or ten persons, possibly of three or four different families; and since the cooking, eating, living, and sleeping are all done in the one room, it soon becomes inconceivably filthy. Except the bedding, the *parflêche* trunks containing the dried meat and extra clothing and finery, a few pots, kettles, and tin cups, there is no furniture, nor is there any attempt at order in the arrangements of even these few articles.

The wealth of the Indian is in his horses and mules. He has no taste or desire for the accumulation of more or other things than are necessary for the wants of his family for the time being. The fall hunt supplies him with robes enough to keep him warm during the winter, and still leaves him sufficient for sale so as to supply the necessities to be obtained from white men.

son brings his young wife. Tnere can be but little romance about a bridal bed on which half a dozen pairs of curious eyes are fixed, and half a dozen tongues making comments. The Indians seem to think it all right, and in their sexual and marital relations they are scarcely above the brute. The husband of one wife brings home another and another. They all sleep in the same bed if it is big enough; if not, the older wives are turned out for the younger favourites. I have never heard of any difficulties or trouble between the wives on this account, and the sentiment of jealousy seems to be entirely wanting. The devotion of a man to a new wife, or his infidelity to them all, seems not to awaken the slightest feeling, and is no more regarded than the infidelities of a cock by his feathered harem.

I have been told by many men, both white and Indian, who had wives in the 'wild' plains tribes, of several curious social and physiological facts, which only want clear confirmation to be both interesting and instructive, as bearing on the theories of unity of races. That when 'the way of women is upon them,' they are regarded as unclean, and retire in summer to the woods, in winter to a lodge especially set aside for their use, where they remain until èntirely well;—that from a period extending from one to three days after she is well, the woman alone has any sexual desire;—that both men and women regard cohabitation with a wife who is *enceinte*, as 'bad medicine' for the family, though the husband's infidelity with another woman in that condition would entail no bad consequences on him.

Either from lack of suitable food or the constant drudgery of her hard life, the Indian woman is not prolific. I have never seen a mother of over four children, and many women are barren. The average is scarcely more than two children to each woman. Red Bead, a Sioux, used greatly to felicitate himself on his large and fine family, his two wives having five children between them. In most lodges the children are not more plentiful than women.

Parturition seems to be a matter of scarcely more concern to the woman than to the buffalo-cow. With the first child she may, or not, have a woman to attend her; but, if she be ordinarily healthy and well developed, she usually does everything for herself. I have been told that in good weather they prefer to go off alone to some retired place in the woods or brush. The whole affair is a matter of an hour or two, and when the child is two or three hours old the mother is most likely at her usual avocations.

Once when on a scout I met a small party of Indians who stopped and chatted for a few moments. The chief asked me where I was going, and, finding that my route took me on his trail, he informed me that one of his wives had stopped a short distance back to have a baby, and requested me not to permit any of my men to molest her. Proceeding about three miles we met the woman alone, riding quietly along the trail, the baby strapped in its cradle on her back.

While the child, either boy or girl, is very young, the mother has entire charge, control, and management of it. It is very soon taught not to cry, by a very summary, if not gentle, process. Its mouth is covered with the palm of the hand, while its nose is grasped between the thumb and forefinger until the little one is nearly suffocated. It is then let go, to be seized and smothered again at the first attempt to cry. The baby very soon learns that silence is its best policy.

Almost as soon as the male child is weaned the control is taken from the mother, and it becomes practically its own master. The mother is never permitted to punish a boy, no matter what its fault. She, however, retains her control over the girls until they are married, and whatever comfort she derives from her children is from them. The maternal instinct does not appear to be very strong. Widows not unfrequently sell their female children, even though not pressed by necessity, and I have known several instances of an Indian woman offering to exchange her baby for a white one.

Some years ago, an officer of the army, with a young wife and lovely boy-baby, was crossing the plains. The Indians were peaceful and he had but a small escort. One afternoon an Indian woman came into camp and, struck with the beauty of the white infant, proposed a 'swap.' The young wife, taking the proposal for fun, laughingly consented, but was soon greatly terrified when the woman laid down her own baby and attempted to take the other. A violent scene ensued, and the woman and her baby were finally put out of camp by the troops, she in a towering passion and vowing revenge. Before sunrise next morning, a large force of warriors appeared with the woman, demanding the white baby, and threatening to take it by force if not surrendered. A long parley ensued, and the Indians were finally bought off by the payment of blankets and sugar.

The widows and orphans of a tribe are cared for, after a fashion, by the ' dog-soldiers,' who, in the general division of meat and skins, set aside sufficient for their maintenance. Among the plains tribes a woman on the death of her husband becomes not only herself free, but the possessor of her female children as property. The sons are independent ; but are obliged to support the mother and sisters, if old enough, or if they have themselves no families. The widows are like their white sisters in their aversion to the sweets of freedom and single blessedness, and if at all young and good looking are very soon married again. I have been told that the old and ugly who have no sons to support them, not unfrequently purchase for themselves a husband, by giving over to him the ownership of her daughters, not as wives, but as so much saleable property. The life of a woman who has

a man to provide for her is so much more secure, so
much freer from the chance of hunger or want, that
almost every woman greatly prefers even the annoyances
of a bad husband to the precarious hazards of widow-
hood.

A grave trouble to the Indians, and one of which I
have heard many complaints, is the number of widows
and orphans left on their hands by white men. The
Indians have this whole matter in their own hands; they
have but to prohibit their women from marrying white
men. But this is not at all to their taste. A father can
get for his daughter possibly twice as much from a white
man as an Indian would pay, and he sells at the highest
price. To prohibit his selling his own property would
be regarded as an invasion of his most sacred and vested
rights. Having sold and got his price, he feels himself
relieved of all responsibility regarding her. She should
henceforth be supported by the husband; and the father
regards it as a hardship, an outrage, a real cause of com-
plaint to be obliged, even partially, to assist in the support
of a woman, his own daughter, sacrificed by his cupidity to
a man whom he knew would abandon her sooner or later.
When the trapper was an institution of the plains, he did
not consider his outfit complete unless he had one or more
Indian wives. When he went back to the settlement
he left them behind. If he returned to the same country
he took them again, but if he changed his locality he got
a new supply from the tribe he happened to be nearest to.
The forsaken dames could not always secure other
husbands; for, though generally the best looking of the
tribe (trappers had taste and money), the women, not
being so constantly exposed to danger, were generally
very considerably in the excess of the men in numbers.
Their fathers would not support them, not being bound to
do so either by affection or custom; so they and their
children became a tax on the strength and energy of the
tribe.

At a council held at North Platte, in 1867, between the Indians and some representatives of the Government, one of the chiefs spoke earnestly and feelingly on this subject. He said that his tribe was poor and could not support the widows and orphans abandoned by white men, and he begged that some special provision might be made by the United States for this class of people.

Our dealings with the Indians have habitually been so stupid that it is not at all remarkable that they consider us very nearly idiots, to be hoodwinked and bamboozled at any time or on any subject by a specious speech or promise. Their belief in our credulity was undoubtedly the cause of their making of that council one of the most remarkable demands ever made in earnest by any people. The spring and summer of 1867 had been a succession of raids, plunderings, and murders. All the plains tribes were loose. Custer, with a considerable force, was scouting between the Kansas Pacific Railroad and the Platte River. It was necessary to communicate with him. A lieutenant and thirteen men of the 2nd Cavalry, with Red Bead, a Sioux chief, as guide, were sent from Fort Sedgwick to intercept him. The lieutenant was very wary and used every precaution against surprise, making no camps, but halting at uncertain intervals to rest and refresh his men and graze his animals. He had, however, to deal with Pawnee Killer, the most redoubtable of all the hostile chiefs (and from whom this account comes). One night the lieutenant marched until nearly morning, then halted, and, without making fires or unsaddling, allowed his exhausted men to lie down and sleep. Pawnee Killer, who was attending him like a fate, crawled with a large force on the sleeping men, and, just at dawn, one volley sent every sleeper, save two, to his long account. Those two men were a corporal and Red Bead. The corporal, at the fire, sprung to his feet, pistol in hand, and, as the enemy rushed upon him, fired two shots, killing two Indians. Before he could do more he was riddled with bullets. Red Bead ran, was pursued, and, in spite of his Indian cunning and endurance, caught and killed. Subsequently, when the Indians came into this council to make peace, they brought an old widow who they said had lost her sons, and had no one to support her, and they demanded that the United States should give her a pension. On investigation it transpired that the widow's two sons were the men killed by the corporal in his last gallant effort.

Judging from the weak-kneed concessions of previous councils, the Indians had good cause to expect that the widow would get a pension. Fortunately there were men in that council who neither feared the Indian nor expected to make money out of him. The demands of the Cheyennes were not only not entertained, but they were met by so fearless and manly a statement of what would result to them if they continued their warfare, that they left the council lodge under the influence of the only sentiment that can actuate them to humanity—viz., fear—and have since then behaved tolerably well.

Though sharp in horse trade and quick to comprehend the general principles of barter with white men, the idea of devoting himself to a particular occupation or trade, and making a living by the exchange of his productions for the productions of others, seems never to have occurred to him. Each man is his own artisan. What he needs he must make for himself or buy from the white man. He has indomitable patience, is imitative, and, with the assistance of his knife and raw hide, he manages to supply most of his necessities. The skins of animals are to him what the bamboo is to the East Indian, or the breadfruit tree to the South Sea Islander. In various forms they furnish house, bedding, furniture, clothing, horse equipment, almost everything necessary to his comfort. Invention seems almost totally wanting.

The old way is the best way, and children do not improve on their father's skill and knowledge. His skill in drawing is very slight; yet, aided by his marvellous knowledge of the 'landmarks,' or natural features of a country, he will, with the ground for his drawing-board and his finger for a pencil, make a map by which any plainsman can travel with certainty.

During his frequent visits to Fort Chadbourne, Sa-na-co would ask an officer to write on a piece of paper the name of some article, as 'sugar.' This paper he carefully put away. Next day he would ask another officer to write, say, 'coffee.' He went the rounds of all the officers, and we supposed he was making 'medicine' of some kind. He left the post. Some weeks after a messenger came in with a letter to the post sutler, which was found to be an order written on a slip of paper, each name on a line by itself, for 'coffee,' 'sugar,' and at least a dozen other articles. The order was signed Sa-na-co, and the signature and each name of an article was so exactly counterfeited, that the writer of the original could not have distinguished which was his own writing.

CHAPTER XXVII.

GAMBLING.

The Indians are excessively fond of gambling. The old games so often described are generally discarded, all the tribes being sufficiently civilised to possess and understand cards. Those who come in contact with Mexicans are well up in all the mysteries of 'monte.' Those who are civilised on reservations acquire a knowledge of 'poker' and 'seven up,' sufficient for all practical purposes, in a quarter the time it would take them to learn the alphabet.

The wilder tribes invent games for themselves, and play with considerable skill. All Indians are arrant cheats at cards, and as dexterous in concealing their manipulations as a 'three-card monte dealer.' Women play also, but I have rarely seen them playing with men. Having but little to lose, or work to do, their sittings are not protracted. The bucks play from morning till night, and from night to morning again. In the winter camps scarcely anything else is done. The stakes are high for a poor people. I have myself looked on at a game between two Arrapahoe chiefs where, it was said, for I could not understand, 120 dollars depended on a single hand. They are possessed of the true gambler's passion, and will, if in bad luck, lose ponies, lodge, arms, robes, blankets, and, finally, wives, and even children (though this is now rare). I have, however, known, some twenty years ago, more than one case among the Comanches where an unlucky gambler lost wife, children, and all. Turning over his property to the winner, the loser started alone for Mexico, to recuperate his fallen fortunes by thieving.

There is no secrecy about the gambling. A blanket spread on the ground, in the open air in good weather, on the floor of the lodge in bad, serves as table. Spectators crowd around, and if a man is losing heavily the whole camp soon knows it. In such case the wives generally put in an appearance, before things have proceeded to extremities, and break up the game, either by bullying the husband, or informing the winner that they will not live with him if won.

DRINKING.

The vice of all others most unhappy in its consequences to the Indian is his love of strong drink. His passion for intoxication amounts almost to madness. To drink liquor as a beverage for the gratification of taste, or for the sake of pleasurable conviviality, is something of which he can form no conception. His idea of the pleasure and the use of drink is to get drunk, and the quicker and more complete that effect be obtained the better he likes it. He is very easily affected, and what would be a very ordinary intoxication without perceivable effect on a white man will make him ' roaring drunk.' To gratify this passion the Indian will go to any lengths, take any risks, or do any dirty act.

The laws of the United States are very stringent in prohibiting the sale or gift of intoxicating liquor to Indians, as well as its introduction into the Indian territory. It is easy to make laws, but by no means always easy to enforce them. When the laws were made, Indian territory was every portion of the country occupied by Indians. Much of that territory is now within States, and the laws of those States protect its citizen in the sale of liquors if he takes out a licence. Decision after decision has been made in the interest of parties who were trying to reconcile the right to permit one man to sell liquor, with the right to prohibit another from getting drunk, until at the present time 'Indian territory' means simply the ground inside an Indian reservation. A squatter who goes over that line to sell liquor subjects himself to fine and imprisonment. If he remains on his own side of the line, he can with impunity sell all the liquor he pleases to Indians who come to him. Whether this is the intent of the law may be questioned, but that it is the actual practical working of the Indian laws is well known to every frontiersman.

The Indian will give everything he possesses for whisky. I have already spoken of the habitual sale by the Brulé Sioux of a wife for a bottle. I have known an instance where an officer was earnestly importuned by a Cheyenne to give him one bottle of whisky for a mule worth $150.

With such profit in prospective, it would require an army of detectives to keep the frontier liquor dealers from trading with the Indians. And when the Indian is as eager for whisky as the trader is for ponies and peltries, it is hardly necessary to say that the traffic is incessant.

Mexicans from New Mexico fit out great caravans for trade with the Kioways, Apaches, and Comanches. The southern part of the State of Kansas is populated with perambulating groggeries. One grog-shop keeper of Dodge City kept, during the winter of 1872-3, several 'outfits' in the field with such profit to himself that a few such winters would qualify him for the highest social or political honours of his State. His regular price for one gallon of watered whisky was one pony, or five Indian dressed buffalo robes. One Arrapahoe chief is said to have bartered at that rate over fifty ponies during the winter.

The Arrapahoes would have been utterly impoverished but for the excess of rivalry among the traders, who, in their eagerness, got over the line into the Indian territory, and were pounced upon by the Indian Department. Sixteen or eighteen were arrested and sent to prison. This broke up the trade for the time, and in good season, for the Arrapahoes were barely saved the necessity of going to war to recuperate.

Texas, Nebraska, Colorado, Wyoming, Utah, and Dakota, all compete with Kansas and New Mexico in this most lucrative trade. Buffalo hunters have come to regard a keg or two of whisky as a necessary part of their 'outfit,' adding immensely to the number of skins. The only wonder is that any Indians are left alive.

The peculiarity of the 'Indian drunk' is, that, if there be only liquor enough, it is quick and complete; consequently he is not 'quarrelsome in his cups.' For the number of drunkards, the very few outrages or murders committed among themselves is very remarkable.

Drunkenness is not a female vice, and in all my experience I have never seen a drunken Indian woman. They, however, look with amiable complacency on the bestiality of their lords, and seem to regard it as a matter of course. On one occasion I witnessed the reverse. A Ute squaw was trying to take home her husband, who had not had quite enough whisky, and was only 'obstinate drunk,' though he could scarcely walk. She was very patient—he, brutal. Finally he struck her. Seizing on a good-sized rod that happened to be lying near, she fell upon and beat him most unmercifully. Thinking he had had enough, I walked towards them to interfere. Seeing me she threw down the stick and began to laugh, while the husband sat upon the ground blubbering like a whipped school boy.

The guide at Fort Martin Scott, Texas, was a Delaware, a faithful and reliable Indian. His pay was forty dollars per month. On drawing it he would go to

Fredericksburg (two miles distant), and spend the whole in 'white man's clothing,' from hat to boots, all complete, even gloves. Arrayed in his new clothes, he would strut about the post thoroughly enjoying himself. He would spend a whole day calling at the different houses ; officers, ladies, citizens, soldiers, laundresses, and servants, all had opportunity and were expected to admire his 'get-up.' This ceremony performed, he asked for leave of absence for two, or perhaps three, days, at the end of which time he stalked into the post in blanket and breech clout alone. All his clothing had been bartered for the means of having a 'good heap drunk' for the time of his leave. This was a regular monthly occurrence.

AMUSEMENTS.

Drinking, gambling, and love making may be said to be serious occupations rather than amusements. Next to this the principal indoor delight of the Indian is story telling. A good story teller is a man of importance. The bucks, squaws, and children crowd to his lodge, or any other where he happens to be, and spend the long winter evenings listening to his recitals. These stories are as marvellous as the imagination of the teller can create, jumbling gods and men, fabulous and living animals, the impossible and the possible in the most heterogeneous confusion. There is little point or wit in them, and scarcely any dramatic power, except the narrator be telling of some personal event, when he also acts the scene with all possible exaggeration. The personal stories are generally very filthy, and the language of the plainest. They have no evasive ways of expressing things ; a 'spade' is a 'spade,' with a vengeance. The presence of women and children is not of the slightest consequence, and imposes no restraint whatever either on words or actions.

One of the most curious of spectacles is a story teller and his audience when the sign language is used. Sitting silent in a circle, all eyes are intently fixed on the story teller, who, without a word of speech, is rapidly moving his hands, now one, now the other, now both together. Occasionally a grunt of satisfaction or approval runs round the circle. More and more eagerness of attention, writhings and twistings of the body, show the increase of interest, and finally a burst of uproarious laughter and applause marks the point of the story.

The sign language is in universal use on the plains, and two Indians who cannot speak or understand a word of each other's language will converse as easily and understandingly as if they had been reared in the same lodge. Such a means of communication is almost an absolute necessity to the Indians, split up as they are into numberless tribes and bands, each speaking a language different from the other. That scarcely any but his own immediate people understand his spoken words, while all are expected to understand a silent language of which he is master, is undoubtedly the direct cause of the Indian taciturnity in the presence of strangers.

The fact that the human voice, whilst the most distinctly marked, is the least common of sounds on the plains, that its use may notify enemies of their presence, and scare game from their vicinity, leads to the constant use of sign language in conversation while on raids, expeditions, and hunting parties, and accounts for their taciturnity at such times. They are silent, but may possibly be 'talking' all the time. In their own camps and families this means of conversation is used at least half the time. I know nothing of the sign language taught to deaf mutes; but I am told that the Indian sign language is very similar, except that, there being no alphabet, the signs express phrases and ideas rather than words.

The outdoor amusements of the plains Indians are

riding, shooting, racing—both on foot and horseback—wrestling, swimming; and with the boys a sort of game of 'tag.' In good weather nearly half a buck's waking hours are passed in the saddle. Riding is second nature to him. Strapped astride of a horse when scarcely able to walk, he does not, when a man, remember a time when he could not ride. Having never seen the riding of Arabs, Turcomans, Cossacks, and other world-renowned riders, I cannot say how the Indian compares with them, but I am satisfied that he is too nearly a Centaur to be surpassed by any.

The bit used is commonly known as the 'Mexican bit.' It is a most cruel affair. The bar is bent in the centre, forming a tongue from two to four inches long, which extends backwards towards the horse's throat. To the upper end is attached an iron ring, which embraces the lower jaw, forming the curb. Long side levers are attached to the bar, and to these the reins of horsehair or raw hide. The headstall is of horsehair, and elaborately ornamented with round silver or plated buckles. With such a bridle the most refractory horse can be thrown on its haunches by one turn of the wrist, and I have heard of one or more instances where a horse's jaw was broken by a violent pull.

The saddle is a light frame of wood, the side pieces shaped to fit a horse's back. The seat is not rounded, but almost perfectly straight, and forms very nearly right angles with the pommel and cantle. These are about eight inches high above the seat. The pommel ends with a rounded knob. The cantle, rather wide at top and bottom, is cut away in the middle to make a depression to fit the leg or heel of the rider, and forms his support when he wishes to throw himself on the side of his horse. The whole is covered with green hide, which in drying binds all the parts together tight and strong almost as iron.

The girth is a broad band of plaited hair, terminating

in iron rings (or bent wood covered with raw hide, if iron rings cannot be obtained). These rings are attached to the saddle on the principle of the Mexican ' Cinche,' by which a man of ordinary strength can almost crush in a horse's ribs.

Great liberties of position are taken by an Indian on horseback, and it is of the utmost importance that the saddle be strong and the girth fail not.

The stirrup is of thin wood strengthened with raw hide, by which material it is also fastened to the saddle. Some slight padding is put between the horse and saddle, the skin of a wolf or buffalo calf; or in these later days a piece of old blanket or grain sack. The stirrups are extremely short, so much so that the thigh of the rider is almost horizontal. They are, however, of little use except in mounting, or as rest to the foot when riding.

Civilised people mount on the left side of the horse, because the knights of old, from whom we get our ideas of horsemanship, wore their swords on that side, and could not, therefore, mount on the right without inconvenience from that weapon.

The Indian mounts always on the right side ; and this is undoubtedly natural and most convenient, as it leaves the left hand free to hold the reins and manage the horse, while the right grasps the mane or pommel of the saddle.

In travelling necessary stores are carried *en croup*, or slung to the saddle on each side. One blanket or robe is around the rider's person, and he sits on an extra one if he has it. His gun is carried across his thighs, resting against the pommel; his bow and quiver are slung on the back, by a strap passing from right to left, but which brings the quiver almost perpendicular with its opening over the right shoulder.

When travelling from place to place, under ordinary circumstances, a more unromantic or less dangerous look-- ing ' specimen ' could not be found than an Indian warrior.

His seat and carriage are particularly ungraceful. The short stirrups force him to sit almost on the small of his back, and the back itself is rounded into an unseemly curve. His head is carried forward as far as the length of his neck will allow. His left hand holds the reins; his right is armed with a short stick, to which is attached a thong of the inevitable raw hide, and with a light blow of this he marks every step of his horse. He uses no spurs; but his heels are constantly drumming on the horse's ribs, with a nervous motion difficult to account for. He scarcely ever turns his head or moves his body, and, even when most watchful, appears to see nothing. He looks stiff, constrained, and uncomfortable on horseback, and yet this uncouth object will perform feats of horsemanship actually incredible to one who has seen only civilised riding.

With his horse at full speed he will pick up from the ground a small piece of coin. He will throw himself on the side of his horse in such a position that only a small part of an arm and leg can be seen from the other side.

One method of racing is to start from a line and rush full speed at a tree, the one who first touches it being winner. Another is to rush at a heavy pole placed horizontally about six feet from the ground, resting on forks firmly set. If the rider stops his horse a moment too soon he fails of touching the pole; if a moment too late the horse passes under the pole, leaving the rider dangling to it or thrown to the ground.

A third method is to fasten to the ground two strips of buffalo hide from six to ten feet apart. The starting point is some 200 yards from these strips, and the game is to run at full speed, jump the horse between the strips, turn him in his tracks, and return to the starting point. The horse which fails to get beyond the first strip with all four of his feet, or which gets a single foot beyond the second strip, is beaten, even though he makes the best time.

The training of the ponies has quite as much to do with the success of an Indian race as his speed or the address of the rider. Great pains are, therefore, taken in training, and a pony thoroughly up in his tricks is highly prized.

The Indian is an arrant jockey, and understands all the tricks of professional horse racing as well as any veteran of Jerome Park. He rarely comes in competition with whites, because his passion being for trick races, as those described, he dislikes to come down to a square and fair race over a straight track. Besides this, it is really exceedingly difficult to hit on a fair distance between the Indian and American horse. The start being always from a halt, the small, quick pony is almost sure to win at from 100 to 300 yards, while the long stride of the American horse is equally sure of carrying him in winner from 600 yards to two miles. A mile or two is then doubtful, after which it is safe to back the endurance of the pony.

A band of Comanches under Mu-la-que-top, once camped near Fort Chadbourne in Texas, and were frequent visitors and great nuisances as beggars at that post. Some of the officers were decidedly ' horsey,' several owning blooded horses, the relative speed of each being known, by separate trials, almost to a foot. Mu-la-que-top was bantered for a race, and, after several days of manœuvring, a race was made against the third best horse of the garrison, distance 400 yards.

The Indians betted robes and plunder of various kinds, to the value of sixty or seventy dollars, against money, flour, sugar, &c., to a like amount. At the appointed time all the Indians and most of the garrison were assembled at the track. The Indians ' showed ' a miserable sheep of a pony, with legs like churns, a three-inch coat of rough hair stuck out all over the body, and a general expression of neglect, helplessness, and patient suffering struck pity into the hearts of all beholders.

The rider was a stalwart buck of one hundred and seventy pounds, looking big and strong enough to carry the poor beast on his shoulders. He was armed with a huge club, with which, after the word was given, he belaboured the miserable animal from start to finish. To the astonishment of all the whites, the Indian won by a neck.

Another race was proposed by the officers, and, after much 'dickering,' accepted by the Indians, against the next best horse of the garrison. The bets were doubled; and in less than an hour the second race was won by the same pony, with the same apparent exertion and with exactly the same result.

The officers, thoroughly disgusted, proposed a third race, and brought to the ground a magnificent Kentucky mare, of the true Lexington blood, and known to beat the best of the others at least forty yards in 400. The Indians accepted the race, and not only doubled bets as before, but piled up everything they could raise, seemingly almost crazed with the excitement of their previous success. The riders mounted; the word was given. Throwing away his club, the Indian rider gave a whoop, at which the sheep-like pony pricked up his ears, and went away like the wind, almost two feet to the mare's one. The last fifty yards of the course was run by the pony with the rider sitting face to his tail, making hideous grimaces, and beckoning to the rider of the mare to come on.

It afterwards transpired that the old sheep was a trick and straight race pony, celebrated among all the tribes of the south, and that Mu-la-que-top had only just returned from a visit to the Kickapoos, in the Indian nation, whom he had easily cleaned out of 600 ponies.

In practising with bow and arrow, the Indian has a short loop of raw hide attached to the pommel of the saddle, which he passes over his head and under his arm when he wishes to throw himself on the side of his horse.

This, with the leg holding the cantle, gives him firm support, and leaves both arms free. He can, however, use only the right side of the horse. In pistol practice, the loop is not necessary, and, needing only one hand with the weapon, he can shelter himself on either side, holding on to the pommel with the left hand.

Compared with the white hunter of the plains, the Indian is a wretched shot. He is about equal to the United States soldier, being deficient for the same reason—lack of practice. The Government and the Indian are each too poor to afford to waste more than ten cartridges a month on drill, and no man ever became an expert marksman on that allowance. The Indian is really much more dangerous with the bow than with the pistol; but the latter gives a longer range, and the Indian does not like close fighting any better than other people.

With all his power of endurance, his life in the open air, and his constant and violent exercise, the Indian is not physically a powerful man. He has not the slightest knowledge of the use of his fists, and the poorest member of the prize ring could carry off the belt from the whole red race.

The boys wrestle a good deal, but without rule or science—a mere scuffle. An average white man will 'get away' with the strongest and most active Indian either in a wrestling match or in a foot race for short distances. In a race for miles the Indian endurance will win.

All Indians swim, as it were, by instinct, and evince great courage and skill in the passage of the plains rivers, dangerous from their swift currents and terrible from their treacherous quicksands.

There are no games of ball, nor any approach to the civilised games of children, except the sort of game of tag mentioned.

The women ride astride, mount on the right side, use the same saddle, and are almost as much at home in it as the men.

It is impossible to say what the amusements of the Indian women are, but it is a fact that they appear very contented, cheerful, and happy.

Where no one can commit a moral wrong, there is, of course, no opportunity to talk scandal. Mr. Chain Lightning can take to his bosom the spouse of Mr. Scarface without causing even a ripple of remark from male or female. I have heard that the gentle sex holds in great contempt a woman who fails to do everything possible for her husband. I have never seen any such thing. Of the several wives of the same man, one may be an excellent worker, another lazy and worthless, another have one or more slits in her nose, but all seem to get along perfectly with each other and with the other women of the band.

Officers have described to me the squaw fights of the Indians of the Pacific Coast, in which every woman of the band was engaged, while the men stood by enjoying the spectacle. I have not only never seen, but never heard of, a fight between two plains Indian squaws. In fact, the Indians seem to herd together exactly as do the buffalo, amicably, each one doing as he pleases without molesting or being molested by others. Two bulls may fight over a cow, or the cow may exercise her natural right of selection, but the affair possesses not the slightest possible interest to any but those engaged.

The little girls are very fond of dolls, and of playing baby-house, and the mothers take great pains and show considerable skill and taste in making and dressing the puppets.

SINGING AND DANCING.

The singing of the Indian consists in the monotonous repetition of a few half-guttural, half-nasal sounds (notes they can scarcely be called, as they form no music), varied by an occasional yell. Whatever the occasion, the 'song' is the same, however varied the accompaniment.

The religious singing over a sick man is exactly the same as the singing in the scalp dance, except that in the first case the interjections are the most dismal and doleful wails, while in the latter they are the yells which accompany the swooping ,charge on an enemy, or the blood-curdling war whoop which proclaims a *coup*.

The dance consists of the alternate raising or putting down of the feet, accompanied by a quick jerking motion of the body. It is varied by bounds and springs into the air; but there is no effort at posturing, nor any set position for the feet. In the ceremonial dances, in which warriors alone participate, the dancers form themselves into a circle facing inwards, and sometimes join hands for a few moments. Any position or contact which tends to restraint is, however, soon abandoned in the excitement to which they work themselves. In the ordinary social dances of almost nightly occurrence in the main camp, and in which men, women, and children may all take part, no positions are taken or set forms gone through.

They know nothing of tenors, or altos, or bassos, and have no idea of either waltz, reel, strathspey, or American jig; they do not even take partners, but each dances by himself or herself to the music of his or her own howls. How such singing and such dancing can give the pleasure they undoubtedly do, is one of the problems of humanity; but for all purposes of excitement, almost indeed of frenzy, they are amply sufficient to the Indian.

I was one hot day sitting in the shade of a lodge in an Indian camp, where all was monotonously quiet, when a fat, jolly-looking old woman in a calico gown, and holding a long staff in her hand, emerged from the door of a lodge near by, and, without a word of preparation or invitation to any one, fell at once into the regular song and dance. In a few moments other women came out of other lodges and joined at once in the accompaniment. The loafing lovers and husbands, lying or squatting about on the ground, lifted their heads, looked, and soon first one, then another, sprung to his feet and struck in just where he happened to be, without joining or nearing the others. In ten minutes from the time the old lady gave her first ' whooah,' the whole camp was full of isolated figures lifting foot after foot, jerking their bodies and filling the air with a babel of ' whoo-ahs.' A more ridiculous and unmeaning spectacle to an outsider could not be imagined.

The ceremonial dances of the Indians have been so frequently and so minutely described, that I can add nothing to the stock of knowledge on that subject, except, perhaps, in a single item, viz., the part of such ceremonial forced on captives.

I was once a spectator at a scalp dance, which was a special and exceptional occasion; for not only had a goodly number of scalps been taken, but two prisoners, a woman of about forty and a boy of twelve, were to grace the ceremony. The peeled wands bearing the stretched scalps had been planted in a circle in the ground. The warriors who had been in the fight, and won the right to participate in the dance, were assembled in a circle around these wands. The prisoners were brought from the lodge in which they were confined, by the warriors who had captured them, and forced to take places in this circle, their hands being held by the hands of the warriors on either side of them. At a signal all the warriors joined hands, and commenced the monotonous song, accompanied by the alternate lifting of feet, as described, all turning slowly about the scalps. The woman prisoner accepted the situation, and in looks and actions appeared to take as enjoyable an interest in the dance as any of the proper performers. Not so the boy. With eyes downcast, without a voluntary motion of foot or body, he was dragged round the circle, taking only such walking steps as were necessary to avoid being pulled down. As the dance progressed, all the warriors became excited, all eyes were fixed on the scalps, as each slayer in turn, springing from the circle and bounding to his wand, vaunted in extravagant terms his own exploits, and acted over again the taking of the scalp. But all the turmoil and excitement failed to produce the slightest effect on the boy prisoner. Not once in the dance of an hour did he lift his eyes to the scalps, to which were directed all the eyes and attention of his captors. Not once did he evince the slightest interest in any of the proceedings, nor make the slightest movement unless forced to it. I could not but admire the proud determination of one so young to resist all the efforts of a crowd of enemies to force him into a semblance of rejoicing over the scalps of his tribe—possibly of his own father.

CHAPTER XXVIII.

NAMES.

INDIANS have no family names. The appellations by which they are known are obtained in the most haphazard way, and changed at the will of the individual or of his associates. The male child is called by some diminutive, expressive of the pride or affection of the father. This name, as he grows older, is liable to be changed by his boy companions either in admiration or in ridicule. On his initiation as a warrior he takes a name, generally of his own choosing, though it may be bestowed by his warrior friends.

From this time until his fame is fixed and mature, he is likely to change his name after every fight or thieving expedition, each change expressive of the fullest appreciation of his own importance and exploits on that occasion. But these changes, though gratifying to his own vanity, are not always accepted by his companions, or the tribe generally. Even the most noted warrior cannot always control the disposition to ridicule or nickname, which all Indians possess in a remarkable degree; and, however he may insist on calling himself or being personally addressed by his chosen title, he may be known and spoken of by a different name given him by the warriors of the tribe.

Any personal defect or deformity of character or person is almost sure to be seized upon as a fit name. Mu-la-que-top called himself very differently, but was known by that title among his own and all the southern plains tribes. Powder Face has won and adopted a dozen names, in well-fought combats; yet he is known to all plains tribes and to the whites by the title which he got from having his face badly burned by an explosion of powder when a young man.

Some of the names are expressive of early peculiarities, others of utter contempt; but it is a curious fact that, however opprobrious the common title by which a warrior is known, he is almost sure in his maturer years to acquiesce in and accept it. The names adopted by the warriors themselves are intended always to be expressive of some particular action or situation, and are generally adopted from the known habits of animals with which they are familiar. Thus a warrior who, brought to bay, has finally beaten off his enemies and escaped, names himself Standing Bull. Another goes off alone on an expedition, from which he returns with stories of successful rapine, and calls himself Lone Wolf.

Girls are generally named by the mothers, and frequently have fanciful titles, meaning or indicating some thing which the mother may think worthy of commemoration, as the Hebrew women of the Old Testament named their children. This name is liable to be lengthened by affectionate diminutives, or contracted into a nickname, but it is not changed as the names of the boys. Married women do not take the names of their husbands, or change their own titles in any way. There are no equivalents for Mrs. and Miss, and in the name, title, or designation there is nothing to show whether a woman is married or single.

When on reservations, or thrown into comparatively close contact with whites, the male Indian is very prone to take to himself some ' white' name; and at a military post in the close vicinity of Indians there is always a lazy lot of Franks, and Bills, and Jims, loafing as an occupation, living by constant and unblushing beggary, and ready to prostitute their wives or daughters for a drink of whisky.

CHAPTER XXIX.

THE Indians, like most people who live in the fresh air, are a naturally healthy race, and, like all healthy people, are very impatient of sickness. A wound is tangible and understood. A slight knowledge of surgery is universal, and the treatment very successful, owing probably to the general good health of the subject and the pure, dry air of the plains.

Sickness is very different. To be burning with fever or racked with rheumatism without external wound or apparent cause, is so wonderful that it can be attributed only to the direct action of the 'bad god.' No idea of diagnosis has occurred to them, for they have not even advanced sufficiently to comprehend that there are different kinds of ordinary disease. Sickness is sickness ; that is all. There being but one disease, there is but one remedy (other than the exorcisms, chauntings, and other religious ceremonies)—that is, the sweat-house. A small structure, shaped like a bake-oven, with one opening in the side, is constructed of rough stone, if possible, on a bank overlooking a pool of water. A fire is built within, and, when a proper degree of heat is attained, the fire is raked out ; the patient, stripped naked, crawls in ; and the opening is closed with a blanket. When almost baked, and the perspiration streaming from every pore, he is taken out and plunged into the water below. In some instances this treatment is very efficacious. In others, the patient enters the water and the Happy

Hunting Grounds at the same instant. This result will not, however, prevent a repetition of the treatment with the next patient. The tenacity of life of an Indian is most remarkable.

He will carry off as much lead as a buffalo bull, and to 'drop him in his tracks' the bullet must reach the heart, the brain, or the spine.

I was once with a force of troops which camped near a large band of Comanches, on the Llano River, in Texas. An Indian came into camp wounded, and our surgeon was asked to see him. When he returned he told me that a heavy bullet had penetrated from the rear, just at the junction of the pelvis and thigh bones, breaking both. The wound was some eight days old, mortification had set in, and the man died that night. It subsequently transpired that the Indian had been wounded in a fight with troops near Fort Inge, had kept his seat, escaped his pursuers, and had ridden alone a distance of over 100 miles (in an air line), crossing the Guadalupe Mountains. A white man would have instantly fallen from his horse on receiving such a wound, and never could have moved, much less mounted a horse.

There was at Fort Mason a worthless old Tonkaway Indian, a beggar and hanger-on of the garrison, who had but one foot. Colonel May, then commanding, told me that this Indian had, when alone, some miles from the post, found a bee tree. On cutting it down to get at the honey his foot was caught, crushed, and held in such a way that he could not free himself. For three days he remained in this condition, hoping some one would find him. He then made a fire of such leaves and twigs as he could reach, and, taking out his knife, dislocated the foot at the ankle joint, stopping the flow of the blood by searing the arteries with fire coals. When free he made his way to the post, where his stump was properly dressed by the surgeon.

I have myself seen an Indian go off with two bullet

holes through his body, within an inch or two of the spine, the only apparent effect of which was to change his gait from a run to a dignified walk. I have heard anecdotes enough of this remarkable character to make a book of themselves.

The Indian, in his natural condition, is almost as little afflicted with disease as an animal in its wild state. Chills and fever in some localities, rheumatism in others, and sometimes, but rarely, a case of consumption, form the principal ills their flesh is heir to. Contact with civilisation has brought its scourge in measles, whooping cough, scarlet fever, small pox, and that worst of all horrors, syphilis, which is slowly, but surely, destroying all that portion of the Indian race which raids upon Mexico.

The occasional attack of a tribe or band by cholera can be accounted for no more satisfactorily than can be the Epizootic, which passed at a regular rate, without contact or apparent cause, from the Atlantic to the Pacific, sparing no herd of horses, however isolated, either of white man or Indian.

The Indians generally are beginning to believe strongly in 'white man's medicines,' and will travel a long way to see or obtain remedies from a post surgeon.

CHAPTER XXX.

FOOD.

THE food of the plains Indians consists almost entirely of meat. Some tribes cultivate a little maize, and sometimes a few vegetables, pumpkins, melons, &c. All are fond of plums, grapes, and other wild fruits and berries, which are gathered in season, and dried for winter use.

The Indians on reservations are furnished with flour by the Indian Department, but not in sufficient quantities to enable them to have their 'daily bread.'

Every animal, bird, or reptile serves by turn the Indian appetite. The entrails of birds and animals are a special *bon bouche.* The smaller are eaten raw and warm with animal heat. As soon as a deer or antelope is killed it is opened, and the successful hunter betakes himself to what, to him, is the most perfect repast ; nor is he satisfied until its bowels, stomach, liver, and not unfrequently heart and lungs, have all disappeared before his astounding appetite. The liver of a very fat buffalo or elk will not unfrequently become granulated and broken up by overheating in a long chase. This, with the contents of the gall bladder sprinkled over it as sauce, is the most delicious morsel that can titillate an Indian palate. A Pawnee Indian, a special friend of mine, once brought and presented me with several pounds of this stuff tied up in a handkerchief, and was greatly disappointed and mortified that I did not swallow it at once. The smaller entrails of the larger animals are also eaten raw.

When a young man—new to the plains, with a heart full of romance and head stored with Cooper's and others fictions of 'beautiful Indian maidens'—I was on the escort of General S——, commanding the Department, on a long scout, or reconnaissance, through Texas. One day, when camped near what afterwards became Fort Belknap, we were visited by a then prominent chief of the Northern Comanches, Pa-ha-yu-ka, who brought with him a few warriors and his family—several wives and one daughter. The daughter was a vision of loveliness, apparently about fourteen, but ripened by the Southern sun to perfect womanhood. Rather below the medium height, her form was slight and lithe, though rounded into the utmost symmetry. Her features were regular, lips and teeth simply perfection, eyes black, bright and sparkling with fun, and the whole countenance beaming with good humour and bewitching coquetry. A tightly-fitting tunic of the softest buckskin, beautifully embroidered with porcupine quills, reaching half way between the hip and the knee, set off to admiration her rounded form. The bottom of the tunic was a continuous fringe of thin buckskin strings, from each of which dangled a little silver bell, not larger than the cup of a small acorn. Her lower limbs were encased in elaborately fringed leggings, and her little feet in beaded mocassins of elaborate pattern. Her beautiful hair was plaited down her back, and adorned with huge silver buckles. The parting of her hair was carefully marked with vermilion paint, and a long gold, or brass, chain was twisted carelessly about her hair and neck. What wonder if, with one look, I literally tumbled into love. She saw my admiration, and, with the innate coquetry of the sex in every clime and of every people, met my eager glances with a thousand winning airs and graces. We could not speak, but love has a language of its own. I haunted that Indian camp fire. Neither duty nor hunger could tear me away ; and it was only when the

Indians retired for the night that I could return to my own tent and blankets to toss and dream of this vision of paradise. Next morning with the sun I was again with my fascination. The general gave the Indians a beef. Some time after a warrior came and spoke to the girl. Rising from her seat, she gave me a look of invitation to accompany her. Proceeding a few yards into a little glade, we came to several Indians standing around the slaughtered beef, which was turned on its back, and the stomach split open. Taking a knife from one of the men, my 'beautiful Indian maiden' plunged her lovely hand and rounded arm into the bowels of the beast, and found and cut off some eight or ten feet of the 'marrow gut.' Winding it about her arm, she stepped on one side, and, giving the entrail a shake, inserted one end in her beautiful mouth. Looking at me with ineffable content and happiness expressed in her beaming countenance, she slowly and without apparent mastication swallowed the whole disgusting mass. I returned sadly to my tent, my ideal shattered, my love gone; and I need hardly add that this one Indian love affair has satisfied my whole life.

When game is plentiful the Indian is choice in his food, eating only the delicate and savoury parts. When suffering from hunger, he will eat anything—snakes, lizards, toads, and sometimes even carrion birds. Dog flesh is regarded as an almost sacred dish, being reserved only for feasts on great occasions. Fat wolf is nearly as good as dog, and not unfrequently supplies his place in the pot when the domestic animal is scarce.

A skunk is a very great delicacy, much prized by squaws in an interesting situation. The odour of this animal is no protection against the Indian, who will seize it by the tail and beat it against the ground until dead, regardless of the fetid discharge which would sicken almost to death another man. The result is that an Indian camp is by no means a desirable country residence for a gentleman afflicted with acute olfactory nerves, the stench being simply abominable.

The offal about the butcher's shop of a military post is greedily devoured (generally raw) by any Indian hangers-on of the garrison. Blood, either warm or clotted, is swallowed with avidity; and I have seen an Indian draw his knife through the udder of a just-killed doe, and, placing his mouth in the gash, suck the warm mixed milk and blood with the greatest pleasure.

Nothing can be too filthy to come amiss to the all-devouring Indian appetite.

Some few animals or birds are protected by superstition (though this is not strong enough to amount to absolute prohibition). Our favourite Christmas bird, the turkey, is tabooed to the Indian, who will not eat it except when on the very verge of starvation. He believes it will make him cowardly and run from his enemies, as the turkey does from its pursuers. The plains Indian depends for his regular winter supply of food on the buffalo. The meat is cut into thin flakes and dried in the sun. It is then pounded up and packed into trunk-shaped receptacles (called *parflêches*), and is the true Indian bread. The children are usually seen munching this dried buffalo meat in the same way as their Anglo-Saxon *confrères* eat with avidity either biscuits or sticks of candies.

CHAPTER XXXI.

CLOTHING.

THERE is no tribe of plains Indians that does not now use more or less civilised clothing, seemingly, however, more from imitative faculty than for any use or comfort derived from the clothing itself.

The natural and ordinary summer dress of the male Indian is breech clout and mocassins. The breech clout is formed by tying a string or belt around the waist ; one end of a piece of very dirty cloth, six or eight feet long by four inches wide, is drawn under the belt in front, passed between the legs and under the belt behind ; one loose end forms a flap in front reaching nearly to his knee, the other hangs out for three or four feet in the rear, like a tail. This is all that is necessary for modesty or decency from the Indian standpoint. In winter the inevitable buffalo robe furnishes all the comfort and warmth that he desires.

Girls wear the breech clout until they nearly reach the age of puberty, when it is exchanged for a buckskin jacket without sleeves, but fitting well up to the throat, and a short kirtle of the same material reaching nearly to the knee. The old women and nursing mothers do away with the jacket, either leaving the body above the waist entirely exposed, or covering it with a loose piece of cloth in the way of a scarf.

These are the primitive fashions. 'Time's resistless course' and contact with white people have so changed those fashions that they are now in vogue only among those of the tribe who are too poor to afford the luxuries of civilisation ; and nearly all the women at present wear gowns of their own make, of calico or costlier material, according to the wealth and affection of the husband.

Even in his most natural and poverty-stricken condition the Indian is excessively fond of finery, and always has something extra for grand occasions. A few feathers tied in the hair, a ring or two of brass wire for the wrists or ankles, and so up to the elaborate display of useless finery that the wealth and position of the individual can afford or is entitled to. Descriptions and illustrations of these articles have so often been made that it is useless to speak further of them.

The common warrior, whatever his wealth, is not permitted to array himself in certain fineries, nor to festoon his shield in certain ways. Earrings are worn almost universally by men, rarely by women. The holes for insertion are made in the upper cartilage of the ear. I have seen an Indian with three or four huge brass rings in each ear, each ring supported by lead-work connections, shells, stones, pieces of bone, until each pendant was at least a foot long, and the whole together would weigh one or two pounds. Of course the ears were dragged out of shape, enlarged to twice their natural size, and much torn.

Paint forms a most indispensable article of dress with all ages and sexes, and no Indian, whatever may be his actual apparel, considers himself in full dress unless his face is besmeared with paint. They show no taste or skill in its use. Each individual daubs it on (using a smooth stone for palette and his fingers for brush) as seems most becoming. The Indian idea of full dress is to heap upon himself every article of finery that he possesses. The result is some of the most incongruous and ridiculous *ensembles* that can be imagined.

I was once present at a council of grave importance, involving peace or war, on the subject of the Pacific

Railroads. Turkey Leg, a chief of some prominence, came into the council lodge, buffalo robe tightly folded around him. Over his head and face he wore a common green veil. Over that, perched on the very top of his head, and at least two sizes too small for him, was a very tall, straight-bodied, stove-pipe hat. When he rose to speak he retained his hat and veil, but dropped his buffalo robe, disclosing his other apparel, which consisted solely and entirely of a very scant calico shirt. The other Indians seemed to think it all right, but I doubt if any white man present carried off any very vivid idea of Turkey Leg's speech.

The Government has for several summers employed a number of Pawnee Indians as scouts. When clothing was first issued to them they seemed to get along pretty well with everything but the pantaloons. In a few days almost every Indian had cut out the whole of the seat and front of his pants, leaving the legs attached to the waistband by the piece of cloth passing up the outer part of the thigh and hip.

There is no such thing as fashion, no idea of incongruity or unfitness. Whatever the white man wears the Indian will wear if he can get it (except boots). He sees the letters on the cap of a soldier. He has no idea that they mean anything, and must therefore be ' pretty ' to the white man. If he can get a hat, however dilapidated, he covers it over with all the broken cross-sabres, bent bugles, and pieces of letters that he can pick up. A gaudy tie may adorn the neck of a man who has no shirt. Another will have a vest buttoned to the chin, and nothing else. No more ridiculous, motley, overdressed, half-dressed, and undressed crowd can be found in the world than a band of plains Indians when ' fixed up ' for company. A shirt will last several years, being worn only on special occasions. As it is never washed, its condition during the last few years of its usefulness can be imagined.

CHAPTER XXXII.

EMPLOYMENT.

WHEN I first came upon the plains only a very few of the Indians were possessed of firearms, and those were of the most inferior kind. The bow was universal. Even the Indians who owned guns still held on to the bow as the more reliable weapon in close fight. All the time a warrior could spare from the difficult task of furnishing food for his family was fully occupied in keeping himself supplied with materials for war or for killing game. A good bow takes a long time and much care and labour in its construction. The best wood is the Osage Orange ('*bois d'arc*' of the old French trappers, corrupted into 'bow dark' by plains Americans). This wood grows in comparatively a limited area of country, and long journeys are sometimes made to obtain it. Only the best are selected, straight and as free as possible from knots. The seasoning process is slow and very thorough. A little cutting, shaping, and scraping with knife or piece of glass, then a hard rubbing with buffalo fat or brains, and the stick is put aside in a warm place, to be worked at again in a few days or weeks. A good bow with fair usage will last many years, but it is liable to be broken at any time by accident. Each warrior therefore possesses several sticks of bow wood in various stages of completion.

The strings are formed of closely-twisted fibres of the sinews of animals. These sinews are cut out their full length. Each is then subdivided longitudinally into strings, and these picked and re-picked into fibres as fine as hairs and as long as possible. With the rude means at their disposal it requires no little skill so to put and twist these fibres together as to form a string perfectly round and of precisely the same size and tension from end to end.

The arrows require in the aggregate much more labour than the bow. Any hard, tough, straight-grained wood is used. It is scraped to proper size and taper, and must be perfectly round. The head is either of stone or iron—of late years almost exclusively of iron, for stone of the necessary hardness is extremely difficult to work, and twenty or more stones are spoiled and broken for each arrow head made.

The Indian has not even yet the slightest practical knowledge of working iron whilst hot, though almost every one has seen it done in the blacksmiths' shops of military posts. His idea of making anything of iron is to get a piece of that metal larger than necessary, and wear it down to proper size and shape by friction on a rough stone. This labour has been also very greatly reduced within the last few years, thin flat iron being in much more general use, as hoops for barrels, binding for boxes, &c.

Under the most favourable circumstances, however, the most skilful Indian workman cannot hope to complete more than a single arrow in a hard day's work. In a short fight, or an exciting dash after game, he will expend as many arrows as will keep him busily at work for a month to replace.

The necessity of making all his own weapons of offence and defence, and of supplying himself and family with food (a matter of serious difficulty and uncertainty with those rude weapons), are undoubtedly the true original reasons for devolving all the other labour on the woman. To keep himself constantly prepared for war or the chase gave the man all the work he could possibly do. Naturally all domestic details, with the labour necessary for their proper performance, devolved upon the woman.

The possession by Indians of excellent firearms has greatly diminished the use of the bow. But ammunition may be scarce, or the gun itself get out of order, and, as he cannot repair it, he has then to take to his bow, until he can find some white man to fix the gun for him. Many Indians are too poor to buy a gun, and have not been lucky enough to kill a man who had one. These use the bow, as also do all the boys ; so that, however rich and well armed a band may be, the bow is even yet an indispensable possession of every male Indian.

The partial introduction of firearms has relieved the warrior of a great portion of his former employment, but he has no sense of generosity or other inward monitor to indicate to him that he ought in turn to relieve the woman of some portion of her labour.

In his natural condition the Indian is a true son of Ishmael, his ' hand is against every man.' Whether his disposition has undergone any change is a question, but the long range breech-loading rifle has certainly modified his habits. He is not nearly so fond of war as he was in the 'good old times,' the game being greatly more dangerous. The policy pursued by the Government tends, however, to keep alive a warlike spirit, by encouraging acts of aggression. The Indians are half starved on reservations, and exposed to the amiable attention of whisky sellers, until too poor to stand it longer. They then break out. Sending their families to the Staked Plains, or some other almost inaccessible refuge, they make dashes and raids on the exposed frontier settlements, killing people and carrying off all the stock they can lay their hands on.

When they have stolen enough to re-start them comfortably, or when too closely pursued by the troops, they either send a messenger to their agent or, avoiding the troops, slip back into the reservation, and declare their willingness to make peace. The proposition is not only eagerly accepted by the Department, but the new treaty entered into is celebrated by many and valuable presents to the Indians. In but one single instance that I know of have the Indians been required to give up the stolen stock, and even on that occasion only a part was actually returned.

At the very moment of writing this several white women are prisoners in the hands of the Indians, undergoing all the hardships and outrages which those words imply, scarcely an effort for their relief being made by a Bureau which finds it more to its convenience and profit to preach humanity in the East than to do right in the West.[1]

The honour of one true woman is worth more than all the Indians on the plains; yet rapes, murders, and pillages go on year after year, simply 'because there is money in it.'

After the almost complete impoverishment of the Arrapahoe tribe, heretofore spoken of, I had an interview with a prominent chief, who in the most solemn manner, almost with tears in his eyes, assured me that his people could not live the next year but by going to war. They wanted to live in peace; but they were too poor to live in peace, and they relied upon the stealings of the summer, and the gifts they would receive for making peace, for means to start again in a condition of comfortable independence.

In October 1874 I took a small party of English people on a hunt from Sydney Barracks on the Union Pacific Railroad. On the second day we came upon a mixed band of Sioux and Cheyennes, numbering about

---

[1] After almost superhuman efforts by the troops two of the girls were recovered on February 25, 1875. When restored to freedom and civilisation, one was seventeen, the other but eleven years of age; yet both had been subjected to 'indescribable indignities and beastly outrages by nearly all the male Indians' from the 10th of September, 1874, to February 1875. The Indians who murdered their parents, brothers, and sisters, and outraged them, are all known, but, instead of being punished, they are now 'good Indians, living on a reservation, fed, petted, and coddled.' The case here referred to is that of the Germain girls.

1,500 souls. They then belonged to a reservation, and should have been upon it. The small escort of troops with me alarmed them not a little, and, in a council talk which we had subsequently, Two Lance, the principal chief present, informed me that he and his people were forced to leave the reservation by actual hunger. 'You may look,' said he, 'through every one of the 200 lodges in this camp without finding a bit of meat, except the fresh buffalo we killed yesterday. We know we are doing wrong in leaving the reservation, but we could not see our wives and children die of starvation. Though in going to the Republican to kill buffalo we know we are in danger from the Ute Indians, from the white buffalo hunters, and from the soldiers, yet we are going because if we do not soon get meat we shall starve.'

With a disposition naturally prone to war, and such incentives as are forced upon him, it is scarcely too much to say that the principal employment of the Indian warrior is war and preparation for war. If not of equal importance as an incentive to manual employment as war, the chase requires even more time and labour. Hunger is of perpetual recurrence, and the work of the Indian in supplying food for himself and family is never done.

Only a few years ago the plains were covered with buffalo, elk, and antelope; white men passed and repassed, killing such game as was necessary for food, or occasionally for the mere wanton love of killing. These few animals were not missed from the numberless throng, and the Indian had no real competition in hunting. The work of getting ready for the hunt was greater, but the hunt itself comparatively easy. All is now changed. The countless millions of animals on which the Indian depended for food, clothing, comfort, and even for life, are gone. Their bones whiten the plains, the fell victims of the universal greed for money.

Slaughtered for their hides!

The Indian is the most patient of men. Were he

INDIANS AT HOME IN THEIR TEEPEES.—DRYING BUFFALO MEAT FOR WINTER FOOD.

as good a shot as he is a hunter, he would lack meat only when he could find no living animal. With his head covered by a cap of grass or weeds, he will lie for hours on his belly, noiseless as a snake, watching the game he wishes to kill; now perfectly motionless, now crawling a few feet; no constraint of position, no fiercest heat of the plains sun, seeming to affect him in the least. He will lie for a whole day at a water hole, waiting for the game to come to drink (though in this case the water must be so situated that hoofed game can get at it from a certain direction, most hunted animals going to water against the wind if possible).

The plains Indian is very susceptible to cold. He therefore hunts but little in winter, goes out only in the most pleasant weather, and but a short distance from his encampment; for at this season he goes on foot, his ponies being too poor to carry him. The habitual hunting of the Indian is desultory, as he may feel in the humour of sport or as the larder runs low.

Every year ' the great fall hunt ' is made for the purpose of killing and curing a supply of meat for winter use. It is in this hunt that he finds his most perfect enjoyments and excitement. Great preparations are made in advance. Runners are sent out to scour the country for long distances and seek out the most eligible situation for the hunting camp. It must be near water, of course; there must be plenty of timber, for poles are to be cut and scaffolds erected for drying the meat; there must be level sward for stretching and drying the skins; and, above all, it must be as nearly as possible in the centre of a region abounding in game. The spot being decided upon, the whole band—men, women, and children—move to it, lodges are pitched, scaffolds erected, and everything put in order for work.

The ' dog-soldiers ' are masters now, and woe be to the unfortunate who disobeys even the slightest of their arbitrary or democratic regulations. All being ready, the best hunters are out long before the dawn of day. If several herds of buffalo are discovered, that one is selected for slaughter whose position is such that the preliminary manœuvres of the surround and the shouts and shots of the conflict are least likely to disturb the others. A narrow valley with many lateral ravines is very favourable. If the herd is on a hill, or otherwise unfavourably situated, the hunters may wait for it to go to water, or by discreet appearances at intervals drive it to the best spot. During all this time the whole masculine portion of the band capable of doing execution in the coming slaughter is congregated on horseback in some adjacent ravine, out of sight of the buffalo, silent and trembling with suppressed excitement. The herd being in proper position, the leading hunters tell off the men and send them under temporary captains to designated positions. Keeping carefully concealed, these parties pour down the valley to leeward, and spread gradually on each flank of the wind, until the herd is surrounded except on the windward side. Seeing that every man is in his proper place, and all ready, the head hunter rapidly swings in a party to close the gap, gives the signal, and, with a yell that would almost wake the dead, the whole line dashes and closes on the game. The buffalo make desperate rushes, which are met in every direction by shouts and shots and circling horsemen, until, utterly bewildered, they almost stand still to await their fate. In a few moments the slaughter is complete. A few may have broken through the cordon and escaped. These are not pursued if other herds are in the vicinity.[1]

---

[1] I have never personally witnessed a surround. The above description is given on the authority of white men and Indians who have assisted in many. The dog-soldiers are exceedingly tenacious of their rights, and object strenuously to the presence of any one who may not be punished for violation of their rules. The chief dares not, without their consent, to give permission for any outsider to accompany the band in a surround. Those who belong to the band by marriage, and a few others specially favoured, are the only white men who have ever been eye-witnesses to this most exciting of

The slaughter completed, the 'soldiers' return to camp to swell and strut, and vaunt each his own individual exploits, while the women skin, cut up, and carry to camp almost every portion of the dead animals. As soon as those skins are stretched, that meat cut up in flakes and put to dry—or, in other words, when the woman's work is done—another surround is made with like result, and this is continued until enough meat and skins are obtained, or until cold weather drives the Indians to their winter camp.

The weapon principally used in the surround is the revolving pistol, though some men may use carbines, and others bows. When bows and arrows alone were used, each warrior, knowing his own arrows, had no difficulty in positively identifying the buffalo killed by him. These were his individual property entirely, except that he was assessed a certain proportion for the benefit of the widows or families which had no warrior to provide for them. If arrows of different men were found in the same dead buffalo, the ownership was decided by their position. If each arrow inflicted a mortal wound, the buffalo was divided, or not unfrequently given to some widow with a family. The head hunter decided all these questions, but an appeal could be taken from his decision to the general judgment of the dog-soldiers. Since the general use of firearms has rendered impossible the identification of the dead buffalo, the Indians have become more communistic in their ideas, and the whole of the meat and skins is divided after some rule of apportionment of their own invention. None but the lazy and the poor shots are satisfied with this arrangement, but it is the only solution of the problem left to them.

Surrounds of elk are made on the same general

Indian scenes. A white hunter, considered very reliable, told me that he had once seen nearly 300 buffalo killed in one surround, that the whole affair occupied less than ten minutes after the signal was given, and that not a single buffalo escaped.

principles. The Ute Indians (a mountain and not a plains tribe) make surrounds of antelope, and are said to be very successful.

In addition to the work required in war and hunting, the male Indian finds employment in some attention to his horses, in making saddles, bridles, lariats, everything necessary for his own equipment.

The work of the Indian woman is almost incessant during daylight. Fortunately for her there is little resinous wood on the plains, and their aboriginal inhabitants have as yet devised no means of making a light sufficient to work by at night. Once in a while they obtain a few candles from a trader or a military post; but these are kept for grand occasions, and are more for ornament than use. The woman makes all the clothing for herself, husband, and family, whether of buckskin or cloth. Until within a few years the needle was a piece of sharpened bone, the thread a fibre of sinew. Now nearly all the sewing is done with civilised appliances. She cooks the food, brings all the wood and water used in the lodge. This last is not a hard task; for they do not bathe or wash the face and hands except on rare occasions, and then they go to the stream. Bloody, greasy, or otherwise filthy hands are wiped on the leggings or other part of the clothing. I have never seen an article of clothing washed in an Indian camp.

I have already said that all the packing of household goods, striking and pitching lodges, as also the packing and unpacking of animals, is done by women. But her hardest work is at the time of the fall hunt. If the buffalo are moving, the success of the hunt may depend upon the rapidity with which she performs her work on a batch of dead buffalo. These animals spoil very quickly if not disembowelled. The bucks do not, therefore, wish to kill in any one day more than the squaws can skin and cut up that same day. No sooner are the buffalo dead than the squaws are at work.

The southern plains Indians turn the animal on its back, and commence skinning, as we do, by a split down the belly. The northern tribes turn the animal on its belly, and make a starting slit down the spine. In either case the skin is removed with marvellous celerity. The meat, cut as closely as possible from the bones, is tied up in the skin, and packed on ponies to camp. The entrails, emptied of their contents, form the principal food of all during the hunt, not only being the most delicious morsel, but not requiring a waste of time in cooking. Marrow bones and hump ribs roasted on the coals serve for most delicious suppers after the day's work is done. All these are prepared by the women and 'brought to camp.

The skins are spread flesh side upwards on a level piece of ground, small slits are cut in the edges of each, and it is tightly stretched and fastened down by wooden pegs through the slits into the ground. The meat is cut into thin flakes, and placed on the drying scaffolds or poles. All this work is done in an incredibly short time. Another surround is then made, and so on, until the winter's supply is obtained.

The hunt being over, or, in the intervals, if game is scarce, the women proceed to 'gather the crop.' Old *parflêches* are brushed up and new ones made. The now thoroughly dried meat is pounded to powder between two stones, and packed in these receptacles. Melted tallow is poured over the whole, which is kept warm until the mass is thoroughly saturated. When cold the *parflêches* are closed and tightly tied up. The contents so prepared will keep in good condition for several years.

The dressing of skins is the next work. No tannin is used, consequently no leather is made. The thickest hides are selected for shields, *parflêches*, &c. The hair is taken off by soaking the skins in water in which is mixed wood ashes, lime, or some natural alkali. The skin is then cut into the required shape and put on a form while green. When it becomes dry it retains its shape, and is almost as hard as iron.

Making a robe is a much more difficult process. The skin in its natural condition is much too thick for use, being unwieldy and lacking pliability. This thickness must be reduced at least one half, and the skin at the same time made soft. When the stretched skin has become dry and hard from the action of the sun, the woman goes to work upon it with a small iron instrument shaped somewhat like a carpenter's adze. It has a short handle of wood or elk horn tied on with raw hide, and can be used with one hand. These tools are heirlooms in families, and are greatly prized, more especially those with elk horn handles. With this she chips at the hard skin, cutting off a thin shaving at each blow. The skill of this process is in so directing and tempering the blows as to cut the skin, yet not cut through it, and in finally obtaining a perfectly smooth and even inner surface and uniform thickness. To render the skin soft and pliable, every little while the chipping is stopped, and the chipped surface smeared with fat and brains of buffalo, which are thoroughly rubbed in with a smooth stone. It is a long and tedious process, and none but an Indian would go through it. Hides for making lodges have the hair taken off, are reduced in thickness, and made pliable. Deer. antelope, and other thin skins are beautifully prepared for clothing, the hair being always removed.

Thus there are four different processes in the preparation of skins, each admirably adapted to the use to which the prepared skin is to be put.

In none of the plains tribes is there the slightest knowledge of traps and trapping. Their invention seems to have stopped short of even the simplest contrivance for catching game, either animals or birds. I have heard of their stealing the traps of a white trapper; but the first time a bungler gets his fingers caught in its jaws, the trap is thrown away as 'bad medicine.'

These seem to be the only aboriginal people in the world who have not some pitfall, spring, or native trap. I attribute this lack to the plentiful supply of large game always to be had on the plains. The Indian never wanted for food and clothing when countless herds covered the plains. He had no ' necessity,' and his ' invention ' was therefore never born.

A few fish are killed by lance or arrows, but until within a very few years the plains Indians had no knowledge of angling with line and hook. They are not fish eaters, and only use them when nothing better is to be had.

CHAPTER XXXIII.

TRADE.

THE trade or commercial industry of the plains Indians is limited to a small barter among themselves, and the annual exchange with white traders, licensed by the Indian Bureau, of their surplus buffalo robes for sugar, coffee, tea, clothing, trinkets and gewgaws. With good management there is a great deal of money to be made by the whites in these trades, and a licence is eagerly sought.

Long before the time of the ' big trade,' each trader sends out runners or drummers to the camps of the different bands to find out how many robes are likely to come in from each, and to solicit trade, with promises of presents to the chiefs and prominent men.

The trading is done under the auspices of the Indian Bureau, and the agent, having control, does pretty much as he pleases. He may permit the traders to go with their goods to the winter camps of the Indians; or he may refuse such permission, thus forcing the Indians to come to the traders. When there are several traders it is almost impossible for the agent to act in any way without his action being for or against the interests of one or other of the traders. However fair and impartial his action may be, somebody is sure to believe himself injured, and equally sure to accuse the agent of interested motives and collusion with his rivals.

When permission is given to go to the winter camps, all the traders are notified at or near the same time, and each starts off his waggons with all possible despatch ; unnecessary, because the runners of each have interviewed the Indians, who are by far too shrewd not to understand the value of competition, and will not, therefore, begin the trade until all the traders have arrived.

Reaching the camp, their tents are pitched, their wares unpacked, and displayed to the best advantage. The bucks stalk gravely from tent to tent, talking business; while the squaws crowd every available space, and admire and chatter with all the eagerness for shopping that the gentle sex everywhere display. But many long talks are to be held, many important questions settled, before the trade actually begins. The traders cannot take advantage of each other by underselling; for the Indians immediately inform all the other traders of a reduction proposed by one. Consequently they are forced into at least an appearance of combined action, although each is doing all he can for himself by presents and personal influence with the chiefs.

Finally, prices are agreed upon. The pint cup is the standard of measure for sugar, coffee, tea, &c. A partial stretch of the extended arms (about one and a half yard), very accurately measured by both trader and Indian, is the standard of measure for cloths.

From the moment that the trade commences it is conducted with something like fury. Each buck rushes to the trading tent, followed by his squaws loaded with packs and bundles of buffalo robes, and each demands to be helped first. The tent is jammed. The trader and his assistants fly round with incessant activity. The robes are not sold by the quantity ; but each is passed singly over the counter, and the price taken before another is passed. This, of course, greatly increases the work of the trader.

Each buck trades first for the winter's supply of necessaries for himself and family, then for articles for his own use, convenience, or adornment ; then he selects presents for his favourite wife, or for a young girl whom he wishes to make a wife, or possibly for the wife of some other warrior to whom he has taken a fancy. When all this is done, if any robes are left, he graciously permits his wives to dispose of them as suits their own pleasure.

For what the Indians have come to consider necessaries—sugar, coffee, tea, flour, Indian cloth, blankets, calico, beads, needles and thread, knives, paint, &c.—the price agreed upon beforehand is rigidly demanded of each trader.

Unless one has purchased at better rates than the other, neither gains any special advantage in this regular trade, except in the number of robes purchased. It is in the sale of trinkets, gewgaws, and articles of Indian finery and Indian luxury, and on which a stated price cannot be set, that the real competition is created and the great profits made.

A novelty has great charms for an Indian, who will pay a hundred times its value for an article new to him which strikes his fancy. He has no real standard of value, and what he will give for an article, not in the sale, is regulated entirely by the greatness of his desire for it. The trader understands this perfectly, and not unfrequently gets two or three robes for a piece of tawdry jewellery which probably cost him twenty-five cents. The trade continues until each family has bought all it needs, or until the robes give out.

In some instances traders have established permanent store tents at the Indian camp, kept open as an ordinary store all the winter. This, however, is not so profitable an arrangement as it would appear; for the Indians are not only arrant thieves, but most importunate beggars, and the trader is compelled to be giving something all the time, or risk losing the favour of the chiefs and head men.

The price of a buffalo robe has very greatly increased within the last two or three years. In 1871-2 it was worth from seven to nine cups of sugar; a red Mackinac blanket was good for two or even three robes; whilst one measure of Indian cloth, or five or six measures of calico, was the equivalent of one robe.

Counting all expenses of transportation of goods, employment of runners, salesmen, &c., the robes actually cost the traders from two and a half to three and a half dollars at the Indian camp. And this, too, when all *legitimate* mercantile advantages are taken. The Indian buys sugar by measure. The trader brings out the lightest and most fluffy article to be found, weighing scarcely half a pound to the pint. The Indian is no judge of coffee, tea, &c. The very poorest article to be found in the eastern market is brought to him. Of the quality of Indian cloth, blankets, calico, and such articles, the Indian is a very fair judge; and in the regular trade, with his accustomed articles, he is not easily taken in. It is when he finds something new and specially adapted to his fancy that his pocket is turned out.

I have said that he has no standard of value. Neither can he comprehend that any other man can have such standard. He will work a month to complete a bow and quiver of arrows, and then probably sell them for something that cost twenty cents. He will gravely offer to 'swap' a broken-down mule worth nothing for a two-hundred dollar horse.

Years ago, before matches were so common as now, a Lipan Indian saw an officer take a box, of what to him were little sticks, from his pocket, and, scratching one on a stone, light his pipe. He eagerly inquired into this mystery, and looked on with astonishment while several matches were lighted for his gratification. He went to his camp near by, and soon came back with half a dozen beautifully-dressed wild cat skins, which he offered for the wonderful box. The exchange was accepted, and he went off exceedingly gratified. Some time after he was found sitting by a stone on which he was gravely scratching match after match, holding each in his fingers until forced to drop it, and then inspecting and examining the scorched fingers, as if in doubt whether it were real fire. This he continued until every match was gone.

In 1867 a Sioux Indian came to Fort Sedgwick, having in his possession a very fine and elaborately painted buffalo robe. Many offers were made by officers for its purchase—sugar, coffee, flour, &c., to the amount of nearly twenty dollars being offered and refused. Some time after a sergeant passed who had in his hand a paper containing two or three pounds of loaf sugar cut into cubic blocks or lumps (cut loaf, then new to frontier people). He gave the Indian a lump or two, and passed on. In a few moments the Indian came running after him, took the robe from his shoulders, and offered it for the paper of sugar. The exchange being made, he sat down on the ground, and slowly and deliberately, with every appearance of the most perfect gratification, ate up every lump.

The laws of the United States prescribe heavy penalties for those who sell intoxicating liquors to the Indian, or even take it into his country without special authority. In prohibiting the regular trader from selling whisky to the Indian, the Government exercises the same supreme wisdom that it everywhere displays in the management of Indian affairs.

It takes the traffic in liquor (which *will* go on as long as an Indian is left) out of the hands of responsible men, in which it could be guarded and regulated, and places it in those of the most grasping, unscrupulous, rascally set of men in the world. The trader is also usually prohibited from selling arms and ammunition. Whether truthfully or not, this most lucrative department of the Indian traffic has come to be regarded by frontier people as the special prerogative of the Indian Bureau and its pets and favourites. Who sells the arms to the Indians will probably always be a mystery; but certain it is that they are always found completely armed with the very latest and most approved pattern of breech-loading rifles, pistols, &c., and, although utterly ignorant of the manufacture of powder or lead, they are nevertheless always fully supplied with these indispensable necessaries.

Where does the Indian get his arms? This is a very serious question to the army and to the frontier settlers, but a question to which there is never an answer. Whoever is responsible is also responsible for the life blood of many a good and brave man, and for the tears and sufferings of many a widow and orphan. There would be no doubt, no mystery, did not the abominable greed for money cover up every crime and every villany.[1]

A few years ago I met a man said to be possessed of a very considerable share of the world's goods, who, in a communicative mood, told me that he had made his first step towards fortune by being selected to pay a sum of money to a tribe of Indians on the Pacific frontier. Going to San Francisco, he proceeded to expend one-half of the money in a most careful and judicious selection of the most suitable goods in that market. The other half of the money (less a sufficient sum for transportation) was expended in the purchase of rifles, pistols, powder, lead, caps, liquor, and articles of finery. He arrived in the Indian country in the most fortunate season, sent out runners, got the tribe together, and, after a talk, opened and distributed his gifts. The Indians were more than delighted. They had never seen such excellent articles, nor had a tithe of the quantity ever

---

[1] The following has been told me as true. If so, it will afford some light on the question, Who sells the arms? The names of all the parties can be furnished :—

A few years ago an army officer of high rank was in command of a force confronting a large body of Indians who were believed to be getting ready for an outbreak. The officer learned from his spies that a waggon train loaded with arms and ammunition was on its way to the quasi-hostile Indians. He immediately sent out and captured the train. He reported his action to the proper authorities at Washington. The Indian agent also made a report, and the result was that the officer received a most decided snub. He was ordered to release the train, and mind his own business.

been brought to them before. When all were in the best possible humour, he opened his cases of arms, &c., and then told them that he was ready for trade. They rushed at it with avidity, sometimes giving furs worth $200 or $300 for a gun which cost twenty. 'I did a pretty good thing,' added he; 'I satisfied the Department, I made the Indians perfectly happy, and I cleared for myself somewhat more than double the whole amount of money given to me in the first place.' I give this story, as I accepted it, for what it is worth. It is entirely within the bounds of probability.

It is well known that the founders of some of the most colossal fortunes in this country started as traders with, or agents for, Indians, and the greatest city of the Mississippi Valley may be said to have been founded and built on the Indian trade.

CHAPTER XXXIV.

DRILLING.

In good weather a very considerable portion of time is spent in drill, and very great proficiency is attained. There seems to be no fixed system of tactics, each chief instructing according to his own particular ideas. There are no ranks, no organisations or units of command; but there are words or signals of command, by which the same evolutions are repeatedly performed, seemingly more by the admirable intuition of the individual Indian than by any instruction that could possibly have been given him. The whole band will charge *en masse*, and without order, on a supposed position of the enemy. At a word it breaks or scatters like leaves before the storm. Another signal: a portion wheels, masses, and dashes on a flank, to scatter again at another signal. The plain is alive with circling, flying horsemen; now single, lying flat on the horse, or hanging to his side, as if to escape the shots of a pursuing enemy, and now joined together in a living mass of charging, yelling terror.

The most remarkable part of the drill is the perfect control the chief seems to exert, not only on the mass, but on the individual, and this in spite of clouds of dust, and noise enough to drown the roar of a cannon. It is done by signals, devised after a system of the Indian's own invention, and communicated in various ways.

Wonderful as the statement may appear, the signalling on a bright day, and when the sun is in the proper direction, is done with a piece of looking-glass held in the hollow

of the hand. The reflection of the sun's rays thrown
on the ranks communicates in some mysterious way the
wishes of the chief. Once standing on a little knoll overlooking the valley of the South Platte, I witnessed almost
at my feet a drill of about 100 warriors by a Sioux chief,
who sat on his horse on a knoll opposite me, and about 200
yards from his command in the plain below. For more
than half an hour he commanded a drill which for variety
and promptness of action could not be equalled by any
civilised cavalry of the world. All I could see was an
occasional movement of the right arm. He himself afterwards told me that he used a looking-glass.

The signal drill is most strong and sacred ' medicine,'
the secret of which it would be destruction to divulge.
Even the whites, intermarried and living with them, are
not admitted to the mystery. I have questioned several
of these and many plains hunters, who could never tell
me more than that such system is in common use. In
the hope of emulating the fame of our renowned chief
signal officer, I have used both persuasion and bribes to
the Indians themselves, but could never get at even a hint
which I might use as a starting point of a practical system
of signalling. They admit the use of the glass, and that
is all.

In communicating at long distances on the plains,
their mode of telegraphing is equally remarkable. Indian
scouts are frequently employed by the United States Government, and are invaluable, indeed almost indispensable,
to the success of important expeditions. The leader, or
interpreter, is kept with the commander of the expedition,
while the scouts disappear far in advance or on the flanks.
Occasionally one shows himself, sometimes a mere speck
on a distant ridge, and the interpreter will say at once
what that scout wishes to communicate. I learned many
of these signals, which are simple enough : as, for instance,
riding rapidly round in a circle means ' danger ; get together as quickly as possible.'

The only really wonderful thing about this telegraphing is the very great distance at which it can be read by the Indian. I have good 'plains eyes;' but while, even with an excellent field glass, I could scarcely make out that the distant speck was a horseman, the Indian by my side would tell me what the distant speck was saying. Indians signalling and telegraphing are undoubtedly only modifications and extensions of the sign language heretofore spoken of. All are offspring of a necessity growing out of the constant wariness incident to a life of peculiar danger.

I have already mentioned the religious belief which condemns every scalped warrior to annihilation, and of the heroism often displayed by the Indian in risking his own life to save unscalped the body of his chief or friend. This superstition is the primary cause of a drill peculiar to the plains Indian. It is to stoop from the horse at full speed, and pick up objects from the ground. At first small and light objects are selected. These are gradually exchanged for heavier and more bulky ones, until some few individuals attain such wonderful proficiency as to be able, unassisted and at full speed, to pick up from the ground, and swing across his horse, the body of the heaviest man.

This, however, is generally done by two Indians. Rushing neck by neck on either side of the prostrate form, each rider stoops at the same instant, seizes the part most convenient, and the combined strength and address of the two swings the body in front of one of the riders, who carries it away to a safe place. The warriors take turns in picking and being picked up, for at any time during a fight each may have to act or be acted upon as foreshadowed in the drill. When drilling as wounded, the prostrate man will assist the others by extending arms and legs. When drilling as dead, not only is no help afforded, but the 'acting' dead man assumes by turns every position, the most unnatural or even impossible that a really dead body might be supposed to fall into. This drill is practised in good weather, most assiduously, on all kinds of ground, until riders, ponies, and supposed dead and wounded are thoroughly proficient in their several parts.

THE NOONTIDE REPAST ON THE WAR PATH

CHAPTER XXXV.

FIGHTING.

FROM the tactical manœuvres described, an idea may be formed of the general characteristics of the fighting of the plains Indian. I have already spoken of his bravery. No man can more gallantly dash into danger when his reward, either in scalps or ponies, is sure.

It is in the higher qualities of courage, the firmness of soul which enables a man to take his chance of wounds and death, for the sake of principle or duty, without hope or expectation of reward, that the Indian is generally lacking. He has, however, exceptional glimpses of this higher order of courage, as when risking his life to carry off dead and wounded comrades ; and I have been told of two instances where a few Indians devoted themselves to sure death, to save large numbers from destruction. As a rule, the Indian relies upon surprise, upon the effect of a sudden and furious dash, accompanied with unearthly yells, to demoralise his enemy and render him a sure prey. In this he has no superior ; nor can he be excelled in the spirit with which he follows up a first successful effort, nor in the remorseless vigour and determination of his pursuit of a flying foe.

Their fights with each other are almost invariably surprises; but if two hostile bands, nearly equal in numbers, should meet on the plains, a long contest is likely to ensue, in which the fighting is done at extreme long range, and consists principally in dashing about on their horses, making short feints of charges, yelling with intense fury, and once in a while firing a shot.

Occasionally a young buck, anxious to signalise his bravery, will dash, well covered by his position on the side of his horse, up to within 200 or 300 yards of the enemy, fire off his gun in mid career, and circle back to his own party. A youngster from the other side will then try his hand with the same result. This goes on until one party shows evidence of weakness, when the feints of charges on the other side become real, and the whipped band gets away as it can. This is not at all usual. Generally the affair is kept up until the ponies give out, when each party draws off to try to achieve by superior craft and cunning what it failed to do in open fight.

I have been told of a *desperate* fight, which lasted four days, in which the bucks on each side displayed prodigies of valour, and in which *one* man was killed. If one party is greatly superior in numbers, it dashes at once into the others, relying on the demoralisation of the weaker side to prevent its doing much damage. Then it is Indian against Indian, pony against pony; and, unless the ground be partially unfavourable, the beaten force breaking up, each man for himself, will get away without nearly so much loss as might be expected.

The first impulse of the Indian, on being surprised in his camp, is that most natural to all animals—to scuttle away as fast as his legs will carry him. He does not, however, forget his arms, nor lose his head to such an extent as to fail to take the direction to the nearest cover. While under this terror, or ' stampede,' as it is called on the plains, he is by no means to be feared, his shooting being wild in the extreme ; and it is only when wounded that he recovers his presence of mind, and becomes again the really dangerous animal that he is. Indeed he is then ten times more dangerous than when unwounded, for in the latter condition he will always sacrifice a chance to

GRAND CHIEF OF THE PAWNEES.

kill for a chance to escape. The moment he receives a disabling wound he becomes utterly reckless; and, seeming to devote his whole remaining energies to the one single object of killing as many as possible of his enemies, he fights with the fierceness of the wolf, but with coolness of aim and desperation of purpose, as long as his eye can distinguish an enemy, or his finger pull a trigger.

Many a white man has been sent to the Happy Hunting Grounds from carelessly going up to an Indian supposed to be dead. An officer of high rank in our service has suffered all his life from a wound inflicted under such circumstances. Stampeded and demoralised, an Indian was running for life, without thought of using his arms. He was pursued, shot, and fell; and the officer, stopping his horse, was in the act of turning himself round to return to his command, when he was struck under the shoulderblade by an arrow, sped with the last breath of the Indian.

I have heretofore mentioned the deadly hate which exists between the Pawnees and the Sioux. Thirty years ago the Pawnees occupied and claimed as their own all the whole vast country from the Arkansas River to the Black Hills. The Sioux of Iowa, Minnesota, and Wisconsin, pushed back by the advancing tide of civilisation, thrust themselves between the Pawnees on the south and the Crows on the north, against each of which tribes an incessant and most bitter war was then and has been since waged. Gradually they spread over the wide plains of Dacotah and Nebraska. The Pawnees, who are undoubtedly the very hardest of Indian fighters, defended for a long time, with desperation and success, the line of the Platte, covering their chosen home, the great Buffalo region of the Republican and Smoky Rivers. One fall, about fifteen years ago, the whole Pawnee tribe was encamped on the south bank of the Platte, near the mouth of Plum Creek. Several hundred of the best warriors, taking with them only a comparatively few of the strongest and quickest working squaws, went over to the Republican for the fall hunt. Learning of this their opportunity, the Sioux assembled every available man, and by stealthy marches surprised and fell upon the comparatively defenceless main camp of the Pawnees, utterly and ruthlessly destroying every man, woman, and child, and carrying off the ponies and plunder to their fastnesses north of the North Platte. The Pawnees never recovered from this blow, and shortly after went upon a reservation assigned to them by the Government.

In August 1873 the Sioux struck another blow at their hated enemies. The Pawnees, in charge of their agent, were hunting on the waters of the Republican. Leaving a few men and the squaws and children to pack the animals, the bucks on the morning of the 4th of August had scattered in search of buffalo. No sooner were they at safe distance, when the unfortunate women were attacked by an overwhelming force of Sioux, and every one butchered. Thirteen men and fifty women and children were massacred. The bodies were all scalped; those of the women violated after death and most horribly mutilated. Even nursing babies were scalped, and their bodies pinned to the ground by arrows. So bitter is the animosity between these tribes that it is difficult to prevent collision when they meet, no matter what the circumstances.

In 1868, when Spotted Tail's band of Sioux was encamped at North Platte station, they by some means learned that a company of fifty Pawnees (then in the United States service) were being transported west on the cars. They immediately flew to arms, and a strong guard of soldiers had to be stationed along the track to preserve the peace.

The Sioux are the meanest, most treacherous, and most cowardly of plains Indians, and, though much petted by the Indian Bureau, are the most constant in their aggression on the whites. Their treatment by other Indians makes the Pawnees the most reliable friends of the whites ; and in any encounter with plains tribes, and more especially with Sioux, the Government can always rely on the services of 100 or 200 efficient allies, unsurpassed as scouts.

The Cheyennes and Utes hate each other with an equally bitter hatred, and fear each other more. The one is a plains tribe, the other a mountain tribe. One can do nothing except on horseback ; the other, though owning and valuing ponies, is essentially a foot tribe. A single Indian of either tribe on *his own ground* counts himself equal to at least three of the other. The Utes go into the plains with fear and trembling. The Cheyennes will scarcely venture at all into any country so broken as to prevent their operating to advantage on horseback. Though constantly at war with each other, few are killed, because neither will venture far into the domain of the other.

In the fall of 1870, Little Washington, with his band of several hundred Utes, went on to the Arkansas, just below the mouth of the Sand Creek, to make the fall buffalo hunt. Buffalo were rather scarce, and but few surrounds had been made, when one day some Utes, who were out on foot towards 'Two Butte Creek,' looking for herds, discovered three Cheyennes on horseback. Noting the direction in which they were travelling, the Utes got in their front, and waylaid and shot them all ; but were in such terror lest other Cheyennes might come on them, that they did not even stop to take their scalps or catch the ponies, but rushed back to their camp and gave the alarm. The whole camp was instantly in commotion, and in an incredibly short time in march ; nor did they stop their flight until safe in the almost inaccessible cañons of Rule Creek. One of the Cheyennes, though mortally wounded, managed to get back to his camp. A large party was at once sent in pursuit of the Utes ; but the moment the trail entered the cañons the plains Indians turned back—not one would risk himself in a place

where he must fight at such disadvantage. All plains
tribes share with the Cheyennes their contempt for mountain Indians on the plains, and their fear of them in the
mountains.

The mixed band under Two Lance, before spoken
of, had to go well upon the head waters of the Republican to find buffalo in sufficient numbers. This brought
them to the edge of the Ute country. As, Two Lance
told me, they feared would be the case, the Utes soon
found them out ; and a few warriors, slipping into the
vicinity of camp during the night, stampeded the ponies
at daybreak, and, in spite of the overwhelming force and
hot pursuit of the Sioux, got safe to the mountains with
over 200 head.

In 1867 almost all the plains tribes were on the war
path, making a last desperate effort to preserve to themselves the great buffalo range between the Platte and the
Arkansas. A company of fifty Pawnee Indians in the
service of the United States, and under a white captain
(Major North), was stationed on the Platte opposite Plum
Creek. A force of Cheyennes, afterwards ascertained to
be 154 strong, came north to capture a train on the
Union Pacific Railroad, and so certain were they of success
that they had with them squaws and pack mules to carry
off the booty. The Cheyennes struck the Platte at Plum
Creek, and, as soon as it was known, the Pawnees were
ordered across the river to engage and hold them in
check until additional forces could be brought up.

The captain of the Pawnees, finding his force greatly
inferior, resorted to stratagem. Stripping his men to
Indian fighting costume, he made each put on his uniform
hat, and throw over his shoulder his uniform overcoat,
buttoning only the top button ; he then advanced to the
attack. The Cheyennes had a most admirable position.
Plum Creek is a deep bed, generally dry, some sixty feet
wide, with high and almost perpendicular banks. The
stage road was crossed by a bridge. The Cheyenne line

was drawn up directly opposite, and facing the eastern end of this bridge, and about 100 yards from it. The right flank, which might be turned, was protected by eight or ten dismounted Indians posted in the loopholed stable of Plum Creek Stage station. The Cheyenne leader undoubtedly believed that the advancing force was United States cavalry. His plan was to permit them partially to cross the bridge, and then, by a vigorous charge, with the usual yells, to frighten the restive and not well-broken cavalry horses, render them unmanageable, and thus throw the whole force into confusion in a most difficult and dangerous position. The Pawnees advanced by the flank, left in front. As soon as the leading files passed the bridge they rapidly inclined to the left, giving room for those in the rear to come up into line. When nearly half the company had passed, the Cheyennes charged with furious yells. When they had arrived within fifty yards, the Pawnees threw off hats and overcoats, and with a true Indian yell dashed at the enemy. The latter, entirely surprised and stampeded, wheeled their horses, and fled in utter dismay and confusion. The Pawnees took sixteen scalps, two prisoners, and a number of animals, without a single man or horse being even scratched. So little danger is there in a ' stampeded ' Indian.

In fighting with white men, a surprise is always made when possible ; when this cannot be done the Indians use other tactics, modified to suit the circumstances of the case. A pitched battle on anything like equal terms as regards numbers is impossible ; first, because the army is so small and so widely scattered over our vast country that it is everywhere greatly outnumbered ; and, second, because the Indians, not being hampered with waggons, pack mules, or other *impedimenta*, can always avoid such a battle, and would never be brought to accept it unless they outnumbered the soldiers at least five to one.

When their very great superiority of numbers emboldens them to determine on such a fight, and a considerable force is engaged, the different bands, each under its chief, are drawn up into an array, not a line— for the bands form no lines—but which nevertheless forms the line of battle. This line may charge altogether or by individual bands. The Indians never receive a charge and very rarely meet one. When charged, the portion of the array immediately in front of the charging force breaks and melts away into individual Indians, while the bands on either side close in to attack or harass the flanks and rear of the charge. The broken Indians, wheeling in circles, form on the flanks to attack, whenever practicable, or break again when charged. Should the attacking force, carried away by excitement, become scattered in pursuit of the flying individuals, its defeat and destruction is almost sure. The magnificent riding of the Indian and his superb drill in this, his favourite mode of warfare, give him an immense advantage. Avoiding, by quick turns of the small and active ponies, the direct pursuit of their more bulky foe, and circling like birds of prey, they collect together, fall upon his flanks and rear, overwhelm him, and disperse, to repeat the process on another.

In small fights the same tactics prevail. I know of one instance where a small force attacked at least five times its number, beat, scattered, and drove them for more than two miles; but, the troops also becoming scattered in the pursuit, the enemy turned upon them, wounded the officer in command, and killed and wounded more than half the party, the survivors saving themselves only by the speed of their horses.

There is one well-authenticated instance of a fair stand-up fight between nearly equal numbers of troops and Indians. A lieutenant of the old 1st Dragoons with sixteen men met a party of hostile Apaches about twenty strong. The two forces approached each other in line, and at about 100 yards each broke into charge, the lines

EMIGRANTS CROSSING LARAMIE PLAINS IN 1868.—THE SIOUX PREPARING FOR THEIR RECEPTION.

passing each through the other. Wheeling, a second and a third charge were made, not a man on either side flinching from his work. On the third charge the Indian chief received a bullet in his brain, and his followers fled beaten from the field.

The Indian and the old hunter or trapper of the plains rarely come into collision. The latter is too cool and dangerous a customer to be attacked without due and careful preparation. Moreover, he is too poor to warrant the almost certain loss that must ensue to an attacking force. The Indians therefore content themselves with watching his camp and stealing his hard-won peltries, his blankets and kettles, the first time he leaves them undefended.

The Indian's great delight is the attack of a waggon train. There is comparatively little risk, and his reward in ponies and plunder most ample. For days he will watch the slow moving line, until he knows exactly the number and character of armed men that defend it. If their numbers or carelessness warrant a direct attack, he selects some place where the ground is unfavourable for coralling the waggons. Here he lies in wait, and at the proper time rushes out with terrifying yells, frightening the teams, which run away, overturning waggons, and throwing everything into confusion. Cool heads and steady hands are required at such moments, and if the whites fail in these their fate is soon decided. If a direct attack involves too much risk, the Indian's next concern is to get possession of the horses and mules.

He will follow the train for days, or even weeks, never seen, his presence never suspected. Lulled into false security, the white guardians become somewhat careless; the herd is permitted to wander farther from camp, or with a too slender guard. Like a thunderbolt from a clear sky, the Indians rush into the herd with whoops and yells, scare it into stampede, and in a moment all disappear together.

One unaccustomed to Indian warfare would naturally

suppose that cover, rocks, thickets, &c., would be the safest place for a small party attacked by an overwhelming force. Unless the thicket is large, no more fatal mistake can be made. In stealth, cunning, and patience the Indian is the white man's superior. However closely the fugitive may hide himself, the Indians will find some means of getting at him without exposing themselves. His only hope is darkness, when the Indian's superstition renders him timid, and under its favourable cover he must put as many miles as possible between himself and that party of Indians.

A party of railroad surveyors at work on Lodge Pole Creek were suddenly attacked by a large force, one or two killed, and the survivors took refuge in a dense thicket of sage brush, three or four feet high and about 150 yards in diameter. The thicket, though commanded by a bluff about 200 yards off, was otherwise very favourably situated, the ground around it being smooth and bare, affording no cover. The whites had run in on the side nearest the bluff, and were congratulating themselves on their good position, when a pony carrying two warriors came at full speed across the open towards the farther side of the thicket. As he passed the edge the rearmost rider threw himself to the ground and crawled into the thicket. Another and another Indian was dropped in the same way, the whites firing at the flying horseman, but failing to hit, either from the speed, the distance, or from not daring to expose themselves sufficiently for a good shot. Several Indians, having got on the bluff, were harassing them with a hot fire; whilst those Indians who were dropped from the horses crawled into the thicket, and surrounded on three sides the wretched men. Scarcely moving a twig themselves, any movement of a bush by the whites was immediately followed by a shot. The protruded barrel of a rifle, or the exposure of the smallest portion of the person, was the target for a volley. When night came

EMIGRANTS ENCAMPED.—THE NIGHT ATTACK.

three men, one wounded, stole out of the thicket and made their way to the nearest post, the only survivors of a party of eight or ten.

Another fatal mistake is to run away. It is a singular but well-established fact, that the mere act of running from an enemy has a tendency to demoralise the person running, and that even the bravest man under such circumstances is liable to ' stampede himself, or lose his head at the very time that all his coolness and judgment are most necessary. Riding furiously and without discretion, he will either throw his horse down by riding him into some ravine or hole, or tire him out so as to be easily overtaken. Fright has rendered the rider helpless, and he is killed without difficulty, or captured alive, to delight the women with his torture. I have known of one instance where a good plainsman, a citizen, who had been in several fights, a splendid rider and shot, became stampeded, and, when overtaken, stood quiet, pistol in hand, and allowed himself to be shot several times, and finally killed, without attempting the slightest defence.

A citizen, employed at Fort Dodge as herder, was one day out, fully armed, guarding the herd, when a small party of Indians dashed upon it. One made direct for the herder, who turned his horse and rode direct for the garrison, but was overtaken and killed within 200 yards of the quarters, without firing a shot.

The safest position for a small party is on a perfectly level plain without timber, rocks, holes, or other cover for an enemy, and large enough for the party to be well beyond fair shot from any ravine. If no such place can be got at, then scan the nearest approach to it.

A good plainsman, when travelling with a small party on unknown ground, is always on the look-out for such favourable positions, and if ' jumped ' by Indians in bad ground he gets back to the last good place without loss of time, horse well in hand, going at a good round rate, but not running. These tactics are always adopted by the old trappers and hunters of the plains, and by all plainsmen, old or new, who know Indians ; and so well have the Indians come to understand it, that when they see two or three men take such a position, dismount, tie the legs of their horses, and sit down on the ground rifle in hand, they turn away and leave that party alone as ' bad medicine.' Of course there are exceptions, when the Indians are very hostile, or the small party owns exceptionally many or good horses ; but these are only exceptions, and rare exceptions. The Indian does not want to be killed or wounded any more than a white man, and he thoroughly counts the cost of all risks. He knows how he himself fights when cornered ; and his experience teaches him that the white will fight just as desperately and even more dangerously, and that an attack on a party so situated will probably cost more lives than the scalps and horses of the party are worth. Besides, as I have elsewhere said, he lacks discipline and the courage that comes of discipline. He argues like a militiaman in presence of the enemy, who, being in line with a thousand other men, sees a hostile line a thousand strong advancing to the attack. ' Heavens,' thinks he, ' what can I do against such a force ? ' and, totally forgetting the thousand men in line with him, he incontinently takes to his heels, not from lack of courage but of discipline. The white soldier going into battle knows that many will be killed and wounded, but always expects that he himself will be lucky and escape unhit. The disposition of the Indian is just the reverse ; each thinks he is the one going to be hit, and every man of thirty or forty charging Indians will throw himself on the side of his horse on the presentation of a single rifle.

To the white defender such position is admirable, not only in affording no cover to the attack, but in bracing and steadying his own nerves. There is no chance of his stampeding himself; and a man is never so cool, nor fights so desperately, as when he has made up his mind to live or die on one spot. Many a life has been saved by this simple proceeding, which would otherwise have been sacrificed. Sometimes the defenders get into a buffalo wallow. This is excellent ; the ground is much broken by these depressions, in which case they can also be used in the attack. If time be given the earth should be dug up with knives, and a rifle pit be made. Even a very slight one is of immense advantage. I know of one successful defence against repeated and desperate charges of an overwhelming force, where the breastwork was the bodies of three live horses, thrown to the ground in a sort of triangle, and their legs firmly tied.

A frontier desperado, having committed a cold-blooded murder at Hays City, was pursued by a party of whites and nearly overtaken. Stopping on a level prairie, he dismounted, drew his pistol, shot his horse dead, and, taking position under cover of the body, he killed and wounded three or four of his assailants, defended himself successfully until nightfall, and then escaped.

In 1867 I was with a party of officers elk hunting on the Loup River. We had an escort of twelve or fifteen infantry soldiers, and six Pawnee Indians. We established our camp in a fine position, and each officer, taking one or more Indians, went hunting as it suited him. One day I was out with one Pawnee, and, not finding game, had ridden some twelve or fifteen miles from camp, when we were discovered by a band of between forty and fifty hostile Sioux, who immediately set upon us.

About four miles back I had noticed a splendid defensive position, one of the very best I have ever seen. Putting our horses at half speed we plunged into the barrancas of the ' bad lands,' and in half an hour emerged on the spot sought for. Here we dismounted and made our preparations for fight. The Pawnee positively refused to fight on foot, and when I was ready I found him ready also ; not a rag of clothing on his body, and nothing but a bridle on his horse. From some receptacle he had

go.' So, after a few hours' siege, we saddled our horses and returned to camp without molestation, but were followed the whole way; and from that time we had no sport or comfort in our hunt, the wretches preceding us by day, driving away the game, and trying to burn us out every night; constantly making their unwelcome presence felt, and yet never giving us a chance for even a long shot at them.

In 1868, when crossing country with one cavalry 'orderly,' I, on rising a little ridge, found myself within less than 100 yards of two Indians, who, going up the ravine at my feet, had just passed the position on which I was. Fortunately, it was a drizzly, disagreeable day, and they, having their heads covered up with their blankets, neither saw nor heard us. Waiting until they had got out of sight, I passed on a little distance, when I saw others and others, until I found that I was actually surrounded on three sides by parties of Indians, whose numbers I could not estimate. Several stopped and looked at us, then went on, evidently taking us for some of their own parties; and it was not until we had obtained a fair start for a high and level table land which I knew of, about two miles off, that they discovered we were whites. The alarm was given, and they came for us. My 'orderly' being mounted on a mule, and the country being very rough and difficult, they had a great advantage in the race, and, on arriving at a good position on the plain, I had only time to loosen the girth, and tie my horse's head close down to his fore feet, when the whole yelling band appeared on the edge of the table land. As soon as they saw my position they stopped, consulted, scattered, and, keeping well out of certain rifle range, went all around me looking for some ravine or other cover for a safe approach. Finding none, they returned to their first position, and had another consultation; after which they rode off in the direction they had come, and I saw no more of them. The whole affair, chase and siege, did not last over half an hour.

In 1871 I was changing stations from Fort Lyon to Fort Larned on the Arkansas, taking, of course, my servants and household property. I had several waggons and an ample infantry escort. About thirty miles west of Fort Dodge the waggon road crosses a portion of the high prairie called the 'nine mile ridge.' This high land is cut by several broad depressions, and towards the river broken by numberless little ravines—very favourable ground for antelope hunting—and into these I, with my coloured man servant, was soon poking after game. It was a raw, foggy morning, and I had been hunting probably for two hours, when the fog lifted slightly, discovering two men on horseback about 200 yards off, whom, as they had on overcoats, I took to be soldiers from Fort Dodge. As soon as they saw me, however, one of them rode the signal ' danger,' ' collect together,' and I began to think of my escort. Looking round I was greatly annoyed to find the spring waggon, in which was my coloured cook, about 600 yards from me, opposite the Indians, while the waggons and escort could not be seen. Making the best of the situation I galloped back to the spring waggon, had it driven well out into the plain, and the mules unhitched and well secured. The driver got out his rifle, and everything was satisfactory except the presence of the cook. I not only feared she might be hit, but I knew the Indians would be more dangerous if a woman were likely to be a prize. Making her lie down in the bottom of the waggon, I packed around her lunch and other boxes, blankets, cushions, seats, everything that might stop a bullet, and gave her positive orders to remain perfectly quiet and concealed, no matter what took place. I then took position with my two men some paces on one side of the waggon, to spare it from shots. During all this time the Indians had been collecting, and, soon after I was ready, a line of about thirty moved slowly towards me. At about 800 yards they broke into a sharp canter. Expecting the charge to come in a moment, I went towards the waggon to be sure that the animals were tied safely, when, to my great indignation, I found Julia (the cook), revolver in hand, and her head thrust out of the front of the waggon. 'Get back there,' I angrily ordered; 'do you want to be shot?' 'Lord Colonel,' she answered, 'let me alone. I'll never have another chance to see an Indian fight.' The earnestness of this, under the circumstances, most unexpected answer set all to laughing; and John, the husband, who a moment before was almost white with apprehension, regained, with good humour, his natural black. Every moment of delay being most important to us, I, when the Indians had got within about 400 yards, stepped forward, made the Indian signal ' Halt,' and displayed a white handkerchief. To my great gratification they halted; and in a moment one came forward with what had once been a white flannel shirt, fastened to the pole of a lance. We met half way—I very friendly, he very gruff; I disposed to talk, he to be saucy. I asked the name of the tribe. He answered by demanding something to eat. I asked where they came from. He answered, ' Powder, lead, sugar.' We could not understand each other well, which I was rather thankful for, as it prolonged the talk. He wanted everything; and asked, not as a beggar, but demanded, as one having right. I am compelled to admit a certain amount of duplicity on this occasion, having, to gain time, promised things which I had no intention of performing.

The Indians had not seen the waggons, which were crossing one of the long depressions below the level of the plain on which we were. They were sure of us; but preferred getting what we had without a fight if possible, especially as we had a good position. While we continued to talk I heard most welcome sounds, and, looking in that direction, saw the waggons coming at the full speed of the mules, while a line of ' the boys in blue,

A story is told of Jack Hays, a captain of Rangers, very celebrated under the Republic of Texas, that once, when his company had charged and put to flight a band of Comanches, his very fine and fast mare became unduly excited, ran away with and carried him alone in amongst the flying savages, who set upon him from every side. Without firing a shot he rode with them for several miles, keeping off too pertinacious assailants by simply presenting his pistol, until finally getting control of his horse, he drew unhurt out of the dangerous neighbourhood.

A very curious and unexplained custom among the northern plains tribes is called 'giving the *coup*.' How the custom originated is not known; but the term indicates that it was at least named by the old French trappers, predecessors of the Hudson Bay Company. When a foe has been struck down in a fight, the scalp belongs to him who shall first strike the body with knife or tomahawk. This is the *coup*. If in a *mêlée* or running fight a warrior kills an enemy, he, in order to secure his proper recognition and reward, must rush at once on the prostrate body, and strike his *coup*, regardless of other enemies that may be at hand. This, of course, renders the Indian less formidable. The enemy being in full flight, a brave and skilful warrior who would press on and on, adding victim after victim to his list, would return at last to find the scalps of all the enemies killed by his hand at the girdles of laggards in the race, to each of whom would be accorded all the honours due to one who had killed his man. While he who took all the risks and did all the killing, and who, in his eagerness to kill, may have passed even the last of his victims, has nothing whatever to show for his gallantry, and is consequently without honour or credit, the cowardly shirks, far in the rear, gain all the glory and applause. The consequence is that, when a foe falls, the slayer, even in the hottest race, and though other

victims are at his hand, must, to obtain the proper recognition of his act, at once give up all thought of further
killing, make his *coup*, and take the scalp.   It can be
readily seen that this custom is entirely to the advantage
of the fugitives, and accounts in some measure for so few
Indians being killed in their fights.

After the return of a successful party, when scalps
have been taken, a ceremony is performed by the
warriors who took them, no other person being permitted
to be present.   I have been a spectator at a distance,
but all to be seen was a number of Indians squatted on
their haunches in a circle.   During the ceremony the
scalps are trimmed, cleared of any fleshy matter, and the
skin partially cured by some process.   Each scalp is then
stretched by thongs inside of a small hoop of wood, and
the hair combed and greased.   Each warrior then
attaches his scalp or scalps in their hoops to a peeled
willow wand, some eight or ten feet long.   All march
gravely back to camp, each bearing his wand and scalps
in his hand.   The wands are planted in a circle in the
centre of the camp.   This ceremony is called ' counting
the *coups*,' and is preparatory to the ' scalp dance.'

A great deal of unnecessary sympathy has been
wasted by the philanthropic world on the killing of
squaws in battle by whites.   In some instances, as the
'Sand Creek massacre,' most horrible and barbarous
murders of women and children have been committed,
worthy the Indians themselves ; but, as a rule, no woman
is hurt except by accident, or when fighting like a man.   In
the surprise and attack of a camp, when all is excitement,
and bullets are flying in pursuit of every flying enemy,
that women and children should be killed and wounded
is to be expected.   In such cases the younger squaws are
very prompt to make their sex known, holding up their
hands and yelling ' squaw,' 'squaw ;' and, even in the
excitement and thirst for blood engendered by battle, I
have never known or heard of a woman being killed

under such circumstances by any soldier of the regular service. The dress and mode of riding of bucks and squaws are so entirely similar, that in conflicts and pursuits on horseback squaws are not unfrequently killed. Many of them, particularly the middle-aged and old women, handle arms with great facility and address, and are fully as dangerous in fight as their husbands and sons. Many a man has received his death wound from a fighting squaw; and if any man finds himself the target for flying bullets or arrows, I think he deserves all he gets should he allow a sentimental squeamishness to prevent his putting an end to the annoyance and the cause of it, whether woman or man.

Few persons visited San Antonio, Texas, between the years 1845 and 1850 who did not know and like jolly ' Tom Howard,' whose rotund person and jovial countenance little indicated the fighting dare-devil that he was. Tom was an ' Old Texan,' whose creed was to hate, and whose first duty was to exterminate, 'Greasers'[1] and Indians at all times and under all circumstances. One day, riding out from San Antonio with a friend, they came upon two Indians, and without a moment's hesitation charged them. One of the Indians was soon disposed of. The other kept on at full speed, sending arrow after arrow at the pursuers, until a shot from one of them brought down his horse. Recovering his feet in an instant the Indian sent an arrow into the head of the horse of Tom's friend, which fell dead on a leg of the rider, pinning him to the ground. Another was sent full into Tom's stomach, dropping him from his horse. All his arrows being expended, the Indian rushed at Tom and seized his rifle, when the friend, raising himself on his elbow, fired his pistol with so true an aim that the Indian fell dead. After some time and with great difficulty

[1] A term of contempt applied by Americans to the lower class of Mexicans.

the two whites got upon their feet. Shaking themselves up, and getting the arrow out of Tom, they went to examine their dead Indian, and, to their astonishment and mortification, found it was a woman. The buck had been finished almost without an effort. The squaw came near finishing both her white enemies. Tom's brother used to tell the story with great glee, adding that, though the arrow went eight inches into Tom, it did not get through the fat.

CHAPTER XXXVI.

CAPTIVES.

THE plains Indians rarely make captives of men unless they have some object to gain or special animosity to gratify. Under ordinary circumstances they content themselves with terminating the existence of a man captive in the most convenient way consistent with a proper amount of suffering. The death of a captive by torture of fire is now very unusual, and since I came upon the plains I have known of but few instances.

In 1855 a small party of the 8th United States Infantry, out from Fort Davis, Texas, looking for timber to build the post, were surrounded by a large force of Apaches, and all killed except a drummer-boy of twelve or thirteen years of age. He was captured and taken to the Indian camp, and, speaking Spanish with tolerable fluency, was questioned at length by the captors, the interpreter being a Mexican boy captured some years before, and from whom I afterwards learned the following particulars. The boy's answers to them proving to the Indians that their scheme of attacking the post was sure to lead to disaster to them, they became very angry and turned him over to the squaws. These fiends in human shape stripped and tied him to a tree, and for some hours tormented him in every way their ingenuity could devise without endangering life. Becoming tired of this, they procured some 'fat'[1] pine knots, and, splitting them into small splinters, stuck them into the skin until the un-

[1] A term applied to wood very rich in resinous matter.

fortunate boy bristled like a porcupine. They then set fire to the splinters, and danced and yelled with delight when the poor boy cried and screamed with anguish. When the fire burned out they left him tied to the tree, exposed naked to the cold of that elevated region. Next morning he was tied, nearly dead, on a horse, and carried with the party, but after going about ten miles was found to be dead. He was then scalped, and his body flung among some rocks, where it was afterwards found by troops sent in pursuit.

In 1868 an attack was made by a party of Indians on a station of the Kansas Pacific Railroad. One man who happened to be outside was captured; the other two or three successfully defended their position, to the great exasperation of the red skins, who, after losing several men, drew off. Just at nightfall they took their captive to a position in plain view, but just beyond shot of the station, stripped him of his clothing, fastened him on his back to the ground, built a fire on his naked breast, and sat around it warming themselves with great apparent satisfaction. The cries and groans of the victim could be plainly heard by his friends; but nothing could be done, and it was not until far in the night that the cessation of his cries proved that life was extinct. Next morning the blackened and half-burned body was found still fastened to the ground, not only scalped, but, being an unusually hairy man, almost skinned, and the flesh cut and hacked from the bones.

I have before said that the Indians are fond of children. In their raids on each other and on the whites those children which are large enough to help themselves a little, and not so large as to be likely to have strong affection or memory, are carried off to the tribe and adopted into it. These foster children are treated by the Indians as their own, grow up, become warriors, or are sold in marriage, exactly as the other children of the families adopting them.

Either the character and customs of the Indians have greatly changed, or Cooper and some other novelists knew nothing of Indians when they placed their heroines as captives in the hands of these savages. I believe I am perfectly safe in the assertion that there is not a single wild tribe of Indians in all the wide territory of the United States which does not regard the person of the female captive as the inherent right of the captor, and I venture to assert further that in the last twenty-five years no woman has been taken prisoner by any plains Indians who did not as soon after as practicable become a victim to the lust of every one of her captors.

The rule is this. When a woman is captured by a party she belongs equally to each and all, so long as that party is out. When it returns to the home encampment, she may be abandoned for a few days to the gratification of any of the tribe who wish her, after which she becomes the exclusive property of the individual who captured her, and henceforward has protection as his wife.

No words can express the horror of the situation of that most unhappy woman who falls into the hands of these savage fiends. The husband or other male protectors killed or dispersed, she is borne off in triumph to where the Indians make their first camp. Here, if she makes no resistance, she is laid upon a buffalo robe, and each in turn violates her person, the others dancing, singing, and yelling around her. If she resists at all her clothing is torn off from her person, four pegs are driven into the ground, and her arms and legs, stretched to the utmost, are tied fast to them by thongs. Here, with the howling band dancing and singing around her, she is subjected to violation after violation, outrage after outrage, to every abuse and indignity, until not unfrequently death releases her from suffering. The Indian woman, knowing this inevitable consequence of capture, makes no resistance, and gets off comparatively easy. The white woman naturally and instinctively resists, is 'staked out,' and subjected to the fury of passions fourfold increased by the fact of her being white and a novelty. Neither the unconsciousness nor even the death of the victim stops this horrible orgie; and it is only when the fury of their passions has been glutted to satiety that she is released if alive, or scalped and mutilated if dead. If she lives, it is to go through the same horrible ordeal in every camp until the party gets back to the home encampment.

Should the Indians not wish to be burdened with a captive, they may, after surfeit of their passions, tie her to a tree and leave her, as I have known in two instances; or butcher her in cold blood, of which there are numberless instances.

The wife of a sergeant of the old 2nd Dragoons was captured by a party of seven. They stripped her naked, staked her out, and all violated her until glutted. They then tied her to a tree, whipped her with switches until her body was covered with bloody weals, and left her. Next morning she was found by troops almost dead. A laundress of the 3rd Infantry, straying too far from camp on the Pecos River, was seized by Indians, thrown in front of one on his horse, and hurried off. Her screams attracted attention. Two or three men sprung on horses and dashed in pursuit. Finding himself unable to escape with his burden, the Indian drew his knife, cut and stabbed the poor woman, and threw her lifeless body to the ground.

A very pretty, intelligent, and attractive girl was in 1867 captured by Indians within a few miles of Fort Dodge. One man of the party escaped and hurried to that post. A force of cavalry was at once sent out, which came upon the Indians in time to rescue the poor girl and save her life, but not until she had been ravished by every Indian, numbering at least thirty. In this case the girl's good looks undoubtedly saved her a worse fate, the

my living among strangers. I shall live the balance of my life with the Indians.' This is the only instance in all my experience of a white woman remaining voluntarily with the Indians.

I could give numbers of well-authenticated instances of outrages as bad, and many far worse, than any here described. I have told enough, however, for elucidation, and I am glad to leave this sickening and horrible subject. I would infinitely prefer to suppress all mention of these fearful atrocities, and I only mention them in the interest of truth. Without some reference to them, it is almost impossible to depict the Indian as he really is, and also to account for the antipathy which exists between those living on the frontier and the red man of the plains.

CHAPTER XXXVII.

SCALPING.

WHEN Indians wear scalp locks the process of scalping consists in removing from the head a round piece of skin of which the crown is the centre. None of the plains Indians wear scalp locks, the hair being parted in the middle from front to rear, all the hair on either side being plaited into a long tail behind each ear. The process of scalping is, therefore, different. A handful of hair is grasped, the skin to which it is attached lifted, and the knife passed underneath. As the long side tails are most convenient to take hold of, the scalp is generally taken from one side of the head, and not unfrequently two or more scalps are taken from the same head. When there is plenty of time the whole portion of the skin of the head covered with hair is carefully removed in one piece, in many cases the ears remaining attached.

Some special virtue or value seems to be attached to hair-covered skin. The Indian has no hair on his face or person, and consequently scalps only the heads of other Indians. The full-bearded white man offers peculiar attractions to the scalper. Every portion of skin to which hair is attached, even to the small bit under the arms, is scalped off. I once saw in an Indian camp a ' scalp ' consisting of almost the entire skin of head, face, breast, and belly to the crotch in one piece. It had been carefully cured, and peculiar value was set upon it as ' big medicine.'

Scalping is not fatal. I have known several persons

alive and in good health who had undergone the process.

In 1867 a party of Indians took up a rail on the Union Pacific Railroad, and laid obstructions on the track. After dark a freight train ran into the trap, and in a moment was a wreck. The engineer and stoker were killed; the conductor and breaksmen jumped off to find themselves beset by the yelling savages. They ran into the darkness, and all escaped except one breaksman, who was pursued, shot, and fell. The Indian dismounted, and, sitting astride of the body, scalped the head, then stripped it of all clothing except shirt and shoes. Early in the morning another train approaching was flagged by a hideous-looking object, which turned out to be the breaksman, who, shot through the body and scalped, had yet walked a distance on the track to warn the train he knew would be along at that time. He was taken on board, and the train moved up to the wreck, which, after plundering, the Indians had left. While examining the condition of affairs, one of the men found a scalp, and, taking it into the car, it was immediately recognised by the scalped man as his own. It was put into water, and, when the man arrived at Omaha, an effort was made by the surgeons to make it grow on again, but without success. I saw the man some months afterwards, perfectly recovered, but with a horrible-looking head. He said that the bullet, although knocking him down, did not render him unconscious, and that his greatest trial in that terrible night was the necessity of shamming dead, and not daring to cry out when the Indian was slowly sawing at his head-covering with a very dull knife.

INDIANS RETURNING WITH THE RESULTS OF A BORDER RAID

CHAPTER XXXVIII.

STEALING.

In the estimation of the Indian, the skilful thief stands very nearly, if not quite, on a par with the daring fighter.

The one attracts the admiration, not unmixed with the fear, of his compeers; while admiration for the other is only modified by envy of his skill and consequent wealth. 'Money makes the mare go' among red skins as among white skins; and the man who owns a big herd of horses and mules (the wealth of the Indian) is a most respectable and respected man, however he got them. Where all are such magnificent thieves, it is difficult to decide which of the plains tribes deserves the palm for stealing.

The Indians themselves give it to the Comanches, whose designation in the sign language of the plains is a forward, wriggling motion of the fore finger, signifying a snake, and indicating the silent stealth of that tribe. This is true of the Comanches, who for crawling into a camp, cutting hobbles and lariat ropes, and getting off with animals undiscovered, are unsurpassed and unsurpassable. But for dash and boldness in thieving, I think the Cheyennes stand first, though closely emulated by the Kiowas.

I have known a Comanche to crawl into a bivouac where a dozen men were sleeping, each with his horse tied to his wrist by the lariat, cut a rope within six feet of a sleeper's person, and get off with the horse without waking a soul.

The corral fence at Fort Inge, Texas, was made of

upright logs set two feet into the ground, the upper ends sawed off level, a plate of timber put on the top, and each picket or log fastened in its place by a wooden pin, an inch in diameter, through the plate into the end of the picket. The stable inside of the corral was built in the same way, but more carefully and of heavier materials. Two sentinels walked around this stable during the night, and a stable guard slept within. One morning after a dark and stormy night it was discovered that several pickets had been removed from the fence and from the stable by sawing off with a knife the pins in the upper end and digging out the earth from the lower, and two horses were taken. Though the work must have taken several hours and the sentinels must have been changed during its performance, not one had seen or heard anything suspicious while on his post. From the fact that the two best horses were stolen from nearly the opposite ends of the stable, with nothing in the position or the stall to indicate favouritism, the commanding officer was inclined to believe that the thieves were white men, who had visited the stables beforehand, and that one or more of the sentinels were in collusion. A lieutenant with half a dozen men and a good guide were soon on the trail, and, after a race of sixty miles, they at daylight next morning surprised two Indians, killed both, and rescued the horses. None but Comanches could ever have taken out those pickets under the very noses of the sentinels, or selected in the dark the two best out of sixty or seventy horses.

The corral fence at Fort Lincoln was made of thorny chaparral bush, tightly pressed between upright posts set by twos. It was impassable for white man or horse, yet not a week of the first summer after the establishment of the post passed that Indians did not cross this fence and cut horses from the picket line. Fortunately they could not get the horses over it after they got possession of them ; and one or two of the thieves having been wounded by the sentinels, they discontinued their attempts, never having secured a horse.

Many years ago I was, when in Washington, requested by a man to help him to procure a commission in the regular army. He based his claim on services rendered during the Mexican War. When I asked what the services were, he told me the following story : ' I raised a company of cavalry to go with Doniphan to invade Mexico. When he started my company was not full, and we did not get off for near a month after him. I started from Leavenworth with a splendid company, well mounted and supplied with everything, and had a splendid march to near Pawnee Rock, on the Arkansas River. Here I went into camp one day rather early. The horses and mules were turned loose as usual, and were feeding in the river bottom close by, without guards. A sentinel was posted in camp. It was a hot day, and I and most of my men were asleep, when the sentinel called out that a herd of wild horses was in sight. I sprang up and saw a herd of forty or fifty galloping swiftly towards my herd. I knew there was danger of a stampede, but, before I could decide what to do, the horses entered my herd, and all went off together. When they got off about 500 or 600 yards, I was astonished to see an Indian rise upon the back of each of the horses we had supposed wild. They left me without a hoof. There was nothing to do but to return. Abandoning waggons and stores, I loaded my men with provisions and sufficient ammunition for protection, and started for the settlements. It was an awful march, and we came very near perishing from fatigue, thirst, and hunger. I think my sufferings on that journey entitle me to a commission.' I helped him all I could by advising him not to tell the story. As, however, he failed to get the commission, I think he probably disregarded my advice.

Nearly every horse of four companies of the old Rifle Regiment were once lost near Fort Davis, Texas, by a brilliant dash, in the face of a strong guard, of not more than half a dozen Apache Indians. The mules belonging to the waggon train transporting the baggage and supplies of several companies of the 6th Infantry were, at Bear Creek, Kansas, in 1871, stampeded and carried off by two Indians, in spite of hundreds of shots. Such instances, though not on so large a scale, occur every summer, and hundreds could be given if necessary.

By turns sneaking and bold, and oftentimes both together, the Indian is at all times and under all circumstances a most dangerous thief, and it is not too much to say that a horse or mule on the plains is never entirely safe from his skill and rapacity.

CHAPTER XXXIX.

TRAILING.

I CANNOT begin this subject without a slight tribute of respect and affection to one who, though utterly ignorant of all civilised knowledge, and to whom the letters of the alphabet were as unintelligible as Egyptian hieroglyphics, was yet full of wisdom and knowledge in all that appertained to his own mode of life ; who, brought up as a thief, was yet honest and faithful ; his boyhood and early manhood passed amid the crime, horror, and licentiousness of an Indian tribe, was yet a firm friend, a kind and loving husband and father.   He was a patient, successful hunter ; and not only the very best trailer I have ever seen, but pronounced by John Connor, the Delaware chief (undoubtedly the most competent judge of the subject on the plains), the very best trailer, Indian or Mexican, on the continent.   Under his guidance I made many a long march and rapid pursuit, and to him I am indebted for my first lessons in plainscraft and in hunting for large game.

Pedro Espinosa was born about the year 1810, of Mexican parentage, in a ranche or hamlet on the banks of the Rio Grande, not far from the town of Laredo. When he was nine years old, this ranche was captured by Comanches, and all the inhabitants put to death with the usual accompaniment of horror, except a few children of both sexes, who were carried into captivity.   On reaching the tribe the children were adopted into it and well treated, but carefully watched.   Espinosa was one of these.   The

Comanches were at that time the most numerous and powerful tribe of the southern plains, and were in a chronic state of war with all the world. When about thirteen years of age, Espinosa was permitted to accompany a party on a raid against the Tonkaways, in which he so signalised himself that at fourteen he became a warrior, and subsequently a distinguished one. Though apparently thoroughly an Indian, identified with all their interests, fighting, stealing, and committing outrages with the others, taking part in all their ceremonies, married and having a family, he had never forgotten his native land and people, nor forgiven the violation and murder of his mother.

He hated the Indians and their ways with the most bitter, unrelenting hatred, and his heart yearned for return to his own country. Whether, in spite of most careful dissimulation, he revealed something of this feeling, or from the natural craft and suspicion of the Indian, no opportunity was ever given him to put his wishes into practice. Though a dozen raids were made yearly into Mexico, he was never permitted to be one of a party that went near the Rio Grande. When he had been with the Indians nineteen years, and was twenty-eight years old, he went with a party into the Guadalupe Mountains to hunt black bear. One night, when the other Indians were asleep, he slipped among the horses, selected the two best (without regard to ownership), and by morning had put thirty miles between himself and his late companions. After a long journey he arrived safely at Laredo, where, the memories of his boyhood being perfect, he soon made himself known to his relatives. In course of time he married and settled, and, when I knew him, was a useful and thoroughly respected member of the community in which he lived

In 1849 I commenced my 'plains' life at Fort Lincoln, Texas, not on the plains, but on a military line established to protect the southern settlements of Texas from the incursions of the plains Indians. Covering the

Bandera and several other much used passes, Fort Lincoln was an important position, and it was extremely necessary that a thoroughly competent and reliable man, well posted in all the wiles of the Indians, should be selected as guide and trailer for the troops stationed there. The choice fell on Espinosa. For many years he served the Government well and faithfully, and at last yielded up his life in fidelity to it.

Some time after the close of the war of the rebellion, a friend wrote me from Texas giving the last scene in the life of Pedro Espinosa. In 1861, when the traitor Twiggs had planned and was consummating the surrender of all the troops and material of war in Texas, Espinosa was selected to carry despatches from Union men in San Antonio to Colonel Reeve, then on his way to the coast, notifying him of the condition of affairs, and warning him to turn back and take his command to the States by way of Santa Fé. While executing this office Espinosa was captured by some of the forces sent to intercept Reeve, and the despatches found on his person; after reading which the captors drew their pistols and shot him to death.

A 'trail' is the succession of marks left on the ground or grass by anything moving to a definite end—as a trail of troops, an Indian trail, a deer trail, a waggon trail. 'Sign' is evidence, more or less positive, that something has been present on that ground. A 'trail' is made up of 'sign;' but 'sign' is by no means a 'trail.' Feeding deer make 'sign;' but it may be impossible to 'trail' them. There may be an abundance of 'sign' in and about an abandoned Indian camp; yet it make take the keenest eye and closest scrutiny to detect the trail by which they left it. The safety of a party may depend on the proper reading of 'sign;' the success of a pursuit upon the greater or less ability of the pursuer to follow 'trail.'

The weakness of the Indian is his trail. Could he get rid of it he would be unconquerable. Fortunately for his enemies he knows this weakness, and the knowledge renders him comparatively manageable.

A raiding party of Indians coming to a recent trail of troops, will stop, examine, hesitate, and follow it for miles. Concluding, finally, that there is no serious cause for fear, they may go on towards their original destination. If another recent trail be struck within a few miles, the party will most likely turn back, and I doubt if there is a band or party on the plains bold enough to put three trails of troops between it and its retreat. It is not that the Indian fears to be intercepted on his return, but the frequent trails show the recent presence and activity of troops. He himself leaves a trail which one of those parties of troops may strike and follow at any moment. He is bold as a hawk to his front; timid as a hare towards his rear. In going on or returning from a raid, he cares nothing for advance guards; but always, when he thinks there is danger, one or two of the most trustworthy warriors follow on the trail as rear-guard three or four miles behind the main body. Surprise is destruction, and surprise is most likely to come from his rear, and by means of his trail.

In crossing a waggon road likely to be used by troops, a war party will scatter out a mile or two and cross singly; and not unfrequently, after crossing, each will dismount and carefully erase the marks, in and near the road, of his horse's feet.

'Trailing' is the art of evolving 'trail' from 'sign.' The requisites of a good trailer are sharp eyes, perfect knowledge of the appearance and character of the 'sign' made by whatever is being trailed, and, when trailing Indians, a thorough knowledge of the country and the habits of Indians.

Trailing is second nature to the Indian, though individuals and tribes differ in their capabilities as trailers in a very remarkable degree. On the plains where large game is (or was) abundant, the tribes which depend for their daily food on small game are those which become most expert ; and of these the Comanches are far superior, except, possibly, the small remnant of the Delawares.

The Indian is taught from childhood to read every mark on the ground, to tell what made it, its age, and all about it of interest or importance to himself. To these are added a thorough knowledge of the habits of game or animals of any kind, and a pair of eyes exquisitely sharpened by constant practice. These enable the Indian confidently to take and keep a trail, where a white man, even with sharp eyes and some practice, would, if he saw anything at all, only see an occasional unmeaning mark. The perfection arrived at is little short of miraculous.

A knowledge of the country and of the Indian mode of travel very greatly facilitate the pursuit of a savage. When anticipating pursuit he will resort to all ruses, keep as much as possible on rocky ground, mount a high hill, only to go down again on the same side. Getting into the bed of a brook he will keep along its channel for miles, going out and getting in again, doubling on his track, doing any and everything which may delay or baffle the pursuit.

As will more fully appear hereafter, Indians travel by 'landmarks.' A good trailer, especially in broken country, will tell from the general appearance of the country what special prominent landmarks the Indian is travelling by. When, therefore, the pursued resorts to ruses and doublings, the pursuer wastes no time in painfully tracking him through all his windings, but goes at once to where his knowledge of his habits tells him that the Indian will pass a certain ridge or go out of a certain valley. There he looks for the trail, and, finding it, pushes on more confidently than before.

The pursued may spend several hours in making a devious trail which the astute pursuer will jump over in as many minutes. The hard ground of the high prairie, marked as it is with more or less of buffalo 'sign,' is peculiarly favourable to the pursued, and the ease with which horsemen can travel anywhere and in any direction renders the 'trailing' of the 'plains Indian' a slow and difficult process, of which the success is always more or less doubtful. Besides, the trailers employed by the Government are generally white plainsmen, no more to be compared to Espinosa in trailing than a bull pup to an English beagle.

One or two of Espinosa's exploits will show better than a fuller description to what skill a trailer may attain. I was once sent in pursuit of a band of murdering Comanches, which had been scattered and the trail abandoned by a company of so-called Texas rangers (a sort of militia in the service of the United States, and resembling the ranger of the Republic of Texas in nothing but the name). On the eighth day after the Indians had passed, Espinosa took the trail of a single shod horse; looking neither to the right nor left, apparently seeing or noting nothing, he silently and patiently plodded on, not a moving animal or bird, not the slightest mark on ground or grass, escaping his wonderful eye. When we were fairly into the rough, rocky Guadalupe Mountains, he stopped, dismounted, and picked up from the foot of a tree the four shoes of the Indian horse. With a grim smile he handed them to me, and informed me that the Indian was going to hide his trail. For six days we journeyed over the roughest mountains, not a man in the whole command being able to discover, sometimes for hours, a single mark or sign by which Espinosa might direct himself. The monotony and apparent objectlessness of this march were extremely trying to my patience, and several times I impatiently demanded of Espinosa that he would show me what he was following. '*Poco tiempo*' (in a short time) would be his only answer; but in a longer or shorter time he would (with a quiet twinkle less marked) show me the clear cut footprints of the horse in the soft bank of some mountain brooklet, or, calling my attention, would point with his long wiping stick to most unmistakable 'sign' in the droppings of the horse. For more than 100 miles, over the most difficult country, did this remarkable man follow the single track, scarcely ever at a loss, and only once or twice dismounting from his horse to examine the ground more closely, until finally we came to where the Indians had united.

Once again, with Espinosa as guide, I was in pursuit of a large party of Comanches. On reaching the head spring of the Perdinales, I found that they had there made a halt of several days, that the whole vicinity was marked with footprints of horses, and that, after the Indians had left, the prairie had been burned, obliterating the trail. Sending Espinosa to work out the problem, I went into camp with my party. He returned at night-fall, having laboured patiently for six or seven hours. He had not succeeded, but was confident. By dawn he was out. About 11 o'clock I rode out on his trail, easily followed in the black ashes, and found him just about to return to me. He had succeeded. We returned to camp. The command, all ready, marched rapidly in rear of Espinosa for a dozen miles, when we struck the trail. That night Espinosa explained how he had managed. Going down the river from the camping ground of the Indians, so far as to be sure he was beyond the range of feeding horses, he made a circuit, the camp as centre, carefully examining the ground. He soon discovered 'sign,' and, dismounting from his horse, he went down on his hands and knees, and with his breath blew away the light ashes, until sufficient prints were discovered to show the direction of the trail. Mounting his horse he continued his circuit, finding other sign, and fixing in the same way the direction of the trails, which he discovered diverged from each other like lines from the centre of a circle. Next day he went out and tried the trails about four miles from camp to find them still diverging. Another trail a mile and a half beyond, discovered them, as he anticipated, converging. Carefully taking the direction of three or four, and finding they all pointed to a common centre, he fixed the direction of that point in his mind; and so beautifully was the whole problem worked out, that if he had been one of the Indians, previously instructed where to go, he could not have gone to that point more directly.

Once when in rapid pursuit of a small party that had made an attempt on our stables, Espinosa said to me, 'Lieutenant, we shall not catch these Indians; their rear-guards have discovered us; they are travelling at night.' I asked an explanation. He showed me where they had sometimes gone under a low branch of a tree, which could easily have been avoided had there been light enough to see, or crossed a ravine at a bad place when a good one was close by, &c. I could give twenty equally strong proofs of his ability as a trailer, but enough has been said to show to what perfection a really good trailer can carry his art.

CHAPTER XL.

TRAVELLING.

THERE is nothing about the Indian more remarkable than the ease and certainty with which he makes his way over the ' trackless wastes ' of plains on journeys of sometimes hundreds of miles. He has, of course, no knowledge of the compass; nor have I ever seen a ' wild ' Indian, who, even with the most careful and repeated explanation, could get the faintest glimmer of an idea of the use of the ' little box.' The reason is obvious. There is no 'north' and no 'south' to him. In all the wide circle of his horizon there are no definite points, no points of reference. He speaks of ' sunrise ' to designate that broad side of the horizon on which the sun rises, and of sunset of the other side ; but he makes no use of either for purpose of direction in travelling. The sun does not rise on consecutive mornings in the same place, and would be to him anything but a safe guide.

The same thing obtains of night travel ; and, brilliant as are the stars of the plains, it seems never to have occurred to his mind that use might be made of them in assuring his journey in any particular direction. His reliance on short journeys, for hunts of a week or more from his camp, is on instinct—the same incomprehensible something that takes a pigeon to its nest, or a bee to its home in the hollow tree. This rarely fails him, and I have heard of but one instance where an Indian got ' turned round,' lost, and wandered for several weeks alone before he recovered himself.

On long journeys to a definite point his sole reliance is on his memory of 'landmarks.' Similar and monotonous as the hillocks and valleys of the plains appear to the uneducated eye, each has its own distinctive features to him, which, once seen, he knows for ever after as quickly and well as the farmer knows the distinctive marks of the cattle which he feeds day after day. When going into a country unknown to him, he consults beforehand with some warrior who has visited it, and it is astonishing how clearly the one describes and the other comprehends all that is necessary for a successful journey.

Espinosa told me that when he was a boy among the Comanches, and the youngsters wished to go on a raid into a country unknown to them, it was customary for some of the older men to assemble the boys a day or two before the start for instruction. All being seated in a circle, a bundle of sticks is produced, marked with notches to represent the days. Commencing with No. 1, the stick with one notch, each is taken in succession. A rude map is drawn on the ground with finger or piece of wood illustrating the journey of the day represented by the notched stick. The larger rivers and streams are indicated, the hills, valleys, ravines, hidden water holes in dry countries, every natural object, peculiar or striking. When this was understood, the stick representing the next day's march was illustrated in the same way, and so on to the end. He further stated that he had known one party of young men and boys, the oldest not over nineteen, and none of whom had ever been into Mexico, to start from the main camp on Brady's Creek in Texas, and make a raid as far into Mexico as the City of Monterey, solely by memory of information fixed in their minds and represented by such sticks. However improbable this may seem, it is not more improbable than any other explanation that could be given of the wonderful journeys made by Indians into countries utterly unknown to them.

A party exploring a country unknown to it, or to

others of the tribe, will, if the new country prove desirable as a hunting ground, set up in rough and difficult ground small mounds of stones to indicate the best route to be taken by those who come after. Many such cairns are to be found in the rough ground of the Laramie plains, and also in the precipitous cañons of Southern Kansas. These cairns are very frequent in the country north of the North Platte, and I have heard many surmises as to their object. It is simply to indicate the position of the trail when the ground is covered with snow. So in a timbered country in the north, stones will be found placed in the forks and branches of trees, on each side of the trail, which could hardly be followed when covered with snow, except by this simple device.

Most of the plains tribes have a comparatively circumscribed country, which they learn by heart. Every mark is known, every precipitous dell affording safety in retreat, every water hole, no matter how hidden in rock or prairie; and, having seen it once, he knows it for all his lifetime, either for his own use, or to communicate his knowledge to his people. The Indian travels comparatively little by night; never as a matter of choice. When advancing towards an enemy whom he hopes to surprise, or when escaping from too vigorous a pursuit, he overcomes the natural distaste for night travel superinduced by his religion. Even in these cases, however, he wants all the light he can get, and the knowing frontier settler or plainsman always takes especial care to guard well his stock about the full of the moon in May or June.

CHAPTER XLI.

CRUELTY.

THE cruelty of the Indian is inexplicable except on the hypothesis that cruelty is a normal trait of humanity. Wild beasts are not cruel; for, although the wolf may tear and devour the entrails of a deer while that animal is yet alive, he does it from greediness alone. The members of the cat family play with and torment their victims, but they undoubtedly do this as practice in catching. Besides, if we are to believe the men who have been in the jaws of these animals, Nature has kindly compensated this exceptional apparent cruelty by inflicting on the victims of the feline race a nervous paralysis, which not only deprives them of any sense of pain, but prevents a realisation of the horror of their position.

The cruelty of the Indian is inborn and inbred, and it clings to him through life as a distinguishing characteristic of his humanity. As a boy, his special delight is the torture of every bird or animal he can get hold of alive. As a man, the torture of a human being gives him more pleasure than any other act of his life, and at no time is his laughter so joyous and heartfelt as when some special ingenuity wrings a groan or cry of anguish from the victim of his cruelty.

For extravagance of delight in the anticipation of a scene of torture, for hellish ingenuity in devising, and remorseless cruelty in inflicting, pain, the Indian woman far exceeds her husband and son; and they can give her no keener enjoyment, when returning from a foray, than by bringing some prisoner on which this ingenuity can be practised.

I have been told that when a female prisoner has been brought to camp, stripped, and staked out for the benefit of all comers, the women will come around, taking the liveliest interest in the proceedings, inciting their lovers, husbands, and sons to repeated violations of the victim, their jealousy (if they have a spark of that feeling, which I doubt) completely extinguished in the pleasure of the suffering inflicted.

Cruelty to animals is equally marked, though of a more passive nature. The torture of a human being is an active, exquisite pleasure. The suffering of an animal is simply a matter of indifference. An Indian will ride a horse from the back of which every particle of skin and much flesh has been torn by the ill-fitting saddle. He will ride him at speed until he drops, then force him to his feet and ride him again. A ' plains' saying is, that ' a white man will abandon a horse as broken down and utterly unable to go further; a Mexican will then mount and ride him fifty miles and abandon him; an Indian will then mount and ride him for a week.'

Once, when hunting in the Guadalupe Mountains, we very nearly lost a bear, because Espinosa failed to fire at a critical moment. After the bear had been killed I took him to task for not firing. He replied, ' I could have killed the bear, but I had only one shot. We may be " jumped " by Indians at any time. I will never be taken prisoner, and always save the last shot for myself.' The answer made a deep impression on me, and I have always tried to act on Espinosa's rule, but in the excitement of the chase rules are often forgotten. Espinosa's experience among the Indians had left not only a bitter hatred, but a most lively fear of falling alive into the hands of these savages. Many a horrible story of their barbarous cruelties has he detailed to me at the camp fire.

As a fair sample, I will here repeat two of these, both of which he knew to be true, so far as a man can be sure of what he did not actually see.

When he was about twenty-four years old, a party of Comanches (from the same camp in which he lived), while on a raid into Mexico, attacked a large ranche. The inhabitants, being poorly armed, made little resistance, except a few men, who, getting into a courtyard, vigorously defended themselves with such weapons as came to their hands. All were soon despatched, except one man, an almost giant in stature and strength, who, although armed only with an axe, killed one or two of his assailants and kept the others at bay. At last an Indian, getting on the wall, threw a lasso over his head, and, jerked off his feet, he was soon bound hand and foot. After the ruthless violation and murder of all the women, the children were fastened in a room, the ranche pillaged and set on fire in a dozen places. Taking with them as prisoner the one man who had signalised himself in the defence of the ranche, the Indians departed for their own country. On the long march the prisoner, though closely watched and guarded by day, and securely bound at night, was treated with extreme kindness. They complimented his courage in the highest terms; told him they intended taking him to their camp, adopting him into the tribe, and making a great chief of him. The trail followed, after leaving the head of the Nueces River, and crossed the southern end of the high table land known to whites as the 'Staked Plain.' At a water hole on this table land the party halted for several days. Telling the prisoner that they wanted it for some religious ceremony, they set him to digging a hole in the ground. Working with knife and hands he, in a day or two, completed a pit about three feet in diameter and over five feet deep. Early next morning a rope was tightly tied about the ankles of the captive and wrapped spirally round his legs and body to the neck, binding his arms tightly to his sides. Rigid and immovable, the man was then planted upright like a post in the hole, the dirt filled in and tightly rammed down around him. When all was completed nothing but his head was visible. They then scalped his head, cut off his lips, eyelids, nose, and ears, danced around, mocked, taunted, and left him. On their arrival at the camp the party described in detail their punishment of the Mexican, and in all the tribe it was regarded as an exquisite piece of pleasantry. The man would live, they said, for at least eight days, revived at night by the cool of the high plains, to be driven mad next day by the hot sun beating on his scalped head and defenceless eyeballs, while myriads of flies would fill his wounds with maggots. This 'joke' gained great celebrity among the southern plains tribes, and the warrior who proposed it was regarded as an inventive genius of the first order.

The Tonkaways cannot properly be called a plains tribe. Very few are now left; but when Espinosa was with the Comanches, they were a powerful tribe occupying all the low country between the Brazos and Sabine Rivers (now comprising the south-east portion of Texas). Incessant warfare existed between the Comanches and Tonkaways, and for many years Espinosa went once or twice or more times each year with parties of Comanches on forays into the Tonkaway country. One of these parties was surprised in camp one morning by a superior force of the enemy, several killed, two captured, and the others dispersed. Espinosa escaped and returned to his camp. Some time after, one of the warriors who had been captured arrived on foot at the camp, and gave the following account of his adventures. His companion in misfortune was wounded. They were bound, placed on horses, and marched rapidly to the eastward. On the second day the wounded Comanche evinced signs of weakness. That night the Tonkaways were sitting chatting about the camp fire, the two captives, bound hand and foot, lying near the ground. One of the Tonkaways got up, walked to the wounded man, took out a knife, coolly and quietly cut a piece of flesh out of his thigh and placed it on the coals to broil. Another and another followed, cutting slices. When the flesh was sufficiently cooked, each man ate his slice, talking at the same time to the Comanche, and complimenting him on the excellence and tenderness of his flesh. The Comanche retorted by hoping that he would disagree with them, wishing that his flesh was poison, &c. When an artery or large vein was cut, the flow of blood was arrested by searing with a firebrand. This horrible feast was continued far into the night, by which time nearly all the flesh of the thighs and loins had been consumed. The Comanche then began his death song, and his life and the feast ended together. The other captive, stimulated by the prospect before him, made, after all were asleep, a successful effort to free himself, and escaped.

The Tonkaways have always had the reputation of being cannibals. Some six or eight were employed as scouts at Fort Martin Scott, Texas, and did good service against the Comanches. I once asked a sub-chief if the tribe ate men. He denied it; but said their fathers ate their enemies, not to satisfy hunger but to gratify revenge. I believe it is the only tribe in North America that practises or did practise cannibalism.

A few years ago I met a gentleman who told me that he was one of a party that went to the front after the terrible Minnesota massacres of 1862. There was no fighting, the Indians having retired, and the party devoted itself to burying the dead and relieving the necessities of those whites who, hiding in thickets and ravines, had escaped the fury of the savages. He said that no words could express the horror of the scenes that must have been enacted. Scalped and mutilated corpses of men and women, and of babes whose brains had been beaten out against walls or trees, were collected and buried. They found at one farmhouse the scalped and mutilated body of an old man lying on the floor of the living-room. On the floor of an adjoining bedroom the corpse of an old woman was found in the same condition. On going into another bedroom a most pitiable, sickening sight met their eyes. Three young girls, the eldest about twenty, the youngest not more than fourteen, scalped and terribly mutilated, were hanging against the walls by large nails driven through the palms of the outstretched hands. They had been in this position for several days. The youngest had been dead some time; another died almost immediately after being taken down; the third lived for a day or two, and gave some account of the massacre. The ringleader of the outrage was well known to the family, and had always been regarded as a special friend. He had often taken meals with them; and on the morning of the massacre he and two or three others came in, friendly as usual, shook hands all round, and asked for something to eat. A few moments after, this friend suddenly drew his tomahawk and crushed in the skull of the father. The women ran into the bedroom and attempted to barricade themselves. A yell brought twenty or thirty more Indians, who surrounded the house, cutting off all chance of escape. The door of the bedroom was then broken up and the mother killed by a blow. The three girls were then stripped of all clothing and successively violated, the special friend being the first to begin the outrage.

The girls were thus kept all day serving the lusts of these fiends, in the same room with the dead body of their mother.

Just before night an Indian came in with some report which seemed to alarm them, and after consultation one went out and brought in an axe and some large spike nails. The girls were then taken singly into their own bedroom, forced into a standing position with their backs against the wall, their arms stretched out, and the hands held open and in position while the nails were driven through the palms into the wall.

After being scalped, their breasts cut off, and otherwise namelessly mutilated, they were left to suffer and to die.

Enough is on official record of the horrors of the Minnesota massacre to take from this story even an appearance of improbability.

Cruelty is both an amusement and a study. So much pleasure is derived from it, that an Indian is constantly thinking out new devices of torture, and how to prolong to the utmost those already known. His anatomical knowledge of the most sensitive portions of the human frame is wonderfully accurate ; and the amount of beating, cutting, slashing, and burning he will make a human body undergo without seriously affecting the vital powers is astonishing. When there is time for the indulgence of the pastime, no wounded man falls into his power but becomes at once a subject for experiment. The bodies of enemies are almost always terribly mutilated ; but it is not generally difficult to tell, from the nature of the mutilation, whether the body fell into their hands before or after death.

If the body is pierced with many bullet holes or arrows, or cut and slashed with deep and careless gashes, the spirit had passed before the Indian got possession. But artistic dissections, partial flayings, dislocations, breaking and splitting of fingers and toes, indicate that the poor fellow went to his long home with all the accompaniments of pain and horror that these devils can devise.

It is a rather curious fact that, while I have heard of but one or two instances of Indians committing suicide, they have a sort of respect for that act in the whites. In one instance, to my personal knowledge, the horse of a gallant fellow fell, pinning him to the ground unhuit, but surrounded by a crowd of yelling, grinning Apaches.

Some had already dismounted to secure him, when, placing his pistol to his head, he blew his brains out. The Indians fled away in consternation, not only not mutilating the body, but not even despoiling it of arms, &c. I have heard of several similar instances.

An officer of the army, blessed with a magnificent ' auburn ' beard, of the length, thickness, and beauty of which he is just a trifle vain, was one day receiving with me a visit from a party of Indians, who professed the greatest friendship. One of the Indians was greatly struck with the appearance of that beard, and his favourable appreciation was so marked as to attract attention. At last, seeming unable to contain his admiration, he reached forth his hand as if to touch and smooth it. The officer, very much flattered, passed his own hand over the ornament, and asked the Indian if he liked it. Compliments were given and received and all was amiability and good feeling, until the Indian unfortunately let out that he so admired the beard because it would be such fun to hang the officer up by it to a tree and shoot at him with arrows. The ' mutual admiration society ' was immediately dissolved, and the officer, turning to me, said, emphatically, ' Colonel, if I am ordered on an Indian expedition this summer, I swear I'll cut this beard off.'

CHAPTER XLII.

PONIES.

MY subject would not be complete without some mention of the pony, the plains Indian's inseparable companion and most serviceable slave. Scarcely fourteen hands in height, he is rather light than heavy in build, with good legs, straight shoulders, short strong back, and full barrel. He has no appearance of ' blood ' except sharp, nervous ears, and bright intelligent eyes; but the amount of work he can do, the distance he can pass over in a specified time (provided it be long enough), put him (in Indian hands) fairly on a level with the Arabian. Though of indispensable value to the Indian, he receives not a particle of attention. He is never stabled, nor washed, nor rubbed, nor curried, nor blanketed, nor shod, nor fed, nor doctored.

When not under the saddle his life is spent in the herd. After a hard day's work the saddle and bridle are taken off, and he is picketed or turned loose, in either case to shift for himself. If his back be bloody and torn by the saddle, a cloth or skin is fastened on it to keep the flies out. When travelling over rough and rocky ground his rider may take the trouble to tie up a tender foot in a piece of buffalo robe. In the winter he is a most miserable object, an animated skeleton. Exposed to the terrible cold and piercing winds of a plains winter, his scanty and innutritious food buried beneath the snow, he would undoubtedly perish, but that squaws cut branches from the cotton-wood tree for him to browse upon. At this season, with coat long, shabby, and rough, matted with dirt and burrs, hips extended in the air, belly puffed out with sticks and bark swallowed in the vain hope of appeasing the hunger that consumes him, forlorn and downcast, he looks an uncouth monster rather than a horse.

But when spring has mellowed the earth and drawn from her pregnant bosom the tender grass, he sheds the rough coat, scours the protuberant belly, and with rounded supple form, head erect, ears and eyes full of bright intelligence, he is again ready to bear his master in fight or foray, worthy to be trusted even to the death.

After endurance the best quality of the pony is his sureness of foot. He will climb a steep rocky hill with the activity and assurance of the mule. He will plunge down an almost precipitous declivity with the indifference of the buffalo. For going over swamps and marshy places he is only excelled by the elk; and he will go at speed through sand hills, or ground perforated with gopher holes, where an American horse would labour to get along at a walk, and fall in the first fifty yards of a gallop.

The amount of work got out of him by the Indian is astonishing. No mercy is shown. Tell an Indian to find out something quickly, miles away, and he will probably go and return at speed, though the distance made be twenty miles. I have seen a party run their ponies for more than an hour in mere pastime. In their drills of one or two hours no halt is made to breathe the horses, which, however, have opportunity at least of changing gait. In the fight, already described, at Plum Creek, the pursuit continued for sixteen miles, and the pursuers returned from it in a hand gallop. And this work is done under apparently most unfavourable circumstances: a terrible bit, an ill-fitting saddle, and a rider as cruel and remorseless as fate itself.

The Indian pony is undoubtedly the same animal as the mustang or wild horse of Texas and the southern plains, and wild life agrees with him. He is sufficiently tractable to the rough-riding Indian; but when brought into civilised ownership he is either a morose, ill-tempered brute, hard to manage, and always dangerous, or he degenerates into a fat, lazy, short-breathed cob, fit only for a baby or an octogenarian. The latter is especially the case when he is stabled, shod, and fed on corn and oats. Prosperity spoils him, as it does many animals of higher order, and his true character, capacity, and value are best displayed in adversity. The variation in quality of powers is little compared with that of our horses; so little, indeed, that 'a pony' is the standard of values.

One may be a little faster or somewhat stronger than another, but these advantages are likely to be counter-balanced by some special viciousness or other defect. Age seems to be little considered, the animal being 'a pony' so long as he has sufficient vital energy to get fat in the spring. The loss of an eye or a permanent lameness is so serious a defect as to render him no longer saleable as 'a pony.' When an Indian buys a number of ponies from another, they are not selected, but 'cut off' from the herd, as one would buy a lot of sheep from a flock. Those 'cut off' are then examined singly, and, if full grown and not defective, are taken. In all large herds there are a few special favourites—riding, war, or trick ponies—which are excepted in all general bargains. Even when a man has stolen another's wife, these are not taken among those he must pay for her.

CHAPTER XLIII.

SQUAW MEN.

THIS is the name given by Indians to those men, not of their tribe, who, by purchase of squaws (marriage), have been adopted by or are tolerated in it. They are of two classes. First, men of some means and frequently of ability, who come among the Indians as traders, and who, as a means of gaining their confidence and obtaining their trade, take to their bosoms a wife from each tribe, sometimes from almost each band. These men frequently become very wealthy and gain great influence among the Indians, and their red wives (being only property) are no impediment to their having wives and families in the States. As they grow old they sometimes retire from business, return to the States, and not unfrequently are respected and influential members of society. Others pass the winter of their days in their western homes, surrounded in patriarchal style by a crowd of admiring offspring and dependents.

Secondly, living with every Indian tribe is a number of outcasts, American, French, Mexican, the lowest refuse, who, spewed out by the society in which they were born, find congenial refuge among these savages. This life is not always a matter of choice, but is sometimes forced upon them by a too eager inquiry after their persons by the myrmidons of the law. Not unfrequently they are accompanied on their arrival among the Indians by a number of horses of various brands, sufficient not only to make friends of some of the principal men, but to buy one or more squaws and a 'tepee,' and enable them to set up housekeeping. These men become part of the tribe thus adopting or tolerating them, and, when near the agencies, send their squaws to draw rations for themselves and their children.

Having more natural shrewdness than the Indian, and a knowledge of the mode of life and habits of thought of the white man, they soon gain a certain ascendency over their red brethren. Being able to go among the white settlements without suspicion, they are accused of acting as spies for the Indians, of informing them where a valuable lot of horses or mules is to be had for the taking, and even of wreaking personal vengeance by inciting the Indians to some act of atrocity. There is scarcely a crime of which they are not accused, and I doubt if there be a crime of which some of them are not capable.

These are the men who trade clandestinely with the Indians. These furnish the arms; these supply the whisky; these are the ready tools of corrupt agents, making affidavits to cover any loss, and swearing to any story that is made up for them. At his own best games, in lying, stealing, drinking, and debauchery, the squaw man is so far superior to the Indian as to gain his unqualified admiration; and he becomes a power among them by the display of qualities similar, but superior, to those held in highest estimation by them. It is from these men that the Indians get their ideas of the character, capacity, morality, and religion of white men.

The Mexicans have a proverb that 'a woman is the best dictionary.' The squaw men prove its correctness by soon becoming adepts in the language of the Indians. All the intercourse between the Government and the Indian is filtered through these men and partakes of their character, being full of duplicity, treachery, and evasion. In all the length and breadth of the plains there is not an interpreter that can be relied on; and no treaty or delicate mission should ever be undertaken without several interpreters, who, moreover, should be required to give each his interpretation out of hearing of the others. There are in the United States about 100 Indian reservations and agencies, at each of which there is an average of about ten of these squaw men. The effect on the Indian of a thousand of such ' Missionaries' as these miserable outcasts may be imagined. A thousand ruffians with their half-bred children are fed and fostered by the Government. They are an injury to the country, a detriment to the Indian, and should be abolished.

CHAPTER XLIV.

CONCLUSION.

THE plains Indian, while not so degraded as many other tribes and people of this and the older continent, is as thoroughly savage as any. His religion inculcates neither obligation nor duty either to God or man. His education teaches no morality. His social life is scarcely a remove from that of the beasts of the field. His idea of right is the execution of his own will; of wrong, the enforcement of another will in opposition to his. But, however savage he may be, it is worth while to reflect that the ancestors of the most enlightened nations were at some time in the world's history as savage as he is now.

Our growth has been the slow development of ages upon ages. It is hardly fair to expect him, even with superior advantages, to change his nature in two or three generations. He has, moreover, never had a fair chance. His advantages, knowledge of and contact with civilisation, are rather apparent than real.

The fur trade of North America has founded and built up some of the most colossal fortunes in England, France, and America. The larger portion of this trade comes from the Indian. Its profits, even with the legitimate traffic, were and still are enormous; and, when advantage is taken of his passion for finery and fire water, these already enormous profits are so far increased that sharp and unscrupulous competition is not to be wondered at. The nature of the direct trade, the small capital required, and its position outside of the jurisdiction of the law, attract to it the very worst class of whites, who communicate to the Indian all the most glaring vices, and none of the good qualities, of civilisation.

That the Indian at this day is the cruel, inhuman savage that he is, is partially the fault of the Government, which has never done its duty by him. Until within a very few years, the agents through whom the Government dealt with the Indians were purely political appointments. A man was selected, not for character or capacity, or knowledge of Indians, but simply as a reward for the political services of himself or his backer, to perform a duty requiring courage, skill, tact, and knowledge of human nature. His tenure of office was the pleasure of the appointing power, and his salary almost nominal—a pittance of $1,200 or $1,500 a year. He was entrusted with more or less money and property for Indian expenditure, much of which he might appropriate himself if so disposed, and his office and contact with Indians gave him the control of the trade in illicit articles, arms, &c. On so miserable a salary a strictly honest man would return from his years of danger, privation, and banishment, if not poorer, at least no richer than when he accepted the agency. The dishonest man in the same position, and under the same circumstances, might return with $100,000 or $200,000. Could there be conceived a more efficient and sure method of converting an honest man into a thief?

Within a very few years a decided effort has been made to benefit the Indian service by leaving the selection of agents to the Christian bodies of the country. This failed necessarily, since the root of the evil—low salaries, and uncertain tenure of office—remained untouched. Experience of life does not teach that men are less greedy of money because they are professing Christians. Temptation comes to all alike, and (leaving entirely out of consideration the crowd of greedy hypocrites who live by the systematic deception of the really good and charitable) Christianity alone will save no one. The man who would steal as a layman, will steal as a Christian. Human nature is very weak in its pocket; and honest, perfect administration is hardly to be expected of men who risk their lives on low salaries and uncertain tenure of office.

The Government makes three vital mistakes in dealing with Indians —

1. In not enforcing its treaty obligations.
2. In dealing with Indians through two different Departments.
3. In yielding too much to the sentimental humanitarian element of the country.

1. *Not enforcing its treaty obligations.*

The treaty system is, in my opinion, entirely a wrong one. The Indians should be treated as wards of the Government, and as such protected, defended, held accountable for misdemeanours, and made to behave themselves. The admirable result of such a system is seen in Canada. The very Indians who raid, and steal, and murder on our northern frontier are well behaved and innoxious just over the line.

The habit of regarding and treating the tribes of nomads who roam about our wide west as independent nations with whom our intercourse must be regulated by treaties, while exceedingly absurd, is now so engrafted upon us that a change is most difficult and can only be made gradually. Let us note what that system is, point out its defects, and try to suggest remedies.

The Government, by Commissioners duly appointed and accredited, make a treaty with an Indian tribe. The Government agrees to pay certain fixed annuities in provisions and goods; to preserve to the Indians the lands inside the limits agreed upon, and to prevent impositions upon them. The Indians agree to give up certain portions of land which they regard as theirs; to restrict themselves thereafter within certain limits, carefully defined and described, and to abstain from war, raids, thefts, and depredations of any kind. This treaty goes to Congress, is approved and enacted into a law.

And with what result?

The Government does not pay the annuities agreed upon, but by its negligence connives at the constant robbery perpetrated by its agents. The amount of money appropriated by Congress is ample for the support and comfort of the Indians, provided they get it or its equivalent.

But they do not get it. Cheated in quantity and quality of rations and of goods, cheated in transportation, the appropriation burdened by *expenses* of numerous commissions, of deputations of a favoured few Indians to Washington and the eastern cities, it is doubtful if the Indians derive any benefit from more than 20 per cent. of the vast sum appropriated.

Again. After the treaty is made, some speculator finds out that there is a valuable tract of arable or timbered lands within the lines of the reservation. A few chiefs are bribed or coaxed into agreement. A 'ring' is formed. The 'lobby' gets to work upon it, and a recession of a goodly slice of the reservation is the result. The Government takes no steps to prevent the encroachment of whites upon Indian territory.

The greed of the individual Indian will cause him to sell his daughter to a white man. That man, while claiming protection from Government and all his rights as a white, yet becomes a part of the tribe. He draws rations for himself and children, as Indians. He builds himself a house on Indian ground, from which Government has promised by treaty that he shall be excluded. He takes advantage of the improvidence of the Indians to buy up their surplus rations in the day of plenty, to sell them back at enormous profits in their day of want.

He makes himself a power among them, to their constant injury and to the detriment of the Government.

He becomes rich, gets special Acts through Congress for the benefit of his half-breed children, and not unfrequently, as he grows old, he returns to civilisation, to a wife and family in the States, takes a prominent position in society, and is looked up to as an authority on all Indian matters.

At this moment almost every agency is surrounded by the houses of these men ; and at Spotted Tail and Red Cloud he may now be seen on ration day, buying *here*, for one dollar, a sack of flour which cost the Indian department seven or eight dollars to deliver, and *there*, a sack of corn on similarly favourable terms.

On the other hand, the Indians, complaining that they are swindled by their agents, that their annuities are not fully paid, that white men encroach on their reservations, cut off their wood, kill their game, &c., make these charges, whether true or false, the excuse for raids, plunderings, and murders. Under the pretence that the agent starves them on their own ground, parties go off ostensibly on a hunt ; really on a foray. The Government complains of the damage done by these parties. The chiefs and head men reply that they are friendly, that they have not left the reservation, that they do not believe that the outrages were committed by Indians of their tribe, that they cannot control their young men, and wind up with recriminations and counter charges.

The agent wants anything but an investigation. He hushes the matter up. The murderer may publicly wear the trinkets of the murdered man ; the thief may habitually ride the horses known to be stolen. Nothing is ever said. No murderer or thief is punished. But little over two months ago a young man herding cattle on Cottonwood Creek was killed and scalped by Indians from the agencies.

Four different plundering raids were made this

summer (1875) by the same Indians on the settlements on the Loup River. And yet we talk about the faith of treaties. The Government does not in good faith carry out its own treaty obligations, nor does it attempt to make the Indians carry out theirs. The whole treaty system is a murderous farce.

It is no easy matter to remedy the faults of a system which have become chronic from long usage, and in the continuation of which many men strong in position and money are pecuniarily interested.

I believe the time has come, however, when the intelligent, humane people of this country are really concerned for the future welfare and good government of the Indians. For their information I will add my opinion as to what should now be done to rectify these faults.

1st. No more treaties should be made with Indians. Those now binding should be abrogated as soon as possible. The system should be gradually changed, and the Indians as rapidly as possible brought directly and individually under the laws.

2nd. Judges or magistrates should be appointed to enforce in each tribe, or on each reservation, the criminal laws of the United States, with power to call upon the army at any and all times to carry out their decisions and orders.

3rd. The squaw men, whites, Mexicans, and negroes should be put away from the reservations, and not permitted to live with or go among the Indians. Cohabitation, miscalled marriage, with Indian women should be punished.

4th. Liquors, arms, ammunition, and property of any kind, taken without authority into the Indian country for traffic with the Indians, should be destroyed on the spot, as also the waggons and animals transporting them. The owners captured should be punished by imprisonment and fine.

5th. Congress should pass laws making it penal to sell

or give arms or ammunition to Indians, even by agents, and thus gradually disarm the Indians.

6th. Give the agent a salary commensurate with his danger, duty, and responsibility, and make his tenure of office ' during good behaviour.'　Grade the agencies as to pay, and establish a system of promotion by seniority or merit.

7th. Establish a proper system of accountability, with inspections for the detection of irregularities.

8th. Give the Indian enough to live on, in his reservation, and see that he gets it.

9th. Regard every Indian off his reservation as a marauder, to be killed, or captured and punished.

10th. When a marauding party is trailed to a reservation, force the tribe to deliver up the individuals composing it for punishment.

11th. Deduct from their annuities a fair compensation for every animal killed or stolen by any of the tribe.

12th. Punish murder, pillage, and other similar crimes, exactly as they would be punished among the whites.

I believe that, if Congress should enact a law dividing the reservations among the heads of families, giving each a specified portion of land as his own, the pride of proprietorship would be a great inducement to permanency of residence. The very first step in Indian civilisation must be to break up his nomadic habits and propensities. Restrictions as to sale or exchange would necessarily have to be made.

2. *Dealing with Indians through two different Departments.*

One of the most serious difficulties in our management of Indians results from there being two distinct controlling influences of entirely different powers and duties.

The Indian Department appoints the agents, buys and

distributes the presents, controls the reservations, pays the annuities, and feeds and manages the Indians.

The army, a pigmy in numerical force, but a giant in endurance, pluck, and power, sits with its mouth sealed, its hands tied, not permitted to speak or act, but as a police force, at the will and discretion of the Indian Department.

The Indian is in the position of a wilful boy, with a powerful but henpecked father, and an indulgent, weak mother.

The latter is constantly saying, ' Now be good, or I'll tell your father; ' or, ' If you do that I'll make your father whip you.' So with the Indian Department. When coaxing, and flattery, and presents fail to keep the Indians in the desired subjection, they are threatened : ' Now, if you do so and so, I will call in the army and have you whipped.'

The result is the same as with the child. The Indian conceives a contempt for a Department which cannot control itself, and a hatred, combined with fear, of an army which allows itself to be used to shield the other's weakness, and do its dirty work.

It is utterly impossible for the Indian to understand the positions of each in their varied circumstances—a fact not to be wondered at when the problem is ofttimes too intricate even for intelligent, cultivated whites. The mother has all the control ; and, however much the father may differ as to the management, he is not permitted to say a word.

Then comes the *dénouement.*

The boy becomes unmanageable, breaks out into ungovernable fury, and does vast damage. The father is called upon ; and, though he may in his innermost heart believe that the mother deserves the whipping, he is obliged, by his position and duty, to ' wallop ' the child. ' Now comes the tug of war.' The boy is light of heel, and seeks safety in flight. He dives into cañons, climbs hills, stretches out on the vast, trackless, water-less wastes, doubles and hides, and covers his trail, killing emigrants, pillaging farmhouses, outraging women, running off stock, and leaving only disaster and dismay behind him.

The more bulky father, patient and indomitable, follows slow, but sure as a bloodhound, certain as fate. He almost has the youngster in his clutches, when by another dexterous double the fatal grasp is eluded, and the boy, realising the sure fate in store for him, expends all his remaining strength in a race for home. Still on the trail, the pursuer relentlessly follows; and when he, too, finally arrives at home, it is to find the truant with his head in his mother's lap, her arms about him as a shield, and he is told that all is made up, that 'the boy is a good little boy, and don't need any whipping.'

This is the actual inception, progress, and result of nine-tenths of the Indian troubles. If, as has been stated time and again on the floor of Congress, it costs a million of dollars to kill an Indian, the reason can easily be seen. An Indian expedition necessarily costs money. If it fails from the defects of a system too absurd to waste argument upon, the blame should certainly not attach to the army.

3. *Yielding too much to sentimental humanitarianism.*

No system of government, either religious or secular, worthy of serious consideration, has yet been devised in which punishment of the wicked and lawless does not bear a prominent part. The strongest of all restraining forces is the fear of punishment. Human nature is so 'prone to evil,' that, but for this fear, the world would itself be a hell rivalling Dante's in wickedness, misery, and horror.

For one person who acts rightly from right and conscience sake, a thousand so act from fear of punishment.

A very large class of 'good' people are restrained from evil by fear of *future* punishment—a restraint not so strong as a hair to the larger class of the ignorant and callous, to whom a year in the penitentiary has more terrors than an eternity of hells as preached from the pulpit. Take from the 'dangerous classes' of New York City the fear of police, troops, gaols, and penitentiaries—in a word, of punishment; how long would that city stand? There are in every community vicious people enough to over-turn the whole fabric of society, were it not for the salutary restraint of fear.

Our boasted civilisation, our enlightenment, the result of ages; our religion, the most perfect yet given to or devised by man : we hold them all, humiliating as may be the admission, by means of the gaol, the penitentiary, and the gallows.

If this can be truly said of a society of which a large, though not the largest, part is composed of educated, moral, and religious people, how much more true is it of a society made up entirely of persons ignorant of any moral or religious restraint, and whose whole standard of action is each his own will. Civilisation has many re-straining influences—religion, morality, honour, pride, and fear. The Indian has but one. This solitary influence is *fear*. Relieve him of this most salutary restraint, and there would be no limit to his crimes, depredations, out-rages, and cruelties.

In an advanced state of society there are always a number of persons of ample means, abundance of time, and kind, sympathetic natures, whose benevolence and philanthropy are only satisfied when exercised at ex-tremes ; men who would do nothing for a poor devil who stole a loaf of bread from hunger, but would move heaven and earth to obtain the pardon of a felon who murders whole families in cold blood, or of a boy fiend who play-fully assassinates half a dozen of his companions. This class of persons is always influential : first, because only the cultivated and rich have time and money to spend on such benevolences ; and, second, because they start right, and are thoroughly in earnest. Their hobbies are good hobbies; and their only mistake is in riding too hard, in pursuing each his own object, without reference to the rights or objects of others. These persons see but in one direction, listen to but one side. Indians murder a family of settlers with all the usual horrors. It touches no sympathetic cord in the philanthropic breast. Troops pursue, overtake, and kill some of the murderers. At once there is a storm of indignation against the assassins of the ' noble red man.'

A large class of most excellent people conscientiously and most firmly believe that the Indian is a supernatural ' hero,' with a thousand latent good qualities, needing but the softening touch of Christianity to develop into a model of all virtue. They are right, only in that he is a degraded human, and can be improved. He will not voluntarily receive improvement, and must be coerced into it, just as among our own people it is beginning to be found out that education must be *compulsory.*

The theories of these good, sentimental hobby-riding people, of exceptional good in the Indian race, must be set aside as amiable, but fallacious; their pleas for constant forgiveness of Indian outrages should be kindly entertained and quietly ignored.

The Indians should be put on reservations, under the control of practical men, who have no pet theories to work out, no fortunes to make. They should be well treated, fed, clothed, and induced, not forced, to work. They should be taught by precept and by experience that an Indian is no better than a white man ; that comfort and plenty will be the reward of good behaviour and industry ; and that crime of any kind will be followed by sure and immediate punishment.

TABLE OF INDIANS

LIVING IN THE UNITED STATES OF AMERICA,

OMITTING THOSE IN ALASKA.

COMPILED AND TABULATED FROM THE LATEST OFFICIAL REPORTS OF THE COMMISSIONER OF INDIAN AFFAIRS,

BY ADO HUNNIUS.

Alseas	108	Alsea Reserve	Oregon.
Apaches.			
" *Aribapa*	384	San Carlos	Arizona.
" *Chiricahua*	290	Chiricahua	Arizona.
" *Cochise*	365	Chiricahua	Arizona.
" *Coyotero*	1514	Camp Apache	Arizona.
" "	175	Camp Apache	Arizona.
" *Gila*	1000	Gila Reserve	New Mexico.
" *Jicarilla*	500	Abiquin Agency	New Mexico.
" "	460	Jicarilla Reserve	New Mexico.
" "	400	Fort Stanton	New Mexico.
" *Lippan*	315	Mescalero Reserve	New Mexico.
" *Mescalero*	1895	Fort Stanton	New Mexico.
" "	830	Mescalero Reserve	New Mexico.
" *Mimbre*	400	Canada Alamosa	New Mexico.
" "	100	Chiricahua	Arizona.
" *Mogollon*	300	Canada Alamosa	New Mexico.
" "	100	Chiricahua	Arizona.
" *Mohave*	678	Camp Verde	Arizona.
" "	828	Colorado River	Arizona.
" *Pinal*	414	San Carlos	Arizona.
" *Southern*	310	Mescalero	New Mexico.
" "	400	Roaming	New Mexico.
" *Staked Plain*	130	Cheyenne Agency	Indian Ter.
" " "	602	Kiowa Agency	Indian Ter.
" *Tonto*	497	San Carlos	Arizona.
" "	94	Rio Verde	Arizona.
" *Yuma*	369	Rio Verde	Arizona.
" "	930	Roaming	Arizona.
Arapahoes, North.	1092	Red Cloud Agency	Wyoming.
" *South*	1644	Cheyenne Agency	Indian Ter.
Aravipais	200	Camp Grant	Arizona.
Arickarees	1646	Fort Berthold	Dakota.
Assinaboines	4698	Milk River Agency	Montana.
Bannocks	600	Fort Hall Reserve	Idaho.
"	1200	Shoshone Reserve	Wyoming.

Blackfeet.....................	1500	Blackfeet Agency	Montana.
Bloods......................	1500	Blackfeet Agency......	Montana.
Caddoes.....................	521	Wichita Agency.......	Indian Ter.
Cakokiams..................	85	Chehalis Reserve......	Washington.
Calapooias.................	24	Grande Ronde.........	Oregon.
Calispells..................	114	Fort Colville..........	Washington.
Cancons....................	149	Round Valley.........	California.
Cayugas	143	Cattaraugus	New York.
"	22	Tonawanda	New York.
Cayases.....................	385	Umatilla Reserve......	Oregon.
Chasta-Scotons.............	200	Malhuer Reserve......	Oregon.
Chehalis....	212	Chehalis Reserve......	Washington.
Cherokees..................	17217	Nation...............	Indian Ter.
"	300	N. Carolina...........	Geor. & Tenn.
Cheyennes, North...........	1202	Red Cloud Agency.....	Wyoming.
" South...........	2250	Cheyenne Reserve.....	Indian Ter.
Chickasaws..................	6000	Nation...............	Indian Ter.
Chilions	400	Camp Apache.........	Arizona.
Chimehuevas................	450	Colorado River........	Arizona.
Chinocks...................	250	Chehalis Reserve......	Washington.
Chippewas..................	2195	Roaming.	Michigan.
" Bad River.......	723	La Pointe Reserve.....	Wisconsin.
" Black River.......	750	Mill Lake Reserve.....	Minnesota.
" Boise Forte.........	3100	La Pointe Reserve.....	Wisconsin.
" "	2000	Boise Fort Reserve ...	Minnesota.
" "	896	Pigeon Reserve.......	Minnesota.
" Fond du Lac.......	399	Fond du Lac Reserve..	Minnesota.
" Grand Portage.....	359	White Earth Reserve..	Minnesota.
" L'Anse...........	1195	Pigeon Reserve.......	Minnesota.
" Lac Court Oreilles..	1253	Court Oreille Reserve..	Wisconsin.
" Lac de Flambeau...	629	Lac de Flambeau......	Wisconsin.
" Lake Superior......	1118	Lake Superior.........	Michigan.
" "	2025	La Pointe Reserve.....	Wisconsin.
" Minnesota..........	450	Turtle Mountain.......	Dakota.
" Mississippi.........	2139	La Pointe Reserve....	Wisconsin.
" Pembina..........	547	Pembina Reserve.....	Minnesota.
" Pillager............	862	Leech Lake Reserve ..	Minnesota.
" Red Cliff..........	660	Red Cliff Reserve.....	Wisconsin.
" Red Lake..........	1141	Red Lake Reserve.....	Minnesota.
" Saginaw...........	203	Roaming.............	Michigan.
" Swan Creek........	825	Roaming.............	Michigan.
" White Oak.........	115	White Earth Reserve..	Minnesota.
" Winnebagoshish.....	1226	Leech Lake Reserve...	Minnesota.
Chocktaws..................	16000	Nation...............	Indian Ter.
Clackamas	57	Grande Ronde	Oregon.
Clatsops...................	138	Chehalis Reserve......	Washington.
" Coast...........	28	Grande Ronde.........	Oregon.
Coahuilas..................	800	Klamath Reserve.	Oregon.
"	150	Colorado River........	Arizona.
Cocopahs...................	800	Port Isabel............	California.
"	108	Colorado River........	Arizona.
Cœur l'Alenes.............	1349	Cœur d'Alene...... ...	Idaho.
Colvilles	1100	Fort Colville..........	Washington.
Comanches.................	2643	Kiowa Agency........	Indian Ter.
" Penetethka........	345	Wichita Agency.......	Indian Ter.
Coosas	123	Alsea Reserve.........	Oregon.
Cowlitz....................	210	Chehalis Reserve......	Washington.
Cow Creeks................	28	Grande Ronde.........	Oregon.
Creeks.....................	13000	Nation...............	Indian Ter.
Crows, Mountain............	3000	Mountain Crow........	Montana.

Crows, River	1200	River Crow Reserve	Montana.
" Other River	1240	Milk River Agency	Montana.
Delawares	30	Kiowa Agency	Indian Ter.
"	81	Wichita Agency	Indian Ter.
D'Wamishes	400	Tulalip Reserve	Washington.
Flatheads	471	Flathead Reserve	Montana.
Foxes, Mississippi	374	Quapaw Reserve	Indian Ter.
" Missouri	43	Great Nemaha	Nebraska.
Gros Ventres, Dakota	600	Fort Berthold	Dakota.
" " Oregon	1100	Milk River Agency	Montana.
Hamptolops	97	Chehalis Reserve	Washington.
Hohs	73	Quinaielt Reserve	Washington.
Hoonsoltons	113	Hoopa Valley	California.
Hoopas	304	Hoopa Valley	California.
Hualpais	620	Colorado River	Arizona.
Humboldts	130	Hoopa Valley	California.
Ionies	85	Wichita Reserve	Indian Ter.
Iowas	226	Great Nemaha	Nebraska.
Kahmiltpahs	100	Yakama Reserve	Washington.
Kansas or Kaws	523	Kansas Reserve	Indian Ter.
Kaskaskias	30	Quapaw Reserve	Indian Ter.
Keawahs	117	Tule River Reserve	California.
Keechies	106	Wichita Reserve	Indian Ter.
Kickapoos	621	Sac and Fox Reserve	Indian Ter.
King's River, lower	175	Tule River Reserve	California.
" " upper	410	Tule River Reserve	California.
Kiowas	1700	Kiowa Reserve	Indian Ter.
Klamaths	550	Klamath Reserve	Oregon.
Klikatats	200	Yakama Reserve	Washington.
Klinquits	200	Yakama Reserve	Washington.
Koo enays	471	Flathead Reserve	Montana.
Kowwassayes	600	Yakama Reserve	Washington.
Little Lakes	169	Round Valley	California.
Lipans	400	Scattered	Florida.
Luckamutes	23	Grande Ronde	Oregon.
Makahs	558	Makah Reserve	Washington.
Manaches	211	Tule River Reserve	California.
Mandans	450	Fort Berthold	Dakota.
Maricopas	300	Maricopa Reserve	Arizona.
Mary's River	32	Grande Ronde	Oregon.
Menomonees	1480	Green Bay Reserve	Wisconsin.
Meethows	626	Fort Colville Reserve	Washington.
Miamies	97	Quapaw Reserve	Indian Ter.
"	345	Scattered	Indiana.
Miscolts	216	Hoopa Valley	California.
Missourias	371	Otoe Reserve	Nebraska.
Modocs	147	Quapaw Reserve	Indian Ter.
"	100	Klamath Reserve	Oregon.
Mohaves	1540	Colorado River	Arizona.
Mollalus	66	Grande Ronde	Oregon.
Molels	57	Grande Ronde	Oregon.
Moquis (Pueblos).			
" Me-chong-a-na-we	225	Village	Arizona.
" Oreybe	526	Village	Arizona.
" Se-cho-ma-we	209	Village	Arizona.
" She-powl-a-we	125	Village	Arizona.
" Shung-a-ya-we	196	Village	Arizona.
" Tay-wah	201	Village	Arizona.
" Tual pis	190	Village	Arizona.
Muckleshoots	100	Muckelshoot Reserve	Washington.

Munsees....................	111	Munsee Reserve.......	Wisconsin.
Navajoes..................	9068	Navajoe Reserve......	New Mexico.
"	2000	Roaming.....	Arizona.
Nehalims, coast..............	36	Grande Ronde........	Oregon.
Nespectums...	100	Fort Colville Reserve..	Washington.
Nestucalips................	200	Grande Ronde........	Oregon.
Nex-Perces.			
" Kamai...........	900	Nex-Perce Reserve ..	Idaho.
" Lapwai....	850	Nex-Perce Reserve....	Idaho.
" Snake........	420	Nex-Perce Reserve....	Idaho.
Nex-Perces, Upper Snake.....	627	Nex-Perce Reserve ..	Idaho.
Nex-Tuccas, coast.............	58	Grande Ronde........	Oregon.
Nisqually....	230	Nisqually Reserve.....	Washington.
Ochecholes................	100	Yakama Reserve......	Washington.
Okanagaus.	411	Fort Colville Reserve..	Washington.
Omahas....................	951	Omaha Reserve.......	Nebraska.
Oneidas, New York..........	198	Oneida Reserve........	New York.
" Wisconsin..........	1279	Oneida Reserve........	Wisconsin.
Onondagas.................	99	Alleghany Reserve.....	New York.
"	46	Cattaraugus Reserve...	New York.
"	58	Onondaga Reserve.....	New York.
Oregon....................	48	Grande Ronde........	Oregon.
Osages			
" Beaver................	237	Osage Reserve	Indian Ter.
" Big Chiefs.............	698	Osage Reserve	Indian Ter.
" Big Hills..............	936	Osage Reserve	Indian Ter.
" Black Dog............	511	Osage Reserve	Indian Ter.
" Clamore.............	239	Osage Reserve	Indian Ter.
" Little	696	Osage Reserve	Indian Ter.
Half Breed	277	Osage Reserve	Indian Ter.
White Hairs...........	362	Osage Reserve	Indian Ter.
Otoes.....................	323	Otoe Reserve..........	Nebraska.
Ottawas...................	3975	Lake Superior........	Michigan.
" Blanchard Fork. ...	1036	Lake Superior........	Michigan.
" " "	142	Quapaw Reserve.....	Indian Ter.
" Roche de Bœuf......	150	Quapaw Reserve......	Indian Ter.
Owen Rivers................	4789	Tule River Reserve....	California.
Papagoes	6000	Papago Reserve.......	Arizona.
Palouses..................	400	Yakama Reserve......	Washington.
Pawnees...................	360	Wichita Reserve.......	Indian Ter.
" Chowees............	759	Pawnee Reserve......	Nebraska.
" Kitkahoet...........	550	Pawnee Reserve......	Nebraska.
" Pet howerat.........	508	Pawnee Reserve......	Nebraska.
" Skeedee............	630	Pawnee Reserve......	Nebraska.
Pend d'Oreilles	1026	Flathead Reserve......	Montana.
Peorias...................	47	Quapaw Reserve......	Indian Ter.
Piankeshaws..............	40	Quapaw Reserve......	Indian Ter.
Piegans..................	2450	Piegan Reserve........	Montana.
Pimas...	4000	Pima Reserve.........	Arizona.
Pisquoses................	200	Yakama Reserve......	Washington.
Pitt Rivers................	64	Round Valley.........	California.
Poncas...................	730	Ponca Reserve	Dakota.
Potter Valleys..............	293	Round Valley.........	California.
Potowatomies.			
" Huron........	60	Lake Superior........	Michigan.
" Indian Ter....	1600	Potowatomie Reserve..	Indian Ter.
" Kansas........	400	Potowatomie Reserve..	Kansas.
Pueblos....................	9500	Nineteen Villages......	New Mexico.
Puyallups.................	579	Puyallup Reserve......	Washington.
Quapaws..................	236	Quapaw Reserve......	Indian Ter.

Qui-leh-utes	234	Quinaielt Reserve	Washington.
Qui-nai-elts	117	Quinaielt Reserve	Washington.
Quits	95	Quinaielt Reserve	Washington.
Redwoods	235	Hoopa Valley	California.
"	71	Round Valley	California.
Renegades	900	Roaming	Oregon.
Rouge Rivers	34	Grand Ronde	Oregon.
Sacs, Mississippi	376	Sac and Fox Reserve	Indian Ter.
" *Missouri*	45	Great Nemaha	Nebraska.
Saint Regis	683	Saint Regis Reserve	New York.
Salmon Rivers	49	Grande Ronde	Oregon.
San Poels	127	Fort Colville Reserve	Washington.
Santaims	71	Grande Ronde	Oregon.
Seapeats	300	Yakama Reserve	Washington.
Senecas	941	Alleghany Reserve	New York.
"	1470	Cattaraugus	New York.
"	632	Tonawanda	New York.
"	207	Quapaw Reserve	Indian Ter.
Seminoles	2438	Seminole Reserve	Indian Ter.
"	300	Scattered	Florida.
Shastas	47	Grande Ronde	Oregon.
Shawnees, Eastern	90	Quapaw Reserve	Indian Ter.
" *Absentes*	688	Sac and Fox Reserve	Indian Ter.
Shoalwater Bays	197	Shoalwater Bay	Washington.
Shoshones.			
" *Eastern*	1800	Shoshone Reserve	Wyoming.
" *Fort Hall*	600	Fort Hall Reserve	Idaho.
" *Goship*	1000	Fort Hall Reserve	Idaho.
" *Kai-da-toi-ab-ie*	425	Fort Hall Reserve	Idaho.
" *Na-hae-go*	530	Fort Hall Reserve	Idaho.
" *Nevada*	500	Muddy Lake Reserve	Nevada.
" *No-ga-ie*	200	Fort Hall Reserve	Idaho.
" *North Western*	2000	Fort Hall Reserve	Idaho.
" *Pa-gan-tso*	172	Fort Hall Reserve	Idaho.
" *Pi-at-sui-ab-be*	249	Fort Hall Reserve	Idaho.
" *Sheep Eater*	200	Roaming	Wyoming.
" *To-na-wits-o-na*	369	Fort Hall Reserve	Idaho.
Shyicks	400	Yakama Reserve	Washington.
Sias	127	Hoopa Valley	California.
Siaywas	200	Yakama Reserve	Washington.
Sioux (Dakotas).			
" *Blackfeet*	871	Grand River Agency	Dakota.
" "	700	Cheyenne River	Dakota.
" *Black Tiger*	150	Roaming	Dakota.
" *Brule, lower*	1347	Upper Missouri	Dakota.
" " *upper*	5000	Whetstone Agency	Dakota.
" " "	320	Red Cloud Agency	Wyoming.
" *Cuthead*	925	Cheyenne River	Dakota.
" *Long*	200	Roaming	Dakota.
" *Minneconjoux*	1655	Cheyenne River	Dakota.
" *Oncpapa*	2976	Grand River Agency	Dakota.
" *Oncpatina*	400	Milk River Agency	Montana.
" *Ogallala*	6000	Red Cloud Agency	Wyoming.
" *Sans Arc*	1527	Grand River Agency	Dakota.
" "	1500	Cheyenne River	Dakota.
" *Santee*	1300	Milk River Agency	Montana.
" "	791	Santee Reserve	Dakota.
" "	150	Devil's Lake Reserve	Dakota.
" *Sisseton*	683	Lake Traverse	Dakota.
" "	200	Devil's Lake Reserve	Dakota.

Sioux, Shooter	900	Roaming.............	Dakota.
" *Teton*............... ..	6000	Milk River Agency.....	Montana.
" *Tatkannais*............	700	Roaming.............	Dakota.
" *Two Kettle*............	1100	Cheyenne River.......	Dakota.
" *Unkapapa*........	450	Roaming.............	Dakota.
" *Wahpeton*............	813	Lake Traverse.........	Dakota.
" "	350	Devil's Lake Reserve...	Dakota.
" *White Eagle*.........	200	Roaming......... ...	Dakota.
" *Yanktonnais*...........	1406	Grand River Agency...	Dakota.
" " *upper*....	2266	Milk River Ageney.....	Montana.
" " *lower*.....	2607	Grand River Agency...	Dakota.
" " "	1200	Upper Missouri.......	Dakota.
" *Yankton*........... ..	1947	Yankton Reserve......	Dakota.
" *Yellow Liver*..........	350	Roaming.............	Dakota.
Sinselaus....................	68	Alsea Reserve.........	Oregon.
Skinpahs...................	300	Yakama Reserve.......	Washington.
S' Klallams.................	575	Madison Reserve......	Washington.
Skokomishes.....	291	Madison Reserve.......	Washington.
Spokanes..................	900	Fort Colville Reserve..	Washington.
Squaxins..................	150	Squaxin Reserve.......	Washington.
Snakes.			
" *Wal-pah-pa*..........	98	Klamath Reserve......	Oregon.
" *Yahooskin*.........	267	Klamath Reserve......	Oregon.
" "	1200	Roaming.............	Oregon.
Stockbridges.................	130	Stockbridge Reserve...	Wisconsin.
Tawacanies.................	125	Wichita Agency.......	Indian Ter.
Tejons.....................	2200	Tule River Reserve....	California.
Terrinos................	56	Warm Spring Reserve..	Oregon.
Tillamooks.................	168	Grande Ronde.	Oregon.
Timpanagos.................	318	Muddy Valley Reserve.	Nevada.
Tonkaways..................	200	Scattered.............	Florida.
Towoccaroes................	127	Wichita Reserve.......	Indian Ter.
Tules......................	1500	Tule River Reserve....	California.
Tuscaroras.................	448	Tuscarora Reserve.....	New York.
Twanas....................	275	Madison Reserve......	Washington.
Ukies......................	181	Round Valley.........	California.
Umatillas	302	Umatilla Reserve......	Oregon.
Umpquas...................	44	Alsea Reserve.........	Oregon.
"	131	Grande Ronde.........	Oregon.
Utes, Capote.................	500	Abiquin Agency.......	New Mexico.
" *Elk Mountain*..........	600	Ute Reserve...........	Colorado.
" *Goship*	256	Uintal Valley.........	Utah.
" *Go-si, Pa-ga-ya-ats*.....	39	Uintah Valley.........	Utah.
" " *Pi-er-ru-i-ats*.....	33	Uintah Valley.........	Utah.
" " *To-ro-un-to-go-ats.*	204	Uintah Valley.........	Utah.
" " *Tu-wur-iuls*......	35	Uintah Valley.........	Utah.
" " *Uu-ka-gar-its*.....	149	Uintah Valley.........	Utah.
" *Grand River*...........	200	Ute Reserve...........	Colorado.
" *Ko-sun-ats*.............	76	Uintah Valley.........	Utah.
" *Los Penos*..............	2100	Ute Reserve...........	Colorado.
" *Muache*................	290	Cimarron Agency......	New Mexico.
" "	650	Ute Reserve....	Colorado.
" *Pai, Ho Knaits*........	34	Ute Reserve...........	Colorado.
" " *I-chu-ar-rum-pats.*.	34	Ute Reserve.......,....	Colorado.
" " *Kai-vav-wits*....	171	Ute Reserve...........	Colorado.
" " *Kau-yai-chits*	31	Ute Reserve...........	Colorado.
" " *Kwai-anti-kwokets.*	62	Ute Reserve...........	Colorado.
" " *Kwi-en-go-wats*	18	Ute Reserve...........	Colorado.
" " *Kwi-um-pus*	29	Ute Reserve...........	Colorado.
" " *Mo-a-pa-ri-ats*.....	64	Ute Reserve...........	Colorado.

Utes, Pai, Mo-quats..	34	Ute Reserve...........	Colorado.
" " Mo-vwi-ats........	57	Ute Reserve...........	Colorado.
" " Nau-wan-a-tats...	60	Ute Reserve...........	Colorado.
" " No-gwats.........	28	Ute Reserve...........	Colorado.
" " Nu-a-gun-tits.....	161	Ute Reserve...........	Colorado.
" " Pa-ga-its.........	34	Ute Reserve...........	Colorado.
" " Pa-qu-its........	68	Ute Reserve...........	Colorado.
" " Pa-ran-i guts	171	Ute Reserve...........	Colorado.
" " Qa-room-pats......	28	Ute Reserve...........	Colorado.
" " Pa-room-pai-ats...	35	Ute Reserve...........	Colorado.
" " Py-spi-kai-vats....	40	Ute Reserve...........	Colorado.
" " Pa-ru-guns.......	27	Ute Reserve...........	Colorado.
" " Pin-to-ats.........	47	Ute Reserve...........	Colorado.
" " Sau-won-ti-aes.....	92	Ute Reserve...........	Colorado.
" " Shi-quits.........	182	Ute Reserve...........	Colorado.
" " Timpashauwagotsits	17	Ute Reserve...........	Colorado.
" " Tsou-wa-ra-its.....	155	Ute Reserve...........	Colorado.
" " U-ai-nu-ints......	80	Ute Reserve...........	Colorado.
" " U-in-ka-rets......	40	Ute Reserve...........	Colorado.
" " Un-ka-ka-ni-guts..	36	Ute Reserve...........	Colorado.
" " Un-kapa-ru-kuiats	97	Ute Reserve...........	Colorado.
" " U-tum-pai-ats.....	46	Ute Reserve...........	Colorado.
" " Ya-gats	68	Ute Reserve...........	Colorado.
" Pah...............	528	Uintah Valley.........	Utah.
" "	1500	Walker River.........	Nevada.
" "	500	Pyramid Lake.........	Nevada.
" Pah-vants.............	134	Uintah Valley.........	Utah.
" Pe-ahs...............	350	Denver..............	Colorado.
" Pi	4000	Shoshone Reserve......	Wyoming.
" Piede...............	200	Spanish Fork.........	Utah.
" Pi-ka-kwa-na-rate	32	Uintah Valley,.......	Utah.
" San-Piche...........	300	Uintah Valley........	Utah.
" San-pits	36	Uintah Valley........	Utah.
" Seuv-a-rits............	144	Uintah Valley........	Utah.
" She-be-recher..........	1000	Uintah Valley........	Utah.
" Tabequache	2100	Ute Reserve...........	Colorado.
" Tampa...	149	Ute Reserve...........	Colorado.
" Tim-pa-na-gats.........	49	Uintah Valley........	Utah.
" Tim-pai-a-vats.........	25	Uintah Valley........	Utah.
" Tim-pa-na-go..... ...	500	Salt Lake.............	Utah.
" Vintah...............	800	Uintah Valley........	Utah.
" Weber...............	300	Salt Lake.............	Utah.
" Wiminuche...........	630	Ute Reserve...........	Colorado.
" "	750	Abiquin Agency.......	New Mexico.
" Yampa...............	800	Ute Reserve...........	Colorado.
Wacoes..................	140	Wichita Reserve......	Indian Ter.
Walla-Wallas............	201	Umatilla Reserve......	Oregon.
Wappato Lakes............	61	Grande Ronde.........	Oregon.
Warm Springs............	304	Warm Spring.........	Oregon.
Wascoes.................	320	Warm Spring.........	Oregon.
Washoes.................	500	Roaming.....	Nevada.
Weas...................	43	Quapaw Reserve......	Indian Ter.
Wenatchepums............	200	Yakama Reserve.......	Washington.
Wichitas................	299	Wichita Reserve......	Indian Ter.
Wichumnies..............	113	Tule River Reserve....	California.
Winnebagoes.			
" Nebraska........	1462	Winnebago Reserve....	Dakota.
" Wisconsin.......	860	Roaming..............	Wisconsin.
Wishams................	300	Yakama Reserve......	Washington.
Wyandottes..............	239	Quapaw Reserve......	Indian Ter.

Wylackies......................	47	Round Valley.........California.
Yakamas......................	400	Yakama Reserve.......Washington.
Yamhills.....	35	Grande Ronde.........Oregon.
Yavapais.....................	4000	Roaming.............Arizona.

CIVILIZED.. 100,000
SEMI-CIVILIZED................................... 135,000
BARBAROUS 81,000

As the Indians are superstitiously opposed to being counted, the taking of their census abounds with many and great difficulties; therefore the strength above given is mostly official estimation.

In each number of the foregoing list are included men, women, and children, excepting the roaming bands of the Sioux, whose warriors alone are given by estimation.

FORT LEAVENWORTH, Kansas, July, 1875.

INDEX